(continued from back cover)

It was an extraordinary three-way partnership, and it produced extraordinary results.

The physical end of the collaboration involved two people:

Rita Warren was a Ph.D. professor of psychology who, after her retirement, spent four years directing The Monroe Institute's laboratory, helping volunteers to achieve and explore altered mental states under controlled conditions.

Frank DeMarco was, and is, an author, a former journalist and an editor with the Hampton Roads Publishing Co., Inc., who had learned to bring forth messages from the other side.

The nonphysical end involved what DeMarco calls "the guys upstairs," a group whose composition changes from time to time, depending upon subject matter and other variables.

Together, in the summer of 2001, they began a series of weekly sessions in which DeMarco entered an altered state and Warren asked questions that had interested her for years, questions for which the volunteers she had quizzed had been unable to provide satisfactory answers. What is the nature and purpose of life? Is there a God? Is there an afterlife, and if so, what is it like? What is the truth behind crop circles, UFOs, etc? In short, how does the world function?

As it turned out, the guys upstairs were more than willing to share what they know. Using a combination of explanation, analogy, pointed questions, jokes, thought experiments, etc., they set out to answer anything that could be asked. This fascinating series of conversations may help you change your life.

THE SPHERE AND THE HOLOGRAM

Explanations from the Other Side

Books by Frank DeMarco

Fiction:

Messenger:
A Sequel to Lost Horizon

Babe in the Woods:
A Novel

Non-fiction:

Muddy Tracks:
Exploring an Unsuspected Reality

Chasing Smallwood:
Talking with the Other Side

THE SPHERE AND THE HOLOGRAM

Explanations from the Other Side

by

Frank DeMarco

and

Rita Q. Warren

"If you see yourselves as holographically part of the entirety of the universe, this doesn't mean that you're a tiny part of something huge, it means you're an integral part of the whole thing, and size is not relevant. It's just really not relevant. And the sphere, again, is only used as an analogy of completion, of totality. It doesn't mean that reality is literally a sphere."

– from Session 18, January 11, 2002

HOLOGRAM BOOKS
www.hologrambooks.com

For information visit: www.hologrambooks.com

or write:

Hologram Books
1270 Roberts Mountain Road
Faber, Virginia 22938

Design by Allen Design Studio

Printed in the United States of America

ISBN 978-0-9820098-5-7

<u>Dedication</u>

Rita's:
with love and appreciation, to my daughters
Laurie Grant
Lesley Grant

Frank's:
To the memory of Rita Queen Warren (1920-2008), friend, confidant,
perceptive questioner, experienced explorer of our communications with the
other side. The guys upstairs were quite explicit: The better the questions,
the better the answers we can receive. Rita's questions were superb.
I hope she likes the form our long collaboration finally took.

Acknowledgements

Rita's:

Martin, my partner of almost 40 years, whose spirit survives and surrounds me
Frank, my good friend, whose joy in writing inspires me
Bob and Nancy Monroe, who left their mark on me as well as on so many others
My many friends from TMI and the New Land, who kept me functioning through rough times and shared my questions and answers in these puzzling times

Frank's:

I owe so much to so many friends, I hesitate to acknowledge any specifically because others with perhaps equal claim are certain to be inadvertently omitted. But I must mention:

Rita Warren, without whom it would not have been possible
Skip Atwater, whose expert guidance through many booth sessions helped me hold the threads
Colin Wilson, who encouraged me to put my experiences into a book
Those friends who read the sessions as fast as I could transcribe them, and contributed comments and questions. You know who you are.

CONTENTS

Introduction

by Frank DeMarco

Probably you don't need this book if the world makes sense to you, if your *life* makes sense to you. But perhaps you are puzzled, depressed, disheartened, by the life you see around you. Perhaps you ask yourself why you were born, why anybody was born. Perhaps you ask what's the sense in it. Perhaps you find yourself unable to believe in any of the traditional faiths that have sustained humanity throughout the ages. Living without faith in any of the revealed religions or in Western materialism, perhaps you suspect that life is by its nature not merely puzzling, but meaningless.

And perhaps – one final "perhaps" – perhaps you say to yourself, "if only I knew how to find the truth! And I don't want to be *told* and required to believe. I'm willing to listen to new ideas, but I want to be able to test them, to find out for myself." If that describes your situation, you've come to the right book.

A few years ago, I wrote a book called *Muddy Tracks: Exploring an Unsuspected Reality*, in which I set forth my tentative conclusions from first-hand experience as to what was real and what was not. Psychic powers? Spirit guides? Contact with other worlds? Was any of it real? Rather than taking anyone's word for it, I had gone looking for myself. The results were conclusive for me, but, in the nature of evidence, for no one else. How else could it be? Until you experience for yourself, you cannot know, you can only believe. In the things that are most important to us, there is no substitute for experience.

The critical experience was a six-day residential seminar called "The Gateway Voyage," held at the Monroe Institute (TMI), half an hour's drive south of Charlottesville, Virginia. In that week, I learned to bring myself, at will, to mental states that were both unusual and useful. More to the point, I learned to approach life from the heart rather than from the head. This proved to be the key to accessing to the psychic abilities I had longed for and half believed in.

After Gateway, I did other residential Monroe programs and learned how to get into touch with internal guidance, and how to contact and assist those who had died and not realized that they were dead. Had I only read about these things, probably they would have seemed little more than fairy tales. It was different, doing them myself, in the company of a score of others. The group interaction and reinforcement was critically important for us all, for we knew that except for each other, we explorers were on our own.

After the programs were over, many of us kept in touch primarily by way of an Internet group called the Voyagers Mailing List (VML), consisting of people who were interested in Monroe's work. And I myself was fortunate enough to have the help of a talented psychic, whose example before and after Gateway was critically important in preparing me for the massive changes taking place, and then absorbing and assimilating them.

But more important than any of these was the influence of those who are by far the closest to me: the disembodied entities I somewhat whimsically call The Gentlemen Upstairs, or the guys upstairs, or TGU. No point in trying too hard to define who or what they are. I think of them as roughly the parts of ourselves that extend beyond time and space. I first made contact with them in the summer of 1989, when I was 43 years old. This began as automatic writing and in time progressed to my being able to allow them to speak to me (and through me) even while I retained full consciousness.

The year 2000 brought two important developments that ultimately resulted in this book. In the spring, I began to become acquainted with Rita Warren. In the fall, I did a series of ten sessions in TMI's isolation booth, what I call the black box.

1) *Rita*. Rita had retired from a distinguished academic career that included an internationally acclaimed research program. This Ph.D. in psychology, following her own Gateway experience in 1979, found herself and her husband Martin running Bob Monroe's laboratory. They conducted hundreds of sessions in which people were put into unusual mental states and encouraged to do some mental roaming, some of which might be called channeling. After a period of four years, they retired again, and the conducting of the sessions was placed into other hands.

I met Rita and Martin because I was thinking of interviewing those who knew Bob Monroe best, to get their views of the man and his work before they passed from the scene. This scheme came to nothing, except that it did serve to put me into contact with them. In April, 2000, Martin died following an automobile accident. A few hours later, as I was writing in my journal thinking to interact with the guys, he contacted me, and in a one-paragraph message, he said in part "take care of Rita. I know you will want to."

Well, with such an introduction, who would not want to? So, she and I fell into the habit of having dinner together each Saturday night. As weeks became months, it became ever more natural to share ideas, feelings, thoughts, memories – in short, to communicate emotionally and intellectually. We spoke the same language and had something of the same background. This was balanced by many differences that added interest, not least that she had been an academic, and I had a skeptical wariness about academics. All in all, it was entirely natural that I would include Rita in my distribution list when I came to post transcripts of my black-box sessions.

2) *Ten sessions in the black box.* In late summer, seeking new adventures, I purchased a series of ten booth sessions at the TMI lab, with me in the box and lab director Skip Atwater at the controls outside the box, controlling the Hemi Sync signals and providing feedback. Beginning in September, we met for ten Fridays out of the next eleven. The series proved to be enormously productive, and (not much to my surprise) appeared to have been orchestrated from the other side to introduce themes, develop them over time, and culminate dramatically in the last session. I transcribed the tapes of the sessions and posted the transcriptions to the VML and to selected others, including Rita.

And there matters stood until July, when for my birthday Rita bought me another session in the black box, which was equally useful, and which led me to say to her that I wished I could do it more often. She suggested that we do the same thing in her home, as by this time I didn't really need the sensory isolation of the booth. So, on the night of Tuesday, August 8, 2001, I lay down on the bed in her guest room, playing a TMI tape to help get into an altered state, and she began to ask questions. This led to an extraordinary series of sessions that brought us far. A few words on what was extraordinary about the information we received.

To me, it seemed like nothing special on my end. Rita would ask questions and I would lie there, relaxed, in a mildly altered state, and say whatever came to mind. I was pleasantly aware of being a bit more fluent than usual, a bit more articulate, but as far as I was concerned, if something special was going on, it was in the nature and persistence of Rita's questions. (For, as the guys often say, the better our questions, the better will be their answers.) But when I told Rita that as far as I could tell I was just making it up as I went along, she told me – in the nicest possible way – that I wasn't smart enough to make up what she was hearing. And in the second place, she told me that in her *years* of experience conducting Explorer sessions, in very few of them had she or Martin been able to get any answers at all to some of the questions she was asking; and in no case had they gotten answers equal in clarity and consistency to what the guys were providing. That was the first time that I began to realize that what we were getting might be of real importance to the world.

Rita and I did not come to this information naïve. Rita had worked with Bob Monroe for years as a volunteer, running his lab, and we each had read his books and worked with the tools he developed. We each had done many TMI residential programs, and we each exchanged ideas, over many years, with many valued friends we had met at those programs, fellow explorers. Besides, between us, we had spent years exploring various aspects of metaphysics, religion, science, psychology, history, and literature in an endless line of books.

But anyone who does any serious exploring into the question of "what is real and what is not" is soon presented with difficulties. It is difficult to envision life on "the other side." How do beings there spend their time? What is it they do, and why do they do it? What if anything is their relationship to us? For that matter, what is our life all about? Questions of purpose have always dogged thoughtful individuals. Can they be answered? What does it all mean? And how does any of this square with what "common sense" tells us about the world?

Rita had accumulated a lot of questions in her time on earth. She set out to ask the guys for answers, and they were glad to oblige. But the difficulties in communicating between their side and our side surprised us, sometimes, and maybe surprised them, too. We, and they, had a lot of translating to do.

Over the course of many sessions with the guys upstairs, Rita and I were given a new way (1) to see the world, (2) to change our lives and, as you will see, (3) to thereby change the world. This promise is not overstated, but is, if anything, understatement.

In this book, we make no attempt to *prove* anything that is said, either by them or by us. I doubt if we could in any case. But we do better than that. We give you the tools you need to test it in your life. It may be that you will come to agree that what has been given to us here is the key to your greater self-development, the key to a better world.

We have not felt it necessary to treat their words (or ours!) as scripture. For ease of reading, we put the narrative into Frank's voice, and in cleaning up the transcriptions silently elided many a false start and "um." Sometimes in the interest of clarity and brevity we have condensed question or answer, but in no case have we changed the meaning. We have chosen (after hesitation and false starts) to present the material more or less in the order that it came to us. After all, if there are no coincidences, presumably there's a reason it came to us this way! Besides, the guys have proved themselves to be good teachers.

Rita and I went into these sessions thinking it was our own idea, as people do. It didn't occur to us that any one step would lead to another, and another, and it certainly didn't occur to us that we had embarked upon a course of action that was being planned out in detail Upstairs (with our on-going participation in the planning process, if TGU are to be believed). Only in retrospect is it obvious that Somebody planned out not only the individual sessions, but the series taken together. Even a casual observer should be struck by the fact that the questions Rita chose to ask did as much to form the pattern – as it turned out – as did the answers. A look at the sort of things that popped up, taken in the order in which they were introduced, shows how quickly certain themes were introduced, and how carefully they were built upon, session by session, until by the end of the series Rita and I were living in a very different world.

Speaking of living in a very different world, Rita made her transition, at age 88, on March 19, 2008. From time to time, I and others have been in contact with her. On one occasion, in the eight days between the time she lost consciousness from a stroke and the time she was able to die, she said of the life she was entering "it's going to be so *interesting*!" That was very much in character.

Although Rita did not live to see this book in print, fortunately she wrote her half of this introduction back in 2002, and so here is her view of the process as she experienced it.

by Rita Q. Warren

The Background

As Frank has reported, Bob Monroe turned his Explorer program over to my husband Martin and me shortly after his new lab was opened in early 1984. Here is how that came about.

In 1979 Bob and his family had sold their home ("Whistlefield") near Charlottesville, Virginia, and re-located about 30 miles south, in rural Nelson County, to build The Monroe Institute (TMI). He opened the first Gateway Voyage program in July, 1979.

A friend and I had read about Bob's work in his first book, *Journeys out of the Body*, and were eager to visit the Institute and participate in a Gateway. Fortunately, we were able to attend the second program given in Virginia, in August, 1979. My world changed in that week as it did for many who have experienced Gateway. [Those who have written about that life-changing event include Joseph McMoneagle *(Mind Trek)*; Bruce Moen *(Voyages into the Unknown); Ronald Russell (The Vast Enquiring Soul)*; F. Holmes Atwater *(Captain of my Ship, Master of my Soul)*; and Frank himself *(Muddy Tracks)*.]

I had thought of myself as a rather stodgy University professor during the 1970s and early 1980s, although I had had some periods showing promise earlier. During Gateway, my life was full of color and amazing adventures, experiences beyond ego. I hadn't planned to retire from teaching for another ten years or so, but when Bob offered lots near TMI for sale in 1980, I couldn't resist. Martin, having already retired, came down to the New Land to build a large house so that we would have room for us and for Nan Wilson (the friend with whom I had done Gateway) and, shortly thereafter, Darlene Miller. Bob offered another Gateway for New Landers (as we were now being called) and although I was concerned that a second Gateway could offer nothing so incredible a second time, Nan and I attended, and I did indeed have more heart-warming and soul-stirring experiences.

At the time we moved to the New Land, in 1983, Bob was building his new lab. He soon was ready to use the help of early residents of the New Land, including Dave and Jean Wallis, Bob Felix and his wife, and ourselves. By February of 1984, the lab was usable for "black box" sessions, although the new isolation chamber wasn't yet ready. Instead, we placed subjects in an old bed with electrodes on their fingers (and sometimes toes). The room had wires hanging about and being fed through the walls to a space on the outside that we called the control room. In the control room were a couple of little machines that were supposed to measure physiological reactions in the subjects.

When the lab was finally set up to begin experimental sessions, Martin and I were asked to attend a meeting that included Bob, Joe McMoneagle, Bob and Lindy Felix, and a few others who had participated in getting the lab set up. Lindy was asked to play the role of subject in the bed. Bob started to ask her questions through the mike and ear phones arrangements. Then he motioned to me to take over the monitor's chair. I was almost dumb-struck, never having visualized myself in such a role. (That was Bob's role!) I stumbled around, hemming and hawing. Finally, Joe took pity on me and suggested several questions that I might ask. (Bless you, Joe.) At the end of this painful exercise, I returned to my original seat at the meeting and Bob, who loved making grand gestures, walked across the room and dropped the lab keys in my lap. He said he would like to have me run the Explorer program.

Two main roles were identified in the control room, monitor and technician. The monitor was in continual contact with the subject via ear phones, while microphones carried the dialogue. The technician listened in and kept track of the physiological readings and briefly reported the content of each session on a minute-by-minute chart, noting important events in the subject's experience. The sessions were, of course, tape recorded.

In getting the lab ready and in our early experimentation, the tone was playful. After all, this was Bob's hobby we were playing with. However, once we were really ready to go, our level of seriousness changed completely. Bob identified our goal as "asking questions that would result in information that would be of value to all mankind." Thus, our questions included such topics as: consciousness, health and healing, environment and earth changes, nature of the universe, and various spiritual and philosophical questions. Beyond that, we asked many questions concerning the process in which we were engaged. What was the source of information we were being given and how was the information transmitted?

Volunteers to become subjects in the new lab were numerous from the start. The volunteers were primarily people who had been able to make good use of TMI programs, people for whom listening to the Hemi-Sync sounds in a protected setting had led to altered states of consciousness and experiences of considerable value to themselves and others. As we all knew, Bob in his earlier lab at Whistlefield had run explorer sessions, using some subjects in many sessions, including Rosie McKnight (author of *Cosmic Journeys*), Shea St. John, and Elisabeth Kubler-Ross. During the four years that Martin and I ran the Explorer program, hundreds of subjects participated in sessions. Most subjects had only one session, though one had more than 100.

When, after four years, Martin and I decided that we wanted to try retirement again, TMI found that they could not find volunteers to continue in our roles. I drew up a proposal for a follow-on program, focusing on booth sessions as personal explorations for individuals willing to pay a fee for the experience, to be run by a psychologist on TMI staff. This proposal was accepted and PREP (Personal Resources Exploration Program) has been operating since 1988.

Our retirement did not mean that we ceased our interaction with TMI. I took most of the advanced workshops that developed over the years; Martin participated in some. We worked as monitors in the lab now and then during crowded times such as the annual meetings of the Professional Division. I also conducted some evaluation research on a new advanced program, and I served and still serve on the Board of Advisors.

During the 1990s we withdrew into the quiet but friendly atmosphere of the New Land, but for a number of years I fell into a spiritual depression. By this, I don't mean that I was without spiritual beliefs. But I had grown spiritually in very active ways during many periods of my life, including the early days at TMI. Now, I felt dissatisfied – nothing growth-stimulating was happening. Martin had been a committed student of *A Course in Miracles* since before the manuscripts became books. I was a student also but did not find all my questions answered there.

One day in 1998, after Frank had been visiting our mutual friend Dave Wallis in the hospital, he exited the elevator as I waited to go up. Someone introduced us and Frank said, spontaneously, "Well, it's about time." Meaning, I guess, that although we had not met, we had heard about each other, as we were both living on the New Land.

Soon after, Frank came to visit my husband Martin and me to ask some questions about Bob Monroe and the early days at TMI. He knew that Martin and I had run the Explorer program and had spent many, many hours with Bob and his wife Nancy, and thus were familiar with "the early days." A couple of conversations, and that was about it.

Martin made his transition in April, 2000, so clear in his spiritual understandings of the process of dropping the physical body, and relieved that his transition-time had come. As Frank has said, Martin came to him that day and suggested that Frank and I stay in touch.

In July, with the help of a gifted psychic, Elizabeth Fitzhugh, I had a verbal interchange with Martin. He explained several events that occurred before and during his transition that I had not understood previously. Even though we believe that the human spirit continues beyond the body, it was reassuring to hear a particular well-known spirit speak of events that I recognized.

Then, over the next year and a half, The Plan led Frank and me through the whole thing, the whole series of meetings and conversations, the e-mails and the phone calls, the laughing and the sharing, becoming comfortable with each other and building trust. But, of course, we weren't told what was coming next. It "just happened" after I was moved to suggest that we try a session in my house.

The Process

All but two of the sessions between Frank/TGU and myself took place in the guest room of my home. (The other two sessions were held in the black box in TMI laboratory, with its advantage of isolating Frank from environmental distractions.) In my home, Frank lay comfortably on a bed. Quiet normally prevailed, although twice during the sessions, a phone rang in another room and had to be dealt with. Light was minimal but still could be somewhat distracting. In early sessions, Frank relaxed by listening via earphones to Monroe's Hemi-Sync sounds and joined the tape in "resonant tuning," a form of humming that helps the process. Gradually, both of these relaxation processes were dropped because they were not needed. Frank was able on his own to drop into an altered state where TGU were easily available.

In each session, for 45 minutes to an hour, I asked questions of TGU using a common interview style of asking broad questions first and follow-on questions to expand the topic. For most sessions I prepared several topics that I hoped we could cover. (According to TGU, the topics were suggested by their guidance or guidance of my own. As we will see, TGU indicate that, in general, we "capture" more of our thoughts than we create.)

I was interested in the structure of Frank's process with TGU. My prior experience suggested that two possible processes took place in this type of communication. In the first, the individual in the booth received questions from the monitor, proceeded to search for this information from whatever source they contacted, then reported it back to the monitor. In the second, following the questions from the monitor, the explorer in the booth simply allowed the information to flow though their vocal cords directly, without the two-step process. Fairly frequently the person using the first process later began to let the information flow in directly, cutting out the middle man, so to speak. This process is often called "channeling."

In the early days at TMI, channeling had a bad name. Bob Monroe insisted that neither he nor explorers in the booth channeled. This attitude seemed to be based on Bob's belief that there was something non-veridical about channeling. I asked Leslie France, who worked with Bob during this period, to describe Bob's attitude toward channeling. Her response was:

"Bob's aim was to demystify the process of interdimensional communication in part by refusing to use any of the currently 'charged' words associated with the various phenomena, even including the word 'spiritual' which is why he made up so much of the language in his books. 'Channeling' fell into this charged word category. Bob felt that if he described the explorer's work as channeling, his audience (readers and participants) would automatically filter the material according to their beliefs and biases about the word, and miss the real meaning of the material."

Frank assured me early on that he did not "channel," meaning that he remained conscious the entire time in a session. His definition of "channeling" and perhaps his attitudes toward it were based on the Edgar Cayce material.

At any rate the issue of awareness during the process of reporting information from contacts with non-embodied energies is not as simple as whether the recipient was or was not conscious. The degree of awareness varies, not only between recipients, but also over a session, and between the sessions of one person. The person reporting the experience may feel as though the words are coming unbidden through his or her vocal cords, or they may be hearing the words as though they are sitting in a lecture hall. In either case, the words may be fully recorded in their memory, totally forgotten, or vaguely or partially remembered.

In Frank's case, he continues over many sessions to feel that he (i.e., the physical Frank) is present but that he is not the source of the information nor the director of the flow. At the end of a session, he may remember very little but will recognize the material when it is called to his attention.

During a session, TGU hear the question or comment from me, often before I have completed it. Frank senses TGU's response – sometimes with a visual, sometimes not. If there is a visual, Frank's job is to describe what it means. If he experiences a "knowing," he attempts to express the ideas in words with frequent use of analogies and metaphors. The language that comes seems to be fed to Frank a phrase or a sentence a time without his conscious mind knowing what is coming.

This process has communalities with others who bring in information from nonphysical energies, but also has unique features. In my experience, the unique feature here is the close working relationship between TGU and Frank's conscious mind. Frank isn't just reporting TGU's responses. He isn't just interpreting what they have to say. The collaboration continually involves both parties as though they are one.

Relevant to the questions of awareness and memory, the issues of other bodily processes intrigue us. Frank feels extremely cold during sessions. Blankets are called for. Even more intriguing, Frank often arrived for a session wheezing, coughing, and having great breathing difficulties. But the minute he was in touch with TGU, all signs of asthma were gone. I did not realize this until a later session, but this phenomenon had become apparent to Frank in 1996 in the course of a session conducted by his friend and business partner Ed Carter. Frank had had Carter ask TGU why, when he was talking to them, he was not coughing, and as soon as communication ceased, he was coughing again. TGU told him that our physical health is actually "a relationship between our various bodies (physical, emotional, mental, astral) and our innumerable mental states," and that health may be affected by changing either end of the body-mind polarity. Changes to the bodies tend to persist but are harder to bring about. Changes in mental state are evanescent but are, therefore, quite easy to bring about.

Frank says that when he was where he goes mentally when he talks to TGU, the specific mind-body combination that had resulted in coughing was in abeyance. One end of the polarity had moved. When he returned to normal consciousness, he moved back where he had been, and the coughing resumed. The guys said this explains why people with multiple personality disorder may have one personality who is diabetic and another who is not. In each case, the body is the same, obviously; but the mind-body equation, so to speak, is not.

Knowing this, why can't Frank prevent asthma symptoms when he is *not* in conscious contact with TGU? As we shall learn, symptoms as well as many other personal issues are there for a purpose.

Working with guidance ought to simplify all our work. TGU recommend just looking to see what's next at hand and doing it. No planning necessary, no designing nor organizing questions, nor figuring out the clearest way to phrase them, no evaluation to determine whether the content of the response was sufficient to complete the information. Don't worry about writing up the experiences and findings; just have fun. Write irresponsibly, they said. Let the intuitions roll.

Interesting that F/TGU asked me to work with them. Scholars like me use all of the processes mentioned above to do the job, hopefully not in a rigid way but in a thoughtful and reflective way. It is amazing that it has worked as well as it has. In reading the transcripts, it is possible to find times when there was a disconnect between questions and answers and questions. But, by and large, the interview sessions went very well. And the writing occurred – easy for Frank, harder for me.

The Sessions

Coming into Session One with Frank and TGU, I was aware that it had been more than ten years since I had interviewed non-embodied energies. True, I had done this many times while working in the Explorer program. And I had talked with Frank about TGU and had read their quoted material in *Muddy Tracks*. I felt a great deal of respect and appreciation for this energy source. I very much wanted to do a satisfactory job of bringing forth their perspective on our lives and their situation. I was highly motivated to find out as much as I could about TGU energy and their role and function in Frank's life and in the lives of us all.

A further question arose for me in trying to understand the process going on between Frank and other explorers and the non-embodied energies speaking through them. Was the source of the information external energies or the "higher selves" of the person reporting? (Some explorers felt that, if the source was internal, they might be making it up. The issue of doubt is pervasive among explorers, including Frank. As a fear, these doubts can only interfere with the whole process.)

While working at TMI, I had decided that the inside/outside issue was irrelevant. Inside/outside is a physical dimension, and we are not dealing with a physical process here. Others have argued that this is theoretically a crucial question. (See Arthur Hastings, *With the Tongues of Angels*.) Most explorers seemed to feel that the source was external, as did Bob Monroe in the early days. In the later part of his career, Monroe clearly felt that he was dealing with other "grander" parts of himself. Transmissions from TGU indicate that they and Frank are one, and that we are always dealing with two points of view: One focuses on our separation as individuals and one focuses on our Oneness. In other words, Frank is both an individual and a part of the Oneness that includes, of course, TGU.

The early interviews felt like training sessions for me. In addition to learning how to see and interpret our world, I was being charged with learning a perspective and a process that was directly relevant to my questioning of TGU. I focused on trying to find out who "the guys upstairs" are. (In fact, I returned to the subject during the whole series of sessions.) The first few sessions were filled with TGU rejection of my questions because the questions were loaded with inaccurate assumptions. They especially rejected questions that suggested that we are separate as individuals and separate from them. They also rejected definitions of themselves as a group, a council or a cluster because those terms imply a collection of individuals. When I asked whether I was speaking with an individual or a group, TGU insisted that it was a meaningless question because it is a matter of viewpoints. They agreed that we could think of them as a task force working with Frank and others. They rejected at first the idea that they had been assigned to Frank, but presented themselves as an affinity group. When I finally asked them if I could call them you-all, they agreed that the term *you* didn't imply singular or plural and was thus acceptable. When I tried to find out how many were in the task force, they began to tease me with suggesting 30 ½ or 29 ¼. The teasing has never stopped.

They also challenged my use of all language that implies space and time. (I had experienced this issue before in our work in the Monroe lab.) The difficulty in avoiding this language is immense and probably not worth working toward. However, it is very useful to hear from TGU the problem it imposes for them. They see us living in "time-slices" whereas they view the whole of time at once. Spatially, we see things in geographical units or perceive phenomena in movement (for example, we see ourselves as moving from our Here to their There as we leave our physical bodies) while they see the whole.

In the early sessions, many areas that required follow-up did not get follow-up at that time, because I didn't understand sufficiently the implications of what they were saying. Fortunately, the big issues did arise again in later sessions so that questions could be further explored. When I confessed my lack of understanding to the guys, they were very reassuring. After all, the whole idea of Frank and I doing these sessions, as well as the timing of them, and the specific questions asked were the result of guidance – either TGU or mine (so far, nameless).

In the past I have known individuals who channeled for a fairly lengthy period of time and eventually seemed to become one with their source. That is, they could no longer separate themselves from their source and could no longer speak for their "Downstairs" self alone. Frank increasingly moved toward this position as the sessions progressed. Some individuals find this a difficult spot to be in since others often assume that material from a channeled source will be superior to that coming from "Downstairs." My sense is that when Frank gets into a completely relaxed state, even when he is not in a reclining position or specifically asking for TGU's input, he can easily speak from an "Upstairs" position.

TGU reported that Frank and I have an affinity relationship that allows for our working together comfortably. Frank's role is that of a journalistic reporter and my role is "professional thinker" who asks good questions. There are enough differences between us to set up a polarity so that questions and answers are needed. And, of course, Frank and I are both willing.

The early sessions with Frank were focused on learning what I could about TGU. Although Frank had worked with them for a number of years, his interest was in receiving information in response to his specific questions. I wanted to know more about how they described themselves as an energy source and how their interaction with Frank and others worked. One of the first things I found out is that they communicate information behaviorally. That is, the nature of the response makes their point.

Time and time again in our sessions, TGU reminded us that we were always dealing with two points of view – one that focused on our separation as individuals or groups and one that focused on our Oneness. They do not see themselves as a group of cooperating individuals, but rather as parts of a unified organism. Even so, when they respond to our questions, there is a specific energy involved, an energy which is most appropriate in responding to that question. So, are they individuals? Yes. Are they a unified organism? Yes.

In further trying to understand the nature of the interaction between TGU and Frank, I asked how they proceeded in answering one of Frank's questions or one of my questions. They said they don't act as a discussion group, deciding how to respond. Instead, they represent a pooling of information and a question to them focuses the information, brings relevant information together for a response. I wondered whether they ever advised Frank to proceed in a certain way or recommended an alternate way. There are rare occasions where they might step in with advice but, there is nothing more respected than free will. Their advice may also remain at an unconscious level. Inevitably, their perspective – since it is larger – is always different from his and they will always make their perspective known to him if he is interested or doesn't block it out. Their information comes in the form of hunches, intuitions, feelings, or emotions.

TGU's view of the world comes through Frank's eyes and the eyes of others. Because they have several sources of information, depth is added to their field and clarity of focus as well. Our perception is based on our choices and our essence or flavor is created by what we choose. We perceive in relative isolation and transmit our understandings to each other in the crude ways. They have a million ways of perceiving from millions of sources, and they can focus on any time or place. So, perceptually, the advantage is on their side. Action potential is on our side. Our "doing" is in creating ourselves and that is TGU.

I asked them about their emotional reactions. We might find their realm relatively chilly emotionally, they report, because for them an emotional response will be spread over a wider area. Would they have a negative emotional response to a catastrophe like Hitler? They would tend to see that more as an interesting natural phenomenon like an electrical storm than as a life and death battle between good and evil. Do they experience something like love? Yes, without the warm fuzziness. Love to them is the interpenetration of being, the fundamental oneness of everything, a binding energy. Then they reminded us that just as everything primarily looks separate until we remind ourselves that it is not, to them everything primarily looks as one until they remind themselves that it can be seen otherwise.

As the sessions progressed and our relationship became more like conversation, the content became more complex. One content area to which we returned a number of times was the discussion of reincarnation. Frank did not agree with TGU's description of the reincarnation process. The problem agitated him and made him crabby. At first, I also wasn't sure I understood the guy's description of the process, but then I had a vivid dream that cleared the picture for me. And Frank finally (after the sessions were over) understood and accepted TGU's interpretation. I think.

In connection with the process of moving in and out of a series (?) of lifetimes, TGU remind us that Earth is not the only playground and that lifetimes don't have to follow a set of rules regarding number or schedule or dimension or kinds of experiences. There are millions of paths and all are valid. What it boils down to, finally:

"You are us. It's just that you're over there right now. Again, of course, most of you *isn't* over there right now! [they laugh] You're still over here! But the part of you that we're talking to experiences yourself as over there."

The Impact of the TGU Material

What has changed for Frank and for me as a result of these experiences? I would prefer that Frank answer this question for himself, but he doesn't seem to enjoy being self-reflective. I have observed in him greater stretches of calmness. He seems more centered and relaxed, and he agrees with this description. TGU have joined him consciously more of the time (TGU would argue that Frank has joined them rather than vice versa).

My self-reflection tells me that I have made some mental, emotional, and psychological changes during our adventures. There have been a number of ways in which the statements of TGU have been particularly powerful for me.

1. Choosing. Our assignment in this life is to choose and choose and choose again. Being exposed to all of the contacts with TGU led to greater awareness that we are continually choosing minute by minute in our lives. After all, if that is our main purpose in life, it is much better to bring it totally into consciousness. It is our way of continually creating ourselves.

Intellectually, I can almost understand the idea of an unlimited number of paths that our choices send us on – choices of specific realities that we make at every moment. I don't operationally comprehend that or it would incapacitate me.

2. Stretching our consciousness. Our current step developmentally is to bring all parts of ourselves to awareness. "Filling our crystal with awareness" is the way TGU phrase it. Looking at everything from an Upstairs (Oneness) and a Downstairs (individual) perspective is TGU's recommendation; I am trying to do that as a way of redefining myself, remembering that the greater part of myself remains in the nonphysical.

3. Losing the dualities of here and there, now and then, us and them. In the timeless and spaceless world of TGU, we are in no way separate from them, and only here and now exist. We can bring our conscious focus on to the here and now, as is often recommended, and it is a useful thing to do since this is really what we have to work with. And knowing that we are One with our guidance is reassuring indeed.

4. Communication with guidance. This whole book is a reflection of how easy it is for Frank to dialogue with his guidance. It has not been so easy for me. In the past my conscious use of guidance has been to ask my guardian angel to help me in a delicate situation; i.e., to speak through me when I felt unsure of my ability to speak appropriately on my own. And, of course, I have often ask for protection for my children. But making requests is a long way from a dialogue.

Recently, I have been surprised to find guidance speaking to me. First thing in the morning before I am completely awake but continuing for a bit after I am awake. Not a dream. The content usually has to do with suggestions for the day, especially in relation to the book. Is this TGU? Is it some form of guidance of my own? I don't know. The voice seems separate from me but I know it isn't. I will continue to give it my attention and hope that it turns in to an on-going communication.

5. The body. I have spent a lot of time grumbling about the body – its needs and deficiencies. I try to feel grateful to it as well; it has kept me functioning for a long time. TGU say that the body gives us a point of view, a set of abilities and

a locus in time and space. That sounds pretty good. The body is holding together all the various bundles of energy that we brought into this life – a life that we had some part in planning. I am feeling more appreciative.

6. Other lives. TGU's recommendation for stretching our consciousness includes identifying and integrating our other lifetimes into our present life. Frank is able to do this with a number of other lifetimes. When he speaks or behaves in certain fashions, he often says: Oh, that's the David Poynter part of me, the Katrina part of me, the Egyptian part, and so on. I have been able to identify one other lifetime in great detail and four others in short flashbacks, but I have no experience with seeing those lifetimes integrated with the present. There is still work for me to do in this regard, another part of redefining ourselves.

7. All is well. All is always well. This is a frequent comment by TGU and one we most enjoy hearing. Stress is released and inner peace supported. Human beings need to remember, for example, that dropping the body is not a tragedy. Just part of the plan the person participated in developing for that lifetime. Remember that we are all volunteers in whatever events occur, say TGU. All is well. All is always well.

8. End of spiritual depression. As mentioned earlier, I came to this project following a period of feeling stuck on a path of spiritual development. A period of waiting may have been important, as TGU suggested. However, I was delighted to move on with the help of F/TGU. The sessions allowed me to move my attention to the process and the content of different ways of thinking about our interconnection with the other side. It allowed me, as well, to ask the kinds of questions that had been accumulating for me in the past decade and a half. As Frank talks about more sessions and another book, I overcome my feelings of being old and tired and rejoice in the opportunity to continue growing with the help of these friends.

My part of the Introduction is over except to say how much joy and laughter Frank has brought into my life. And I want to express my gratitude to TGU for ending my spiritual depression.

The Sessions

We begin with two extracts from the afterword of *Muddy Tracks,* written (about a year apart) by The Gentlemen Upstairs themselves.

1) We well realize, from dealing with Frank "over many years" of change, that you in your position find it difficult to understand us in our position. It tempts you to think that those who are not encased in bodies are all-knowing, all-powerful, all-anything. Conversely, it tempts you to think that we do not, because we can not, exist. It is hard for you to envisage us as we are. Impossible, probably, because you cannot even envisage yourselves as *you* are. This is said not with contempt, at all; nor with sympathy which would be undeserved, nor with despair which would be unwarranted...What we're saying is, different environments reflect themselves in different modes of being, which reflect in different externals such as language.

To put it more plainly, we on our home turf are different from you on your home turf, more because the turf is different than because of any inherent differences between ourselves and you. If you will think through the implications of this very true statement, you should find them very encouraging...

We will put it this way, you are already part of a larger being. It is in the larger being that you exist, for if you were cut off from it you could not live one second. And this is what your theologies have been telling you; only they could not give the reasons in a way that could be heard by you. This was no accident, for it is time for new conceptions, in order to make possible new ways of being.

Every age has its own characteristic way of seeing things, of reacting to what it sees, of becoming. The Middle Ages had possibilities closed to you at the new millennium. Similarly, ways that are open to you are closed to it, and for good reason. To allow anything to manifest, contradictory manifestations must be suppressed. You see? The life-force that is moved into vortexes to produce a rose must, in so doing, suppress everything that is *not* rose. Can a rose be a rose while also manifesting daffodil, or turtle, or elm tree? Yes, it is true that on the highest scale, everything is one; it is also true that that distinction is meaningless in nature, in what Frank calls 3D Theater.

2) We end as we began. There are not *two* worlds, but *one* world, not *two* realities, but *one* reality containing an infinitude of seeming realities. Not a dream world and a real world, but a world that is a real dream. That is, reality is a dream; the dream is the reality. Same thing, said seemingly differently because of the difference in starting point and emphasis.

You – we, everyone, everything – are part of *one* indissoluble reality. Thus everything impinges on, colors, everything else. Nothing can exist in isolation, because there is no isolation to exist in! All is one; separations are illusion. Not that it is a magic trick, or a delusion, but that the appearance of separation masks and blurs an underlying connection. Just as space is not separate, just as time is not separate, but each is considered to be made of separate parcels so that they may be apprehended, so reality in the widest possible sense is not separate, but all one thing.

Live in that knowledge. Know that you overlook any one facet of reality only at the price of to that extent disregarding what is. "I say, ye are gods." Of course. How could it be otherwise? Ye are also rocks, and sky, as actors in a movie might be said to be individual actors but might be also said to be "part of" that movie. Is either view of things untrue? Is either view the only valid way to see it?

We say to you, see things as they are. The only way to do that – since neither the one viewpoint nor the other is the only correct way to describe reality – is to alternate from one to the other, or to overlap them (dealing with the slight resultant confusion and fuzziness), or to *see* one way, while *remembering* the other way. Then you will be whole.

Session One
August 8, 2001

[Rita and I decided to meet Tuesdays at seven P.M., which gave me time enough to get home from work, check my email, change clothes, and have supper. Then I'd drive the short way to her house, and we would talk for a bit, and then I would stretch out on the bed in her guest room/work room, pulling a cover over me to protect from the temperature drop that comes with altered states. I would lie with my head toward the middle of the room to be close to the tape recorder's microphone, and she would sit on an uncomfortable-looking chair nearby, with her note cards spread out on the seat of another chair in front of her.

[We went into these sessions thinking they were our own idea. It didn't occur to us that maybe the idea of sessions, and the content of the sessions, might be prompted from the other side. In retrospect it is obvious that somebody was planning it, or was improvising pretty smoothly as we went along. For the questions Rita asked introduced certain themes, and theme built upon theme, pretty smoothly.

[For the first session, she lent me a portable tape player and a Monroe tape to bring me to an altered state. Like the black box itself, the tape was a handy crutch, but not really needed. After a few sessions we dispensed with it as unnecessary. At first, Rita asked to talk directly to The Gentlemen Upstairs rather than me, and I had to explain that although the words come through me in "their" voice, as though from them, I don't ever space out entirely. I am not "elsewhere" during the process. But I did suggest that she address them directly, so as to make it easier for me to remain receptive, passive, neutral. Think of me lying there, saying whatever comes into my head, holding myself in a middle place where I was neither censoring the material nor trying to shape it.

[During the first sessions, I lay there listening to a Monroe Institute free-flow Focus 27 tape on earphones [Focus 27 is a Monroe term for a non-physical state that closely tracks Earth activities], to help me to get into an altered state and remain there. After a couple of minutes, I told her that I was ready to go.]

Rita: I'd like to talk directly to The Gentlemen Upstairs. Can you do that?

Frank: I can't guarantee that I won't be here but I'll relay what I get. What I mean by that is that I'll be here, but the words will just come through like from them. I don't ever space out entirely.

R: You don't need to space out, you can just move over a little bit, and let them speak directly to me, if that's acceptable to them. I'd like to have a little more information about them, from them. About who they are, how they relate to you,

[I moved into an altered state.]

TGU: What would you like to know, as a starting place?

[Rita's very first question plunged us into deep water.]

The Gentlemen Upstairs – Individuals or a Group?

R: Are they a group, or a solo individual?

[I suggested that she address them directly, rather than talk to me, so as to make it easier for me to remain receptive, passive, neutral.]

R: All right, I'd like to speak to The Gentlemen Upstairs and ask them to tell me a little more about themselves, whether they represent themselves as individuals or a group –

TGU: Well you might find it hard to understand, but individuals versus a group is a meaningless concept even on your end, but much more meaningless on our end, because it's a matter of viewpoints. If you look at it one way, it's all one thing with individual nodes, and if you look at it the other way, it's all individuals who are closely cooperating. It's the same on your plane, but it doesn't seem like it to you because your physical bodies hold you apart and you have the illusion that your minds are separate because they seem to you to be in different heads. You can look at us either way and be partially correct.

R: Is there a spokesman who talks to Frank in response to a question he asks?

[I got a visual image that I found hard to describe. Think of a circular ring filled with marbles, as an omelet would fill the bottom of a frying pan. At any given time, the one that will come forward will be the one most closely attuned to the question or the questioner. I expressed this, and then shifted back into their voice.]

TGU: It isn't a hierarchy or a rigid structure, it's more like, if you had a cloth and the cloth were woven this way and that way, the warp and the weft, every intersection point of the thread could be represented as an individual. There's no hierarchy there, it's just all interconnection.

R: Yes, I wasn't thinking of hierarchy so much as, on a particular topic some one might be more relevant to answer.

TGU: That's right. It's not necessarily predictable who that'll be. Some are sort of permanently stationed here [chuckles] from your way of looking at it, although of course, you know about multi-tasking; that's what we're doing too. But when you're interested in talking, we're interested in talking. Some aren't necessarily part of that, they are doing other things, but they are on tap when we need something more specific. But that's more or less transparent to you, because you don't have the skill at hearing nuance as to who's different.

Some people would be unable to function with the metaphor we just gave you. They would have to have a metaphor of individuals cooperating. So they would get a story that would allow them to function. The more sophisticated the understanding, the more sophisticated the metaphor that we can use to then stretch you.

R: Do I hear the suggestion that some of the energies are usually with this group, and others come and go?

TGU: That's right. You might think of us as a task force, or connected individuals. And of course this is not the only thing we do with our time.

R: So it isn't always Frank that you work with then?

TGU: Hardly. Think how often he doesn't use us, even unconsciously.

R: So you have this kind of responsibility with other individuals on earth?

TGU: Yes. Not just on earth.

R: Not just on earth. But are all the individuals that you work with in physical bodies?

TGU: Not necessarily *human* physical bodies. And not necessarily aliens as you're thinking, but more like, if something's in another dimension, it has a sort of a body, but there might not be a sort of a body that would be recognizable to you.

TGU's Work

R: Would you think of the work that you're doing with Frank and others as an assignment that you've been given?

TGU: [pause] Too many definitions. "That we've been given," particularly. You could say it's more like a location that we gravitate to. It's somewhere between a hobby and an endearment. It's a way of fulfilling our own nature. It's not a one-way street. The giving is the receiving, you know? So, we once told Ed Carter [my friend with whom I did many TGU sessions] we're teachers. He understood it that way, and we knew how he'd understand it. That's close enough. We do it for the satisfaction of doing it.

There *is* the nuance, now that I think of it, of being assigned, but if there is an over-arching assignment pattern, we don't necessarily notice it. [pause] Interesting thought. We might think about that ourselves.

R: With respect to the work you're doing with Frank and with others, are you involved in other activities that are very different from this particular activity?

TGU: [pause] We don't mean this in any disrespectful or impatient way, but it's nearly impossible to talk about it because our and your frames of reference are so different. Frank always says we go around the barn [in explaining things], but sometimes it's necessary to take a long perspective. Let's try a metaphor.

If you were to ask a similar question of various organs in the human body – the liver and the pancreas and the white blood cells, say – each of them might have an entirely different concept of what it is they were doing. Depending on their mood at the time, they might say, "well, yes, we do x," or they might identify with a different part. A muscle cell might define itself one time as muscle, another time as part of the right arm, another time as flesh, you see. All those are true; they're all inadequate. You must remember that we extend into your dimensions. You all tend to think of us as being in Focus 27, or somewhere. But that's only sort of true.

R: Are you rejecting the notion of space?

TGU: More, rejecting the notion of limitation. We're everywhere as you are everywhere, and we would say you don't, we don't, nobody really *moves*; it's a question of where your attention is. And so perhaps you ought to think of us as a localized part of all that is. Part of us is in your physical matter reality and part of us isn't.

You've been told that you exist in every dimension, because you couldn't exist in height and depth but not in width, say. Well, if reality were 30 dimensions, let's say as an example, then everyone must be in all 30 dimensions. So it isn't really true, from our point of view, that you are *there* and we are *here*, but it's that we are – where we are. We're in the only place there is. We're *all* in the only place there is, because there's only one of us, maybe, or maybe there's a million of us. (Definitions!) We know that sounds vague, but it's the best that can be done. It is, in fact, worthwhile to break down the unconscious assumption that there's a "there" and a "here," there's an "us" and a "them," there's a "now" and a "then." It's all one thing. It's all the only thing there is, but it can only be experienced as separations and distinctions.

R: I think I see what you're saying there, however that leads me to difficulties.

TGU: We did warn you. [chuckles]

TGU and We Co-Exist

R: When Frank speaks to you, it's as though he thinks you are seeing things from a somewhat different perspective than he is, or perhaps a higher perspective than he has. So the different perspective suggests that there's some separation there.

TGU: Think of it as a difference in emphasis. If you are partly *in* time-space and partly *outside of* time-space, as you move your emphasis, you move your experience. We – meaning what he calls the guys upstairs – are primarily outside of time-space. You are primarily *in* time-space. We both extend both places, because there's no other way it can be. Everyone is everywhere. Everyone is the only place there is. But if our emphasis is over here and your emphasis is over there, yes, it is going to change the point of view. We would suggest to you, though (which will shake up everybody's concepts, we hope) that we can slide our point of view down toward you, and in fact we do it all the time. You can slide your emphasis up toward us, and *you* do it all the time. As would have to be, because it's the same thing!

It's difficult for us to explain how it is, because everything you see is divided by time-slices, and a reality that is experienced in time-slices, or space-slices, can only be experienced as sequential or fragmented. There's nothing wrong with that. But we once showed Frank that it was difficult for us to kind of remember where he was, because if you had a five-foot long fish, and you had to find one scale on the fish because that's where he happened to be, you could have occasional difficulties finding that scale on the fish, you see. [they chuckle] We know that he doesn't like the analogy much, but that's too bad.

R: Were you available to Frank before he recognized that consciously?

TGU: Oh, certainly! It would not be possible to live in 3D Theater, as you call it, with only the resources that you have [on your side]. You don't recognize the help you're being given every minute. You can learn to, but you don't necessarily.

R: Was there an effort on your part to get Frank's attention?

TGU: [laughs] We would hardly say *an* effort! [they laugh]

Frank: I think they've insulted me enough, we can go on. [Rita and I laugh] They were implying stubbornness, if you didn't hear it. [We chuckle again, then it's back into TGU mode.]

TGU: In fact one of the things that makes him the most valuable made him the most difficult, and that is the repeated, "I don't want to be fooling myself, I don't want to assume something's true which may not turn out to be true, I don't want to be a dupe, I don't want to be a victim of wishful thinking." It required demonstration after demonstration after demonstration. But that exact trait also makes him a better witness, because it gives him a place to stand. Nobody could possibly be as stubborn resisting him as he was resisting us.

R: That sounds in character, there.

TGU: [chuckles]

Blurring Distinctions

R: In Frank's book Muddy Tracks, *he seemed able to clearly distinguish between when he was speaking and you were speaking. When he speaks now, or when he's in laboratory sessions, I find it difficult to know who is speaking. Is this increasingly true for Frank?*

TGU: No. What's happening is that he was required to make a Copernican world-view shift first, and to do that found it either necessary or convenient to almost over-emphasize the difference between us. That was the only way he could conceptualize it. But he began realizing that we're often speaking through him, perhaps to say something important to someone else who had to hear it from a human voice because they weren't able to hear it inside. Once he realized that, he began seeing it more, and then he began seeing other aspects of himself – other lifetimes, as you call it – going in and going out, in and out, and then he began to deduce, correctly, that he does the same thing there [i.e., speaking from other lifetimes' point of view], unconsciously usually. The more he looked into it, the more he realized, it isn't "me" versus "them," it's really I/them, or it's us, or it's me. You know, all the distinctions blurred.

Which is good! Because the distinctions were never accurate in the first place. They were, shall we say, a necessary detour, because if you are entrapped in a given logical structure, the only way out *may be* to go to an equally inadequate structure which nonetheless is different, so that the comparison frees you from both. So he initially said, "this is me, this is them," then went to "well, maybe this is me, maybe this is them," and as time went on, found that in ordinary life – there's *only* ordinary life.

That was another distinction that he had made as a halfway house, you know, the ordinary life versus talking with us! But there's only ordinary life. Or, there's only talking to us, whichever way you want to look at it; it doesn't make any difference. Or there's both. Or there's neither.

R: So, then this has to do primarily with the extent to which Frank is conscious of it?

TGU: [pause] We would say it has primarily to do with a re-structuring of mental structures. Your mental structures are ordinarily transparent to you, and therefore they are an almost infallible way of warping the world. That's not necessarily bad or good, but it's the way it is. Getting through the structures is always provisional, always incomplete, because you really can't live in 3D Theater without structures. But it's worthwhile to exchange them, to remind yourself that in fact you don't have *the* structure; you know, *the* truth. [pause] That didn't quite answer your question, did it?

R: [laughs]

TGU: Want to re-phrase it, then?

R: No, I think that's fine. You answered a better question.

TGU: We heard the doubt, though. The hesitation, anyway, the reservation.

R: The doubt has to do with my next question.

TGU: Ah.

The Concept of Levels

R: Recently Frank has talked as though he understands that there are many levels. Many levels of what I'm not quite sure, but a suggestion would be that because he's in a physical body, he's in a certain level. At another level you might be viewing things from a different perspective. Is this an appropriate way to think of him?

TGU: [pause] Well, we're not sure what you mean by those things. Do you mean levels of being, or levels of – ?

R: Well, to the extent that Frank's on one level and you're on the next level, my next question would be, is there another level beyond that, and beyond that, and – ?

TGU: No, no. We even said specifically in *Muddy Tracks* that the difference be-tween us and you is much more a difference of the turf that we're on than of any other thing. You in our place would be like us. And we in your place would be like you. And what we didn't say but could have, is that it isn't that it *would* be that way, it *is* that way. The part of "The One Thing That Is Us" that is in time-space functions as you do *because* you're in time-space. The part of "The One Thing That Is Us" that is *not* in time-space functions as we do because we're *not* in time-space. But there's no difference between you on your end and us on our end other than just where we are.

Now, if you're talking about the difference in levels of being, that's a different thing, but if you're talking about you on your level and us on our level, you all tend to put us up on a pedestal, and it's a mistake, because it not only removes us from you conceptually, but also under-rates what you're doing. What you're doing is difficult, and requires skill, and is valuable, and requires courage. So we respect it highly. At the same time – it's us! You see? In all of these things, the way your language is structured – and you do hear the word "your" [chuckles] – the way your language is structured continually, quietly, between the lines, emphasizes divisions that are not real divisions. They're *circumstantial* divisions. There is no "you" and "us"; it's an "all-us" kind of thing. But there's almost no way, in fact there probably *is* no way to speak without using such language, because the language was developed in your circumstances.

R: I think that Frank's notion of levels has to do with the suggestion that there are a series of levels that each have a larger perspective than the previous level. Is there a series of these that you're aware of, and are you aware specifically of a level just beyond your own?

TGU: [pause] A spatial analogy might be that of climbing a mountain, where each new level gives you a broader view, at the price of reducing your grasp of detail. You can see more, but you can see less detail. We would say that's the major difference in terms of difference of level.

That's if you look at it one way. Now we'll take it all back and look at it another way, and say that if you were to imagine yourself as "an individual" – which we know is the way you see it – if you look at yourself as if you really were an individual, there's a part of you in time-space and another part of you outside of time-space. We would say this is illusory, because there's only one thing. But take it that way. If, then, you said that one percent of you is in time-space and 99 percent of you is outside of time-space, then the first step would be to increase your awareness of what is beyond time-space. Maybe you could double your level of being; you could be a broader, deeper person with more resources and more awareness. There would always be more and more and more until you were the absolute maximum person that you could be.

That would involve many different lifetimes. But we want you to remember, we're trying to cram all this into this time-space analogy. To say it closer to right we would have to say something like, "all of your lives at the times they're there, and the time between times at the times that we're here in non-time . . ." [laughs] It's very clumsy. And it's misleading. But you see the idea. We think.

We would go further than that and say that since we're all intimately, literally connected, we can't conceive of any end to the level, because we can't conceive of anyone being able as an individual to extend to all that is. On the other hand, just as in that movie *The Global Brain,* Peter Russell speculated that 10 billion things make a new level of complexity, we suspect that when x number of us come to know what we are – if all of us come into our full flower – we will probably realize that we are part of something bigger, starting all over again. Just as the cells in your body are part of a larger being and some know it and some don't, and you are part of a larger being, and some of you know it and some don't, we are part of a larger being and some of us know it and some don't. It goes on forever. We don't know the ultimate, any more than you do, either ultimate small or ultimate large.

R: I see. So do you have questions in your own mind about this? The idea of the larger and larger being, or the larger and larger entity, or energy?

TGU: Well, if we were humans we'd call it idle curiosity because our day-to-day work is in what we're doing. Everything tells us that this is what needs to be done to go to the next step, but what's beyond the next step is as blank to us as it is to you.

The Next Step

R: And the next step is – ?

TGU: The next step is this current step, this bringing all parts of ourselves to awareness. Once that happens, something else happens. In fact, Bob Monroe said the same thing. He was talking to someone and they said that whenever they got their elements to a level of awareness, something happens at that point. Now, the something that happens takes them out of our viewpoint, out of our reality, in a way, so we don't really know. But there's no sense of apprehension about it. It is clear to us that that is the next part of the process, as death is to you, only without the resonance of fear of death that is often the case with the physical body. We know that we are participating in this process in order to bring this on, but what happens after that, we'll let you know. Except you will know too, because you'll be –

R: Part of that process as well.

TGU: But the thing that's hard to get across to you is, you're part of *this* process too! [pause] It isn't like you're the slow pupils and we're trying to bring you on so we can go on to the next grade. It's more like you're the explorers and we're listening to your reports and learning from them partially vicariously, and partly by participating. This is as much learning for us as it is for you.

R: Okay. Have all of you in your realm been through a process of physical body –

TGU: Oh, you don't have any conception of how many of us – if you want to look at it individually – there are. It would hardly even be possible. This is a...[pause] A moment. Let's think about this.

Supposing you looked at the surface of a globe of the earth, and you looked at Greenland. That island might represent the amount of reality that's physical, and all the rest of the globe would represent the amount of reality that cannot be described as physical. There are people doing things everywhere.

R: Then I guess the answer to my question is no.

TGU: The answer is there are many more things to do than be in the physical, and relatively few people are in the physical. Except – we keep coming back to it – another way of looking at it would be to say that a very small portion of our body is in the physical. Because you could look at it, we keep reminding you, as one thing. When you look at as one thing we have a few fingertips in various physical matter realities. But those fingertips, by their nerve endings – to carry the analogy further – report to the whole rest of the body. At the same time, they're nourished by the whole rest of the body. That's not a bad analogy.

R: I'm talking now about your own experience, either as a group or individual: Have you had the experience of the physical?

TGU: Well, some of us have. If you look at us as individuals, you're talking right now to about 30 individuals. Sort of.

R: So it isn't necessary to have had a physical body for you to be in your realm of experience.

TGU: Oh no. No, no, not at all, any more than it's necessary for a fingertip to have had experience as a white blood cell, or as a lung tissue. You see? In a way, it's specialization of function, but in another way, it really is just a matter of definition. It's so simple, it's hard to get across. But we assure you, it's easy, once you cross the line. [chuckles]

The Nature of Individuals

R: Once Frank crosses over, is there some reason to believe that he won't join those of you who are speaking to him?

TGU: Well, he couldn't help it. Oh, you mean, in our function?

R: In the functions that you're engaged in right now.

TGU: [pause] Well, he's an explorer and a teacher by inclination. It's part of him. But he has lots of other parts that are other things. [laughs] We'll give you a choice of answers: yes and no. [they laugh] Yes, in that that particular atom of our being will be on call for a specific person who needs to talk to him, when he's the closest resonance to someone who's talking. But the difference between him and Frank is so –

You think, because you're in bodies, that the body makes a unit. But it doesn't. The body has huge amounts of stuff inside it that function as a unit, sometimes better, sometimes worse. But the body holds together disparate things. Basically the body gives a point of view and a set of abilities and a locus in time and space. That's really what the body *does!* So take away the body, and all those strands of the bundle – well, the analogy breaks down, but you see where we're going with that?

R: There's no reason to believe that these parts will hang together –

TGU: Well, they're not *going* anywhere, but "there's no reason to think of them only in that way" would be a better way to put it. Katrina would see them from Katrina's point of view. It's the same bundle. But there's plenty more of that bundle that's unsuspected and that does not manifest in that life, that would manifest somewhere else. So –

[At this point the tape ran out and a few seconds worth of plastic leader ran through until the cassette clicked off. Seems like we always ran out of tape in the middle of something interesting, and so often lost a few words or even a couple of sentences. This was before the days of digital recorders. We changed sides of the tape.]

R: Feel okay?

Frank: Yep. Where were we?

R: We were talking about the various bundles from different lifetimes. We could have a part of the energy moving across temporarily into the "there," although that's a time concept, which I assume you don't want.

[TGU again]: The point is just that individuals are so much less individual than you think they are because they're enclosed in a body. It would be like thinking that the electric components inside of a tape recorder are all inherently part of that tape recorder, but they're not. They *are*, while they're in a tape recorder, but the tape recorder could be taken apart and all the components reshuffled somewhere else. It's a clumsy analogy, because that's mechanical and not alive in that sense, but you understand.

So to talk about will "he" be doing this or that later, in a way we'll say no, "he" is only here between the time that he's born and the time he dies, which is a finite thing. That's a slice of reality during which he functions in a certain way. That slice of reality doesn't go away; it's just that you're not experiencing it. Thomas Jefferson functioned as a particular bundle in a certain place. He's still doing it in that place, it's just you can't access that place.

R: You've talked a number of times about the idea of other lives, with the suggestion that parts of the energy field that represent Frank now have participated in other lifetimes – other experiences in different physical bodies.

TGU: With the exception of the tenses of the verbs, we agree with that. It's more like, "are participating," although we know that's nearly incomprehensible to all of you.

R: Well, it is nearly incomprehensible, but I can understand that there is such a concept.

TGU: It's so easy once you step outside of where you are, but – that's why you're there! [laughs] New Jersey doesn't cease to exist when you move to New York, but you can't access it. And in the case of time, you don't have the ability to go backwards to where you were. Seemingly.

The Merit of This Work

R: Okay, now I'd like to ask, is there any merit for Frank in the kind of thing we've been doing this evening?

TGU: Sure. There's no substitute for experience. This is like going to school, or like reading. It's input. If you experience something, and think about what you experienced – or even if you don't – it changes you. The more of it you do, the easier it is to do more, and it becomes more efficient. Besides, he enjoys it.

R: [pause] Exploring his relationship with you has been a main topic. Is there something else that would be good for us to explore?

TGU: Well, you haven't said anything about *your* reasons for doing it, what *you* are getting out of it.

[Again I left the altered state for a moment]: I have no idea what that means. I'm starting to fight some emotional resistance now, because I feel like an eavesdropper. I hope that meant something to you.

R: Yes, I thought I understood that. What am I up to here? Why is this something that I want to do?

[TGU again]: Not that we want to know the answer to that, but to show you that we already know the hidden question – which we're trying carefully to conceal! [they laugh]

R: – and too well! This a role that I've played a lot, and enjoyed a lot. It has to do with another way of looking at a human being in all his complexity and glory. And it is always a combination of learning something about a specific human be-

ing and learning something about the nature of things generally. This is a very positive experience.

TGU: We suggest to you that you have yet to decide whether to consider yourself honorably retired, or to go on and do some more pleasurable but perhaps strenuous explorations. We also remind you that all paths are good. We're not making any implied push – although we've been known to do it in a certain direction, but he's more stubborn. [chuckles]

R: Well, that sounds awfully like Frank.

TGU: Well, but, you know, this is one of the things that began to erode his artificial concept about the difference between him and me, is to realize –

[Frank, suddenly]: "Him and me"; did you hear that?

R: I did hear it.

[TGU again]: Is to realize that when you say "that sounds like him," we *often* sound like him, because we're often coming through – and not only *we*, but David, or Katrina, or John, or whomever – and obviously the same for you and everybody else. That was a realization that began to erode that artificial separation for him. Finally.

R: Well, retirement means that you stop working for pay and go on doing what you want to do.

TGU: Mm-hmm. If you're lucky.

R: If you're lucky, and I am very lucky in this regard. And I'm not about to go out and apply for a job as a monitor of people for these kinds of experiences.

TGU: [chuckles] We'll make it a little blunter. [they laugh] You could take this as a self-chosen assignment and structure it in any way that you wanted, and here you have the unique opportunity to do it either reciprocally or at the same time; you can do it once a week, once a month, once a year, every 25 minutes – and you could explore whatever you wanted to explore, without any external considerations of utility – which is what Ed Carter did [with Frank, talking to TGU], some years ago.

Or, as we say, you could regard yourself as honorably retired and you don't need to do any of this. You're not required or even expected to do anything at all. You're required and expected at this stage in your life to do what you want to do. The difficulty is deciding what that is. We would say to you that in the present state of development in August of 2001, the vast majority of seeming individuals are *not* doing what they want to do.

R: Well, I don't have other questions at this time.

[Frank again]: No, I just got the same feeling, that that's like a natural end to things. [yawns]

R: I guess you were awake the whole time.

Frank: No, I'm *very* rested. Shall we stop?

[Note this final exchange. I didn't notice it at the time, but it showed that Rita and I were not yet fully on the same wavelength. She, from years of experience working with people in altered states in the booth, still expected that when we were talking to the guys, I would not be there, and to the extent that I was still there listening, we were somehow not quite where we should be.]

Session Two
August 21, 2001

[We skipped a week – can't remember why, now – and then we were back in another session. You will note that Rita had a habit of referring to discarnate personages as "energies." It was a long time before I asked her about it. Turns out, someone in sessions long before had recommended that phrasing.]

TGU's Mission

R: *Last week I was trying to find out your sources of information, and your relationship to them, and I'd like to continue that. I got the sense that they are a group of energies. The number 30 came up. I didn't understand exactly what 30 represented. Were those aspects who specialize in certain kinds of information, or play particular roles with you, or –*

TGU: No, that was about the number of what you'd call people that participate at any given time. It's as though you are talking to about 30 of us more or less, at any given time.

R: *Do the 30 of you specialize in certain kinds of information?*

TGU: Well, we were trying to make clear that it isn't so much what we *specialize in* as what we *are*. This is a different way of saying the same thing, but we want to make that nuance clear. If you're an historian by occupation, you could look at yourself either as an historian by occupation or as resonating to that particular kind of information. We're specialists in the same way that you all are specialists; not by occupation, by what we are, what we resonate to.

R: *And this particular cluster of energies has been brought together because of their relationship to Frank?*

TGU: This again is something we were trying to get across last time, and it can be very difficult because you all start from the assumption of separation, and so you think of us as being separate up here, but it isn't that way, this side. It would be like you trying to make more of a distinction between the kinds of cells in your hand than there is. You could say that everything up here is available, and that would be true. You could say, *some* things up here resonate to a particular situation, and *that* would be true.

R: All right, I'm trying to think of you not in your individual-ness but in your cluster-ness. Does the cluster of energies that you represent have a specialty mission?

TGU: [pause] We feel that it would be misleading to answer the question in the terms it's placed. We know of Jane Roberts [who brought forth the Seth material] and the way they were explaining things, but we think that it came filtered through her language, because it has to come through language. And we think it's time to clear that up a little, because it still sounds more like cooperating individuals than – how else could we be described? The only analogy that we can think of is as parts of one organism. We're objecting to your saying *a* cluster, because the associations in your languages bring the idea of being an individual in through the back door. [pause]

Think of computer timesharing. You have one major computer and all those terminals. To a person typing at a terminal, it would look like he was dealing with one cluster of that machine, and in a way that's true. But it isn't really true. Do you see why we're gagging at this? To call us a cluster is to sort of bring the idea of individuality back in through the back door, in a way that's more misleading than it is representational.

R: I'm searching for another word that doesn't suggest bringing in individuals but representing a totality of some kind, in its operation with Frank, for example.

TGU: But, in its operation with *you* it's not necessarily totally different. It's not a different individual, it's not overlapping, it's not shared, it's not separate. The words have to keep in mind the difference of what we call the playing field. And your language doesn't do that because your language describes *your* playing field. We're trying to...[laugh] We're playing an away game. It's difficult to describe.

We know that it's probably a little irritating for us to constantly be quarreling with the question, but if you see more from our point of view, a lot of your questions will fall into line. If we try to answer your questions and leave you in your point of view without also bending it, or extending it, or alternating it, let's say, with *our* point of view, all it will do is reinforce your point of view, and it will warp the picture.

R: Okay, I accept that, as long as we can keep struggling, trying to get an answer.

TGU: Well, this is good work, in fact. We *approve* of the work!

TGU and Frank

R: Do you have a mission with respect to Frank?

TGU: You say "a mission." When you say "a mission," there are two kinds of missions; one mission is your life. But you are asking, do we want to accomplish something over and above the living of the life. Yes?

R: Well, in the sense that it provides direction, or has some impact on the life that we value.

TGU: [pause] To use your expression, we're trying to wrap our mind around the concept, because it's incomprehensible that there could be a separation between what a person's life is...[pause]

The mission that we sent him on, or that we sent *you* on, could be described, and if that's what you want we can do that; but it isn't separate from the life.

R: So that one could say that the mission hasn't developed with his experience and training, but rather that he brought the mission with him?

TGU: The mission flowers as you live it, but you go into it knowing the flower that you plan to grow, even though you don't remember that when you're here, necessarily. So that's the mission, you know? He is a living-out of certain ideas, abstractions, ideals – and that is the importance to us, because that's how we live it out.

R: Considering where he started when he came into the physical body in this life, how is the plan developing? Is it developing as expected?

TGU: [pause] Well, he's missed some opportunities but he's grasped others, and we don't mean to be evasive but, the plan was more to put him in place, and the plan *is* for him to choose among the options. He might have been more forthcoming and overcome more tentativeness. On the other hand, he could have been unable to grasp the opportunities at all, and turned away from it. None of it is ever predestined. It can be set up as a preponderance so that the chances are, you're going to follow the path up to a point, but to predestine it would be to destroy it. Nothing can be done without free will; you're here to choose. That's the point of the thing.

Planning a Lifetime

R: To what extent did Frank have a part in developing this plan before he came into this lifetime?

TGU: Before he was created into this lifetime he was part of us. You could look at yourselves as bubbles that come up off a boiling sea, or as wheat sprouts in a field. Don't make the distinction between us and you as firmly as you're making it. Because, you *were* us. And you *are* us, in a different environment.

He was not so much sent as created, just as all of you are. That is, a little of this, a little of that, a little of that, put together – those tendencies and abilities, and disabilities, and inheritance and all of those things are put together in a package. When the package dissolves, all of that original material is still there, and can be re-mixed to make a new cake. When you die, if you've crystallized your soul you remain crystallized. If not, the ingredients can go back and do it again. There's nothing really lost in that way, but nothing new has been created. We don't know if that's very clear or not. That's not lifetime by lifetime, either.

R: I was asking about lifetime to lifetime. You have talked about the choices that are presented to him in life, and I was asking about the period when he is not in the physical body, operating with you – and I assume he's making choices.

TGU: Well, when he's not in a physical body, he *is* one of us; as you. He's already crystallized, as are you. We were attempting to make a fuller statement, is all. You're beyond the point of trying to decide whether it's going to crystallize or not. When he's done with the body, he's back with us.

R: And, I'm asking about how that process continues. He's become part of you. There's some point at which there's a decision made for a part of you to move into a physical body, or not?

TGU: Well, let's back up just a little bit. We'll be a little more precise. We said last time, we extend there, you extend here, and there isn't movement as much there's change of focus and attention. So, your ceasing to have a functioning body is less movement than a movement of your consciousness back to the part of you that it never had left. And so it isn't like anything needs to be created again except another opportunity for you to come back into a body – either on earth or somewhere else, or in other dimensions, or whatever seems appropriate.

By our living, each of us is a different flavor, a different frequency. Certain situations are more appropriate for a given flavor. It's for the benefit of the individual part of us and for the benefit of the general situation. It's for both the actor and the play.

R: At some point the focus of attention is going to shift from the Frank that's part of you to, let's say, another body, another lifetime. Can you say some more about the process of choice that goes on there?

TGU: [pause] You mean the process of deciding *where* to go next? Or the process of deciding whether or not *he* should go next? Of course he may not be a he, but you understand.

R: Yes. Well, either of those, but somewhere there are some decisions made that either result in a part of you taking physical form again, or not.

TGU: Again, resist the temptation to think of us as individuals. However, to conceptualize easier, you could look at it as a committee of people, including yourselves, looking over where you've been, seeing where you are, weighing what's needed for growth or balance – and what could be contributed, and when. But you might do better to think of it as more of an intuitive process than a thinking process. In other words, all-of-us or maybe a part of all-of-us saying "oh yeah, here's a good slot over here"; deciding, you see? We're trying to give you the sense of a collective weighing of opportunities and progress without weighting it so that your minds take us to be individuals because of the analogy.

You, or he, and a portion of The Great Us – that's the best we're going to do – will come together, weigh and review, look for progress, take into account what he wants, and take into account what the opportunities are. Sometimes, if there's a serious enough deficit, he may get overruled and sent into a situation whether or not he particularly wants to, perhaps because there's an asymmetrical development of the personality. Someone sufficiently developmentally one-sided might get to the point where it would be impossible to choose the experiences that would widen it out. They would be assisted [laughs] whether they want the assistance or not.

[This certainly seems to be an explicit and definite statement about reincarnation. It seems to say that we live, die, and are reborn. However, coming sessions will repeatedly blur the picture before finally providing another way to look at this, as you will see.]

R: I've heard it said sometimes that a group energy can send out a representative to be in certain kinds of experiences that will bring back to the group the final experiences needed so that the group can in some way move on, and not continue to be sending –

TGU: Individuals. Eventually. That's the theory. We get tired of this too. [laugh]

R: Get tired of – ?

TGU: Well, how long do you want to be in sixth grade? At some point you want to graduate to seventh grade.

R: I see. Okay. So the group at some point will move into something beyond what it's now –

TGU: Yes, and what you heard before is our understanding of it, accurately broad. We don't really know what goes next, but we know that *something* goes next. And there's a sense of trust in it, you know. There's no dread of it, it's just, some things have to be finished before new things open up.

R: A difficulty that I'm having is that last time I understood you to say that the membership of your totality changes from time to time.

TGU: The membership of those that are dealing with you; with earth; you know, with him, at any given time.

R: So there's not a fixed composition of this totality.

TGU: You could say there's like a center of gravity, but no, not absolutely. If you start talking about Cardinal Richelieu, we'll bring in our specialist on French history. [laugh]

R: Uh huh. I don't think I'll do that. [they chuckle]

Variety of Lifetimes

R: Is there some continuity in the role in the physical world that Frank, or anyone else, experiences in a series of lifetimes?

TGU: [pause] We know what you're asking, but we're thinking about answering something slightly different, because the answer to your question as posed is "yes, but no." We are going to rephrase the question.

Suppose you had a hundred lifetimes. Say that five had a common thread. There might be another five with a different thread, and another ten with another thread. When you are in a body at any given time, some easy resonances would come through. In his case, the only ones that have come through with details are modern, and either American or Western European – because they are the closest.

On the other hand, the Egyptian [an ancient priest] and the Englishman [a medieval monk] have come through in a different way because their resonance is closest, you see? The externals are very different but the internal dynamics are very close, so they can come in. So if you're saying "is Frank always of a monastic or a warrior or a scholastic disposition," no. But if you were to say "is there a line of continuity from him back to several of his other lives," yes.

You wouldn't gain much if you came into life after life after life always with the same bias. You want – and believe me, when you're not in, you *do* want – to be balanced in many ways. You want the spice of life; you want the experience. You wouldn't want to be a schoolteacher for 33 lifetimes. You wouldn't want to be a galley slave, or a king, or whatever. No matter what, it would get old, because you couldn't learn much from it. This particular life is an experiment of sorts, and a difficult one.

R: [pause] Say some more about that?

TGU: Oh, it's nothing he doesn't know. It's a life being led without external props, more or less, and therefore continuously uncharted grounds. In fact, when he was in charted grounds, it didn't fit, which made it uncharted grounds, you see. To spend an entire lifetime not fitting in to things – without being a professional misfit, which would fit into things, you see –

It isn't a question of playing Hamlet when you're actually in *Macbeth*. It's more like…[pause] playing a role with blinders and earplugs. You are walking into a stage and for all you know they're playing Hamlet or they might be playing Macbeth [laugh] or they might be playing anything. And you're doing what you can do.

This is not an accident; this was designed this way, but – you asked.

R: What could be accomplished in that?

TGU: It is a trying-out of abilities and of patterns that many people will probably have to learn if we're going to move on to the next thing. To get people relatively quickly out of existing patterns, it's helpful to give them a pattern of not living in a pattern. [pause] Does that actually resonate?

R: I think so. We are trying to be developed to move into doing that.

TGU: Don't misunderstand us, though, to think that it's necessarily something that Frank's going to become famous for! It may not be ever known by anybody but himself, but that, still, is in the mind of man, and will put him in the human subconscious. Everything that's done, however unheralded or alone or totally anonymous, adds to the potential for everyone else, because we are all one, and it can all be drawn on.

R: It becomes part of the human library, so to speak.

TGU: Exactly. Or, better, you might say that each of you is a neuron in the human brain. Another way to look at it, a little more active and interactive analogy.

Wholeness

R: Mm-hmm. [long pause] People sometimes talk about collecting parts of them-selves together. Sort of some aim, I suppose, of self-definition?

TGU: Becoming more whole, yes.

R: Is that a meaningful concept from your perspective?

TGU: Yes it is, but we see it not as *movement* but as a movement *of consciousness*. If a part of oneself has split off – well, even psychologically you understand that. When you bring the split-off parts back into wholeness with the rest of the bundle, the *brain cells* don't move. The only thing that happens is that the *consciousness* wraps it back in with the rest of the bundle, and that's pretty nearly the same thing as what happens when people bring back parts of themselves.

In fact, in a larger sense that's what you all are doing for us, or we are doing for you, whichever way you wish to look at it, in the whole scheme of things. At some point we will have brought everything back into full interactive consciousness. At that point we will have brought all of our pieces back together. We will have recovered them all.

And, from your end, to the degree that you expand your interactive awareness to all of your other lives, and all of your other dimensions into which you fit, and all of your connection with us, you're doing the same thing. It's more than a lifetime job. But you have time.

R: This kind of session we're having here is different from what we did in the lab, where we would be asking you to go to a state where important information is available to you, and ask for you to comment on that.

TGU: We're open to whatever you want to do. The mechanism wouldn't be much different because unless Frank becomes a trance medium he's going to feel the answer and then say it. But you're certainly welcome to experiment.

R: One aspect of doing it the way we're doing it is that I get information that I'm interested in, and it may well be that there are other areas that would be helpful for Frank to get in touch with through these kinds of sessions, where presumably –

TGU: If we may paraphrase you, you're saying perhaps you're asking the wrong questions by chance and coincidence. [they laugh] We're not concerned about it. We recognize the unselfish intent, but it's misplaced. You're being directed, too.

R: I assume that that's the case, but I don't know whether I'm being directed on Frank's behalf or not.

TGU: Well, you know, we don't actually see a distinction there. And if you're interested in that, we could look at it a little.

R: I would like to hear it.

TGU: People get in trouble because they allow their personal interests to override someone else's interests, because they feel they have to force something to happen. You know, "there's only one acceptable solution." If you don't do that, you can't *get* in trouble. Your highest good and his highest good will mesh. They can't help mesh. [pause] If that's not clear, we'll say more, but to us it's *so* clear. [chuckles]

R: Well, I liked hearing that, but I'm not sure exactly how that works.

TGU: Suppose you had a bunch of large goldfish in a pond. They look perfectly orchestrated. They don't bump into each other, and there's nothing clumsy about it; it really looks like a dance. This is because everyone makes second-by-second adjustments, watching the other ones. They know where each other are and they just get out of each others' way. To get awkwardness into a situation like that, just have one fish say "by God, I'm going this way right now, and you just stay out of my way." Now, even there, you could conceivably still have harmony, with everybody else just saying "okay, well fine." But when you have two of them [chuckles] the odds are less, and if you have three of them, the odds are less. You see.

Whenever you have people who are drawn together out of an affinity, and are each operating out of the place that you're operating out of, rather than [self-]assertion, what's good for you is good for him, and it will always appear serendipitous. When you're out of that place, anything can happen. But when you're in that place, there's nothing to worry about. Literally nothing to worry about. We can't conceive of a way in which two people, operating on the beam, can wind up where one has to win and one has to lose. It's like saying black could be white. [pause] So don't worry about it. [chuckles]

R: Okay, here's something else. I've been somewhat concerned about the possibility of these sessions getting in the way of sessions in the laboratory monitored by Skip [Atwater]. Is there something to be done to make this process easier?

TGU: Is it even conceivable that you might actually be following directions in doing this? [they laugh] In other words, why after so many months did you think of it just now? And why after so many months did it become possible, just now? And not only possible, but effortless. We think those are pretty blatant clues. [they laugh]

R: I can appreciate that. As long as that's with this situation in mind.

A Difference in Voice

R: All right, now I want to clear something up. You've indicated – you, Frank – that essentially I'm not directly speaking with the guys upstairs, and, whoever I'm talking to, you are answering me.

[As Frank]: Mm-hmm. I'm never out of the picture. I can hear it, let's put it that way. Go ahead.

R: You're hearing it. The voice that's coming through is the voice that I heard when you wrote in your book that it was the guys upstairs speaking.

Frank: Hmm. Okay. So you can hear a difference in voice, huh?

R: My assumption has been that I've asked you to move your energy slightly aside so that it can be as direct as possible, and I thought maybe tonight you were saying that that really wasn't possible. That it's all coming –

[Back in the altered state, letting the words flow through as TGU]: No, that's not quite what's meant. There's an extreme, which is the trance medium, who will be asleep and won't know anything that comes, because literally their consciousness will be elsewhere. The consciousness will not be participating.

The other extreme is an everyday consciousness with no intuitive input, strictly rational thinking, aware on a conscious level. In between is this vaguer area, and Frank lives in that area normally. Just as Edgar Cayce's talent was to be able to put his personality aside and bring it through, Frank's talent [laughs] – talent or predicament – is to be here *and* there, to be every day in a conscious level at some point functioning instinctively rather than rationally. There's not a word for it. Well, if there is I don't know what it is. [Edgar Cayce (1877-1945) was, of course, the famous psychic known as "The Sleeping Prophet."]

R: It's constantly a communication that's coming out of you and Frank together.

TGU: Yes. To a varying degree. And when he speaks, as usually, without first knowing what he's going to say, that is very much close to what's going on here. And that is rather unusual in our experience. People usually stop and decide what they're going to say, and say it. They decide what image they want to project. We don't mean that as a criticism. There's an interposition of their personality that will shape it, whereas with him it just comes. Usually. That's what's going on here. That's why the difference is less than you might expect, and it's why he's easily able to go in and out, but it's also why he didn't recognize it for all those years. It was so normal that he was looking for something that would be un-normal! He was looking for trance mediumship.

R: I think that's all I had for tonight. Unless you have something useful to add to this?

Good Questions Get Good Answers

TGU: Yes, there is, actually. Your input you undervalue. And we'll try to give you a sense of the input from the outside, to give you something to chew on intellectually. From outside, it would look like a person with acknowledged and undoubted intellectual ability, and emotional trustworthiness and rational trustworthiness. In other words, smart enough to know what to do, good enough to do what's in everyone's best interest. Frank was a reporter professionally and can use those reporting techniques. You use the academic techniques. The professional thinker. And by so doing you can bring better answers out of us because you ask better questions.

If someone asks a vague question about good or evil, they might get better than a vague answer, but the chances are much better if you ask a sculpted, or a crafted, or a thought-out question, and follow it through. The differences between the two of you set up a helpful polarity. If too much were understood already, there would be no need to articulate it, and you can't learn as well. So actually two people who don't understand each other intellectually can learn better than two people who do!

This pulling-out process, the teasing-out of the implication of things, will make the product for the end reader. So, we just want to give you that kind of reassurance, because a) it's not *necessarily* your idea [laugh] and b), you're not scunching on other people's time or interests. And we'll leave it at that.

R: That was a statement that I really appreciate. And I appreciate the whole session tonight and I am full of gratitude.

TGU: Well, if you can realize it, so are we. It isn't everybody who can do this, or will do this, for us. With us. Against us. Whatever.

Frank: [stretching] Oh, if they think I'm going to talk about gratitude to them, they're wrong. [we laugh]

Session Three
August 28, 2001

Gender Polarity among TGU

R: [Watches me yawning] All right, nice and relaxed; that's good. I've been asking a lot of questions about the nature of The Gentlemen Upstairs. I have another one.

Frank: I can hear them groan.

R: I've been wondering whether in your state there are male and female energies, or an absence of gender phenomena in your state.

TGU: Well, you're going to get used to hearing this, but the answer is, it depends. We and you are different mainly by the terrain that we're on, so therefore everything that's a part of you is a part of us, and vice versa. In that sense, we do have the *relative* – and we underling the word "relative" – polarity that you experience physically and psychologically. Each of us, considered as a node, has both halves of the relative polarity within ourselves in different proportions. And considering all of us as one, the totality of all of us as one also includes the energy, and in a balanced form, just as it would electrically with positive and negative.

R: I see.

TGU: So you could look at it as, a balance with local fluctuations. Local and different times, different equations.

R: One thing we had talked about had to do with specialty nodes – if that's what we can call them – within the totality. Do you have experts on maleness and femaleness? Would one node of your group be more appropriate to respond to that kind of question than another?

TGU: We have to see the question. It's hard to imagine. It would be like any other polarity. It's a little abstract.

R: I see. So okay, so that answers that.

TGU: If you ask the right question, we'll probably learn something ourselves. Surprising you though that may –

R: Yes. If Frank or I were to ask a question about the nature of maleness or of femaleness in some respect, I was asking, does that cause certain members of your group –

TGU: Ah. Well, you're making a jump that we wouldn't say is warranted. One needn't be predominately male to be an expert on maleness, so to speak, just as one needn't be a tree to be an expert on forestry, although having been a tree would be an advantage. Does that make sense?

R: Yes. I think I understand that.

TGU: In general, ask what you want. We'll do our best to oblige.

Free Will and Conscience

R: You have explained that Frank is part of you and vice versa, but do you sometimes act as a council in order to advise Frank about something?

TGU: That would be one metaphor, but we would move more toward the metaphor of the automatic habit systems in your brain. It's more like he is an extension of a certain neural function of the brain that is all of us. Rather than thinking of it as a council, which implies not only individual wills but conflict and clashes, we would think of it more as an automatic adjustment of energies. For instance, you asked this question. We don't need to sit around and discuss how to answer the question; the question polarizes the answer. It's a pooling of what we know from what we are. In fact, you could argue that you in bodies are largely responsible for our consciousness *because* you are limited, and because you're pointed.

R: Implied in my question was the concept of you sometimes responding to something without Frank included and other times with him included.

TGU: Well, with him conscious and other times without him conscious. He may be off doing other things, too, from our point of view. And frequently is.

R: So the situation wouldn't arise where Frank would be doing something and you all would be saying to yourselves "boy this is not a good thing for him to be doing."

TGU: [laughs] This is a less theoretical question than you might think! But there's nothing more absolutely respected than free will, because that's what you're there *for*. We can watch you play in traffic, and we can say "that is *not* a smart thing to do," but we will almost never step in. There are occasions where we'll step in for overriding reasons, but in general the rule is, "no, if you go play in traffic, take the consequences." Even though we don't like the consequences.

R: Okay, so that I understand. He's operating on the principle of free will and you're having some reaction to this, which doesn't include him, at least at a conscious level.

TGU: That's a very good qualifier, "at least at a conscious level." Exactly. That's the nature of conscience. It's not only "did I do the right thing or the wrong thing," but it's also "am I on the beam or am I off the beam" in a morally neutral way. If your conscious mind wants to do something, and unconsciously you're hearing, "no, this is not the best thing for you to do," or "you could react better to the situation than the way you are," the thinness or thickness of the barrier between that realization and your will determines how easy it is for you to stay on the beam. So not only we, but also another part of yourself, in a more direct way, is trying to give you guidance, and it's always up to you to say yes or no.

R: This suggests that you may have an opinion of something that is quite different from Frank's opinion about it, and different from his interpretation of events, and so on.

TGU: Oh, sure. In fact, even when we agree with what he's doing, we have a different view. That's inherent in the situation. Outside of time and space the threads that are separated by time-periods might seem clearer to us than the moment of time you're in. To you while you're in a body those threads in different times seem to be absolutely different. So we're just saying that yes, we always see it differently.

R: You suggested a bit ago that by and large you wouldn't call these differences to his awareness.

TGU: Oh no. We will always call it to his awareness if he's interested in hearing it. That is, if he doesn't block it out. But we almost never would override his will. That could happen, but it's somewhat a last resort. For instance, supposing someone's lifetime has important ramifications for the people around them, and for their own sake and the people around them it's really important that they stay on the beam. If they are about to fall off the edge, it could happen that it would be decided, "no, that's too disruptive to the whole pattern. It can't be allowed to happen." In that case it would be more a matter of that person's own self over here invading his consciousness, you might say, and causing him to act in ways that would be inexplicable to the conscious person. But that's a very rare situation.

R: Would Frank be aware of this intervention that occurred?

TGU: Well, it would depend partly on introspection, partly on the dissonance between the action and what that particularly active part of his own mind wanted to do. [pause] A lifetime of introspection will help you in that regard. It will make it clearer when you are receiving transmissions, shall we say.

R: But more typically, he's asking for your input when you give it.

TGU: [pause] We're talking about something a lot more than input. We could theoretically override what he wanted to do, so that he would not have his free will available to him. And that's what is forbidden, almost always. That's what we're talking about. The input is always offered, and is always available. [pause] The input is really in a way only a more sophisticated version of his own – or anyone's own – pondering and experience and wisdom and thought. It's just from a larger perspective.

Higher and Lower Impulses

R: So I guess the experience would be, more typically, he's thinking things through and some of the things that occur to him are coming from his experiences in this life and some of them are coming from input from you and all that's coming to him, undifferentiated?

TGU: Yes. Not only thinking but also – in fact more – hunches, intuitions, feelings, emotions. Predominantly the non-rational impulses of a person's mind come either from the body or from us, rather than from the personality in the middle. In fact, your language says, lower impulses or higher impulses.

R: I'm not sure if I'm following all that.

TGU: Well, from the body you might have a sex impulse, or a hunger impulse, or an attraction to a feel or a touch or taste or smell – those things. Nothing wrong with them, one way or another, but those impulses, preferences, attractions, can come from the body, what we would call a lower impulse – or from the other side, from us, what we would call a higher impulse. A higher impulse might be, "why don't you study Greek?" Or, "it's really neat to put things together," or "I'll bet learning to play the violin would be good." You see? And some of them could blend so that it would be hard to say whether it's a lower or a higher. And we do not mean that in a judgment or hierarchical way; it's just that that's a way of describing. You could say body or spirit, same way; it's about the same thing.

R: Body or spirit. Do you consider yourself a spiritual force?

TGU: Well, we used body or spirit, but if you'll notice, originally we said higher or lower. "Spiritual" in that we don't have a three-dimensional body, yes. Any other associations the word might have are problematical. But after all, you're spirits in bodies.

The Mind

R: What about when we add the mental level? The brain is obviously part of the body but there are mental processes going on at your end too, right?

TGU: The mind and the brain, as you well know, are very different things. You have a brain in the same manner that you have a kidney or a lung. It is a physical organ to transmute energy. But your mind – well, you *could* look at us as the spirit, and the body as the organs and all, and *you* in the middle as the mind. It's more or less true, but only *more or less* true. It's *sort of* true. You are the focus, centered in one time and place, that continues for a certain amount of time. That's the best we could describe what you call the mind.

Now, when the body dissolves and the spirit returns to us, the *content* of the mind goes with you. In other words, the content doesn't get destroyed. But the mind itself is more of a habit than a living function, if you can understand that.

R: It's hard to understand that the mind is a habit.

TGU: You are familiar with the concept of ghosts. You could look at the ghost in the bodily form as a sort of a habit of the body. It can't eat, it can't function – although it *can* touch things – but you understand, it's more like a habit of the body than the body.

The mind when it is divorced from physical associations that hold it into certain patterns – the neural synapses, the habits, the real, the actual connection with the body – is brought as a memory back to us. And so if you were then to talk to "me," whoever "me" may be, when "me" is dead, it would have the same flavor but it wouldn't be the same thing.

Let's do this way. Frank dies today; tomorrow you go upstairs to talk to him; you talk to his spirit through the habit system of his mind, but it's not the same as his physically connected mind is now. The spirit's the same. We're not saying it's a delusion, but you aren't dealing with quite the same mind, any more than you can hear with your physical ears his voice, once he's over on the other side.

R: I feel like I understand that from trying to communicate with my husband. It seems familiar, but it's not the same.

TGU: That's right. Nor could you expect it to be. Nor will *you* be. *You* will be in an environment in which you are unlimited sideways. That is, you'll have unlimited access not only to every part of yourself in the lower sense, but every part of yourself in the sense of all of us! And that moment-to-moment unlimited access means that rather than a small intensely focused consciousness, you'll be a part of a large, less intensely focused consciousness. A totally different flavor.

If someone from Downstairs then calls you, and you wish to respond, and talk, you will express in a way that will feel different to you up There, while you're doing it. It'll actually have a nice little flavor to it. But at the same time the person talking to you will say, just as you did, "familiar but not the same."

How TGU See the World

R: All right, now let's see. I think this is another way of phrasing what we've been talking about. Would you say that you see the world – the physical world here – through Frank's eyes?

TGU: Well – not exclusively. You see?

R: Because you're also seeing through the eyes of others.

TGU: Exactly.

R: Okay. But it's not a perception of those in physical body.

TGU: [pause] Are you saying, are our only eyes the eyes of those who are in the physical?

R: Yes, that's what I mean.

TGU: No, we can't say that. Just as you're aware of things in Focus 27 , as you say, without being dependent on one of us to filter it through, we're aware of Focus 1 without having to have *you* to focus through. This is worth pursuing perhaps.

Every point of reference, every point of view, adds to the depth of field and clarity of focus. So if we're looking through one person's eyes *and* another person's eyes *and*, shall we say, through the trees, or through the general ambiance of the moment, those are all different viewpoints and – coming back on this side, they're all integrated.

In fact, you could say that *everything* is perceived from over here. It's all *here*; the question is which cluster (as you like to say) knows what or is focused on what at one given time. If we wanted to see Caesar crossing the river somewhere in France, a part of us is doing that. But that doesn't mean that's *us*. Our lives form a library, and the libraries are all interconnected. Everything's here, but whether this book and that book ever happen to be on the same shelf – well, it's getting tangled, but we think you understand.

All of you are valuable, but primarily by what you create by what you choose. It's the *creation* of your essence, the particular flavor that you become by the way that you consistently choose things, that is the achievement here, not the allowing us to see the world in 1948 or whenever.

Different Perspectives

R: Okay. [pause] I will come back to that, if I can remember. But I want to back up a little bit, to ask about reliability. You say, "just as we can perceive Focus 27 and see what's there." Well, I have great questions about the truth of what I see when I look at 27. I think of it as an interesting idea, but I don't confuse that with the truth of what it is.

TGU: Well, we have the advantage over you in this sense. [gesturing] On our side of the barrier, there are millions of us – or, you could look at it as "I," we, whatever – going through the barrier in a million places, in a million ways. All of this is all connected, for us. We all get it first-hand. On your end, each of you acts seemingly in isolation, so you have only the crudest of ways to transmit to each other your understandings of what you've seen. That's the major difference in perceptions.

R: That must be quite an advantage.

TGU: Well, it is. [they laugh] In fact, we could throw in one more thing: That *is* the advantage. *Our* advantage on this side is perception; *your* advantage on your side is action. And that's the difference. You can act. But we can perceive. But you can also look at it the other way around: We can perceive, but you can act.

R: But it seems to me that we also perceive and build our whole experiential life around what we perceive.

TGU: That's right. And we can also act, but not in the same way. That's right. It's a matter of emphasis. Our primary advantage is the ability to perceive huge amounts of things as one; your advantage is primarily the ability to form what you are by repetitive conscious choice. But obviously you can't choose without perceiving. And obviously there'd be no point in our perceiving and not *using* that perception, which is to say, acting.

R: Okay, now I want to go back to the other point and see if I got it. You were saying that what you receive from us is not so much our perceiving the world so that you can see it through our eyes, but what we do that adds to the mix of the perception and the action.

TGU: Your "doing" is in creating yourself. That's all we mean by that. It's not an external thing like "do you paint pictures." Everybody who lives, even if only for ten minutes, to some degree creates that person. And that person is what we perceive and that's our gift from you.

Emotions

R: Yes, I like that way of putting it. [pause] You had mentioned something called emotional states before; I wanted to ask a little more about that. Do you all react emotionally as Frank does, say, or is there an absence of emotional experience in your reactions?

TGU: [pause] It's a hard balance to strike. We would say there's an absence of *isolation* in which to act emotionally. That is, if an emotion arises, it doesn't play out in an isolated individual.

Supposing something raised the temperature of one of the cells of your skin. If that cell were in isolation, it could get exceedingly hot, or burn, or whatever. To the degree that that cell is connected with other cells and is able to spread the iso-therm, then it will sustain proportionately less damage. The effect when you are connected is not the same as it is when you are in relative isolation.

However [pause] beyond that we would say that if you were able to come here as you are now, you would find this realm relatively chilly, emotionally. But you won't, because you will – be here! [they laugh] And it'll be normal.

R: Well, suppose there's a world-wide catastrophe like Hitler, would you react with some kind of negative emotion to that?

TGU: Well, we wouldn't see it the way you see it. Would you react emotionally to an electrical storm, say? Or would you react emotionally to – oh, a random number generator generating more ones than zeroes for a while? We tend to see it more as an interesting natural phenomenon than as a life and death battle between good and evil. You see it that way, but – you *need* to see it that way, that's what you're there for. But we do not.

R: Do you experience anything like what we would call love?

TGU: If you could take your understanding of love and divorce it of the, shall we say, warm fuzziness, then yes, of course, that's what makes the world not only go 'round, as you say, but it's what makes the world! But – love to us is the interpen-etration of being. It is the fundamental oneness of everything. To us, you see, love means *not* rejecting Hitler, and the war, and the suffering. Love means incorporat-ing that as well as everything else. It's the binding energy. Gravity worked as well for Hitler as it did for Gandhi, and so does love. We can't put it better than that. It isn't quite the same when you're not in isolation, because your way of judg-ing things is different. Just as to you everything looks separate until you remind yourself that it is not, to us everything looks one until we remind ourselves that it could be seen otherwise.

R: Okay, so your experience of love is the common phenomenon, so to speak. It's the common state of being.

TGU: It's what makes the world – everything; life, the universe – possible. It's what it is. It is to life what flesh is to bodies. No love, no life. [pause] We don't get warmly fuzzy about gravity, either. [they laugh]

Helping Others

R: Okay. A bit of a change of topic here. Sometimes Frank seems to feel very dissatisfied with his life. How do you react to that?

TGU: Well, we're used to it. [pause] There's nothing wrong with dissatisfaction, there's nothing wrong with any state.

R: So this isn't a situation where you might give him some advice, or –

TGU: Oh, we'll always give him advice! Will he *take* it? Or will he be able to take it? And, – [pause]

Supposing you have a child and you want the child to perform some intricate task. You might make it harder for them to learn by hovering over them than by giving them a little distance. You might, by giving them a little distance, reduce the pressure on them, actually. So, in other words, we hear you saying we could help if we chose to by being closer, but actually not. Not in our judgment, anyway. But we're always there when he asks. And we've certainly given him plenty of clues over the years. Plenty of nudges, really.

R: Do you understand the source of his depression?

TGU: Certainly.

R: In a way that you could help those of us who care about him, help him out in some way?

TGU: [laughs] Well, the problem is, how does anyone know what is good or bad, what is right or wrong, what is helpful or not helpful? We appreciate the intent, but this is really his bicycle to learn to ride, and other than running along with the bicycle holding the seat until he sort of gets his balance, there's not much one can do. Otherwise, he won't really learn how to ride the bicycle. He may get to the end of the driveway, but he won't still have learned how to ride the bicycle. It will actually have crippled him rather than assisting him. This is not to say that it is bad to offer someone help. Of course it's always good.

R: But it sounds as though your recommendation would be to take the same stance you're taking, which is feel supportive but let him live his own life.

TGU: Well, you wouldn't have any choice about that anyway. No one can live another person's life.

You could – theoretically – find the source of someone's depression, or someone's anxiety, or someone's rage, or any other strong emotion or dominant emotional pattern, but as we say, it might not be a good thing. The impulse to help is always good. The care and compassion is always good. But there may not always be a point of application, and if there is a point of application, it may not always be really what's needed. Supposing one had a fever so that certain germs could be burned out. Reducing the fever might *retard* the process of burning out the germs. On the other hand, reducing the fever might prevent death, you know, so it's always a matter of judgment.

To give you the bluntest answer, there's no way that you can get at his sense of the meaninglessness of his life. He fights that out, but if it were easy enough for someone to give him an answer, *he'd* have got the answer.

Life's Goals

R: I asked last time about whether the roles that we tend to play in our various lifetimes are the same, and you said no to that. I was wondering about life goals, overall purposes. Does that tend to be the same, in a series of lifetimes?

TGU: [laughs] Only if you're slow learners. [they laugh] No, there are so many goals –

It's so easy to do that you can accomplish a lot quite easily sometimes. And then it's so hard to do that sometimes it can take a long series of things to work out different nuances of the problem. That is to say, to experience not only a complicated emotion or series of emotions, but the working out of them. Because the working out of them can cause – *will* cause – other problems, and others. It's a long, long road. Sometimes you'll need to be the downtrodden and sometimes the downtrodder.

You might have several lifetimes in a row in which you were a hard-driving executive type. But those lifetimes might not be at all consecutive in time. So it's very hard for you to *see* a pattern like that.

R: I had thought, though, in terms of overall purpose in life, not at the level of being an executive. For example, what is Frank's overall purpose in this life? Can you state it in such a way, or are there too many to even speak about?

TGU: Well – there are some things we *won't* speak about, only because some things need to be pursued not self-consciously, between the lines. But we can certainly say that an experiencing of life in a very cloistered, almost monastic way, that profoundly alters the balance between this side and that side is a major portion of what he's doing. We'd rather not say any more than that. He more or less knows that anyway. There are things that can only be done if you don't know what you're doing ahead of time. For one thing, it takes all the steam out of it if you know what you're doing.

Now, let's go a little further. Let's say he has six goals, and by the end of this life-time accomplishes anywhere from zero to six. In another expression, they won't be the same set of goals. Even if they were the same set of goals, they wouldn't be in the same circumstances. Even if they were the same goals in the same circumstances, they would be in the personality that shaped around the new person. So, there's less seeming continuity than you might think.

But also supposing all six goals were accomplished and he/she/it/we/they, whatever, were to come in again, there would be a new agenda, or a partly new agenda, or the old agenda in a different set of circumstances. So, what you're asking has logic behind it, but to us it looks a lot different than it does to you. [chuckles] You may have heard *that* before!

So we would say, every time you go in, you have a different mix. That's the best way we can put it. [pause] We can put it in terms of an emotion. You wouldn't expect someone to come in choleric, time after time after time after time. At least *we* would not. We wouldn't expect one to come in who was scholarly, or monastic, or contemplative or artistic or executive or military. We wouldn't expect the same thing *all* the time, although there might be predominant strands within a certain – even several.

In fact, look at the way that Frank has been able to discover his other connections, and you'll see that he started with the ones that were the closest to him now. If you come up with six monks in a row, that doesn't mean you're always a monk; it means that's the easiest thing for you to relate to this time.

Scripting

R: [pause] I don't know if this is a meaningless question or not. Does the extent to which a person is able to fulfill their purposes in a particular life have to do with the next assignment? I mean, are there certain purposes that ultimately have to be achieved?

TGU: Again, you're looking at it from an individual point of view. We would have said "well, if that particular tool wasn't shaped just right, there'll be another and we'll use that one, and even if there isn't another, we can make do with something else." We don't look at it as individually as you do, because to us the individual is almost an illusion. We know where you're going – it's not a meaningless question, at all, but perhaps that's the theme of these sessions, the difference in appearance from our side and your side.

R: Well, you've just suggested that if the one tool doesn't quite fit, there's an-other –

TGU: We're always making do. [they chuckle]

R: Does that suggest that there are certain patterns on your side that need to be filled, and that you're looking for the right tool to fill those?

TGU: You could say that we're performing extemporaneous drama, and trying our best to script it despite [laughs] the best efforts of all the actors! And there could be certain events –

Okay. Take a civilization as an event. If we now create Western Civilization, with its mechanization and its desacrilization and all of the various attributes that are the West – to create that involves moving a huge number of pieces on the board. Now, if you have to do that while preserving the free will of all the pieces, it becomes a very interesting question.

Now. The other part of that is, all those pieces come in with a part to play. However [laughs] in the middle of the play they forget what their lines are, and they improvise. Or they choose not to play their lines, or they play them badly. So really your question is, do we on our side have a purpose on your side. And the answer is yes, but it's not so much to get the painting painted as it is to have you all have the experience of being painters – which gives *us* the experience of being painters. That's the best we're going to do with that.

R: What about the purposes on your side, then? You have purposes as well.

TGU: Well, the overriding long-term purpose is to get everybody back into full connection, so that we can see what happens next. That's our meta-purpose, I suppose. Within that purpose are all kinds of specific flavors of experience where we decided, "if we did this, we could put this together." Now, [pause] how to explain this?

You have, as you know, a reality in which at any given time there are x number of realities that can be chosen. Those alternate, or possible worlds, are not quite as real as the one that's chosen, in the eye of the beholder. They're equally real ultimately. And I'm sure that doesn't make any sense.

R: Well, it sounded more like an individual than a totality responding to purposes here.

TGU: For each individual, there is a realer and an unrealer path. You're actually here today. That's what feels real. Another individual is elsewhere and *theirs* feels more real. On our side, it's all equally real, but on your side, it is not.

TGU's Purpose

R: We're almost through, but I wanted to ask just one more question. It's just a little question. How do your purposes get established?

TGU: They emerge. As things happen, they emerge. We know that you're in the habit of thinking that outside of time-space there's no time, but you can't wait without duration. It's just not the same kind of time. We grow as you grow, unevenly, in reaction to what happens. And as we grow unevenly, a lack, or an urge, is felt, and in the exploration of that the next thing emerges.

R: *You're exploring that as a totality? Or are you getting guidance from somewhere?*

TGU: Ooh! [pause] [chuckles] That's an interesting question. We have experienced it as, "it emerges." And now you've made us very suspicious. [pause] As soon as you say that it becomes obvious that, in fact, that's *exactly* what's going on. But why, out of *our* experience, would we not have understood that? [pause] Oh, wait a minute. [pause] The suspicion is that there are other parts of us that *do* understand this. Which means, either we haven't gotten into contact with them, or it means that we may be more specialized tools than we happen to think of ourselves. [pause] We're going to pursue that, and we'll let you know.

R: *All right. That's good.*

TGU: By the way, you two – just to scratch this itch – you said, and he says it all the time, too, "this may be a meaningless question…" That's literally not possible. Every question has a unique origin, even if it's the same question on different days. The origin and the penumbra of thought or emotion or experience around it will be different. It doesn't mean they're always productive, but it does mean they're not meaningless. [chuckles]

R: *Thank you very much. I appreciated this discussion tonight.*

TGU: Well, thank you for participating.

Session Four
September 4, 2001

[Beginning with this session, I ceased using a TMI tape to go into an altered state. As we begin, it is clear that Rita and I have different ideas about what is going on, as she again asks me if I can move my conscious mind out of the way to let the guys come through.]

R: This is an experiment tonight, we're trying without your listening to the Hemi-Sync, and without doing the resonant tuning, but you're doing a good job of being very relaxed and willing to let The Gentlemen Upstairs come through.

Frank: They always come through. I don't need a lot of preparation.

Filters

R: I had a kind of leftover from one of our earlier sessions, about their way of perceiving things and our way of perceiving things. I have these experiences – and I think a lot of folks do – of being aware of other energies in our field, that we catch out of the corner of our eye. When we turn and take a closer look, there seems to be nothing there, but I have had the feeling that those are other energies somehow operating on an earth plane but not in ordinary physical dimensions. Do you have some comments on that?

TGU: Well, yes, we would say two or three things are going on. What you see is seen through filters, and the filters are transparent, so it's hard for you – for anyone – to realize that there *are* filters. Seeing out of the corner of your eye, metaphorically as well as literally, may be the only way that you can see something that your filter says doesn't exist. And then as you look at it more closely, your filter will totally close it out. That can be overcome simply – simply but not necessarily easily – by informing all levels of your being that you wish to remove those filters. You need to reassure other parts of yourself that it's safe to remove the filters and that it will be interesting to do so. This is basic shamanism as you would call it.

There are two other things going on. One is, your range of frequency varies from day to day and from moment to moment, and sometimes as your frequency extends a little bit it is easier for you to see something that you wouldn't ordinarily see. So there's two things there. One, there's the filter that's partly blocking it out. Two, you have to be at the right resonance to see it anyway. And the third says "I don't really believe in this, so it's obviously not there, so I'm not seeing it," which is what prevents the vast majority of people from seeing these things. This is the overriding one.

R: I'm not sure I understood that third point.

TGU: The third one doesn't particularly apply to you as an individual. It is a complement to the filter. The filter is a totally unconscious way of not seeing things, of not bringing in data. But the third thing is a conscious, rational, logical decision that "they don't exist, so I'm not seeing them."

R: And does [the fact that we're perceiving energies] suggest that there are others operating in this physical earth plane in some way but not visible to us living lives as we live them?

TGU: Well, yes, but the problem is the spatial analogy [that enters into discussions involving non-physical awareness], which is almost unbreakable. There's only one "here," and it's here for Focus 27 as it is for Focus 3 as it is for Focus 1. There isn't any other "there," so yes, all the various frequencies are here, and as you move your receiving set you perceive different ones – filters and other things allowing.

All of Focus 23 is right here. Focus 27 is right here. There's not another "here" to be.

Other Energy Systems

R: In our physical bodies, we have a civilization, in which we see each other and interact in certain ways. Is there another such body of energies working in a similar way but unavailable to us?

TGU: From your point of view, there are many others. From our point of view, they're slightly different variants of the same overall energy. So – looking at it from your point of view, there are many many many many many– not just *another* but an infinite number of others. If vibrations had steps, every step is filled.

R: And are these groups of energies operating just at different vibrational levels, is that why there isn't this kind of contact?

TGU: The contact is perceived by you as being separate, and so sometimes it could be experienced as ghosts, or fairies, or different spirits, or earth spirits, or energies or – or – or um…

[Speaking as Frank]: I don't quite know what they mean. It's like affinity, but that doesn't make sense in context.

TGU: It's only an analogy, but it *is* an analogy. Some frequencies resonate to yours, and with those there can be interaction. On your end the interaction might be perceived as proceeding from your own mind, rather than as coming to you. Ideas, for instance, are actually the interaction of your own energy system with other energy systems. This is one reason why you can have an idea, and if you don't grasp it, it goes away. It's an interaction between two things. You wouldn't think of an idea as another energy system, but it's the product of one.

R: And in our ordinary thinking process, when one idea leads to another, is this something that we're not creating but just picking up? Something that is there, that we become aware of?

TGU: Your thinking process is more like choosing than like constructing. And your various filters make it impossible for you to think certain things.

R: Makes it impossible for us to think certain things? What is it that's limiting us? Just our ability to choose alternatives?

TGU: Well, both as a civilization and as a family and as a individual (which means a collection of things), there are agreed-upon understandings of the way the world is, and those understandings make possible a common language. In making possible a common language, they therefore make *impossible* certain other perceptions. If you are going to agree that green is green, it makes it impossible to agree that green is sound, you see? Or that green is the Lone Ranger. Nonsensical things are examples of things that you *can't* think. They are self-evidently not even wrong, just nonsense.

R: These agreements that we've made: Is this the history of our language development?

TGU: Well, we would just say it's the inevitable result of living in a limited time-space. You don't really have any other way that you can live, because the infinitude of reality is too great. You have to pare it down to a manageable subset. That's the best we can do with that. Different civilizations have different subsets, and they overlap, but some of them are radically different. That's one reason for different civilizations.

R: Are you talking about differences in civilizations that exist at one time on the earth?

TGU: Well, at one time, at many times. In a way you could look at it as a larger view of the difference between what seem to you to be individuals on the earth. Each of you as individuals lives different lives, comes up with different viewpoints, and you have therefore constructed different things. The same thing happens on larger and larger scales.

R: Okay, I was thinking now of moving on to another subject, unless there's something else that you'd like to say on this topic that we've been on.

TGU: Well, our sense is that you understood it very well.

Control over Health

R: I want to move to the health and healing area, and first I'd like to ask the extent to which our physical health is under our own mental control.

TGU: Well, we hate to be pedantic, but it depends on what you mean by all of those definitions: "we," "control," "physical" –

Let's go back over the definitions.

You are human beings, of course. But what *are* you as a human being? How many levels? If you mean "what kind of control do we have as conscious Downstairs individuals [that is, those who are primarily conscious only of the physical world]," it's an entirely different question from "what kind of control do we have to the extent that we are at a larger and larger integration with other parts of ourselves." You see, the question determines the answer, really.

Those who are not in touch with their own unconscious mind and not in touch with the intuitive perceiver that you call the right brain – in other words, those who are logic-oriented and sense-driven, have only the most indirect control over their own health. They really can do very little other than physical things that will have a physical result. Their best bet is to stay out of the way and let the automatic mechanisms of the body do the best they can. And the best way to stay out of the way is to maintain a cheerful attitude, follow sensible rules, and if they have a physical problem, deal with it in physical terms. Because they have such a limited tool chest.

Now, those who are working only Downstairs, but are highly intuitive, will extend their tool chest. They will have the ability to know what they should do, what they should eat, how they should be; and what they're doing to harm or help their health. There'll be no conflict between their intuitions and their habits. They won't get sick as often. They'll have everything the first set had, but they will seem to be "lucky." It'll look like they're always fortunate.

At the next higher level are people who have integrated intuition and logic, they're living in a sensible and an intuitive way and beyond that have become aware of other resources. Other modalities as they say. Energy-body work for instance. They'll be able to do everything that the second ones can do, and more, because they will be moving their control to another level of being. As Frank says, they'll be able to "load the dice." They will be able to assist their own unconscious processes by focusing them. They'll say – and you've done it many times – "you need some healing energy here." They may not know how to do it exactly, but they don't need to know how to *do* it; they know how to *direct* it, and that's all that's needed.

Then, next level up after that is more conscious control of more of the automatic mechanism. Beyond that is greater, wider, deeper, surer, more constant connection with what you call Upstairs, and it is as though it puts control of the health in the hands of a wiser, more far-seeing part of the person. When you do energy work, you are running the energy through yourself and help heal yourself while you're helping someone else heal. The ultimate is when, as Jesus said, "I and the father are one." What he meant was, "that energy is coming right through me." Flowing through, and without the distinction, it gives the ability to raise from the dead. Literally.

Now, we know that's a long answer, but it's the real answer.

R: As more and more control is given over to the higher energies, is it an automatic state, in that one has turned over that kind of control to the higher self?

TGU: When we say turn it over, it's not throwing up your hands; it's like being a steward of larger energies. The greater energies are there to be used and you are able to channel them more. Before you have the access to the wider energies, there's nothing for you to use. You know, it's kept out of your hands, as you keep sharp instruments out of the hands of children. More energies become available to you, but you're still the one using them. What you said is not wrong, it is true that a lot of it seems more automatic.

We would caution you however that the purpose of life is not necessarily the avoidance of illness. Illness or disease or accidents (so-called) are not necessarily failures, but, as Jules Verne used to say, "incidents, not accidents." They may have their own purpose.

Problems and Opportunities

R: One brought some physical difficulties into this lifetime for certain purposes.

TGU: Well, you could look at it like this. You have physical and mental legacies from where you've been before. And the whole purpose of life, of course, is to accumulate those legacies. You have mental predispositions, you have talents, you have innate things that you know, because you've been there and done those. A concomitant of that, which cannot really be divorced from it, is that some of those are injuries. Injuries can be fixed at any time. They're not necessarily brought in as lessons so much as they're brought in because this is a time that they can be dealt with, perhaps. If in any given lifetime you were to bring in all of the physical disabilities, all of the mental problems, all of the emotional hurts, all of the lessons to be learned [laughs] you couldn't live!

R: It would overwhelm you.

TGU: It would overwhelm you. So, as a given lifetime is, certain things seem to go together. "Well, she can work on this, this, this, and this." "All right, in that case, she can also do this, this, this and this." "Well, do you want to do this as well?" "Well, maybe that one. Maybe this too." So there can be some physical things, some emotional things, some mental things. And many of those will be tied together, because it is after all one organism. But it's always selected before you come in. You couldn't deal with *all* of them. Therefore, you could look at all of your problems as opportunities. We know it's a cliché, but – they really are. They're only here because you are capable of dealing with them. Now, by your wrong choices, you might make it impossible to deal with them, but, you know, "wrong" choices still lead somewhere.

R: We also have the factor of genetic disorders that come to various members of the same family.

TGU: Well, you're born into a family that offers you that opportunity. You will remember that members of those families inexplicably *skip* those tendencies, too. Those members didn't need it. You might not think of it, but in the shaping of your lives, a lot of compromise goes on, and you say, "we can do this, this, and this, but if we do that, the problem is, we have to accept *this*." And we say "well, that's worth it because it's so advantageous otherwise." You know? So you might wind up in a family that has even a disability that doesn't really impact you one way or the other, but it comes with the territory. We mention it just for the sake of completeness. That's a sort of a rogue factor, you might say. There's always a little chaos inside the pattern. [laughs]

R: In order to join a certain family you might decide to put up with some other aspects of it that would genetically be present?

TGU: Yes, that's a way of looking at it. They may not be physical, they might be attitudinal, emotional, they might be anything. But, you're not going to find a perfect situation. Well, every situation can be *considered* perfect but sometimes the perfection has to be looked for carefully. [chuckles] In other words –

R: Not necessarily obvious.

TGU: Well, it isn't necessarily what you might have chosen had everything else been shaped that way, but then "since it's there, okay, we'll use this and we can use this to develop patience," or something.

R: Why is that there are inherently some physical or mental or attitudinal difficulties? When a person is choosing a lifetime why not make everything perfect, or as perfect as possible?

TGU: Well, you could say that it *is*, given that the purpose of the lifetime is to exercise your muscles and choose. It's the old analogy of the baby bird coming out of the egg: If it didn't have to struggle to get out of the egg, it couldn't develop the muscles it needed to fly. The whole purpose of being in space-time is to have delayed consequences. And it's true – and we really do understand this; we *know* what pain is, and what suffering is, from your point of view. But –they're just so useful to you. Which means "to us," but it means "to you," too.

Life As Choice

R: So that we don't have to think of it in terms of learning lessons, necessarily?

TGU: [pause] Well, in your society right now, we think the whole "school" thing is way overdone. It isn't as much about learning lessons as it is making choices and becoming what you become by the choices that you make. Now, if you make choices, you're going to learn, but the learning is the byproduct. The making choices is the product. The becoming, the fashioning. We would say that your overeducated see everything in terms of learning and schools.

Your life itself – apart from any lessons or morals or retrospection – is the gift you bring us, because that's your shaping. If a child sits down and colors a picture, and gives it to the parent, the *picture* is what she gives to the parent. It's not a lesson, to the child. Now the child may learn something, making the picture, but the picture is the picture. Your lives are the gift.

It's true, you can't very well live without learning, and you wouldn't want to. And you can't live long enough and thoughtfully enough without gaining in wisdom. But the end result of gaining wisdom isn't the important part; the end result is the living. A person who lives as a drunk and dies in the gutter has still created a picture. We know that's hard –

Mental Health

R: I like that. Well now, my original questions had to do with physical health. I assume all those things that you've said apply equally well to mental health. Emotional health?

TGU: It's hard for us to see what you mean by mental health. Look at it for a moment from our point of view. [pause] To us, your concept of lack of mental health implies someone whose mind is malfunctioning. But other than a physical malfunction, a brain malfunction, it really looks to us like what you call mental ill-health is people who don't do what you want them to do, people who scare you because they're not predictable, people who live in such a different world that it's hard for you to adjust to them, and impossible for them to adjust.

So take Alzheimer's, for example. That to you looks like a mental health thing that's caused by physical health. But you only see it from the point of view of a person looking at another person. You can't, of course, see it from the point of view of – of – how shall we say it?

You're all tentacles on one octopus, so to speak. It's not a tragedy. It's not a malfunction. It's a series of choices and an activity, let's say. It's not a deformed picture, any more than a person who dies of cancer is; it's just a picture.

R: When I think about mental health, I include things like the ways in which childhood experiences affect the rest of a person's life in negative ways, causing a grownup to always choose the wrong marital partner, for instance, or always to be in a state of anxiety, or –

TGU: And why do you suppose those events happened and had those effects, when someone else who experienced the same kind of thing would *not* experience that effect? That's not an accident, that's what the person had set up, for a reason. That lifetime of what seemed like dysfunction could be looked at as a mold, that constrains them in certain ways, so that they'll come back against the same situation again and again and again, and have to choose. There is learning in that, but we would say it's the choice and not the learning that's the important part there. The learning is important in that it helps them to choose.

So a person who spends an entire lifetime in total frustration in a certain direction may come out of the lifetime *extremely* benefited. We can give you an example. Edgar Cayce [the Virginia Beach psychic] lived his life under *very* severe constraints, which purified him and protected him from the temptation to misuse gifts that, misused, would have only damaged him. The picture that he chose to paint was painted against a background carefully chosen to help him paint it.

Now, that's talking of poverty and anxiety and depression, but still, what looks to you like mental problems looks to us like a person adapting as best they can to tangible and intangible circumstances.

R: Part of the picture for me has been that one sees similarities in certain childhood crises; certain childhood patterns seem typically to be worked out in the same way by adults. There's no reason why the matter of choice couldn't still be in there, but there seem to be typical choices for certain patterns of response. And –

TGU: Are you suggesting that the patterns are beyond their control?

R: I don't believe that they are without choice points, somehow. It may be inevitable that there is some disruption or some discomfort in adulthood that follows from childhood patterns.

TGU: They may lead a life of total frustration. Seemingly.

R: But you're saying that there's meaning in that.

TGU: Given that you're here to create a flower, or a picture, it can't be *without* meaning. *Nothing* can be without meaning. This is one deeper sense in which the expression that "all paths are good" can be seen. It doesn't really matter what the final picture looks like. To a large degree, what matters is that the picture is painted. And if 999 out of 1,000 paintings are failures, so called, they're still painted. It's better to paint than not to paint. [chuckle] We've been lured into a really terrible analogy, because it's constrictive. A better analogy – if you had a thousand leaves of grass in a field, some might be blighted and some might be prematurely brown and some might be broken, or eaten by insects – but it's still the perfection of a field of grass. And part of that perfection *is* the very irregularity and the very unpredictability of it. There *can't* be a failure in a leaf of grass.

R: So when we have children and we consider their early life experiences to be very important and we try our best to give the child, the person starting out here, as positive a picture as possible to move ahead with, are those unreasonable concerns on our part?

TGU: Oh not at all. Don't forget, that child picked that family for that reason, for that concern. Those matters cannot be dealt with *except* in terms of 3D Reality. It's true that from *our* point of view, all paths are good. But from *your* point of view, it is certainly not equally good that the child fall under the school bus or that the child be safe. That's where a lot of people are going wrong, because they're sensing that there's more to life, but it doesn't negate what's all around them. You do the best you can in every circumstance, and – anyone's best is none too good, you know?

Everyone deserves the very best, so no one's best can ever be *too* good for the person. But there's a limit to your responsibility, because you are a part of a situation in which that child is an equally sentient being, who is there by consent. As you well know.

Now, we'll say this as well. To the degree that a society cares more deeply about its children, that society as a creation is different from a society that treats them as consumables or is indifferent. That's another aspect of the creation thing. The care that you as a parent give to your child makes a difference in terms of the flavor of the society, so to speak, as well as the individual reaction.

R: In some ways it seems like things are getting better in that regard. Children used to live in much worse circumstances than they do now, being put to work at very early ages; those kind of dimensions that seem to create a lot of unhappiness and health problems.

TGU: Well, we wish we could agree. We don't, though. We don't think there's much difference. The difference is in the flavor. Chocolate is not better than pistachio, just different. We know where you're going with this. You're thinking of the children who were basically thrown away in mines and things, and died at age 10 or 15. But we would point out to you your sex industries in your cities. You're doing the same thing, but even worse. It's different, but it's not "better." It's different. And your children of privilege are actually in many ways perhaps the most underprivileged. They are being cut off from their emotional roots. But again, they're in that situation because that's the situation they chose.

[Pause] That was very interesting; you actually brought us into your framework for a moment. Quite interesting. You understand? We swung down, so to speak, into your seeing it as individuals. Very interesting.

R: Mmm. I see. As a result of that –

TGU: Well, we felt emotions! Which is your largest gift. Very interesting.

R: Uh-huh. [laughs, perhaps in perplexity]

TGU: Well, you see, you mentioned good and bad, better and worse, and, in thinking about it, we encompassed it. We *felt* it to, the degree that we *were* it. And our sadness for the children was as if we were there. It's *very* interesting! Surprised us, actually.

R: So that you were also thinking in terms of better and worse.

TGU: Yes, precisely. Well, no! Not *thinking*, because we're *well* capable of *thinking* it, but we were *emotionally* thinking it, if that's not a contradiction. *Very* interesting. And of course, that's a major thing we get out of you being there.

R: All right. Well, I appreciate that being brought to our attention.

TGU: You see, we keep saying, we're *not* any different, we're just in a different place. And we just sort of visited. [chuckles]

How to Make a Better World

R: One of the things that we think about is how to improve our world for the masses of individuals in it. And we think about that in terms of children, and how children's lives are led, and how it impacts them and doesn't. Millions of us have lived our lives trying to make a better world, if you will. And I'm hearing you say well of course, it makes sense that one does that with children. But the whole goal of making a better world doesn't seem to make any sense from the perspective that you're speaking.

TGU: We'll try to say this carefully. Your trying to *make* a better world is good work, because of what *you're* choosing. But "better world" implies that you know how to *make* a better world. Your ability to know what a better world would be is very great for yourself; it's pretty good for your family and friends; it's somewhat good for your neighborhood; and it's less good the wider the circle goes. Now, it's true that abstractly you can have preferences and some of those preferences may be absolutely right. Certainly you want to have clean water rather than water that's not safe to drink. But in actual human terms your ability to know what's good and your ability to know what will bring the good is really very limited. We would say your major ability to make the world a better place to live in is one simple thing: Be a beacon.

R: Say that again?

TGU: Be a beacon. Shine what *you* are. It's very powerful. It's very subtle and seemingly inconsequential. Many of the results are not in the physical plane at all. The closest we could come at the moment would be to say that your reactions – what you are – resonate with others, and that resonance is not just within time-space. We've never tried to express this, because you don't have the words for it. The what-you-are mingles with other people who are the same thing, and it creates a warp, a pattern, in the energy system.

Let's go back to the basics. By being a beacon, your example – not so much what you *do*, although that's how it shows, as *through* what you do, what you are – encourages other people to be like that as well, and that creates a better world. Now, it's true that "goodness is as goodness does," but the "is" and not the "does" is the essence of it. A person could do good works and actually be a *negative* beacon. A person could do no good works, or none that were apparent, and be quite a positive beacon. So it isn't the works, it's the choosing to be what you are.

R: Somehow your essence is communicated out there.

TGU: Yes. Yes, yes. You're broadcasting your essence every second of the day. You haven't any choice about that.

Healing

R: I want to move to the idea of distant healing. It seems like that's related, the idea of our trying to use ourselves as a beacon to send healing energy to someone at a distance. How can one best use one's self here, with a purpose of healing someone who is not present?

TGU: The simplest thing is to overcome the illusion of distance. That's really all you need to do. You and the other person are part of one thing, literally. Not metaphorically, but literally, there is no distance between you in another dimension, no matter what there is physically. The idea of distance that's in your mind because of physical bodies tends to unconsciously make you think you have to *overcome* the distance. But you don't. All you need to do is remember that there *is* no difference, and it's an easy, simple thing to then just be at a level of being that is healing, and resonate with the person so that they can rev themselves up to that level again. That's really all they need to do. You're acting as a tuning fork for them, so to speak.

R: So we don't need to make the distinction between the distance healing or side-by-side healing.

TGU: There *isn't* a distinction. It *appears* to be, because you're in bodies, but there's no distinction, it's the same thing.

R: Okay, well how does one best direct this being-ness to be helpful in some way to someone else?

TGU: Your easiest way is to look at your religious traditions. They show you a very good way to do it. They would not put it this way, but they're saying, "my personal power, brought up to a higher power, and brought down again to the other power, to the other person." And so you might think in these terms: You, at all levels, in contact with the other person at all of their levels, and helping them. Assuming that they *want* the help. (Assuming that you're not actually interfering with them. That's an important thing. It gets overlooked.)

That's really all that needs to be done. To the degree that you can remember how great you are, and not think of yourself as a limited physical body, then you'll know that you have all you need. And they have all that they need to be able to receive. It's really just strictly a matter of love. That's all there really is. Lots of complicated techniques are invented, and these things really are belief crutches. And if they work, that's fine. But they're not needed. Jesus was not a Reiki master.

R: I can see that the belief systems tie up with particular techniques or strategies for doing this.

TGU: And to the degree that they work for the people, well and good, but they're not necessary – unless they're necessary for that person.

R: When you say that the healer is trying to connect with a higher power –

TGU: That is to say, other levels of themselves. It's not a different person.

R: Yes. Higher self, or whatever language one uses. Bringing forth energy through the person, or sending it directly, would seem to be the only difference between distant healing and –

TGU: It *seems* to you that you're sending the energy, and there's nothing wrong with that seeming. It works for you, and there's no reason not to use it. But that's not *really* what's happening. What's really happening is, you are resonating at a state of health, as we say, like a tuning fork, and the other person is being able to lean on that resonance in order to get back up to speed. Terrible mixed metaphor, but you see the idea. However, we recognize that for people in general it *looks like* sending healing. And there's nothing wrong with that; it works. We're just stating that's not really what's happening. Not from our point of view, anyway.

R: *Well, I guess another way of going at that is, when one is aiming to do a healing with another person in one's presence, and has a sense of energy flowing through them, say into their hands or through their hands to another person, is this imagery that we use? Is it unnecessary to use the imagery that way?*

TGU: [pause] Well, we're tempted to say that people don't do things that aren't necessary. As your world changes, the experiences that you have change. You'll notice that in the healing that you're doing back and forth [i.e., Frank and Rita], the experience changes unpredictably. Neither of you know what's going to happen, necessarily, until it does. That's a pretty good sign that neither of you is intending it, you are just removing the barriers from it. Which is fine. You know, the *intending* is that help shall be given and received. But neither of you could *do* it in the way that you could write your name, or do any skill that you perform. It's not so much a skill, it's a being. So sometimes you'll perceive it as tingling, sometimes as heat, sometimes as transfer of energy, sometimes as something else.

The experience is more a function of your concepts than it is of what's really happening. So if you have a concept of putting energy in, and having the energy come in and rearrange things, there's nothing wrong with that, and it works. Someone else with a different concept would heal in a totally different way and it would work. Neither one is invalid, neither one is imagination, it's just that the phenomena are the product of your states of being, really. A good Catholic at Lourdes might have a broken arm instantly restored, and that would follow a certain unconscious expectation. If you were in another context, it might be a slower process, like the laying down of new nerves and things. The healing will manifest as a result of the belief systems. But it's only a manifestation, it's not the actual thing.

R: *As you know very well, [chuckle] Frank is very interested in healing – others.*

TGU: [laughs] That's so true.

R: *I'd like to know if you have any suggestions for him.*

TGU: "Physician heal thyself." [laugh]

R: *Is that happening? With him?*

TGU: Unpredictably. Or should we say, in a quite scattershot manner. Not at all systematic. He has no interest.

R: Then what kind of suggestions do you have? More frequent, or more frequent occurrence?

TGU: Well, he is what he is. He's doing all right. I mean, he's not going to take the advice anyway.

R: He's not?

TGU: [laughs]

R: How about when he's working to try to heal my leg? Do you have some suggestions for him there?

TGU: No, you're both doing fine on that, because we give the suggestion second by second and he follows; he's learned to just go with it and that has unblocked the channel. There's still more to be done, but what you're doing is fine. And by the way, if you haven't guessed, you're part of a demonstration that the two of you have set up.

R: Good.

TGU: That's with him and N———, same thing. [chuckles] They're two of a kind, those two. Neither one cares about healing themselves. [laughs, and they laugh] Just interested in healing others. Which is of course why they're there: mirrors.

R: Why is that? Why is there this resistance to self-healing?

TGU: Well it isn't so much a resistance to self-healing as it is a matter of self-definition. They take themselves somewhat for granted, and they say "well, this doesn't bother me much, it's not worth fooling about – but *that's* interesting over there." [chuckles] This is literally what's going on.

R: "It's my pain so it's not important," or something like that? "I can handle it because I'm tough?"

TGU: No, no, there's two levels here. When they're really in trouble, they're not in a position to help themselves. It's very difficult. When they're *not* in trouble – [laughs] You know what it's like? It's exactly like the man who never fixed the roof that leaked [laughs] because it was too wet to fix when it's raining and when it's not raining it's not leaking. [they laugh] That's *exactly* what they're doing.

Well, to be a little more serious about it – what we said is true, but there's another aspect of it as well – they can see and understand when they have a place to stand, to move, working on someone else, because they can get outside of it and work on it. But not when it's themselves.

Although, Frank was doing something very interesting last night and little by little we got it across to him to actually move his awareness within his own body. We can't say too much about this. [chuckles] Hostile ears are listening. [laughs] We don't want him to know certain techniques.

The whole essence of healing is love. Everything else is just added on to it.

Separation and Oneness

R: All right. In this process that we're doing, here and now – Frank's conscious activity seems to move in and out. Sometimes I feel like he really is able to step aside enough so that I can speak directly to you, and other times I feel him coming back in. I'm asking questions about this generally without a very good way of putting it, but – what's going on here? Is this to some extent a matter of Frank's needing to or wanting to control what comes up, or is it just not wanting to miss anything? I'm asking why he comes back in when he does, I guess, and does this in effect get in the way?

TGU: No, you're not seeing it right. It's not going in and out at all. He's never not *here*. And *we're* never not here. [pause] The manner of expression alters so that sometimes it seems him and sometimes it seems us, but it's always the same thing in different proportions. That's the best we're going to be able to do with that. You're never going to get all him; you're never going to get all us. It's *always* going to be mixed. And the *reason* is, because that's how he lives. That's his normal life.

This disappointed him, when he was younger. There is no "him stepping all the way aside and us talking," because there's not that much separation between him and us to make that possible. Or even desirable. But also, oddly enough, there is no talking to him and not talking to us. Because the separation is not there and not desirable. So even when you're talking to him about tuna fish, we'll be popping in and out all the time, because he's not got the barrier there. You see?

R: And yet it seems sometimes that you bring up information that Frank is not aware of.

TGU: Oh absolutely! Absolutely. That's the value, you know. Well, not so much information, the value is that we are a corrective point of view. Actually, he might not see it that way. He would prefer *more* information than we usually *can* bring. He tends to think of us as having all knowledge and access to all knowledge, which is theoretically true, but in practice it isn't true, because it depends on the questions. You see? [pause] We wouldn't answer for the results if you were to ask us a question in Mandarin Chinese. Given the right circumstances, we suppose we could go find somebody. But it would have to be real and not theoretical; I don't know how to explain that.

R: Okay, so my question really was aimed at what we're doing here, and I'm hearing you say that there's nothing that interferes.

TGU: That's right. What you're getting is hard for people to believe because of your concepts. It's only a very slight exaggeration of your own life. In your own life, your own Gentlemen Upstairs – your Ladies Upstairs, whichever you prefer – are popping in and out all the time. Well, they're not so much popping in and out as they're there but they're not always contributing. It's just that your language and your civilization doesn't encourage you to recognize the fact. And that's one of the things that he's here to do. Perhaps he'll accomplish it, perhaps not. If you all realize that *you* are *we* and *we* are *you*, and that it's *not* a question of a great occasional leap across a barrier, but of everyday intercourse, that will change your civilization radically.

R: Yes, that's certainly true. And I'm encouraged to think in those terms. And yet people are encouraged to pray, to ask for help –

TGU: Yes, but, look what's implied there. A prayer implies distance. You know? You're praying *to* something else, which is a very strongly different nuance from opening your own channels. You can call 'em the guys upstairs, you can call 'em God, you can call 'em anything you want. But you also would be better off to remember that it's part of you, it's not something different. It is but it isn't; you're always going to get that. Because of the difference in playing fields, every answer is going to be, "well it is but it isn't," because it depends on where you are when you ask the question. You *are* the same as your higher self. But you're not. But you are. You pays your money and you takes your choice. [pause]

The whole mode of operation that assumes that there is a Frank and that there's an "us" is incorrect. It's a useful fiction, but that's all. Because when there is identity, there can only be relative distinctions. There can only be polarities, let's say. So, to say "well Frank, you get out of the way, we want to talk to the guys," sets up a willingness to open up a little more, and a willingness to speak without pre-intent, and to let come whatever comes, but it does not in any *meaningful* way substitute one personality for another.

R: Or create any kind of separation.

TGU: Exactly. There is none. Now, for many people there *is* that separation, but it's only of their own concepts. The separation vanishes when it's desired to vanish, on a deep enough level. If you define yourself as Downstairs, there *will* be a difference between Downstairs and Upstairs, because you will systematically ignore, or not recognize, or distort, the input that comes from other than inside your definition. As you loosen the definition, the distortion lessens. That's probably the simplest way to put it.

R: And at the same time, at the level at which we are all one, an additional set of factors come in that we interpret as meaning that we are individual and separate. And while you and Frank are the same thing, Frank and I are the same thing, and –

TGU: And you and *we* are the same thing, yes.

Barriers between People

R: And then the whole process of getting information from one aspect to another seems relatively meaningless, and yet information isn't available across what seem like these boundaries.

TGU: Well, we would argue that if you want to get information between one individual and another, the most efficient way is to remove the barriers between yourself and other layers of yourself, so that you *do* interact over here where everything is one, and then you'll both know. And in fact you all do that, to an unrecognized extent.

R: We don't necessarily take advantage of that, even though we would like to in many ways.

TGU: Well, you do, more than you realize. There's much more telepathy going on down there than you think. You take it as intuition, or as instinct, or as hunches or whatever, but you know because you know, and one of the ways you know is, on this side, there are no secrets. If you're both willing to listen, and both willing to interact, then you can both have all the common knowledge that you wish. It's not *quite* that simple, but it's close to that simple. The only other complicating factor is that, to bring into consciousness things in your world requires a certain ma-nipulation, but you can unconsciously know things quite easily. That is why you can have a hunch about someone instantly, and that hunch can be *entirely right*, with no data. But it's much harder to have a factual knowledge about that person without data. The forming of concepts and of articulated knowledge is very much a 3D thing, but the instincts and the knowing is very much from our side.

R: What would happen if we did have the totality of our selves available to our-selves, with secrets not existing. Is there some advantage to having part of our-selves secret from other parts of ourselves?

TGU: Not from *our* point of view. [pause] There will come a day when you will live your lives as individuals knowing that you're connected. Knowing – not believing, but knowing – that you're connected. And this is a small example of what it's like, but it's only a beginning state. And in fact right now you can see more of the complications than the promise of it, but you could live your lives, and someday will, knowing that you are individuals and knowing that you are *not* individuals. Simultaneously. That life would be paradise to what you have now, and will be. It's a new stage you'll come to. There's no advantage to being sealed off from the other side. It's a consequence of many things.

R: Well, living in a world of secrets is about the most uncomfortable thing that I can think of.

TGU: It's a subset of control. People keep secrets to try to keep control. They don't succeed, of course, but that's what they try to do. In other words, secrets are the byproducts of fear. Fear is the byproduct of perceived lack of control, which is the byproduct of perceived separation. Eliminate the separation and everything else goes.

However, there will still be complications – it will still be interesting down there. But life won't be the pain and the isolation and the cross-purposes it is now.

R: Well, I thank you very much. This was another interesting session.

TGU: We thank you at the same time. This, as you say, is interesting. You gave us a new experience as well.

Session Five
September 11, 2001

[Between sessions, Rita prepared a list of questions, which is why this evening's session was not taken up entirely by the day's events.]

R: Well as you know this has been a sad day for us and we're checking in to see if this is a good thing for Frank to do a session with us tonight.

TGU: Good thing for him. He tends not to get in touch with emotions.

Holding One's Center

R: We've had an extraordinarily large number of people moving from the physical into the "there" today. And this raises for us questions about the best way for us to deal with such things as a disaster. Do you have some comments you'd like to make about that?

TGU: That's an excellent question. It's the best question you could ask, because this is only the beginning, as you know. From your own points of view, the central necessity will be to monitor your reaction to the events that are coming. Your choices are constrained by your prior emotional reactions, so that were you to react in fear, or in rage, or in any of myriad ways, certain lines of development would be opened and others would be closed. This is said less for the particular people who are in this room than for the record, because this is – as we've said before – a record for others.

Our primary advice would be, hold your center. Stay on an even keel. And this does not mean do not react, but, in the midst of your reaction, remember who you are – for your own sakes, but also because of the part that you came here to play.

R: I'd like to come back a little later to question what happens from your perspective when we have this kind of disaster, but go ahead now with questions around what you suggested, which is how we handle this kind of turmoil and fear-arousing incidents. Is there a way in which we can be helpful in counter-acting fears and anxieties – both our own and others'?

TGU: Yes. Maintaining what you *are* has its effect on all the rest. You must remember that you are *a* part of *a* thing, and a part can affect the whole, by what you are. You aren't isolated individuals who can only influence each other by thoughts or words or actions. This looks innocuous and ineffective, but in fact it is the most effective response possible while you are in bodies.

R: It's one thing for us to be here in Virginia listening to events that are happening elsewhere. It's really hard to imagine that if we were closer to the events we wouldn't be in states of fear and anxiety ourselves.

TGU: Oh no. There are people on Manhattan Island doing the same thing you're doing, but for the same reason that they will not hear of you in the news, you will not hear of them. You were not left as a little island off to the side.

R: I understand that, but we talk about the idea of releasing fear, releasing anxiety, and that sounds great, but how do we do that? That seems a very difficult thing to do.

TGU: How did *you* do it?

R: Well, I'm at some distance from it. If my children were there, if I were there myself, I can't imagine that I would be feeling as calm and relaxed and as centered as I feel here.

TGU: Well, that's true – but there have been times in your life when you *were* in the center of things, and at those times, we ask again, what did you do? It's only a rhetorical question, but the temptation in your country will be far greater from anger than from fear. Granted, the anger will stem *from* the fear, but more people will be in anger than will be in fear, and it will be a much stronger emotion, more easily manipulated.

However, if you ask, what can *you* do to help others maintain their centered-ness, we say again, maintain your own. It's not ineffective.

R: Yes, that's kind of the same theme we have for a lot of things; when we're trying to heal, when we're trying to send others good wishes, or love. You were talking last time about being a beacon. That struck a great nerve with me all week. And I thought about it in connection with the exercise that a research group used to do here, trying during a disaster to open a path for those individuals who were ready to move over [to the non-physical] with minimum anxiety and minimum fear; representing ourselves as beacons leading to a simple pathway for people to pass through. Children would be the easiest to think of moving in that way, because they wouldn't be loaded with fear, and expectations.

TGU: Well, the children don't miss anything, but they often misinterpret, of course. The beacon is an excellent way to do. You weren't so much leading them through as you were, by what you are, letting them change to resonate to what you were. A minor point.

R: It seemed as though we were just pointing to an opportunity for them. In that sense just being a beacon.

TGU: In the sense that you were a stabilized point, that got them through; helped them get through. You understand, you were a stabilized point, and that is what we're asking you to do now. Being a stabilized point helps smooth the waves and the sloshings around.

The Manner of Death

R: It seemed as though that would be something that we could do that might be helpful for those people who were easily ready to move to a non-physical state. But for all the others, we often did what we called rescue missions. Do you have some comments to make about that?

TGU: You could say that the period you're coming to now is unprecedentedly different. You are loaded with volunteers who came in to do just this part of the drama.

Okay, let's go back. You will remember that the last time we were talking about a person bringing in the things that that person could handle – that you couldn't bring everything in to deal with at one time. Well, another aspect of that is, the kind of death someone has can also help to put them into a situation *on the other side*, that they can learn from, that they can grow from. It'll help them to smooth things out for themselves. Not that being smooth is the ultimate result, but you understand: Just as you come into this side, into a situation that is sort of planned for you, giving you certain opportunities so that you can grow, so when you go to the other side it's the same thing. You're being born into the other side, into a certain limited situation, and so just as in this life you might come in with cerebral palsy, in that life you may come in with a traumatic death in an explosion or something that gives you no time to make sense of it.

Interacting with your belief systems at that time – which is another way of saying interacting with the product of what you have made yourself – sets up the situation on the other side. We realize that it looks like all the action is in 3D Theater, but there's as much action going on on the other side as here. The interaction between the two allows changes of scene, so to speak. But when you go to the other side, that isn't taking off the makeup and sitting in the back room, kicking your heels. You're involved in another play over there. It's just different terrain, you understand? Time and space are different over here, but you're not *without* constraints, they're just a different kind of constraints. So all of that's very complicated, but what we're trying to say is, the deaths that people die are part of their birth on the other side. It's neither meaningless nor accidental.

R: *So I guess that's why the Buddhists have so many ideas about what death should be like. Seems to me the Buddhists – I don't know if others besides the Buddhists – are very concerned about the nature of a death of a physical person.*

TGU: Well – we're smiling. It's true. All we can say is that people by what they are form preferences, without even knowing it. And so smooth will look preferable to someone as opposed to rough, but it's only a preference. We wouldn't say that the Buddhists have the final word on the subject. They have *a* final word, *a* way of looking at things. It is a productive way; it's not the only way.

Preferences in the Manner of Death

R: *I've noticed that when people get to my age, they begin to think about death much more frequently than in earlier years, and often state preferences for ways of dying. Does that kind of preference make any difference?*

TGU: Does it affect how you will die, you mean?

R: *Yes.*

TGU: If you want it to. [pause] But the joker in the deck is, "who is you?" Unless you put a gun to your head, you're not going to have the final say in this. Upstairs will pull the plug.

R: *People state preferences for a sudden death, for example, versus long lingering illnesses, or things of that sort.*

TGU: But it's also true that people don't know what's good for them, too! [laughs]

R: *Ah. Okay. People so often state a preference for conscious death, or fear conscious death. There seems to be a lot of concern about the nature of death.*

TGU: Well, we hear you saying – and we would agree – that people's preferences are a flowering of what they are. But their preferences may not be what they know and want at a different level. If we had one bit of advice, we would just say "relax about it" to all of you, because it may or may not be what you consciously want, but it isn't going to be by accident, and isn't going to be at random. We have a saying, "all is well, all is always well," and we really do mean that, all the way through. No matter what it looks like.

Span of Consciousness

R: *I'm going to go back to your point about having a lot of activity in the There as well as the Here, and is this also a matter of choice on the other side.*

TGU: Well, the short answer would be yes. The longer answer would be, again, keep in mind who *you* refers to. Supposing we took just one tentacle of the octopus. [Their octopus analogy compared any one life to one tentacle of an octopus, with the rest of the octopus representing the total being.] Just you, yourself – but you in your totality, up to the point where you connect with all the rest of us. You'll see that here you have an animal that's quite different from the animal that *you* think you are because you're dealing with this one little slice between your one birth and your one death. You have all the rest of this to be conscious of and then there is the consciousness that *is* all that, and of course beyond *that* the rest of the octopus. So when you talk about you (or she or he or whatever), a lot of misunderstanding slides in there, because you tend to slide that definition in the middle of your sentence without even recognizing it.

We haven't lost sight of your question, we're saying yes, it's planned, but not by the little-you on this side, *and* not by the little-you that just got born on the other side.

R: Because you have become part of the totality in a more conscious way?

TGU: [Sigh.] Well – well – again, it depends on which part of the "you" you're talking about.

Let's suppose that your total "you" is 100 square miles. Maybe *one* square mile of that is lit up and is a seemingly separate consciousness. The other 99 percent is conscious of itself but is not necessarily apparent to the one. There's a reason for that, because it makes the experience possible.

When you're born into either side, the overall being is conscious, but the newly born being is not *automatically* conscious of anything. To the degree that you increase your consciousness over here, consciousness will be increased over there, you see? You're widening your field of action. That can be a relatively permanent gain, so that you could say that your span of consciousness becomes larger with practice. You have more control over larger things, more awareness of connection. Does that answer that?

R: Well, yes. It's not the little-you that's here, but the expanded-you that's on the other side when you first move over, say. But you're saying that that "you" is again a small part of the totality.

TGU: Mm-hmm. You all have a tendency to assume that once you get to the other side you know everything and you're connected to everything and on one level it *is* so, and on another level it isn't; just as when you're over here. It's just that the constraints are different. There are different kinds of constraints, and they operate in different ways.

R: Then are you talking about an increasing consciousness of the you as you live a life and then live between lives and again repeat the cycle over a number of times, that there comes increasing awareness of the totality?

TGU: There can. Depending on your choices. You can also lose ground, of course.

R: But where are you in this process?

TGU: Well, we're mostly graduated. [laughs]

R: You're graduated from the circle of in and out?

TGU: Mm-hmm. Mostly. I suppose we could be enticed back in, given the right need, but not from our own need. You have your examples of your bodhisattvas like Jesus who came in, not of their own need to incarnate, but out of a need to play a part, to show the way. You could look at it like a natural cycle in which the seed is planted, the seed goes a certain way and flowers or doesn't flower and then drops down, dies down, and the seed could come up again. Your souls are like that. You have a time at which you've been planted and you need to grow and increase and experience, but then when that cycle's completed, you don't need to keep doing that. You see? Once you've got it, you've got it.

R: And are we talking about here many, many lifetimes, or does it vary?

TGU: It varies because it somewhat depends on choices. To a degree it depends on circumstances, but really that's saying choices too. You remember we said about drawing pictures? You can have complicated pictures or simple pictures. A simple picture doesn't take as long to draw. And if you extended this beyond one lifetime and looked at the whole overall pattern as a picture, some come in and go out with a simple picture. Others do more complicated things. (Except of course, it isn't "others"; a part of us does this, a part of us does that.) Again, the analogy of the field of grass. If all the stalks were identical, it wouldn't be perfect, but artificial.

R: Well, as you know, I'm always trying to find out who you are. Are you then a totality of individual parts who have done this in a very simple way, a very complicated way, have lived many lives, have lived few lives, all of these alternatives in the "you" that's responding to these questions?

TGU: Yes as long as you remember that the "you" that's responding to these questions is also you. We're all one thing. It just looks separate on your side.

R: Yes it does.

TGU: And [chuckles] therefore all possible variants are part of us. Or we are part of all possible variants. We could say it either way.

Individuals: A Convenient Fiction

R: In an earlier session I was getting the sense that if one were to look at what I'm calling the totality of the energy who's speaking here in terms of individual energies, we would be talking about 30 or so. Somehow that number came up.

TGU: That was what was there then. It's different at any given time. [pause] From a certain point of view it's true, but from another point of view it isn't at all true. It's difficult to know how to put it. Even when *you* are an individual you're not, and you're not *a* unit. You are a collection of things, and at the same time you're only a part of something larger. The whole idea of a unit is just a convenient fiction. We can't make you see it as we see it. For instance, you comprise billions of cells and over the lifetime of your body there's no unity to it, if you wanted to look at it that way. You understand? It's just a flow.

R: Units come and go, yes.

TGU: Now, within that, you have somewhat more stable organs that are composed of these cells. You could say, well, this village is composed of x number of so-called individuals, all of whom are born and die and move and all sorts of things. So *it* flows, too. And to carry the analogy just one more step, you are part of something which lives and dies many times in different places, and so there too there's flow. In a very real sense there is no individual in the way that it looks to you because you see everything in time-slices. If you could only see it not sliced, you'd look like a worm, sort of, you know, a long, long, long thing that goes on. Well, you get the idea. You're attempting to see us as individuals, and we can't even see *you* as an individual except as a decision that it's more convenient to think of you this way. That's the best we can do on that for the moment.

R: Well, it's very easy to understand the theory of this, but it's very difficult to organize our thinking around that. So the questions come out with implications that we would rather are not there, but they are there.

TGU: Well, you are in time-space; you can stretch yourselves to envision it, or to imagine it, or to approximate it, but by the best gymnastics you can do mentally, you can't do what we can do just simply *only* because we're just not in it.

R: I'm intrigued by this point which seems reasonable and yet I don't think that I really have ever thought of things this way, that in the There where you are, there are many things going on. You're not just observing life or observing your existence or planning for a future life, but there's an existence there that includes many activities in the same way there is here.

TGU: That's right. It's not just an intermission.

Affinities

R: *[laughs] Okay. I asked this kind of question before, but I want to ask it again, because it's such an intriguing question, and that is the question of assignments, or missions, or duties or whatever that you have at that level. I've gotten a sense that there are variations in what those assignments are, but I've not gotten you to admit that there are assignments. [laughs]*

TGU: Well, supposing someone were to ask you, what's your assignment for Friday the 14th of January? Whether past or future? Your whole day of the 14th of January has so many things in it, and the relative importance of those things depends strictly on the person who's judging them. You couldn't answer the question except arbitrarily. And to answer it arbitrarily would be to misinform the person asking the question, because it would imply to them that the question made sense in a context where it doesn't. So you want us to say "we're teachers," and there is an aspect of that, in a way, but – what if we said we were roofers? [they laugh]

R: *But I have the sense that you have an assignment with Frank, so to speak; that he's part of your group and while he's living his life in the physical, you have a certain relationship to him.*

TGU: Now remember, this is more a relationship of affinity than of assignment. Those closest in nature to what he's doing at a given moment will seem to be drawn there, but it isn't like they've been assigned. It's more of an ad hoc affinity, in a way. Now, some of us are connected more closely over time; that's a different level of affinity. There could be an affinity of task, an affinity of soul. We'd rather not go into that any more at the moment but – we can at another time. You have other fish to fry tonight. We're only saying that we ourselves have many other things to do besides him. And again, because we're not constrained in the way that you are, we can be with him and for him any time he needs us, whether he's aware of it or not, without taking up all of our time. So –

R: *I had understood that you had a similar role with others besides Frank.*

TGU: Sure. But this is not a good night for this discussion. Let's bookmark this question of spiritual affinity as opposed to task affinity, and we will be glad to answer this at another time, but it's not the right night for this. It's for reasons of the constraints on you, not for the constraints on us.

R: *Well, I'm going to ask one more question about that, and you may want to rule this out for later too, but I didn't mean an assignment in the sense of being told to do this specific task or something I only meant it in the sense of, in the existence that you're now in, is there a specific purpose that you have. You're not purpose-less.*

TGU: Could you answer that question if we asked it of you? If we said to you, do you have an on-going mission, or do you have even a center of gravity, so to speak – in this case, not just in this one lifetime but for yourself as a whole, would you be able to answer that question?

R: Well, I'd be able to take a stab at it for a current part of my life.

TGU: That's right. But suppose it were for the whole thing.

R: Well, I've never been able to do other than what seemed like fantasy about the purpose of the total life.

TGU: Well see, it isn't the vagueness that's the problem, it's that what you're do-ing slices what you are by time. As we say, it's natural, but to you what looks like a unit – Rita's life – is *not* a unit. It can be *seen* as a unit, particularly if you're stuck in space-time, but it isn't really a unit. So, once you got to the place where you didn't see a part of yourself as if it were all of yourself, you'd find the ques-tion – as we find the question – pretty nearly unanswerable. Our mission is to be. Is to live. We'd be willing to consider that further sometime, but I don't know what else we could say. At any given time one or another task might become more important, but over time you're going to find that growth is growth and it leads now here and now there.

The Effect of the 9/11 Event

R: Okay, let me ask this. Would the events that happened in our time and space today change the energy at your level in some ways?

TGU: Well, you know, we're not surprised by any of this. We know what's going on that hasn't happened in your area yet. We know converging probabilities to the degree that it might as well be set. [That is, the probabilities are practically certainties.] So, how should it change our energies?

R: Well, I'm saying that there may be on the earth level lots of demand for your attention today.

TGU: But, you know, how many people died? When you have 15 or 20 or 30 bil-lion at a time, then you might start taxing our facilities, but – you know how many people there are? Or, how many ex-people, or part-people, or whatever you would call them? World War II didn't tax us, this isn't going to tax us, in terms of a drain on our attention, if that's what you mean.

R: This would be a small event, compared to the kinds of events in your –

TGU: In a way, you could kill everyone on the planet on the same day, and – the mission of the planet off to the side, just considering that number of people –if we had to we'd react to it.

R: Well, all the suggestions you made tonight about the future on our planet sound very grim.

TGU: You knew them a long time ago.

R: Well, I haven't known them. I have really been an optimist. And when the question has been, "are we going to end with being blown up by atomic bombs, or are the earth changes going to wipe us out," I haven't come down on the side of either of those. But it sounds like you're saying I'm wrong about that.

TGU: We didn't mention either of those things. [stops, starts and sputters]

R: Well I was using that as an example of the kinds of questions that had to do with how it all ends.

TGU: Well it *doesn't* all end. [they laugh] It always goes on. It's curious to us, how while you're in bodies it seems to you that anything that takes people out of bodies is not an optimistic end, given that you're all going to come out of the body anyway, and if you didn't you'd be stuck. You are going to have extensive disruptions, but your whole lives have been extensive disruptions and you've lived them fruitfully and with purpose. Looking back on them, one might say, "oh my God, it's been one damn thing after another," and in a way that's true. But in another way it's, "wow, it's been the removal of one chain after another." And in a way *that's* true.

If your systems were currently functioning in an optimal or even a sustainable way, then disruptions to the systems would be bad in the sense that you would find it not only uncomfortable but retrogressive. But your systems aren't sustainable, and most of them aren't even humane. And disruptions of those systems we cannot see as anything other than a way forward, not backward.

R: By systems you're talking about social institutions and ways of defining our livelihoods.

TGU: Indirectly, yes. Primarily, we mean the way people are defining themselves, what they think they are. What they think the rules of life are. What they think the purpose or purposes of life are. All of that is very dysfunctional, although – within the overall context, anything that happens is a flower, as we've said. But we prefer other flowers, and to see this one destroyed…Well, we'll ask you a rhetorical question. Would you rather see your civilization destroyed, or the earth? Not that that's the real choice. But you see what we're saying. There are times when something being destroyed is not only the lesser of two evils, but in fact is not an evil at all.

R: Okay, something I want to follow-up on has to do with what's happening on your side. Do you have events occurring that are similar to, say, our disaster today? Are there events that kind of seem to shake your universe on that side?

TGU: The immediate answer is, yes, when they occur in time-space. In other words, we're not unaffected by this. We're getting direct feed, so to speak. But there can't be the collision of forces when – not as an abstract thing but as a real thing – we know that it's all *one* thing. When we're all connected, and all aware of the connection, and we form our purpose not by tension between component parts but by a sort of a bubbling forth, a sort of an emergence, there is no mechanism for the equivalent of that on our side. Although Milton thought there was a war in heaven, there was a misunderstanding of the nature of things.

R: Okay, let's take the collision of forces out of it, and ask if there are events that seem to simultaneously affect everything in the There in a way that events can have that impact here.

Rubber Glove Analogy

TGU: Well, it still looks to us like a false distinction. The events on your side *do* affect us on our side. We don't need anything more direct than that, because it's as direct as can be. We've never talked about that, but supposing you were wearing rubber gloves, and you've got them into water up to the wrists. The fingers inside the rubber gloves wouldn't recognize each other as being part of the same thing, because they would be separated by the rubber. But, down the nerve pathways, they would still know they were the same thing. So, we extend into time-space by way of you, and it's a direct extension, so everything that affects you affects us. [sigh] You remember the time we visited emotions, briefly?

R: Yes.

TGU: Well, that was a visit; because we don't experience it that way usually. That was very unusual. It isn't like 3D Theater is off to the side somewhere. It's as central as anything else. So the major events that rock our world are the same ones that rock your world.

R: But in saying "it's as central as anything else," you're saying something else affects you besides what happens here.

TGU: Well – [pause] If you've got your hand in a glove and it's in the water, there's still the rest of you that's *not* in the water.

R: So what are the nature of the events on your side that don't involve it [i.e., the physical world]?

TGU: You might not *recognize* these other events, but we'll try.

All right, look at it this way. We ourselves – the ones that are talking to you – which last count was 29 ½ or maybe it was 31 ¼ . . .

R: [chuckles]

TGU: We ourselves are the product of many things, many experiences, many choices. Now over here there's another part that's the product of many choices and all of that – it may look to you like the blending of colors. That's probably the best analogy, for the moment anyway. Our interacting with them – now, understanding that there's not the separation that those words imply, but if one is a light blue and the other's a slightly different shade of blue, the intermingling could either change both or could cause either to maintain itself against the other -- in other words, increase this feeling of supporting the identity. And of course that happens in all directions. We know that's vague, but how else could we describe that?

R: Well, that's speaking still to the interaction, I guess.

TGU: That's all there is.

R: [Musingly] That's all there is.

TGU: Well. Well, it's not a one-time thing, it's a continuing thing. So every time something changes, everything around it potentially changes. You see? If something goes from blue to light green, then everything around it either changes, decides not to change, or experiences itself differently, or looks steadfastly in another direction. Because everything affects everything else. But there's not the delay that there is with you, where you have time and space slowing you down to do your part. We can't talk to you about politics and wars and commercial trade or anything; that's not what goes on. But –

Rita's Balloon Analogy

R: Mm-hmm. Well – you'll have to excuse the spatial references but that's all I've got – the way I'm getting it now is that you and we are all inside some great balloon, or wall. And there may be things going on outside of it, but they don't involve all of us in the balloon.

TGU: Well, we suspect that there *is* something going on outside, but we don't experience that first-hand, any more than your blood cells experience your skin. We think you're right, there's more going on beyond the part of it that we all share, but we're not the ones to know what that is. Again, we're not all-knowing or all-anything.

R: Do you have any thoughts about what might be out there at all?

TGU: Well, we know – we think we know – we feel pretty confident – that we're a unit. One unit, so called, implies others, and we wouldn't be surprised if all those so-called units are not part of a larger thing as well. But it's mostly supposition.

R: You don't know of your own experience.

TGU: Well, we don't. [pause] Supposing you look at us as the continent of Asia. We may live in – Bangkok but we don't necessarily know something that happened in Sinkiang. You know? We know that from your end it looks like we should, but that's not the way it is. There is locality *here* as there is locality where you are, except that there's not any illusion of distance and firm separation.

If you can envision alternate localities without spatial analogy, let us know. All right, another way of looking at it: Areas of affinity? Or different vibrations? There are all kinds of analogies that can be drawn. But what it means is, it's not one homogenous thing. It's a very *heterogeneous* thing, and that's the richness of it. That's encouraged, that's not discouraged. And one way to get even more heterogeneous is to run you through time-space, which means all those choices, which produces all those flowers – even if some of them are ragweed.

R: All right now. But that statement you just made was all encompassed by this bubble.

TGU: For all we know, this bubble is a corpuscle in somebody's veins.

R: Yes. Okay, I thought of that possibility. [chuckles] I find it not a very rewarding thought, but –

TGU: [laughs] Why not?

R: It doesn't sound very interesting.

Interest Is in the Moment

TGU: [chuckles] Well, we'll see. [chuckles] "Interesting" is in the moment. If you put your interest only in the future, or only in the past, you lose the only reality there is. The reality is in the present, right now. Now, if you spend "now" thinking about the past, that's okay as long as you're "now." And if you spend "now" thinking about the future, that's okay as long as you're "now." But it's when you forget it, you see, that you lose the reality and you become – almost ghosts of yourselves. Happens a lot.

R: Well, I feel like I've had an interesting life –

TGU: So far.

R: So far. And I feel like I've had a more interesting life than a lot of people, and I don't know exactly what interesting means in that context, but I would hate not to have had an interesting life. [laughs softly]

TGU: Then you're not liable to have that problem, are you?

R: Oh. Okay. Again, that's one of those choices.

TGU: Well, unless in the larger sense you decide "I need a boring stretch so I appreciate interest more." But we'll say it again, it's always well. There's really nothing to worry about. Even though worry itself is an interesting experience. [they laugh] If only by contrast. If you're worried about, "when I die am I going to be bored?" we would say you're wasting your time. [laughs]

R: Bob Monroe described such an experience of sitting on a cloud and being bored.

TGU: But, don't you *see*, the *only* way he knew he was bored was because he had grown to the point that it was boring. That by itself tells you, it's not static unless you don't want to move. Those who didn't want to move are *still* there listening to the same cloud and the same music. And that's fine for them too. There's nothing wrong with that.

Rules

R: Okay, let's go back to the process of moving from a life into a hereafter and then returning and so on? We always hear that we've lived thousands of lifetimes and we don't hear about those energies that have lived one or two or five. And I thought I heard what you said before, but I think I didn't understand it.

TGU: Well, we would add that just because people *think* they've had thousands of lives, doesn't mean that they have, necessarily! And because they would *like to* doesn't mean that they even think it, but that they sort of persuade themselves. All we're saying is, this is not the only playground.

All right, this is too arbitrary, but we'll do it just to keep it simple. If we say that our life overall is a seed that grows and dies at a certain point (we're talking from *our* point of view) and that the process of the growth of that stalk is a series of lives, those lives don't all need to be on earth, they don't all need to be even in 3D Theater, and they certainly don't need to have x number of them, or x number of years between them, or x number of different kinds of experiences. All those rules are just rules. They don't have anything to do with real life.

R: Okay, but then on your side, the repetitions. Do those accumulate in ways that are different for some than others?

TGU: Mm-hmm. Because – this is a very strictly limited analogy, don't take this too literally –we're all specialized tools. So what we are helps determine what we choose and what we do, which helps determine what we become, which helps to determine what we choose. So a person who is a monkey wrench is going to have a very different life from someone who is a hammer, or a screwdriver. An inelegant analogy, but you get the idea. And, there could be somebody who's tired of being a screwdriver and in the middle becomes a hammer. Or decides to alternate, or to become part pliers and part hammer, you know; something like that, to create something new. There are millions of paths. Every path is valid, because it's all interesting. Anything that anything wants to become, is fine. It adds to the picture.

R: Okay, then that's true where you are, as well as where we are.

TGU: We would say it almost couldn't be true where you are if it *weren't* true where we are. We *would* say it. You are us. It's just that you're over there right now. Again, of course, most of you *isn't* over there right now! [they laugh] You're still over here! But the part of you that we're talking to experiences yourself as over there.

R: This has been an extremely interesting session.

TGU: Well, we'll tell you again, you're doing good work and we on our end appreciate you on your end's doing your work. You're coming to a very interesting time. Don't worry about it, or fear it, just – *be* it. Just do the things that are closest to hand, be yourself and don't lose yourself, and know that by so doing you're doing what can be done. We approve.

Session Six
September 18, 2001

R: I'd like to pick up on one of the topics from last time. We were talking about all the disaster issues last week, and one thing we're hearing lots about is the idea of evil. I wonder if you can talk some about the idea of evil as regards human behavior.

TGU: Big subject.

R: Well, yes.

Polarity

TGU: As usual, we have to start a long way away. Suppose you look at the whole universe as a balanced system. In electrical terms, it has positive and negative, all right? Now, for the moment we're not talking about good being positive and evil being negative, but as positive and negative. As polarity. And every polarity has to balance out. Otherwise, there'd be something left over, you know [laughs] and it couldn't be.

Taking the universe as a unit, its various polarities all have a positive and negative end to them. And in various local parts of the universe – this is a spatial analogy, but we don't know how to avoid it – there might be more negative or more positive. And certainly the negative and positive could be intermingled, they could fluctuate, they could go back and forth – like everything else, they form fluctuating patterns.

There's no such thing as being able to eliminate all the negative, and have even one atom of positive more than negative. It just can't be done, you see.

Now, you could concentrate all of the positive as a *super* positive, and have all the negative as a sort of spread out negative, so that the negative would have more area and the positive would have more intensity, or vice versa. You see what we're saying, you can change the local formulations, you can change the ratio from a local point of view, but overall it's an equal mix because it has to be.

Now, we'll come down to 3D Theater. In 3D Theater, you have time separating it all into slices, as we've said, and because of that the fluctuation is much less obvious to you; the overall balance is not at all obvious to you, and the symmetry of it is something you can conceptually pick up but have a hard time really internalizing, at least, as far as we can observe.

So, when you think of the state of the world in the year 1950, it doesn't occur to you to balance into that the state of the world in the year 1450. You see? Vastly different times, totally unconnected things. Just as geographically, if you're looking at a soil sample in Virginia, you're not taking into account the soil of Mongolia, and yet from a properly large enough perspective, they *are* interrelated.

So, you have what you might call evil times and good times. Now, there are so many aspects of this to deal with, but we'll start with this one, and let us know when we get you lost.

Let's for this moment take "good times and bad times" as though they were, abstractly, good times and bad times, rather than people's preferences, or people's illusions. You might have a century in which there was an overwhelming preponderance of positives, or one in which there was an overwhelming preponderance of negative, or one followed by the other; any conceivable choice. That's all intrinsic to the play of it, but again, it's not ever true that the balance could be disturbed.

Neither is it true that you're moving toward a future in which there will be a disturbance in the balance, in other words where the future all will be good or all will be evil. Except that – and you knew this was coming, didn't you? – when you consider all of the time-slices as one big orange rather than a series of slices, it could very well look as though there was a tendency or trend in one direction. But to think that you're going to go to a future that's going to be all positives and no negatives – the only way you can do that is to have all negatives in the past and no positives, somewhere. Now, and we're weaseling there a little bit, because it does occur to us that given that things are a matter of choice, you *could* skew the balance.

All right, now let's back up again and start all over again for the third time. Aren't you glad you asked?

R: I am.

Moral Relativity

TGU: There is another more difficult question, and that is good versus evil as a matter of preference. This subject raises emotions, because it raises fears and uncertainties. More than that, at a very deep level, it seems to some of you to be evil, and we're sorry about that. We understand the mechanism, but it's more important that you know what's right, what's real, than what you prefer. Again, Rita, we're saying this as a record for others. We know where you are.

When one looks at reality, one makes judgments from one's viewpoint. A slave-holder in Charleston, South Carolina, in 1820 has goods and bads that are *radically* different from yours. But someone looking from the year 2130 in Denver, Colorado, has goods and bads that are vastly different from yours. There was a discussion started years ago about moral relativity, and some took that to mean an abandonment of standards. They took it to mean that there *is* right and wrong, but people prefer to do what they want, rather than what is right. And we would say this is because they're not seeing that they themselves, always, inevitably, unavoidably, live by standards that are equally relative. And here's why.

Which of you would be content to be judged by the standards of Victorian England? Or of Elizabethan England? Or of the Roman Empire? Or of Saddam Hussein's Iraq, or Stalin's Russia, or any oligarchy anywhere in South America? Common sense says that all of those moral standards that the people lived by – and we are disregarding hypocrisy here; we're talking about those who had a moral standard and lived by it – common sense should tell you that they can't all be right, because they're all conflicting. But we would go beyond common sense and say, they were right in a sense.

Everyone's standards may be regarded as a rule-of-thumb balancing of positives and negatives. Today you condemn slavery. Perhaps in a hundred years people will condemn the wage-earning system. But the slave owners saw no acceptable substitute, and nor do you. Now how can you or anyone tell that what you're doing is better or worse than the alternatives without trying them? But if you try them, then how do you know that that's better or worse? You see? It's endless. There's nothing wrong with that, we're just telling you the fix that you're in.

If there were one standard of right and wrong applicable to every truly moral person, in the first place the game would come to an end, not by bringing it to its proper alignment, but by arbitrarily freezing it somewhere.

Searching for an analogy, here. All we can think of is, supposing you have a swirl of black and white marbles. You can stir them or you can blend them or you could do whatever you want with them. What is *the* right pattern for that bowl of marbles? There *isn't* any *the* right pattern! There's a pattern that's more acceptable to *you*.

In *any* moral issue, there are always compromises that have to be made; there are always shadow sides to positives, and it becomes a preference – it cannot be anything *other than* a preference – as to which drawbacks to accept in order to receive which gains.

An honest politician, should you chance to find one, might be too inflexible to prevent evils that he could prevent with some flexibility. A dishonest politician might be more flexible and might prevent a war, or some evil. A corrupt cop may be the way in which society, behind its own back, stitches together the underworld and the upper world.

We're not advocating or dis-advocating any of this, we're just saying, there are always costs to virtues, or to desired outcomes. Sometimes they're acknowledged, but usually not acknowledged. When your society eliminated red light districts, prostitution then did not disappear, it changed forms. There was no other way that it could be. When you reached certain limits of toleration and moved against something, it mutated. It didn't disappear. Or where did you get your child sex industries in the cities? [pause] Aren't you glad you asked that question?

R: [laughs] I am, but I am feeling overwhelmed with all that quite wonderful material. I'll be glad to read that when Frank can type it up.

TGU: You can hear him grinding his teeth. [they laugh]

Values and Conflict

R: I have been quite surprised to hear the extent of attribution of evil to the forces that attacked the United States last week. I believe that all human behavior could be explained if we understood the background and the dynamics of a person in a situation without attributing dimensions like evil, or even goodness. And it sounds from what I've heard that you're accepting the idea of the continual existence, in some proportion or other, of at least positive and negative forces. And at one end of that continuum of negative forces – we might call that evil. What is my question? [they laugh]

TGU: It sounds like you'd like a little more on good and evil.

R: Well, the underlying question is, can human behavior be described in terms that don't involve the concept of evil?

TGU: Easily. That's how we do it. But it requires – You want to know how?

R: Yes.

TGU: Okay. This might actually be a shorter answer. We did say "might." [pause]

You all look out onto the world from the cave of your mind, through the windows of your senses, and you interpret what you see or hear from where you are: There's no other way you could do that. Where you are is what you were raised to be, plus what you came in to be, plus what you've done with it since. You've created a set of values that come out of your point of view; they're the same thing. If your value says, "thou shalt not kill," and it's an absolute, you become a conscientious objector and you may or may not call warriors evil, but you are saying that they are *doing* evil. If your emphasis is more toward protecting people, protecting society in general, more toward the willingness to sacrifice yourself because you're bonded with your own people, then to *not* fight may be evil to you. And it's a very thin line between saying that a thing is evil and that the person who does the thing is evil.

But it is not an unwillingness to make judgments that brings people to say "there is no evil as such"; it is a statement of fact that everyone is doing his best, pathetic though it may seem. People don't do things for no reason. When they act in ways that are individually scary, they are labeled as mentally ill or as criminal or as – at the most charitable – inexplicably eccentric. The labeling serves the psychological function of putting a distance between you and them. When a society is at war, its enemies are its enemies; but they're not thereby evil. Except, how do you kill them? It's easier to kill them if you regard them as evil. When American boys who were raised not to kill people were shooting and killing German soldiers who were defending Nazism, they did so believing that those soldiers were evil.

[pause] Well, but were they?

The cause was evil. The cause was better destroyed than preserved. But if an army or a society couldn't move against the enemy until it itself was pure, it couldn't move.

The systematic, persistent, and resolute ignoring of one's own shadow side is the chief cause of labeling something or someone else evil. Young children are the most prone to do this at the least cause, because they have no sense of their own shadow, and they must believe, for their own psychological well-being, that they are good. The child who becomes convinced that he is bad has been broken in a very critical place.

However, most in your society, most of the time, in most of its ages, are still children in this respect. They want so badly to be good that they are almost literally unable to bear to see their own shadow side. The accumulated pressure forces them to find scapegoats that to them seem most obviously evidently evil.

If an American, in defense of his own country, were to fly an airplane into a building in Afghanistan next week, he would not be seen as a coward or evil. He would be seen as a hero, because his motivations would be understood, his patriotism would be identified with. But hatred and the attribution of evil to the enemy are rooted very firmly in intolerant self-righteousness stemming from weakness; stemming from the inability to recognize one's own imperfection. If the line between good and evil could be drawn *between* people, then all the good people could stand on one side of the line. And that's what people very naively think *can* happen and maybe some of them even think *does* happen.

But the line between good and evil runs *within* you, because good and evil are the same polarity. We're using the words for lack of an ability to do otherwise, but they're not really separate things.

R: Using this kind of language, it seems to me, takes us back to our religious concepts and particularly the fundamentalist religions that so clearly define good and evil, as opposed to many religions that seem to be a little more moderate in those definitions. And in the kind of conflict that's going on now, it seems that we do have a culture of those who can easily find good and evil, versus those who up until this week I thought had definitions that were much more approximate and mixed, made up of the kind of definition of partial dimensions that you've been talking about.

TGU: Yes, we understand. You know, of course, that under stress people revert. And when they revert, they never revert to a *higher* level of functioning; always to a *lower*, to a simpler level. If you wish to draw lines in the sand, rather than drawing them between good and evil you might more productively draw them between those who look for an external source of rules and those who look within to what *feels like* the right thing to do.

Those who personify evil in others think that they're on one side of a line. By having seemingly objective standards – the Ten Commandments, the laws of the country, whatever it may be – they say that to be good, one need only follow these rules. And when they get in a situation in which two rules are in conflict then they either ignore one or the other – or both – or they get under psychological stress of a quite unexpected sort, which can turn them quite murderous.

The others, who are more inner directed as you say, function that way until *their* stress level gets greater, and they are tempted to revert to their own religious training. That religious training doesn't come from the churches, in your society, so much as it comes through the air they breathe. Your society, we should point out, means more the West than only America, but anyway – it's one of the givens.

R: Within an ethical framework, you're saying.

TGU: It may be dressed up in other ways, but it's basically the religious idea of the Ten Commandments. The entire idea that there is a code that one can follow which will lead one infallibly to be right, assuming one can follow that code infallibly – that whole way of looking at things is embedded in your society, because your society was founded as a Christian society. The ostensibly religious trappings have been stripped from it, but that only really leaves it all the more jagged when people come to it in moments of stress.

R: It seems like most of the people that I am in contact with do not have this strong dividing line between right and wrong, or good and evil. You're saying that that's a tentative stance, that a crisis of sufficient dimensions could change that.

TGU: Well, we won't disagree with what you just said, but let's rephrase it. We would say that your friends tend to have a pretty good integration of their shadow side, and that integration could potentially be warped under stress. It's really saying the same thing, but it's a little different.

R: Makes it a little more acceptable. [they laugh]

TGU: Well, you saw through that!

R: Still makes us the good guys.

TGU: Well, but you see, you're *all* good guys. There aren't any bad guys in the sense that people mean. There are plenty of malicious people, but their malice comes from what they think are good causes. That's the thing. You can have someone like Hitler who's corroded with hatred, who seemingly warps his whole time, and spreads misery in all directions. He did those things thinking that he was good, that he was doing good. He served the values that he chose.

Now, in order to drive the point home – and alienate anyone else who's listening – we would point out to you that there was hardly a thing that Hitler did that the Americans hadn't done in connection to slaves or Indians. Rather than using that to feel guilty about the slaves and the Indians, it would be more productive to use it to get a genuine insight into how people's values can lead them to do things that later their descendants or contemporaries will look at aghast, and say "how could you possibly have done that?"

How TGU Experience Emotion

R: Okay, so many things came up in connection with what you were talking about, but I'd like to postpone going on with that until we can read the transcript.

TGU: That's okay with us.

R: This is another question that came up around the disaster questions last week. You had said that our 3D Disasters had some impact on you. I wondered if you could talk some more about that. Here we are experiencing fear, other emotions, questions about how to behave, how to feel and so on. What happens for you?

TGU: It's almost too simple to be able to get across to you. What happens to you is what happens to us, with the caveat that it's what happens to *all of you,* including trees, rocks, oceans, and air, all of which are sentient, as you suspect. What you feel *is* what we feel, but you only feel it one tentacle at a time, and we feel the whole octopus.

R: But without the emotional impact. Or is it the totality of the emotional impact also?

TGU: [sigh] Well, that requires – have you guessed? – another lecture.

What you experience as emotions are gradients. This is difficult, because Frank doesn't have this language, really. Let's move back up a little bit.

You know what a gradient does; a gradient takes something from one state to another. The slope of a hill could be considered to be a gradient between a high place and a low place. It connects them and at the same time its own nature describes *how* they connect. If you have a total discontinuity – a mesa, say, out west – that rises straight out of the surroundings, the gradient is radically different from the gradient in a gentle prairie that might still gain a thousand feet, but take a thousand miles do it.

Well, your emotions are gradients between what happens and what you would prefer to happen. This is very crude and it's not *exactly* right, but it's an entry into the subject.

We don't have emotions in the way that you do because we don't have the preferred option in the same way you do. We are trying to steer things in certain directions, and hoping that you all make certain choices, but we ourselves don't identify with any one of you in the way that any one of you *has to* identify with yourself. You as an individual may become aware of your other lives and your other dimensions and expand the size of the part that you identify with, but while you're in the body you're only identifying with one part of the whole.

[interruption]

Perhaps the purpose of the interruption was to allow us to regroup. You will remember that we say that your purpose on earth in physical matter reality is to choose and choose and choose and to create yourselves, and that the creation of yourself is the gift. Well, it isn't *only* after you come back as part of us. It's a gift while you're doing it. Now this is an analogy, this is not literal, but just as *we* taste cherry pie when *you* eat cherry pie, so *we* can experience the emotion of hatred and fear when *you* experience the emotion of hatred and fear. With the major exception – which invalidates the analogy – that we don't experience things in one slice of time after another, and we don't experience things in one slice of individuality, so-called, after another.

So the way we experience it is so different from the way you experience it, that until people make more of an effort to understand the difference in terrain, they'll never understand that both sides are doing the same thing at the same time. If *you* have a life largely lived in fear, you will still experience that life moment by moment by moment. If *we* are experiencing that life largely lived in fear, we'll experience the fear more as a color or a tint or a flavor or a shade, tingeing the whole thing, rather than one specific moment at a time. Now, that doesn't mean we don't *see* a moment. We're here, with you, in this moment. But it means that what's fluid for us seems solid to you; what's fluid for you seems solid to us. As an example, your whole life looks to us as one unit, and we have to sort of focus carefully to get you at any moment in time.

Okay, now we'll go back and start again. Keeping all that in mind if you can – it'll be easier when you read it – your emotions are a gradient between what is and what you want. Now, you could also say, it's a gradient between what happens to you and what your previous experience has led you to *think* would happen to you. We're not going to get very far here without examples, so let's go with an example. Give us an example that occurs to you of a strong emotion.

R: Well, there are people right now getting onto airplanes in a state of terror. They have to go someplace and yet they're very fearful about that.

TGU: Now let's explore. What is it we want to look at about the emotion?

R: Well, my original question was, what are you experiencing on your side, when we're seeing a disaster in terms of these strong emotions?

TGU: Well, the person boards the airplane in a state of advanced fear. The person next to them boards the airplane *without* fear, because they live in a different reality. They have a different belief system. *You* experience the moment as the overriding thing, because you live moment by moment, or rather, you live in the continuing now. But *we* experience the overall *flavor* of it – the lengthwise flavor of it. So what *we* see is that person being brought to an opportunity-point of dealing with an ingrained pattern of fear that maybe until then has been unsuspected or has been dealt with casually. So that where you look at it as "how they feel right now," we look at it as, "what opportunities does this give them to choose?" That's really the way we look at it. Thus, we can be made to look very cold-blooded, to you. We assure you that we're not.

R: It doesn't sound that way when you explain it.

TGU: [lightly] We have good lawyers.

Prayer As a Phenomenon

R: I've been interested in the current research on prayer and its impact on groups of individuals who have some sort of illness. How do you make sense out of this kind of phenomenon.

TGU: Well, oddly enough it would be *almost* accurate to say they're praying to us, because they're praying – although they don't know it – to themselves! And we *are* themselves. Remember, we've said that the key to healing is to remove the illusion of distance, and that the way to remove the illusion of distance is to love. It's the same thing, really, but it looks different.

So these people are gathering in a sincere, loving way, without intent to get something for themselves – in other words, it's an altruistic way. (Speaking of good and evil, this is a good example of positives.) They don't *intend* to create a group mind; they don't *intend* to destroy the illusion of distance; and they don't *intend* to provide a supportive electrical field, or magnetic field, against which the person can lean and regain the vibrational level they need, but that's another way of describing what happens. There doesn't need to be anyone they're praying *to*, and there doesn't need to be anyone to say, "well, yes, I think I'll grant your prayer," or "no, no, you're not really worthy." That's not what's going on. When people pray, when they love, when they love without thought for themselves to erase the distance, with the intent of helping another, in fact it is *literally* true, that's when miracles can come. It's not the *only* place, but it's certainly *a* place.

R: Well, I like that. That really pulls that material together.

A Symbol of Togetherness

R: There are lots of people who have been recommending that we all go outside and bring candles at 10:30 tonight, that with all these candles, it will be observed from our satellites, and parts of the earth will be all lit up. I don't know if it's possible to see candles from space, but –

TGU: It's possible to see light. You won't see the individual candles, you'll see the light. In places where there's enough light. So the question is?

R: Well, I don't tend to question that sort of thing. It feels like to me it's the same sort of thing, decreasing distance between you and others who are in need as the result of disasters.

TGU: To make everyone feel less alone.

R: Yes. That one seems easy to accept. Easier than the prayer one, for me.

TGU: And the underlying question tying the two together seems to us to be a matter of what would be appropriate for you, given your belief systems?

R: Yes, and that's a continuation of what we were talking about last week. What do we do in the face of the disasters? What's the best way for us to think of ourselves?

TGU: It would be a lovely image if all the people on the earth could hold the candle outside with the same intent, not one against another but saying "we're all on earth" in the way that you did at the New Year [2000] when you were afraid that you would lose everything. And you watched the New Year come, from the Pacific all the way around the world, and it was the first time ever, in *our* opinion, that it really got to all of you on a visceral level that in fact you are one planet.

So we wish the lighting of the candle could say not, "I'm an American, don't push me around," not even, "I am good and I stand against evil." We wish it could say, "I am part of the whole [pause] and all parts of the whole are equally – um – well, my brothers."

The Current Crisis

R: You said a bit ago that you had preferences for the choices we would make. Are you speaking of preferences like you would prefer the earth to continue rather than be destroyed? Those kinds of preferences?

TGU: No, a little more manipulative than that. We are talking about near-term problems and solutions and things that are being set up. For instance, this current crisis is not about America. This current crisis is about the future of the earth civilization that isn't yet quite created. It *looks like* it's America versus some terrorists, or possibly the West versus the Muslims. Or possibly good versus evil. But really it is our attempt to correct certain manifestations that we think will make the earth unsustainable – which is not in *anyone's* interest.

And therefore we manipulate situations to attempt to precipitate situations in which people will choose in certain ways that will change them. We are *continually* doing that, and remember, now, "we" are also "you" – and when you go into your life, you say, "okay, here's the things that I can accomplish." Well, those are not only on a personal level. Dwight Eisenhower went into his life, you know, with the probability that at some point he would be used in a certain way.

So, we have very strong preferences. Our strong preferences are: that the earth continue; that the human plant, if you want to call it that, continue; that you move toward greater unity of being, greater unity of action, so that you increase your own awareness of all parts of yourselves and then become more aware that you're all one thing. It's important to us that ultimately we get to that point. We will get there, one way or another, but there are preferable ways and less preferable ways. It's important that we get to the point in which we are all reconciled in the sense of recognizing that we are one. In other words, you're taking off the rubber glove, so to speak.

There will be a day in which humans live on the earth in full awareness of all of their own extensions *and* in full awareness that they're all part of each other, literally. Not in your lifetimes, or anywhere near, but that's what we're moving toward, and we continually create new scenarios to try to adjust the course as we go along. But because the very number one essential is freedom of choice, we can't just set it out and know that it'll go that way, so we're continually having to make new adjustments.

We know people very well. We could say, "if we do this, this will probably happen." And so your hijackers and your airplane pilots and passengers were all part of that scenario. They were all playing a part. Not knowingly.

TGU's Awareness and Manipulation

R: I've heard two things from you here. The second one I'm hearing tonight, the first one I heard before. What I heard before was that you are aware of what will be happening to us. That you have a preview, somehow. You know before we know what's happening. And now I'm hearing you say that you actually arrange this.

TGU: Both of those are true, but neither one of them is the full thing. Let's back up a little.

You remember that all possible – not just outcomes, but procedures; you know, situations – have their reality. [The concept of multiple simultaneous realities.] That should be just mind-boggling, because it's just staggering complexity. It all has its reality, and the question is, which of those will you go to? And so, looked at one way, yes we know the future because they're all there, we can see where you're going now. But tomorrow you might go in a different direction. In other words, we can predict the future, but you may not go there! [they laugh] But that future still exists!

R: So you're trying to move things, but they don't necessarily go your way. At least in the short run.

TGU: Well, it's not that simple either.

R: Of course time doesn't exist, so that doesn't apply either.

TGU: Well, more than that, both halves of every choice exist. So how can anyone say it *did* go our way, or it *didn't* go our way? [laughs] It did both! It always does both! Only – not a both, it's an infinite, you know? It becomes almost impossible to explain it.

R: Well, you're saying that you have preferences for how it goes –

TGU: Yes. We're trying to steer it.

Time, There

R: It's hard for me to think about that without thinking about a time dimension. Because it seems like when you move things, that's obviously a time dimension.

TGU: [slowly, with emphasis] *This is an absolutely major misunderstanding* [that others have]. Absolutely. We live outside of time, but that doesn't mean we live outside what we should call duration. All right?

R: Okay, now you said something like that before, and I didn't understand it. Would you try again?

TGU: Let's closely define the word "time" to mean time in the way that you experience it [in three dimensions], where you have no choice, you're dragged along, piece by piece by piece. You experience time in slices. Another way of looking at it is, it's the eternal now, but you have no way of changing that. You can't make Tuesday come after Saturday until you go all the way around again. You know what we're saying. You are on earth in the thrall of the time machine, and time is going to go forward one moment at a time, click, click, click, click, click, click – and you're not going to be able to skip around in it.

Now, *that* kind of time, we are not at all enmeshed in. As you very acutely pointed out, there's a difference between that kind of time, and duration. There *is* duration, otherwise there couldn't be change. Absolutely. But how do we define it? How do we talk about it? Everything that we will say about this will all have to fight against all of your prejudices, totally unconscious, based on the fact that your entire life is lived with one experience of time.

Now, if you can stretch your mind to envision a kind of time in which you can go backwards and forwards at will, in the way that you on earth can go north, south, east, west, or southeast or southwest at will, you might get a sense of it. The duration is still there, but we're not *stuck* in it, like flies in amber. All right?

Now, [pause] we'll use as analogy the situation you're used to on earth and we'll just throw in one variable. Let's say you live fifty years, from 1950 to 2000. In those 50 years, you are present in every single moment. You couldn't *not* be. You couldn't exist from 1950 to 1973 and then not exist until 1978 when you come back into existence again until 2000.

The only principle that we want to establish here is that as you are in time, we are in duration: *in every moment of it.* We can't *not* be in *any* moment of it.

But – whereas you can't move from Tuesday to Saturday other than by waiting, and you can't go back at all, except in your mind, we can. If you were to look at us as a string, from the first moment of duration to the last, we could move anywhere along that string, because it's not movement, but a movement of consciousness. We *are* wherever we concentrate on *being*.

R: I see. I think.

TGU: Well, you'll see until you think about it some more, and then the logical paradoxes will overwhelm you. Because you'll say, "how can that *be?* How can there be any meaningful action when in a sense it all has to be done ahead of time?" And we'll say to you, that there is no movement here either, it just looks like it. You are in the middle of a crystal that contains all possible choices, paths, and outcomes, and where you move your own intent, your consciousness, is what makes it look like the situation it is. Given all that, the only difference between you and us is you're stuck in slices of time and slices of individuality, whereas we can see the whole thing at once.

If you can make sense of that, hearing it once, we're surprised.

R: [laughs] I feel like I've gotten in very deep water tonight. You're saying that you can see everything at once. From our perspective that would mean over time and over space. I don't know, is space a dimension in it for you at all, or is there just a form of time that you deal with?

TGU: A better analogy would be the difference between you as a grown up and any given child that you were dealing with. It isn't that you live in any different environment than that child, but your mental outlook is so much greater, and your ability to draw connections is so much greater, that you're really not living in the same world as that child. That's why you have such an advantage over it in terms of understanding, even if the child has an advantage over you in terms of perception. So you, here, in time-space, may have the advantage of us in perception, because you're right on the moment. But *we* have the advantage in perspective because we *see* wider and broader.

R: You simply understand more. Is that –

TGU: Well, [pause] we would think so, but the question does give us pause, because everyone thinks so. [they laugh] [pause] Get back to us on that another time. It's an interesting question. It's a longer question than you have time for tonight.

Is It All an Illusion?

R: [pause] I want to ask about illusion, but that might take a bigger chunk of time than we have tonight, also.

TGU: Well, begin, and we'll see.

R: Begin? All right. Many people think that all is illusion, on this plane and perhaps elsewhere. And usually they mean by that, physical objects are illusions; we as human beings are illusions. It's never quite clear to me what advantage there is to thinking that way, except in the sense of immutability. The notion behind it is seemingly that the only reason we perceive physicality at all is because we have learned to perceive physicality, and it doesn't just exist in its own right, and that we would somehow all be better off if we were aware that this is so.

TGU: [pause] Well the short answer to that will be to tell them that their belief is an illusion. [they laugh] A somewhat longer answer would be, they're shifting a definition in the middle. Because something is not what it *seems* to be is not the same thing as saying it doesn't exist. We see you all as – remember we used the definition of octopus and tentacle, or a long worm –

R: [laughs]

TGU: – and those are not accurate definitions of you either, but they're as accurate as your own. The fact that our definition is not accurate and yours is not accurate doesn't mean you're not there! It's true that what appears to be matter is actually energy bound in forms, but that doesn't tell you anything, that's just changing words. What's energy?

R: Well, that's a good question; I'm going to ask you that. [they laugh]

TGU: Well we're not going to go into that at the moment, but the point of it is that it's important and valuable for you to see that things are deeper, broader, wider, different, more mysterious than they appear, but to our mind it serves no purpose to therefore define them out of existence, even while – continuing to eat!

R: [laughs]

TGU: They are professing in one world and living in another.

Appearance and Reality

R: Okay now this is associated but different. One of the big events in my life was being told by the physicists that things that we perceive as solid are in fact in great movement within the molecules. It was a very powerful bit of information for me, because it meant that our perceptions are so incomplete.

TGU: Inadequate, yes.

R: Inadequate, yes. [pause] How'd we get in this fix? [they laugh]

TGU: Who's we? [they laugh]What's a fix? [they laugh]

R: The human race has come along for a long time, and not known that solids were not solids.

TGU: [quietly] We deny that.

R: Oh, do you? Okay, I'd like to hear about that.

TGU: *Western civilization* has come along, for what seems to *it* a long time, and denies what all the rest of the society knew, but knew in a fashion that was not recognizable to Western science. Your natives, so called, the people who live close to the earth, have an invisible technology of mental communication, as is well known now even to your scientists. Those people did not live in the same world that your scientists are living in, and there was little or no communication between them. But when someone can communicate with the heart of a tree, or the DNA of a bird, so to speak – these are metaphors but not *only* metaphors – they learn things that they may have no way of saying, but that they live. Your scientists in the West have no way of living it, but they learn it. Those are two very different ways of being in the world, and the world has use for both of them. They came into being for a reason and they will endure for a while for a reason. But we deny absolutely that for most of your existence people have had this illusion that what appears to be solid, is solid.

Having said that, we'll back off from about half of it and say that what appears to be solid *is* solid – sort of. You go to the refrigerator and eat. You're as solid as the refrigerator and the food, and as nonexistent as the refrigerator and the food. It's all in which end of the continuum you choose to concentrate on. The continuum exists regardless of the fact that you're ignoring the other end of it.

R: Well, you know, one way of thinking about this is to think about something that we haven't yet experienced, or have so minimally experienced. Take the Big Bang. We have an assumption that there are physical objects out there in the universe that came as a result of the Big Bang or something else that we don't understand, but that created these physical bodies that are functioning, and that when we get the transportation that can take us there, we'll find out that there they are. And they will be real, and they aren't illusions and this is an example of something that's distant enough that we can't verify it in the way that we can verify that the table seems solid.

TGU: But [laughs] listen to your statement. Listen to your statement! You said, "we can verify that the table *seems* solid." [they laugh]

R: Okay, right.

TGU: That's *exactly* what you can verify! [they laugh] That's *exactly* what you can verify, and nothing more. There's no need to go to Jupiter to see if Jupiter's as real as your refrigerator. [laughs] It's equally real and unreal. If you look at it from one point of view it's real; if you look at it from another equally valid point of view, it's not even there. If you look at it from our point of view, everything is one. If you look at it from your point of view, everything is separate. They're both sort of true.

And as to the Big Bang, we don't believe in that either.

R: You don't, huh?

TGU: You have your mythology of Bob Monroe's emitter. [Monroe's explana-tion of creation.] Now if you will think about the emitter mythology in terms of the Big Bang, we think you might find that productive. We know full well there was no Big Bang out of nothing. Now there might have been a Big Bang out of *something*, and you might want to think about that, but if you're looking for the ultimate creation of everything, we suspect that you don't have a telescope big enough. [laughs] Or a microscope strong enough, you understand. As Frank often says, you're in the position of a fish at the bottom of the ocean trying to imagine a man on a mountain watching television. There's too many levels between where you are and where the ultimate is, for you – or for us, for that matter – to really be able to see. There's too much. Look at the difficulties in translation between our side and your side. There are some things that it's interesting to speculate upon, but not too profitable. [pause] Ask us next if there is God.

R: I'm not going to ask you that tonight, you'll probably just have a long lecture prepared on that. [laughs]

TGU: No, we're *known* for our brevity. [they laugh]

R: I want to stay with this Big Bang thing for a minute here. [pause] Did you ar-range that?

TGU: Which is the same question as asking you, so we'll ask you: Did *you* ar-range it?

R: Well you seem to have a broader perspective for giving these responses than I do.

TGU: Well, but we're all one thing. Did we arrange it? Use your logic for a mo-ment.

R: Well I – you're saying as a totality, including us and you and whatever –

TGU: If we're living in it in a matrix, how could we have arranged it? If we're the fish in the fishbowl.

R: But that calls for a lot of assumptions on my part, which I don't think I can make.

TGU: Ours too. [they laugh] Okay, let's go through it slowly. We would look at us – us meaning you and us – as fish in a fishbowl, and we strongly doubt that the fish created the water and the fishbowl. That doesn't tell us a thing about who *did* create the fishbowl – but it gives us a pretty strong inference as to who probably didn't. On the other hand it may be a terrible analogy and this may be something *we* don't know anything about. We did remind you that we don't know everything. Well, we could probably find out, but we might actually be told no.

R: You couldn't find out? Is that what you mean by no?

TGU: I mean, we might be told, no you're not going to get this information at this point.

R: Oh. Okay.

TGU: We're not an undivided thing, we're a – oh, a federation of parts of something.

R: But this is still all us in a bubble.

TGU: Maybe. Maybe we extend beyond the bubble.

R: Well that's what I really would like to know.

TGU: Us too.

R: Well I tried to get at that, one time, with asking you if you had a source of guidance, and I don't know if that would mean leaving the bubble but – I don't know. Do you and does it?

TGU: We can only say we don't know, and we'll tell you why. The only reason that *you* become aware of a source of guidance is because you're divided into time-slices and individual slices. If you were not, what you knew would be what you knew. Now if some of that were being planted, how would you ever know? Think of us as how one giant physical brain would look: One huge, complicated set of individual cells. This may not be the best analogy, but we'll go with it. Suppose that, for the moment. If we had guidance external to ourselves, how would we know it? And we're not even sure that "external to ourselves" is a phrase that makes sense. Well, it does make sense, but we don't know what sense to make of it. If you think this is unsatisfactory to you, try it on this side.

R: Well, you're implying there that the only reason we know that we have guidance is because we are –

TGU: You're sharper than we are.

R: We're all inside this bubble together.

Suspicious Footprints

TGU: You're sharper than we are. And we mean that without sarcasm. You are pointed. You are on one moment of space-time. And that's why when you ask a question of us, *we* have the knowledge, but *you* can elicit the knowledge. Because on our side, it's a little more – fuzzy, or – well it's just not focused.

Supposing you were to look at us as the equivalent of your unconscious, or as your subconscious. We might have vast knowledge and less awareness, and therefore when you bring your awareness into it, the vast knowledge is enabled to crystallize around the question. If we can be regarded in that way – and I think we can – then we would almost by definition be less likely to observe subtle injections of thought or

Well, isn't that interesting? The word that came to mind was emotions. Which suggests that we have emotions and that we're not – [chuckles] The answer to your question is yes, we're beginning to see their footprints, and wouldn't at all be surprised if part of this is not designed to bring us to greater awareness of this. Well, well. You remember the incident with us experiencing emotions?

R: I do.

TGU: And now the next little step. Suspicious footprints. You are increasing our own – either our paranoia [laughs] or our self-analytical abilities.

R: Well you put it in terms of increased focus. That would help you look for footprints, I guess.

TGU: Well – *you*'re helping us to look for footprints, because the focus comes in relation to you. This is puzzling and interesting.

R: Is this a good time for us to stop tonight?

TGU: If you mean in terms of Frank, he's fine. If you mean in terms of us, we're fine. It's up to you. If you mean in terms of the matter of how deep the water is we're about to get into –

R: [laughs] Well, I guess I'm thinking of that, because I feel there was so much material here tonight that I had some difficulty keeping up with not just remembering it but getting it in the first place.

TGU: Well, look at it and see. We can stop and – we'll be back.

R: We can always come back another time, if you're willing.

TGU: Don't underestimate the value of your function to us as well as to yourselves. This is *very* interesting. [pause] But if you've had enough for the night, we'll bid you good night and see you the next time.

R: Thank you so much. I feel so grateful for this contact.

Frank: Well, I rather think they do too.

Session Seven
September 25, 2001

R: I was looking back today at some of the notes and thinking we have a few leftovers I should pick up on tonight. [pause] I have understood from you Gentlemen Upstairs that you have a great deal of information – maybe almost all of the information – and that our job is to suggest a focus for identifying the information by asking questions.

TGU: You will have to pardon us if we always answer literally what you say, because we're so aware of slippage in communications. We would say we have access to knowledge and probably have access to further knowledge when you want it. We're trying to emphasize, we don't ourselves know, but we can find out. That's the way to put it. It's one of our usual nit-picks.

How TGU Access Knowledge

R: Okay, well, one question that arises for me is, how does all this information become available to you?

TGU: [pause] To us the process is more or less what it is to you when you're thinking about something without needing external resources like books or conversation. It's as though we're ruminating, only we're kind of gravitating toward the information. Don't know a better way to put that.

R: So it isn't as though the information has to be collected.

TGU: Well that's how the information *is* collected. It's the same way that you do when you associate ideas, or when you hook a fantasy to a dream to an idea to a thought to something you've read. It could be looked at that you're collecting information. It's really a very similar process.

R: And then does the information get organized in some way?

TGU: It does if you organize it. *You* organize it.

R: But you don't have the sense of speaking out of organized files, so to speak.

TGU: Well – we speak out of the knowledge in the same way that you speak out of the knowledge when you talk and don't censor in advance what you're saying. It's really about the same thing. You've heard us begin to say something, stop, go at it again from another way to organize the same material that will lead to a slightly

---

.erent nuance. You all do the same things when you speak – or even when you think, but it's more obvious when you speak.

R: You started out last time, in response to my question about evil, by saying there are three different ways to look at this material, something like that. That's what I was meaning by the organization of the material in some way.

TGU: Ah. Well, wait, let's look at the process. This isn't something we had to go fetch, so to speak, and therefore you could look at it like these are organized thoughts in the way that you have organized thoughts when you discuss a subject you've thought about before. You know how the first time you try to explain something, you make a jumble of it, and by the third or fourth time you try to explain the same thing it has organized itself, seemingly spontaneously? The same with us. When you ask us something on which we are pretty firm, we can say, "well, it's this, this, this, and this. And we'll talk about this first and then this and then this."

We keep coming back to the fact that it's *almost* too simple to get across to you that you and we are the same thing, with more or less the same ways of being, and the main difference is the time-space matrix that you function in and we do not. So, any time that you're wondering how we operate, start with the assumption that it's the same way that you operate, and then see that if you can intuit how that would be without the time-space constraint. You may not get it right, but it'll be very productive. And – as Frank's very fond of saying – it'll have the meta-purpose of accustoming you to thinking at a deeper level about how similar we and you are, how it isn't "them and us" it's just us. [pause]

And you have to realize, that was a short answer, for us.

The Record and the Needle

R: [chuckles] Right. Well, we've heard the term Akashic records. Does that term mean to you the total knowledge that's available to you to tap into?

TGU: Well, it's not a library building, the way some people like to think of it, and, you know, it's not a computer terminal, but it is there, objectively written (so to speak) in the fabric of time-space, and you probably will stump us if you ask how we read it, we just – read it. But if we were to ask you, how you remember last Thursday, could you answer? You don't know, you just do. It's such an automatic mechanism, it would be very difficult to trace out. The Akashic record is not separate from time-space, it *is* time-space. It's the same thing. So if you're looking at it, there it is. But how we get to looking at it – we do it by intent, same as when you talk, and as when we talk. Just as it is your intent that points this conversation. [pause] Have we confused you?

R: I am following that, and I'm thinking about it and making sure that I understand what you were saying. You were saying that you from your perspective have the advantage in perspective, so to speak, in that you're seeing it all at once, and the totality of it –

TGU: Well we didn't quite phrase it as an advantage; it's just a circumstance. There are advantages to being quite pointed in time-space, and disadvantages, and obviously, the other way around. Our disadvantage is a somewhat diffused consciousness. It's an advantage, it's a disadvantage. It depends on how you look at it. We would not at all say it's an absolute advantage over you; it's an advantage in certain ways.

R: Well I think you were saying you had the advantage in the perspective and we had an advantage in the perception, or the focusing.

TGU: We have an advantage not so much in perspective as in totality of access. You can provide the needle to play the record, we can provide the record to be played by the needle.

R: I like that. When I interpreted you to have said that you understood more, you asked us to get back to you on that. That didn't seem to be quite the way to put it. You were using an analogy of a child and an adult.

TGU: Our meaning would be that a child sees probably more clearly because it's more clearly focused: It's absolutely right at the moment. But what it sees it may interpret badly for lack of context. This is the only way in which we would make the analogy between us on this side and us on – you on your side. It is like a parent-child relationship, *in that respect* strictly, not in any other way.

But our perspective is tempered by our experience, and the experience is relatively vast because we have vastly expanded access. Your awareness is perhaps more acute than ours, because where we see somewhat fuzzily because our consciousness is less intense, you see sharply as anything, and your struggle is to be able to provide a proper interpretation to what you see so clearly.

[pause] We do want to stress, that's the *only* aspect of the parent-child analogy that applies. We're not saying that you were created from us or anything on that order. [pause] Although, that would be another metaphor, actually, [chuckles] but we don't want to muddy those waters.

The Matrix and the Individual

TGU: We're working hard to be sure that people get out of the habit of worshipping us as all-knowing, all-being, all-important, because all that does is degrade yourselves and it is what could be considered false humility, because it makes you think of yourselves – if you'll pardon the expression – as worms. [they laugh] No matter how *we* see you.

You'll find that's a constant refrain with us, because at the moment it is so important. People who have the gifts have to *give* the gifts, and if they think they have no gifts, they don't.

This is the time in which you're not only giving the gifts of what you make yourselves, but you're contributing specifically to a set of situations that we are working hard to design, in order to bring your whole society to a new place. We mean to provide the external circumstances that will lead to what seemingly is internal development, which is more important to us. [pause] We don't need to pursue that, but we can if you want. Wherever you want to go.

R: That was development in human beings, is that what you mean?

TGU: You [humans] are going to become a different thing, and the social developments are important because they contribute toward your becoming a different thing, but they're not important in themselves. They're not the focus of the play. If you're mining for iron ore, you make a big pit in the earth. The pit is important because it gets you the iron ore, but it's the iron ore that's important, not the pit.

R: So the meaning of that analogy for what's happening here is –

TGU: That it is important that we twist and turn and manipulate so that society changes in certain ways, but we're not primarily interested in *society* changing; we're interested in changing the society to provide a matrix in which *individuals* will change in certain ways. To provide a supportive external environment is not the important part. That's the hole in the ground. It's the *people* that are the iron ore. It's the new way that they will *be*, the work you've been doing, brought to another level.

R: So that answers my next question, which is how are we to proceed to move to this different level. Our role, anyhow, is to do this sort of thing.

TGU: You will find that the important thing to do is always right there. You don't have to step across a thousand-foot gulf, it's always right there by you. And you do that faithfully and it leads you to the next thing.

The work of self-transformation is nothing more than self-development, because you're just becoming aware of what it is that you already are, potentially. That work is always available, and it can be shirked if it's put off in response to seemingly more urgent claims elsewhere. But those urgent claims elsewhere can be met in such as manner as to very much further the work of self-development, or self-transformation. Self-remembrance, is really what we would say. [pause] Rita, you as an individual know all this; this is just for the record.

Secret Schools

R: Well, I'm wondering. You know, there are some specific places in the world where some things are happening, like the Monroe Institute training process and other similar things, where people are getting some direction in this process, but it seems as though most of the world isn't there, so are we talking about building little islands here that will somehow spread?

TGU: There are always secret schools, and secret schools may not even know that they are secret schools. They may have their attention firmly placed on something else, but of course from the other side we can direct the opportunities and we can suggest to people the lessons to be learned from things.

So, you know the parable of the leavening of the loaf. It takes only a tiny bit to leaven a huge loaf. If the leaven were absent, the bread would not rise. If it were all leaven, it wouldn't be bread. If all the leaven were in one place, it wouldn't rise evenly. It's a matter of proper proportions in the proper place.

You are a member of one secret school, although it may not *know* that it's a secret school – some do and some don't, depending on their perception – and this secret school is being supported from our side in order to provide a cadre of people with improved access to certainty, so that they may be anchors of stability to those around them. But there is no necessity to have 13,425 Monroe Institutes around the world. There's no necessity to have that same number of Trappist monasteries throughout the world. Or Buddhist monasteries, or Islamic study centers, or synagogues. You see? Secret schools are secret for one reason – because they're right out in the open. That's the only way to keep a secret. They're secret because people can't see what's in front of them.

And in a secret school – we're using that word meaning a school that teaches secrets – it is not necessary that the people in that school, on a Downstairs level, understand what they're doing. It is only necessary that they change. So their Upstairs component is leading them gently to do this, that and the other, and some are good Catholics and some are good Muslims, and there are innumerable members of secret schools who consider themselves to be atheists. [they laugh] It doesn't matter to us! And in fact, it is an old law of nature that safety is found in diversity. So, if you need your secret schools to continue and to be invulnerable to the vagaries of history, scatter them out in 50 million different ways. Make them look nothing like each other.

R: And some will survive.

TGU: More than some. And it's not so much a question of surviving, that's a little too grim. It's more a question of, some will have greater influence than others. You're not in a situation where it's beginning to rain and there's only one ark.

When Things Seem Stagnant

R: Before Frank came along and we started this process, I felt I was in a state where nothing was happening. I assume on principle that what looked like a delay to me had some purpose. I'm willing to accept that on faith. But, you know, it's a big step for me not to feel like there is something we should do to push, rather than just to sit back and say "well things come about in their proper time," you see.

TGU: It is a serious question, but we look at it – as so many things – somewhat differently. [pause] When things appear to be not moving, sometimes it's a process of settling in, sometimes it's a process of preparation. Sometimes it's a necessary rest, sometimes it's stopped *here* because you're working *elsewhere*. Sometimes it's waiting for external circumstances to come around. And sometimes, of course, it is that you are *refusing to do* what you know you *should be* doing. But those are all very different circumstances, all of which may look the same.

When things seem like they're dead still in the water, you can always find out whether things are stagnant or whether they're fallow. Examine your feelings. Is there something that you know you *should* do that you *don't want to do* and you're *not* doing?

We don't mean this in the sense of "I *should* be a better person, I *should* be more helpful"; those are just beating yourself up. But if you're saying, "this job *has* to be done, I *know* I have to do it, but I don't want to" – that's not necessarily wrong either, but examine your feelings about that. If you're shirking something that you legitimately should do, you'll know it. And if at the same time things feel stagnant, there *may* be a connection!

Now, your comments brought up two things to talk about, and that was one. The second is, it's a common mistake to confuse doing nothing externally with doing nothing. A monk in a monastery who is not even speaking to his fellows, who is sincerely and intelligently striving for whatever his own goals are – he would call it, probably, getting closer to God, but you might call it self-development – whatever the goal, someone who is sincerely striving, is *not* doing *nothing*.

It may look from the outside that they're not doing anything productive, or that they're even shirking their job. But we would say, if you're shirking your job, you always know it. We would also say, there's an awful lot of wasted energy going on because people think they must "do something." But you never have to "do something." If there's something you really have to do, you know what it is, you don't call it "something." You see? [laughs] So beware of people who say that "we need to do something."

R: Yes. Well there's sometimes a sense also of feeling impatient that things aren't happening, as you suggested, and not knowing what it is that one's supposed to be doing.

TGU: You always have that knowledge available. Just sit quietly and meditate and ask sincerely. You may not get, "you should go do this," but in the absence of "you should go do this" you'll know "no, no this is fine, what I'm doing." You see? Waiting sometimes is what you need to do. And while you're waiting on one level, you're working on another. [pause] What would you like to do?

R: I would like to do what I'm doing now, but I felt there was a period of time when I was describing myself as spiritually stuck.

TGU: Ah! Well, then we suggest that for your own amusement, or for your own reassurance, go back and look and ask yourself, "what would be different had this happened before that period?" and that will, by reflection, tell you what you got out of that period. And the answer may be, "well, I had to wait for the time to be right." Or the answer may be, "I had my attention focused in the wrong place and that delayed it." But the answer very well may be, "because of this I've been changed to this," you see. We're not predicting what the answer will be, but we say it's a good exercise.

R: Well there's some sense where you feel that something came so close to not happening, and you feel so pleased that it happened, but it might not have happened!

TGU: There are innumerable realities in which it did not. But you chose the one in which it did. Your choice.

R: That's good. All right, I wanted then to go –

Countless Realities

TGU: That *includes* the World Trade Center situation. Everyone who's here chose one of the realities in which it happened – by definition.

R: And it's always so mysterious to us that 6,000-some people have chosen the path they chose of being in the way of that falling building plus all –

TGU: Well in this case we're talking about the *rest* of you, who are living with the aftermath of it, rather than having chosen to live in the realities in which that didn't happen at all, you see. You are not in any different circumstance from the people who were in the plane or people who were in the buildings, in one respect, and that is, all of you chose *this* particular reality rather than others. And of course the others are in the same fix relative to theirs.

R: It's so hard to imagine that without having a sense of somebody directing that.

TGU: Well that's fine, but you're the director. [laughs] You, Upstairs. [pause] Well, you Upstairs puts you Downstairs into situations and you Downstairs choose, and where you choose shows where you go. Now, you didn't *know* anything about that, ahead of time. The situation was on its way, but you chose –

Okay, how do we do this? [pause]

See yourself as not only that part of yourself that is Downstairs, as you call it, but also that part that's Upstairs. At the same time, remember that there are countless versions of you in all the various different realities. So in a very real sense, you don't *choose that* at all. Everybody takes all conceivable actions, or inactions. The only question is, where is your particular consciousness in that maze of choice? You have a version of yourself living in worlds that didn't experience that crash – but also didn't experience World War II! You have versions of yourself that have no Korean War. You know, all the infinite variety of things, good and bad. It isn't that you chose and chose and chose – although that's the way we always put it, because that's the way it seems. You're only choosing in the sense of choosing to put your consciousness through one door or the other door. But in the sense of you actually being an actor in each of those realities, you've made *all* the choices! And all the non-choices. [laughs] There's no – if you'll pardon the expression – choice about it.

Now we know full well how impossible it is for you to understand how there can be millions of variants of yourself living, breathing, walking, dealing with all those situations and you be aware of only one.

Because you are in all conceivable paths, all the dilemmas – and particularly the moral ethical dilemmas – that you all think are inherent in a situation, aren't. They're not real. It isn't that you chose this path or that path and something might have happened. The paths all exist; you exist; you chose to identify for the moment with this particular you in this particular path.

It's the best we can do. You can stretch your mind that far, but we know you can't make it as real as the moment of time-space you're in, because that's how it is.

R: Well, I'm confused here. You're saying that in viewing all those possible alternatives that we chose among, all those choices were not only potential, but in fact occurred.

TGU: Exactly. They exist. Not past tense, not future tense. The whole thing is one big present. At least to us.

R: It's very difficult to perceive things from your perspective. [laughs]

TGU: Well, in fact, it takes a certain skill to keep in touch with where you are. It's like a homing device, you know. We have to sort of keep a bookmark on you. *You don't ever have trouble finding us only because we find you.* But if we *didn't*, you *couldn't*.

Now, you can extend that a little farther and say, if there weren't the inherent tie between us – if we weren't *really* all one thing – well it's difficult even for us to imagine that! But if we *weren't* all one thing, how *could* we find each other?

R: And you have the same ties to us in all those other alternative –

TGU: Sure. We know the question that arises is, "all right, if I'm here, this by definition is real, and those other alternatives that I didn't take are by definition theoretical, let's say. Are they less real than this one?" Well…[pause] this is the only way we can say this. All of the terrain is, let's say, theoretical. All of the terrain, including where you are. Your *consciousness* makes it real. It isn't like there's one reality that's *really* real and the others that are only *potential* or are only *theoretical*.

[laughs] It's the best we can do. One viewpoint is that there is only one place where you are at a given time, one path that you're walking, and that path by definition is always real to you. By definition you're always *in* the reality, and the others are either theoretical or hypothetical or they don't exist. To you.

Stretching Consciousness

TGU: And it's only a function of your consciousness! If you stretch your consciousness to the point that you actively experience other lives, for instance (which is typically a first step, because it's easiest, it's closest) you begin realizing, "time's not really real in the way that I think of it," and you realize "well, they and I are part of something bigger than either one of us; they're not really me; I'm not really them" and you start to realize that the thumb is not a past life of a finger, but they're both part of something bigger.

As you develop your consciousness, your effective world expands. If you can get your consciousness to the point where you see that you really are on all sides of all those choices, then your world will expand in a totally different way. And – *this* is what magic *is*. Magicians are people who learn to move from one to the other on demand. If in your reality you have a broken bone and you can figure out how to do it, you can move to another reality in which your bone is not broken. It's just as real, because the reality of it comes from your consciousness, *not* from anything external.

R: But can one change a specific instance without changing the whole pattern?

TGU: Well, you aren't really *changing* anything; you're changing where you stand in relation to it. Nothing really moves. The only thing that moves is consciousness.

R: [pause] So you're saying these patterns that we put together in a lifetime are alterable –

TGU: Well they *seem* alterable, yes. But you don't so much alter them as just go to a different one.

R: Well it's not going to a different one but changing the events or the perceptions within one of those.

TGU: Well let's look at that a little. Every time you come to a choice point – which in practical language, means every second –

R: Every nanosecond.

TGU: Exactly. A leaf falls this way or that way, there's two paths. You look this way or that way, there's two paths. So – the choice points are infinite. And the possibilities are infinite. Therefore there isn't really *a* path and *another* path. Those are conveniences of speech, but really, you're walking in a maze of freedom. You're walking in an absolute maze of freedom. You can have, do, be whatever you want, provided you know how to do it. Or provided you can do it without knowing how, which also happens.

To say, "I'm on this particular path, but I want to change this," is true enough, but it's no more meaningful than saying "you're in a maze of freedom and you can go where you want to go." One way is saying that the path is more real than the part not on the path; the other way is saying a path is just an arbitrary definition among this wilderness of choices. You see?

R: But because of this duration-of-time phenomenon, there are going to be consequences to choice, are there not?

TGU: Well, if you continue down that path, sure. There are if you want them to be, believe them to be, think there have to be. But if you believe in miracles, miracles you get. That's what a miracle is, a sudden movement from one place to another place without any transition. Well, there could be transition, but you see what we're saying.

R: An unexpected –

TGU: Well it wouldn't even have to be unexpected. If you expect a miracle, it's still a miracle. And in fact there are people who *do* expect miracles every day, and they get them. They live in faith. That's what living in faith *is*. That's one form of living in faith. [pause] Living in trust perhaps would be a better way to say it.

And there are people who live in trust negatively. They fully expect bad things, and of course they get them. They choose the path nanosecond by nanosecond, as you said.

TGU and Guidance

R: I want to come back to where we ended up last session, in which we were talking about your seeing footprints of your guidance. We ended at some puzzling questions around that, I thought.

TGU: *You* thought! [laughs]

R: You at one point said "how would we know?" Well, we sense our guidance in some way. We sense that you're there, we have a sense of being able to dialogue with you. We find that things work out better if we get some word from you and follow through in that kind of way. That's all what I would think of as a sensing of guidance, and I got the feeling that you didn't have a similar sense.

TGU: Well, I think you saw an example of the fact that your consciousness is somewhat more pointed than ours. Because you're more pointed, you are of course more limited in input, but you're also more aware of nuance, perhaps. And so guidance has a different flavor than your own thought. Seemingly.

Well, if we're [laughs] – you know, we can hear his [meaning my, Frank's] pleasure at this one. If we're somewhat in a fog [they laugh] we need to become more pointed in order to recognize such things, and speaking to you, someone who's in time-space who can focus these things, is a very good way to get more pointed.

But it had not occurred before that someone focused it back on us. And when they did, and for the duration that they did, we thought "yeah, you know, maybe so." Now, this leads us to the suspicion that we have our *own* Gentlemen Upstairs, which implies that they would have a wider breadth of knowledge than we do. We don't think that makes much sense, because – here's why. Unless –

Frank: [laughs] That was so startling my eyes popped open! I mean, I got a sense of *them* being startled.

[Resuming as TGU]: Unless, just as our reality is less pointed than yours, there may be another – No, we don't know. Come back to us on this. We'll examine this a little bit. Or – come at it from another point of view; maybe that'll give us something more.

R: The implications would be that there are some hierarchies here of –

TGU: [slowly] Well, you know, you know –

We told you that we know we're waiting to sort of complete ourselves to go to the next stage? It does make sense that there still is only one thing, and we're a part of a larger thing. And perhaps we're one of *its* slow learners, as you're one of *our* slow learners. [they laugh] We don't know.

But – but, we *do* know. Here's what's going on here. There is one thing. We are like a conduit to you, as you are a conduit to, say, your blood cells or something. That is, just as you are part of us and we are part of you, both of us – being part of the same thing – are also part of *it*, whatever *it* is.

This has the flavor of infinite regress, but all of a sudden we would say, "yes, there's definitely another level." And the suspicion arises now that – ah hah [laughs] that in fact *they're* waking *us* up. They're manipulating this to help wake *us* up, which would make us –

If we were actually to wake up...Let's assume that we're half asleep. Let's assume that we could make our consciousness as pointed as yours – well, well, who knows? That may be what's going on. But you've made us aware that *something's* going on.

R: *Can you say something about what the footprints were, what was giving you this awareness?*

TGU: Oh, well, once we began a little self-referential thinking about "where did that idea come from, where did this bright –" You know? Just like when you do your retrievals and you say, "what made me get into that scenario" and you finally realize the scenario is all set up for you? Well – [they laugh]

R: *I see.*

TGU: It's only speculation, but it's very persuasive at the moment. We'll get back to you. Or you'll ask the right question and it will come to us as well. Oh, that's a very nice sub-purpose of this. It's good to remind you how valuable you in bodies are to us. You constantly tend to put us on pedestals and it's not warranted.

R: *But if we keep asking questions this will cause some kind of movement somehow.*

TGU: Well, it sort of illuminates *us*. Your question provides focus, and things come [to us] around the focus. And because we are in communication with you at the time that you're providing the focus, we think differently than we would if we were just giving you guidance. It's all the difference between looking outward and looking inward. If we're concentrating on setting up a scenario and walking you through it, we're not necessarily aware of behind-the-scenes constraints on us. But if you ask us something in a way that focuses our attention that way – we have access to lots of data, and we have the ability to make sense of that data. *You have the ability to light up the corridor.*

R: Would you see any resistance on your part to becoming aware of an additional layer of guidance now?

TGU: We have no resistance of will as far as we know – in fact, it intrigues us quite a bit. The circumstances are that it can be difficult for us to hold this self-referential thinking. However, we'll see. The funny thing is, we're well aware that all of this discussion is couched in terms in time, but as we said, there is duration and we need to think some more of that. We all need to think more of that. It will answer lots of questions, and pose more questions. It's important. If it doesn't do anything except get you off this eternal idea of us sitting on clouds and having haloes and all of that, or of being perfect sources of information who – blah blah blah, you know – if it helps to bring a better sense of the reality in which we live, it'll be all to the good.

A Future Life on Mars

R: Okay. I'm going to move on to something lighter here. Here's something I wondered about, when we were talking earlier about the different aspects that make up the thinking within that totality. We talked about some component parts, or some aspects. And as I recall your response was that it would be composed of a whole variety of things, some energies that at some point had been in a physical body, either on earth or elsewhere; and some that would not have been in. I won-der, is there some aspect that has been in what we would call our future.

TGU: [pause] Sure. Because the whole thing is in all the dimensions in all the possibilities, and that includes of course all time and all space, which means all futures, all pasts, all presents, dimensionally, in all possibilities, and what looks to you to be only probabilities. So the answer is, by definition we have to exist everywhere. And so do you. Because you are us.

Just as you as one individual in one time on earth, in one path, as you call it, or a probable moment – just as you experience the separateness of that, that's fine. That is your pointedness. At the same time, you're all part of one and therefore are part of everything. Is that unnecessarily complicated?

R: No. I just wonder if there's somebody there that I can talk to that's lived on Mars. Maybe having gotten there from the earth.

TGU: More the other way around.

R: [pause] Meaning the Martians have come to earth? Is that what you –?

TGU: You the Earthians used to live on Mars. That is, in other words, a Martian would look upon this as their future. [pause] However, having said all that, let's see if we can find someone who was on Mars. [pause] But you really want an Earth person who lives on Mars in the future.

R: Well that's what I started out with, but I'm willing to phrase it some different way if that's a more productive question.

TGU: Whatever you want. You choose.

R: Well, this gets into the question of whether people from earth eventually will be able to transport themselves to Mars, to have an existence there.

TGU: Well, sure, in some realities.

R: And in terms of the probabilities of this happening. I mean, you said you know what's going to happen –

TGU: Everything's going to happen. It's absolute. All probable possible theoreticals happen. What is capable of being put into odds or probabilities are more "what will the local probability go to?"

Well, no. We need to back up a little.

There are realities in which Wernher Von Braun did or did not develop rockets in Germany. And there are probabilities from there in which he did or did not begin to work for the United States. You can see where that all goes. So, yes, you got to the moon, and no, you didn't get to the moon. It depends on which reality you look at. Your question actually would boil down to saying, "is it 100 percent? Are there no places at which humans ever lived on Mars? Ever got to live on Mars." You see? That would be the only way in which we could give you an answer other than "yes you do, no you don't." And that isn't so.

But it's really a meaningless answer. [pause] If one says, there are probabilities, there are realities, in which humans live on the surface of moons of Jupiter, those realities almost by definition preclude other things that you might find preferable. Which doesn't matter, but we're saying the realities that extend in space may be considered somewhat less likely to extend their consciousness. That being so, they're more likely to be the detour realities rather than the one we're most interested in, which would be, to get all of us back together again. That's not an absolute at all. In one respect, we don't care if you go visit Pluto.

R: [chuckles] That would be a detour in your thinking.

TGU: It would tend to be. Wouldn't absolutely have to be. And of course there's more than one way to visit Pluto. You could visit Pluto without having to carry your body along in a rocket. But at the moment only a very few of you could do that and come back with a fix close enough that it didn't fluctuate all over the place, which means it would be a mixture of reality and unreality in any given existence. In any given reality. You see what we're saying?

R: Yes. I get that.

TGU: Swedenborg conversed with beings who lived on the planet of Jupiter. Well – not in this reality. But he wasn't wrong either. But it's hard to hold that focus! You see the point. Now. You want to communicate with – what?

R: Well I think I'll drop that, unless there's something you want to tell us about that that I am not now asking.

TGU: All right, the only answer we'll give you is, yes, you can do that. We'll find 'em. So whenever you're ready –

R: Whenever I'm ready to talk to someone who has lived on Mars.

TGU: How about someone who's lived in Virginia?

R: [chuckles] I don't want to talk about anybody like that.

TGU: They're just as mysterious; no more, no less.

Vengeance

R: I've been listening in to people's reaction to this disaster, on the issue of striking back against what's perceived as the evil forces of Osama bin Laden. And it's presented often in terms of "this is what we need to do to balance things out." And I'm asking about this issue of balancing things out in a worldwide sense. You've talked about the fact that you see this without the slices of time. You're looking at the totality, and in the totality everything is balanced out eventually. And the "eventually" means – ?

TGU: A long time. [laughs]

R: So I'm –

TGU: You're asking, are they right in any sense?

R: I guess.

TGU: Well, if the world had been created the day before yesterday, maybe. But given the history of the planet in any given reality you choose to investigate, once you look at it carefully – once you look at it even consciously at all! – it becomes obvious there's no way to balance it out, because every society on the face of your planet is the result of some past aggression somewhere. Forget the present moment. Everyone has or could have grievances. Everyone wants to get one last blow in and that'll make them even.

But the people who are saying that aren't very good at mathematics. Because there's no way. The entire point of breaking the cycle of vengeance is that the cycle cannot be completed; it can only be broken. It can't be completed because every new retaliation creates the seeds of new retaliation in the future, because it can never *balance out*. It's foolish talk. Besides, that's not what they mean. What they mean is, they don't want to feel that they have been weak, that they have been taken advantage of. That's all that really amounts to.

R: You know, we talked about our visualizing ourselves and being ourselves a certain way as a way of dealing with this kind of thing. Is there more that we could do? For example you said one of the factors in understanding this process is people's inability to see their own shadow sides, or integrate their own shadow sides. It's hard for me to think about how we would go out on a campaign of teaching people to see their shadow sides or to integrate their shadow sides. [chuckles] Is there something in that kind of a realm that we could be doing?

TGU: Well, each will be impelled to do the work that's proper to each. You will know; you'll meet the opportunities that come to you. And some people will be called upon to teach, and some to organize and some to stand silently and protest, and some to fly warplanes. There are millions of roles and everyone will know the role that's there that's available to them. However – [pause]

Frank: That's funny, that doesn't happen often. I know there was something else coming, but it just went away. Wait a minute. [pause] Hmm. I'm going to re-say what they were saying and then maybe it'll come out again. It just disappeared. I know what they were saying was everybody will have their own thing to do – and that's obvious. It'll be obvious to the people. Well, there was another point that wasn't like that, but…What was the other part of your question?

R: The question had to do with, is there something more that we can do besides try to be the best of ourselves, so to speak. Is there something we can do in this world where everyone is worried about –

Frank: Oh now I know what it was. The other thing that came was that, yes there is a campaign to have people recognize their shadow selves, and that campaign is being orchestrated on their side, not on our side. [laughs] That's what they're saying.

R: Okay.

[Resuming as TGU]: The impact of events is a bigger teacher to you than anything that one of you could say to another, and so you are a different country today than you were last month. The difference has been created by your reaction to the events. We can create the events and we can lead you toward – but it's up to you to choose the lessons to be learned from events, and the ways to change from the events. Because the airplanes hit the buildings, there are people who are a little more chastened and a little more self-reflective and sober today than they were before. There are others who are totally lost in rage, and there are some who are lost in fear. You see? Millions of reactions. And you needn't worry too much about that, we will provide the opportunities. You can each spread the word, first and foremost by living it, because you'll spread it on the internal internet, so to speak. First and foremost by living it. There are many people preaching it and if some of them would do less preaching and more living of it, they would be more effective.

But having said that, there are specific things that some of you can do, and you'll know it. And there are specific things all of you can do and you'll know it, but some of those may not be external things. They may seemingly be tending your garden in peace, so to speak.

R: What did you mean by a campaign on the other side to orchestrate –

TGU: Well, we're orchestrating the opportunities, you know.

R: Specifically having to do with people becoming aware of their shadow side?

TGU: Specifically being concerned with creating the situations that allow the opportunity for some people to wake up in response to the situation. So when we create what you are all fond of calling a disaster, it has impact around the world in the unpredictable way that Princess Diana's sudden death had, or the killing of the Kennedys. Those orchestrated incidents, shall we say – and we remind you that those who participated in those incidents were volunteers – those orchestrated incidents couldn't have *specific* effects because the specific effects are more the result of people's conscious choices, which are free by design. But they set up the circumstances in which people could make the choices. It sort of stressed them toward it, it biased the –

Frank: It's a visual of pushing on a screen, you know, to push it sideways. I don't know how to translate that.

TGU: Your choices are always free, as individuals and therefore entirely. All that we can do is set up circumstances and give you opportunities, and it's up to you to take them. And as soon as you take them or don't take them, then we scramble with Plan B, you know? [chuckles] We're always on Plan B.

R: Well as I'm hearing this, I'm wondering, what's the advantage to free will.

TGU: Because free will is what allows *you* to create. Free will gives *you* the opportunity to choose what you will be, what kind of flower you're going to present to us.

R: But you're doing so much of the creation on the other side –

TGU: We're creating the matrix for the free will. [stutters several times]

You're saying to yourself, "that isn't quite fair, we have free will but you're pushing us in certain directions," and that's true if you look at it in any one reality. But you need to remember, if you can, that it's happening in *all* realities, and you can move to the reality you want to move to. [pause] Well, theoretically.

R: But it seems like since you have preferences about how we choose and how we move, that you're creating the situations... What is this process all about?

TGU: All right, we'll talk about that. Let's make a theoretical example. Supposing you as an organism came into this world intending to get a little experience with selfishness. Both the satisfying of it and the overcoming of it. We and you – but you will no longer remember, because you're down here in it – we and you set up an endless series of obstacle courses that present you with those situations in which you will choose about selfishness. And choose and choose and choose and choose and choose. Now your choices might cancel out! Or they might radically alter you, or they might leave you the way you were. Don't forget, you're in on this process, it isn't us doing it *to* you except that in any moment of time, it's us doing it to you because you're functioning in the moment of time, and so we're the ones holding the score, so to speak, or holding the –

R: A plan that we've agreed to.

TGU: But you know what? "We've agreed to" isn't quite right, it's "we are agreeing to" continually, because you're continually up there with us as we're modifying into Plan B. But you Downstairs – some of you do and some of you don't connect Upstairs to be part of that planning. There are actually people who remember the planning, moment by moment. And you could too. It's a matter of requesting access and getting it. You might find that an interesting process. Takes a lot of the blame away, though. [laughs]

R: I'm just really asking myself "how'd we start on this process anyway, and in the larger sense what is this all about?" Why are we doing this?

TGU: We remind you that you don't like being bored.

R: Oh. [they laugh]

TGU: You are seeing calculus that was invented because people mastered the times tables. Okay?

R: I see.

TGU: And as we master calculus, then we'll move on to other games. They're not meaningless games, but they are games. They're games in the sense of stretching our abilities, of enjoying it, of playing it, you know. They're not games in the sense of one wins and one loses, but they're entertainment. They're engaging, let's put it that way. Remember that the next time you get bad news on the television set, it's better than being bored. [they laugh]

Valuable Process

R: Okay, I think I've run out of questions for tonight, is there something else that you would like to comment on?

TGU: Well, we know we're a broken record on this, but we want to say it again, this is a very valuable process. You're thinking of it now in terms of a book and we can steer it that way, but it's valuable just for its own sake. Valuable to us. Valuable to you. And as your little bonus for the evening, we will tell you that you could, when you go to bed, give yourself the instruction that you want to remember your participation in the planning.

R: All right.

TGU: And do that a little bit on an on-going basis, and then we'll talk. [laughs]

R: Okay. All right. Thank you very much.

TGU: Thank you very much. [stretch]

Frank: We now return to our normally scheduled programming.

Session Eight
October 2, 2001

[I was sick quite a bit for a couple of weeks: heavy coughing, wheezing, all the fun that accompanies asthma. But throughout this session, as previously, as long as I was talking to the guys, my breathing was easy even though I was lying on my back – which is an impossible position for an asthmatic to be comfortable in! The reason I mention this will become apparent.]

TGU: [coughing]

R: *All right, good evening to The Gentlemen Upstairs.*

TGU: Good evening to the ladies downstairs. [they chuckle] [coughing]

The Meaning of Disasters

R: *I had mentioned in an earlier session, on the 11th, that I wanted to return at some point to ask about what we think of as disasters like our recent events, and other times when there's been loss of life on the earth, either human beings or other life forms, and ask, to the extent that you're able to alter things in the 3D world, what meaning do these kinds of events have?*

TGU: Hmm. [pause] That's a hard question to answer, phrased that way. It's rather like asking us what meaning does a day have. Because what *you* see as all the same kind of things, putting the title of disaster or atrocity or war or whatever around them, to us are infinitely different, and so it's difficult. We'll give you an example to show you the difficulty, and then ask you to rephrase it, really. [pause]

If you have that disaster at Bhopal, where people died because of corporate indifference, and a disaster in New York where people died because of an act of war, and a disaster resulting (seemingly anyway) from nobody's fault – the bridge over St. Luis Rey, if you remember that old example – if you only look at the fact that there is relatively widespread, seemingly indiscriminate death, then you might say those three incidents are three of a kind. And we would say they're nothing like. [coughing]

R: *Can I add to that list the meteors crashing into the earth and causing major death among the dinosaurs?*

TGU: [laughs]

R: *That would be another disaster for the dinosaurs.*

TGU: Relatively few of the dinosaurs asked questions about it afterwards. [they laugh]

All right, well, see, that's an interesting example of what *you* would lump together. To you those four things have something in common, and we can understand the abstract pattern of it, but we don't see it as inherent. It would be as though you grouped the people of a city who were all wearing sneakers. Yes, they would have that in common, but it wouldn't necessarily be a meaningful "in common." If you could ask that question in a more pointed way – and we can't tell you how, because it's your question that will elicit the answer, but –

R: Well let me try a different emphasis, then. I've heard you saying that you have some role in deciding things that happen here. And those things include a major loss of either human life or of other kinds of life on the planet. Why would you want to do something like that? What would be accomplished?

TGU: First, let's point out that we don't so much "decide" as we "plan." We absolutely respect the free will of the individuals involved. They are planning it with us, but if they decided not to do it, we have to run around for Plan B, C, or D. We don't decide it, we plan it. Having said that, suppose you want to build a new building on a lot that already has an old building. You destroy the old building first. Of course, it depends on what's going on, but you understand the analogy. If you have an old wooden building on a lot that you intend to build a skyscraper on, the destruction *has to* come first. [pause]

You all tend to think that death or even injury is necessarily a bad thing, which perplexes us. Although we understand it intellectually, we can't really empathize with that attitude, because – it's so funny. It would be like regarding every sunset as a tragedy because it was the end of the day. You're all going to die, you're all going to get injured in one way or another, probably, on the way. And when you die, so what? Then you come back, either here or somewhere else.

So we really can't share your views of the finality of it or even of the importance of it. A sudden death or an accidental death, so-called, or a violent or lingering death – there are a million ways to die – each of them can be molded in such a way as to help the soul that's experiencing it. As we said, the thousands who died on the same day, on the 11th of September, were volunteers in the first place, and in the second place, you know, thousands of other people died that day who weren't noticed. So, we know it sounds cold to you, but it's not a big deal to us.

Now, the orchestrating of an event that can have long term, hopefully positive, effects on society – which, as we have said, only interests us in that it helps to mold people closer to their potential – that's worth an awful lot of transient human suffering, because the alternative is not a lack of suffering, the alternative is suffering of an entirely different kind. [pause]

R: Yes, you've mentioned that point before. I was thinking not so much about the tragedy and the loss of human life as the impact that that loss has. I hear you now saying that can be a very positive impact, in that it has some altering effect on those who are still running around on this earth –

TGU: Yes. Let's search through the old memories here. Frank's got all kind of historical analogies. The attack on Pearl Harbor led, by way of an entire war, to a generation of men who were given college educations who never could have had college educations without the war and the GI Bill of Rights. That generation of men, mostly men, in turn had a vastly expanded life in terms of their earning potential and their intellectual horizons, and they added to the intellectual capital of a whole generation of Americans, which affected the whole world.

Now, that isn't an *excuse* for Pearl Harbor, and it isn't the underlying *reason* for Pearl Harbor, but it *is* one of the *effects* of Pearl Harbor. So we think it's very misleading to look at those who were killed in the attack as if that were the full story, when in fact the story is darker – in that you have all of the 50 million people who were killed in that war – but it's also lighter in all of the things that followed after the war cleared stuff away. It's a matter of how wide you spread your net when you do your accounting.

R: You said "although that was not the reason for the event," as though the reasons for the event are somewhat different than the long-term effect.

TGU: [pause] We're saying an event has initial consequences and then the secondary consequences and tertiary and quaternary. It goes on and on. You can't say that the event was caused for the sake of the tertiary consequences. But you can say that those consequences came because of the event. Again, it's a question of how carefully you do your accounting when you are attempting to see.

Again, you all see things necessarily in time-slices. Because you see them in time-slices, you can't possibly see them the way we do. What you call the tragedies of World War I and World War II, and everything in between, not to mention the Cold War afterwards, we would look at as the seismic interruption of a world culture that had kind of reached a dead end. This resulted in the freeing of many countries that had been colonies – which in turn had good and bad effects. The level of civilization often dropped. But it's still better for people to work out their own destiny than to be held as children. [pause] It's not that simple, but we're trying to give you a simple example.

R: These are consequences you're talking about, but implied is that there was also a reason for it. I'm saying that presumably those reasons are something that you're dealing with at your level.

TGU: An easy way to talk about it is as a demolition job. That's perhaps tactless given the fact that the two buildings collapsed, but when a society encrusts itself with certain institutions or corruptions or even virtues, it can be impossible to pull them down, no matter how necessary it may be to do it, without some violent, or in any case catastrophic, discontinuity.

R: Well what about the dinosaurs?

TGU: What about the dinosaurs? The dinosaurs were cleared off the face of the earth.

R: Yes. That was with intent, I guess you're saying. I can't imagine what the intent was.

TGU: Well, you remember Robert Monroe's very productive analogy about Someone in his garden Somewhere. Remember, the garden of loosh? [This may be found in Monroe's second book, *Far Journeys*.] He began by sowing a crop, a second crop, and a third crop. He – Someone – destroyed them successively as he discovered disadvantages and could think of new ways that might be more efficacious. He either destroyed the whole crop or reduced it in importance. This is an analogy, a fable, but in many ways it's exactly on the mark. What good would it do to have the world continue with dinosaurs in a Devonian world that could not go where it has gone in the meantime?

R: But one might want to ask, why were the dinosaurs here in the first place?

TGU: Well, supposing the dinosaurs were here as a necessary intermediary step. *Or,* supposing that dinosaurs were a dead end that could have gone someplace else, and didn't. *Or,* supposing the dinosaurs were a whimsical play, just to see how big we can make a bird that doesn't fly.

R: [chuckles]

TGU: It's not relevant, really. Teleological thought can be extended too far. (Something Frank tends to do, in fact.) You don't always need to know why a leaf falls on one side of a fence rather than the other. [pause] We don't object to the question, we're just saying, that's our answer to the question. We can bring the dinosaurs back if you want, but where are you going to put them?

R: Okay. One could assume that you were talking about planting seeds of animal life that evolved eventually into dinosaurs, and perhaps that was somebody playing a game. I kind of like that explanation best.

Evolution and Creation

TGU: Well, just as long as it's clear that we don't believe in *meaningless* evolution because that is one of the silliest things you've come up with. Not you personally, fortunately. [they laugh] Nothing happens without purpose, and to think that it does is to overestimate your own intelligence and to underestimate the intelligence of the universe. Evolution is –

You know, there's a tendency among your scientists to use that word as though it were a *deus ex machina*, to actually – not quite consciously – make it into a person. "Then Evolution walked onto the stage," rather like Someone. And that's not what happens. What happens is, we play, and not just we; whoever created us, as well. But inherent in the nature of true creation is always the inherent uncertainty of the result. Otherwise you're not creating, you're just following a design. So when you truly innovate, you produce unpredictable results. That's *why* you innovate. You know which way you *want* them to move, but that doesn't mean that's going to do it.

R: Is this always a situation of co-creation, where the thing that you're creating also has a creative force in itself?

TGU: A lot depends on your definition. We could agree with that, but let's look at, say, a tree. A tree's role in the co-creation is to follow its own nature, to become the best tree it can be. To pursue the nutrients, to produce the leaves and the chlorophyll and all that. So to that degree – and actually to a larger degree than most of you right now understand – yes, that tree is an active co-creator, although it would be truer, probably, to say trees, as a one-thing. Before beings get differentiated up to your level, the whole thing is really halfway between us and you in a way, you know? Supposing you had 10,000 maple trees; that's more like one generic maple tree than 10,000 individuals. Now, it's not quite, but you see the point. I hope. Did we tangle this up entirely, or should we make it worse?

R: [laughs] No. No, I think that's been a useful discussion, for me.

TGU: Good. We're glad you can't sue us, every time a train goes off the track.

Changing Humans

R: [chuckles] All right, I wanted to ask again about another life – from another previous session. I'm going to quote you here: you're "interested in changing society to provide a matrix in which individuals will change in certain ways." What do you feel are the main ways in which the human being could change in order to be improved?

TGU: We wouldn't say improved, exactly, but let's say developed. Let's say that you're ready for your next – um – growth spurt? You two are actually working on this right now in your own way. That is, first will come the firmer rooting in our side while you're still in your side. This will give you a firmer rooting on your side – well, wait. [pause]

At the moment, people on earth are mostly having to *believe* that there is a purpose, that there is connection, and that there's meaning. And they do or don't believe, to greater or less extent, depending on the circumstances. We're moving, and trying to move you; and you're moving, and trying to move yourselves, in the direction of more firmly rooting yourself where you are *by* rooting yourself more firmly with us. By increasing your access, you see.

Now when you do that, you destroy the fear of death, you destroy the fear of accident. In fact, in general you could say you destroy fear, because once you realize that you are creating what's around you in a *real* sense, not in a *theoretical* sense, then you don't have to worry about being hit by flying bullets.

Once the *fear* is eliminated, *curiosity* enters, which is again another thing that Bob Monroe said very clearly. He saw that. Mainly because he had to overcome a lot of his *own* fears. It's important for you all to realize that pioneers are not fearless. They're intelligent enough to be afraid, and stubborn enough to do it anyway, and playful enough, and curious enough.

Well. The easiest way to start this is as a civilization, as a society, because most people want to fit in and they can more easily do it by fitting in than by going against the crowd. So those of you who go against the crowd actually serve the purpose of *changing* the crowd so that then all those who fit in then will do it, at which point you're uncomfortable, and you go off and do something else! [they laugh]

But that's fine. That's meeting your purpose. Once you in general have been more firmly grounded in the way things really are – once it's no longer a wild-eyed theory propounded by Seth or propounded by the perennial philosophers, you know, and seen and interpreted variously by religious figures, who are then thought to be either soft-hearted or soft-headed, by the people who think of themselves as realists – once you've changed that basis, and the fear is gone, and the connection is increased, and the curiosity and the access and the ability to *satisfy* the curiosity is increased, then you go on to the step after that. (This is not going to happen in two days.)

So you see, we do have very clearly a sense of where to go next. And you can see that you're going to be an entirely different species. You're going to be the same species, and you're going to be entirely different, just as you are entirely the same species and entirely different from what you were in the 1500s, or the 1000s. Or in Asia as opposed to Central Africa, or – Greenland.

Frank's Struggle with Health

R: I have another question I want to go to, but first I want to ask you why it is that Frank is now doing so well with his breathing. He's lying down, which is ordinarily difficult for him. And he seems to be totally relaxed and comfortable, which hasn't been the case for quite a while, but during these sessions this happens. Can you explain that to us in a way that will help him generally?

TGU: Well apparently we can't! We explained this five years ago, and he understands it, but he's missed the practical key. He must have told you – we seem to remember him telling you – about his sessions with us for his friend Ed Carter. It wasn't asthma but Frank was having a very wracking cough, and a very similar thing happened, and as soon as the session was over, he was back with his wracking cough. So he asked his friend to ask us why. And he got the answer immediately, and they got it on record, and they got it correctly. And that is that your health is a ratio between your mental states and your physical states. If you need to change your health instantly, you can do it by changing your mental state. It's hard to *hold* that, though, because your mental states change all the time. They move. They fluctuate. That's what consciousness *is*.

He knows all that. The difficulty is that given his biases, which are very very very strongly in favor of mental and spiritual powers rather than physical powers, it would not be in his best interest for us to encourage him to do that, given that he would ignore the physical even more.

So that when he burns himself, or when he cuts himself, as he has remarked to you, he can cure that right away. And we certainly don't have any objection to that; that's fine, and this is something you'll all be able to do. But you see, that does not in turn tempt him to burn his finger again.

But to be able to suppress the symptoms of a chronic illness would not be good. It would actually make things worse, requiring more illness in order to get the attention, you see. So perhaps we should say that we're sabotaging it a little bit, in his best interest. Were we not to, do you think there's any chance he would have gone to the acupuncturist [in an attempt to cure the asthma]?

R: It was very difficult, clearly, to get him to do anything that seemed sensible to some of us.

TGU: Well, he's fighting quite a different war than you are, and he's fighting it after he's already won it, but he's a little hard-headed. He'll probably never have told you this story, so we'll tell you this story.

When he was a boy, probably 12, 13, 14, he read a story of Theodore Roosevelt being a sickly boy with asthma, building himself up because his father gave him a gym set when he really wanted a book! His father gave him a gym set to build up his body, you see, because his father was afraid that the boy would grow up sickly. Now, from that story Frank proceeded to promptly get all the wrong messages; he turned it around entirely to his own bias, without even realizing it until much later. Now, fancy this. The young Roosevelt was sickly, he was bookish. He wanted to continue to be bookish; his father intervened and had him build up his body. Which in turn cured Roosevelt of his asthma. So the lesson Frank learned was, "this can be controlled by your mind without medicines."

R: Without the gym set.

TGU: Without the gym set! Absolutely! See? That came to *you* right away. That didn't come to him for ten years or more. And he still doesn't do it. So we're saying this is a –

Well, this is a real long story, do you want more of it?

R: Of course.

TGU: He…[pause] came into the world with the knowledge, with the certainty, that mind is the important thing and everything else should follow it. We're not talking about intellectual demonstrations, but – you know, mental powers. Spiritual abilities, so to speak. You see, he came into this life in touch with the man who had brought someone back from the dead, who knew all this. But *he* had no sense that he was being influenced by that. He was a boy, mentally, not just physically. He was a boy who was sharing a mental space with something that knew absolutely that everything that he was being told in the 1950s was wrong.

So, there was this civil war within him about healing, and about maintaining his own body. And there's much more. He tended to blame the body for its problems. (It's only in the last couple of years that he's actually realized what he's been doing.) None of this is a dead end. All of this is instructive to him and will be instructive to others. We seriously doubt that he would even say it was too bad, you know. Anyway, that's the background of what's been going on. That's why it was so difficult for him to go to any modality at all. [laughs] If acupuncture were more widely accepted in the United States, he'd have had to find something else. [they laugh] It was only marginally disreputable enough. [they laugh]

The Value of Struggles

R: All right, that all computes. However, he's here still trying to play some role in the physical life, which seems to be interfered with by these symptoms.

TGU: Well, now you see? Your question goes right back to your first question about catastrophes. And it's absolutely mistaken. It starts from the assumption that if nothing "bad" happened, everything would be fine. But it's not true. All this struggle that he's had with the mental aspect of this, the spiritual aspect of it, the physical aspect of it – none of that has been wasted.

R: [pause] All right, so it hasn't been wasted, and if continued it still won't be wasted?

TGU: Well, if he were to continue without making any progress it might be wasted, but that's not going to happen. His difficulty is not getting stuck, it's trying to jump *too* far forward.

R: Okay. So trying to figure out how he can spend more of his time in the state he's in now is not necessarily a good plan.

TGU: That's right, because, you see, you don't know but that that struggle will all of a sudden turn on the light bulb and he will make a great stride from it. Or, that in hearing this transcript, someone *there* will make a great stride from it. You know? It's not something anyone can know about anyone else's life.

It's a common mistake. You look at the other person's life and because *you* see the things that are hidden from *them* – because they're too close to them – you think, "ah if they would only do this." But of course there's a *reason* why they're not doing this. Whether or not *they* know what the reason is. One of our mantras is, "people don't do things without reasons."

R: Okay, well I'm taking all that literally, and I assume the listeners and the readers of this material will also.

TGU: We hope that neither you nor they will consider yourselves rebuked. We're just trying to give you a course correction.

R: No. No, we're trying to understand this, and this makes great sense as you say it.

TGU: Think of Jane Roberts, dying! [She had spent many years channeling Seth.] [She was in] great pain, over a long period of time, at the same time that Seth, coming through her own vocal cords, is saying, "you could get up whenever you wanted to. You could still get up now." She was in a fix that is inexplicable to any of you. She obviously *believed* in Seth. She obviously was a person of great refinement and great sincerity and great intellect and great will. So why wouldn't it work? You don't know, because you *can't* know, what was going on inside, what the larger purpose is, what will happen to her three lifetimes later because of this, what will happen to the people who read it – you see? There's all kinds of ramifications. [pause] All is well. If we could just reassure you of one thing, it would be that all is well, even when things are going badly.

Living in the Now

R: All right. Back to our Plan A.

TGU: [laughs] Well, you're doing better than we are, we're on Plan C12. [they laugh]

R: We talked earlier about improved societies. I was asking about them as goals, and aware that we're a very goal-oriented culture. And yet we're constantly being told to live in the moment, not analyzing our past or anticipating our futures.

TGU: We don't think that's the proper understanding of that statement.

R: Could you expand on that?

TGU: If you don't mind. You can plan for the future and be in the present. You can review the past and be in the present. Conversely, you can be walking down the street doing nothing and not be in the present at all. The emphasis on that is to *remember yourself continually.* To keep your consciousness – conscious!

Let's say you're planning for the future, planning to build a house, say. While you're working on the architectural design, you can have your attention shoot outwards toward the architectural design to the degree that you forget yourself. Or, being mindful, you can work on the architectural design. Externally they look like the same thing. But the second one is "in the now."

"In the now" does not mean incapable of planning or remembering. In fact, to the degree that it was possible, it would be extremely undesirable. What it *does* mean is that no matter where you send your consciousness, *you go with it.* [pause] That's our understanding of it.

R: So just in that statement, if you're totally engrossed with the architectural plans, forgetting who and where you are except for that future, you're putting your total consciousness on the future event.

TGU: Well, it's more like you're *dimming* your consciousness by *only* thinking of the future event. Just as you can be very much aware of yourself, and you can be very alive, eating an ice cream cone, without at all detracting from the taste of the ice cream, in fact enhancing it, by being conscious *of yourself* enjoying the ice cream cone – so you can do the same thing while you're totally involved in an artistic or creative or an academic or any kind of endeavor that requires you to focus outward.

It would be desirable for you to learn to focus outward *without* dimming the lights inward. That's really what's meant there. Or if it isn't meant, it's what *should* be meant. You are *always* here to choose. The more consciously you choose, the more you will get out of the experience. Now, having said that, there are some things that people deliberately *don't* put their consciousness in. People in a lynch mob withdraw their consciousness from what they're doing, although they don't know it. That's why mobs are so much less intelligent than individuals.

So, we would say, by all means live in the now. And while you're in the now, do what you want, which includes planning, remembering, fantasizing, daydreaming, active thought, scholastic comparisons – all of that can be done with you sitting in the middle of the spider's web enjoying yourself. [pause]

[Humorously] First we called you a worm, now you're a spider. We don't know how this is going. [they laugh] You haven't been a dinosaur yet. [they laugh]

Personality and Affinity

R: *Okay, in an earlier session [session five] I asked a question that you declined to answer at that time.*

TGU: Because you had other fish to fry that night.

R: *Yes. I'm asking whether this "later" is "now" on this question, and if it's not, we'll move to something else. My question was, when we talked about the relationship between you and Frank, you indicated that you're not working with Frank as an assignment, but rather what you called a relationship of affinity. Can you say more about that?*

TGU: The part of that assignment idea that we don't like particularly is the implied person who assigns. However, we have to say that since we declined to answer that, you've also made us wonder whether or not we're being more directed than we thought we were.

All right. By now you are more in tune with reality as we see it over here, which is that it's sort of a floating coalition of individuals intimately linked, and more fluid than it is where you are. Therefore Frank's advisors – and of course yours, but we'll stick to Frank– [pause] All right, let's back up here just a little bit.

Have you ever noticed, in yourself or in others, that in different parts of yourself you seem to be radically different people? You have interests that are all-consuming, and then you rather lose interest in those interests and others take their place, or maybe nothing takes their place. And you have propensities or you have avocations or you have...You know, the *flavor* of your life changes from time to time, and it's almost as though there were someone else living it, in retrospect.

Well, as those shifts happen on your side, different members of the poker club over here horn in on the game. If you become interested in stock car racing, those of us who resonate more with motors and noise and mechanics and competition and living on the edge – that kind of thing – will move in because that's the affinity. When the person loses interest in stock car racing and develops more interest in drinking beer [chuckles] there are others who resonate with more quiet (not necessarily quiet, but could be quiet) perhaps introspective, perhaps emotionally nurturing, perhaps [pause] Hmm, you're going to get us on a lecture on drink here in a moment.

But whatever a person's proclivities are at a given moment, there will be those on our side who will resonate to that, and they'll move in (except of course there's no movement). So it wouldn't be accurate to say anyone was assigned to do anything, except in the largest sense of all of us being assigned to all of you. You see? It's much more like, we're invited to kibitz.

R: So there's not a core group that you would say was –

TGU: Only in the sense that there's a core to any of your personalities, which there is. But only that. If you radically change your being because of internal or external or combination of circumstances, then the guys, as you say, on the other side will change as well. Not because they're required to, but because – it's so automatic it's hard to even give you a sense of it.

R: You also said something that was more difficult for me to understand. You said that some of you are more closely connected in an on-going way; an affinity of soul.

TGU: That's more or less the same thing. Because the core essence of a person doesn't really change during a lifetime, those of us on the other side that are the closest in affinity to that core don't change either, but we don't mean more than that.

R: Okay. You're calling that a spiritual affinity rather than a task affinity, or something of that sort.

TGU: That's right. A person's task affinity can change radically because they can in the course of their lifetime change what they're doing. They could start off being a politician and wind up being an artist. But their core being is less likely to change, and they could be a dreamy introvert of artistic proclivities and spend 20 years in politics, sort of working against their own nature, and then move into becoming a painter and be more comfortable with what they are. But their internal essence hasn't really changed much, and so a relationship of affinity is less likely to change, merely because the underlying personality is very unlikely to change. It can develop, it can have snags, it can even go in the wrong directions, but it's liable to be the same thing.

Between Lives

R: Was Frank a part of your collectivity between his earth lives?

TGU: [pause] Well, you're going to get tired of hearing it, but – yes and no. Yes, in that all of you are a part of us even right now. No, in that there *was* no Frank.

There was the underlying being that is now Frank and in other times is Bertram or David, you see. Remember we said that when you are on the other side you're not quite the same, even mentally, as you were when you're on this side, because you're in different circumstances? Well, when you go on the other side, you won't be the same. The penumbra of you, that *flavor* of you, will remain, as we said, but maybe that penumbra goes to, oh, San Francisco in the 1940s, and hangs out. You know? Has fun for a while. And then maybe goes elsewhere and fools around, and then maybe goes into another lifetime. During all that, that part of that existence can't be said to be one of us in that respect. However there, as here and now, a part of that existence *is* us, and we are it. Impossible to explain using one perspective, but we think you're getting the idea by us continually *shifting* perspectives.

R: Yes, but one of the things that seems to happen between lives is that there is some energy or other doing some planning about the next –

TGU: Remember, we said you're doing that now, as well.

R: Yes, you did.

TGU: You're planning, moment by moment. So you're always planning.

R: Mm-hmm. But that energy becomes a more diffuse energy once out of the physical?

TGU: [pause] Let's say the center of gravity shifts. While you are on your side and you have a body to coalesce around – a body that sort of holds the various pieces together – you have more of a specific gravity, so to speak, than you do when you *don't* have the body holding it together, and your various bodies can go in various directions, and various parts of your consciousness can become relatively dissociated. (Not in a pathological sense.) So that the part of you that is living in a belief system territory then may forget what it knew about us while you were here. That's the *nature* of the belief system territories, really. [Monroe terminology for non-physical recreations of physical environments.] And the people who can remember being part of us, avoid all that. That's the point. The point of many things, really. [pause]

There's nothing wrong with doing that. We don't want to say that it's a detour or that it's unhealthy or anything like that. People go to those vibrations because that's where they're vibrating. By definition. And so it's the appropriate place for them at that time.

But, on the other hand – to contradict ourselves as always – from our point of view it's better if you can remember yourselves. If you remember yourself and *don't* do that, and *don't* let your consciousness diffuse, then yes, you'll be on our side with us and you may not come back. [pause] Avoiding the wheel [of reincarnation], in effect.

R: So that sounds as though the planning aspect would be easier done while we're in body.

TGU: Well, easier in the sense that –

R: We're more coherent somehow.

TGU: More coherent in the sense that you have a continuity to your consciousness that is upheld and supported by your bodies. But less so because you're stuck within the space-time-slices mentality, or matrix. So it has advantages; it has disadvantages.

R: So I guess, deciding to come back in physical body or not is clearly one of the choices.

TGU: Well – [pause, chuckles] You're never going to get a straight answer out of us, you might as well just resign yourself to it. The question there depends on who's making the choice. If a person is in a position to make the choice, fine, they can make the choice. If their mind is too clouded or too diffuse for them to make the choice, another part of themselves will make it for them, and it will seem to them like it's made beyond their own control. All right?

R: Another part of them –

TGU: Just as we're another part of you, say. So when your Downstairs has been razed because you're dead here, you're on the other side, what *was* your Upstairs has not lost its clarity of vision, or its wider view. But *you* may well have lost the pointedness that you had because you were in one slice of time and one slice of space. In that changed condition, you may be very much dependent upon what is what you now call your Upstairs to put you back into the earth to give you another place to stand. It's not a punishment, it's not a reward; it's the only place for you to apply yourself, if you're in certain mental situations.

If you have developed yourself to the point that you can hold your mental clarity and your mental focus without a body, then it becomes a matter of choice whether you come back or not. But if you can't, in the absence of coming back, you'd be unable to develop, you'd be unable to function, really, beyond a very minimal way, because that part of yourself wouldn't have enough consciousness to function.

Again, the thing that will clarify this more than anything else, is to listen to all these explanations and then rephrase them from the opposite point of view. We just gave all of this as though we believed that all of you were individuals. Now, rephrase it, starting with all of us as one, and you see that what you have is that we, as one, developed individual pieces of ourself, as best we can, and when those pieces need to be cooked a little more, we put them back in the frying pan. [they chuckle] If that doesn't make sense, tell us and we'll pursue it.

R: *I'm following, but I don't know if I'm getting all of my questions answered about this.*

TGU: Pursue, by all means.

The Uses of Physical Matter

R: *[pause] It's seen by some religious groups as though having the choice of not returning to a body is somehow the ultimate reward, or the ultimate state to seek, and I'm not hearing that from you.*

TGU: Not at all. We think they're making a basic mistake. Perhaps not such a big mistake, but we think they're confusing the fact that those who achieve and are able to hold their consciousness on the other side don't *need to* come back – which is clearly a gain – with the thought that not coming back is *in itself* a gain. Which it is not. You see? The appropriate place and the appropriate time *is* the best place and time. Sometimes being in 3D Theater is, sometimes not. What is gain is the ability to hold yourself away from it if you want to.

Now, they've got that, but they've sort of tangled it up with the idea that earth is inherently painful, diversionary, illusory, and in general undesirable. And we would say earth is inherently painful and illusory and eminently desirable. [pause] It's not the only game in town, but it's a nice game.

R: *And the other choices are very limited from our view here. We think, well, maybe we could be living on another planet or something of that sort, but the choices beyond that aren't very clear to us.*

TGU: You must understand, when we say coming back to earth, we don't necessarily mean *this* earth. To us, all physical matter is physical matter. We ought to make that clear, probably. To us, if you come back on another star system, you're still living on an earth; you're living *in* 3D. Even if the physical laws are somewhat different.

R: *And is it true that while we're in this state, we would be totally unable to understand what some of the other choices might be that didn't involve living on a star system?*

TGU: Well [pause] it will be more understandable the more you're able to reflexively see things both from an individual viewpoint and at the same time the contrary-seeming "all is one" viewpoint. The more you get stuck in one viewpoint or the other, the more distortion comes in. You see, here's why: because if you think of yourselves as monads, as individuals, as really the center of the universe for you, there's nothing wrong with that, to a degree. But if you're then going to try to envision what it will be like when you're not in a body but you still think of yourself as an individual, you're making a basic logical shift in the middle of the sentence! And of course it's going to invalidate things. However, since you can't really envision what it's like to be over here, as part of one, without having lost your individuality – a good halfway house is to go back and forth between the two. [pause]

A better question, a more pointed question, will get a more pointed answer about what the possibilities are. We don't know where to go with this at the moment. You might –

R: Let's leave it for now. I want just to comment that these sessions have given me what seems like a much better notion of what it would be like to be in the oneness state where you are. This undoubtedly is distorted in lots of ways, and yet I have a sense of beaming in on something there that's much more understandable than it's ever been before.

TGU: Well, we're delighted for two reasons. One is that your basic integrity deserves to be responded to, and two is, you're also a very powerful lens, and you can focus this for others. So again, you're part of the Plan B.

Shifting Consciousness

[Rita and I had told people on the Voyagers Mailing List, a Monroe-oriented computer group, and others we sent transcripts to, that we would welcome hard questions for the guys about life, the universe, and everything, to test TGU's limits.]

R: All right. A group of questions have come in to Frank, based on the material from past sessions. I'd like to ask some of these.

This came from a person who's asking can he simply shift his consciousness, becoming one of the other versions of himself, and thus I guess be in a much happier life circumstance.

TGU: All right, that's an interesting question. It's founded, though, on a misunderstanding, we think. [pause] We'll back up, as always.

Let's say there are 50 versions of you – a vast understatement, but let's say there are 50. We're talking about 50 versions of you in your present lives, just because of different choices. All those versions exist and always did exist. It isn't like they were created only when you chose, because when you chose you went down one or the other that already existed. To say "can I change my consciousness to move over to another life that took better choices" – which is in a sense what he's asking – is to think that he can leave any path. And in fact the actual reality is you *all* are on *all* paths. As we've said earlier, we can't answer a question that says "will this happen or will it not happen" because the answer is always "yes it will" and "no it won't"! [laughs]

So we know where he's going, and we're not avoiding his question, but it's important to say first off that in fact he *is* on *all* those paths, because there's no other way that it could be, just as you can't not be in three dimensions. You can't on Tuesday the 14th decide you're not going to be in height that day, you're only going to be in depth and width. You *have to be* in all dimensions, all the time. *We* have to be. And all those alternate possibilities are, from our point of view, dimensions. Given that he's in all those dimensions, it becomes a matter of him moving his consciousness to something that's actually there. Remember we talked about miracles being the moving from one state to another state, as moving from one reality, basically, to another reality that's identical to the first except in the way that one wants it to be changed. Yes he could, but no he probably can't.

"Yes he could," because the potential is there. "No he probably can't," because the belief required would probably be overwhelmingly difficult for him. If he wants to try an experiment, we suggest that he try changing very little things. [pause] Change the weather from moment to moment. Or change insignificant trifles, that can't be accounted for logically. It would be impossible for him to verify it, and he should forget about verifying it. But he can *experience* it, and that will get him on his way. Bearing in mind, of course, that his question that "he" thought of to ask was undoubtedly prompted, [laughs] which means that it's probably an important question for him, as well as for those listening.

Focus of Consciousness

R: *Now, all of those alternative paths have a consciousness attached to them, or not?*

TGU: Remember, we said that all of those paths could be considered to be theoretical until and unless you move your consciousness to turn them into reality? There's no inherent difference in them. The inherent difference is in you, is in where *you* put your focus now. If you visit the insane asylums, you will find people there who have inadvertently expanded their consciousness to the point that they are experiencing several fluctuations at the same time, or in close proximity, and they have no idea what's happening to them.

R: *That's interesting.*

TGU: And there's no way for them to explain it.

R: I don't know if I got my question answered or not; let me ask it again.

TGU: Mm-hmm. Always a good procedure. It will always be slightly different.

R: All these alternatives are possible for this man who is asking about changing his consciousness. But the other alternatives don't have a consciousness attached to them?

TGU: That's not exactly true. [pause] The logical difficulty for you all is that you are aware of what you're aware of, and you're very much unaware of the huge amount that you're unaware of. That's what we're talking about, about expanding the limits of your consciousness. You have your consciousness on *all* those paths. When you pop out of this lifetime, you will have experienced all of those paths, not just one. Sort of. Well, wait a minute. [pause, laughs]

Frank is arguing with it. No, that's what we mean to say. [pause]

All right, it will be easier for you to understand if we confine it to seemingly inanimate objects. There is a reality in which a leaf falls on one side of a fence, another reality in which the leaf falls on the other side of the fence, a third one in which it doesn't fall at all, a fourth one in which it never grew in the first place. All those realities are equally real. They're real, as far as you're concerned, only when, as, during, and because, you're walking down that reality. When you pick a path, or wander down a path, or get diverted down a path, the other paths might as well not exist for you, but they *do exist*. In each of those paths, there's a version of *you*. And *you're* choosing which version you wish to animate, so to speak, by your choices. So that when you come out of your life – remember we've said you're here to choose and choose and choose and choose? All of those choices will have in their aggregate determined your path. They will have determined the flower that you are by what has happened to you out of all the myriad possibilities, [pause] most of which by necessity are only shadows to you. The path not taken is always a shadow to you. But that *doesn't* mean it's a shadow to an outside observer seeing you walking down it.

R: But the reason it's a shadow is because you're not putting your consciousness on that other path.

TGU: No, not exactly. It's more like it's a shadow *to you* because you're not aware that in fact your consciousness *is* on that path. Your consciousness is *everywhere*, but your *focus of consciousness* is only on one at a time. It's very difficult to make that clear, we understand that. The easiest analogy for you who have Monroe backgrounds is to say that all given possibilities are Focus 23, and walking any one of those turns it into C1 temporarily, for yourself.

Okay, this is interesting, we'll go on a little bit. Let's suppose that the three musketeers are in Focus 23. Any three friends, relatives, whatever. They all take different paths, and let's say they all take paths in which they all stay together. But they all take *different* paths in which they all stay together. From any one of their points of view, this is the only real thing, because there are their friends, there are they, they know they're conscious; this is what it is; they and their friends could not have taken a different crossroad.

Another one of those friends, having been in the reality that took a different crossroad, sees it exactly the same way: "This is obviously, self-evidently, the only real *real* choice. The others were theoretical choices. Because here I am, here are my friends. I can see them, I can touch them, I can feel them" Okay? But the outside observer looks and he sees all three paths, all three paths taken, all three paths animated. But there are paths a, b, and c; there are friends 1, 2 and 3, and – well, back up a little.

Tell us when this starts to lose you, and we'll back up a little more. But, for each of you, if your consciousness could extend outside of time-space, as ours does, you would see yourselves so radically differently that you'd realize that you are simultaneously in all possible realities; you couldn't *not be* in any of them. (Except the ones in which you don't belong, you know. If there's a reality in which you're dead, you're not in that reality once you die.) In all the ones that you belong, you're in all possible realities. Always. You have to be.

R: Along with your consciousness.

TGU: Yes. But, *you* only are aware of the consciousness pertaining to wherever you are. The other ones are only aware of where *they* are. And so your next question – we can hear it – is which one is the real one. And the answer is, yes! [they laugh]

R: That wasn't my question. My question is, you've made a distinction between consciousness and point of consciousness.

TGU: Yes. If your full consciousness is a hundred units, your effective consciousness at any given time may be only 3 units. The other 97 units are closed to your awareness. There's no absolute change, it's just that your light doesn't shine that far.

R: Well, it seems an odd definition of consciousness, that one can be conscious in multiple realities without being aware of that consciousness.

TGU: Good! This is a perfect example of how shifting your analogy back and forth between our side and your side will help you see this.

From our side, it's perfectly obvious that at any given time, only a small part of your consciousness is lit up, even in *one* reality. But it's also perfectly obvious that the other consciousness is there. Now, you often call it the subconscious. When you're asleep and dreaming, what you call your conscious awareness hardly flickers. But you're not any less aware from our point of view than you are when you're in full waking consciousness.

Again, and again and again, and not just for you but for your readers, it is *so helpful* to keep shifting viewpoints, because it stops you from making those inadvertent redefinitions in the middle of a statement. Well, it won't *stop* you, but it'll correct you after the fact. [they laugh]

R: Well then, how do we think about your consciousness?

TGU: How *do* you think, or how *should* you think? [laughs] [coughing]

R: How would we? How is it possible to think of your consciousness? When you're seeing everything, and you're conscious therefore of everything, I guess –

TGU: You'll remember, we said that our consciousness is a more expanded version than yours, but less of a pointed version than yours. And we know we'll never hear the end of it, but we're somewhat in a fog *in that sense.*

R: [chuckles]

TGU: And so you could look at it perhaps that your ordinary consciousness is a background light, and your full awareness is a flashlight, or a beam of some kind, that is more intensely aware. Your conscious intent – your flashlight – is brighter than ours; it's just that our background lighting extends forever. The difference between your flashlight and your background lighting is so great that it often seems to you that there's no light but the flashlight.

R: I see that. All right, let's see. I'll move on to another question here.

TGU: You're making us work tonight.

R: Yes, that's good.

TGU: We think so.

An Exercise

R: This notion about Seth has come up a number of times, equating what is happening here with the Seth energy that came through Jane Roberts. Is this an appropriate analogy here?

TGU: We'll set you an exercise, actually. We'll answer this at another time, but in the meantime we'll set you an exercise. Look at that question from our side. In fact, look at it from your side, then try to move your mind around it and see how we would see it from our side, and then move your own to see how you would respond to our theoretical response. Do this with pencil and paper, if you wish. If you don't wish, that's fine. This is a *good* exercise to get you started, because there's no point in just listening to us. This is a good exercise to get you started to see how you can learn to *dig*. So if you don't mind, let's do that. Leave that as an exercise. We'll answer it later, but in the meantime, people may find themselves surprised at how much they know that they don't suspect they know. It would be better, when they're trying to do it from our side, to get into a mild meditative state. Those who have tapes, put them in Focus 10.

R: All right.

TGU: That'll fix 'em.

R: [chuckles] A little challenge there.

TGU: It's – it's a *big* challenge. Because this habit could change their life, much for the better. We know that's a large statement, but it's true.

TGU and Using a Body

R: All right. [pause] Another questioner of Frank's was asking him what your energy sounds like to him; how do you speak and so on, but he goes on to ask what are your limits if any in regard to use of the body. [pause] Do you understand that question?

TGU: Oh yes. Well, Frank already answered that question on the internet.

R: He answered about the nature of the voice and how that came across and sounded.

TGU: No, the other answer was actually a sufficient answer, and that was that because he's there, we're not going to get away with too much. Meaning, in order for us to move his body, we would need his permission to such a degree that it would be the same thing as him moving the body, really. You, Rita, will notice the gestures we make are his gestures, because we're translating through him. If we were to be like – no, we're going to stay away from Seth until we get people's answers [laughs].

Without violating free will, we can't take over a person. If we take over a person with their full consent, we can't do as good a job as they can do, because it's a complicated diving suit you're wearing. It would unnecessarily take a lot of our attention and energy. Try running *us* from *your* side! [laughs]

R: Well that wouldn't be a fair challenge. Maybe the Seth challenge is a fair challenge. By the way, Frank doesn't make many gestures when you're coming through.

TGU: That's because *we're* not Italian.

R: [Ignoring that] Very, very limited, practically none at all. He talks about them as his normal gesturing, but there isn't any gesturing to speak of.

TGU: Well, hardly. There's occasional movements.

R: Very, very few.

TGU: Very few. That's right. And this is because when he first began listening to the Monroe tapes, he made a particular effort not to move a muscle, out of what... Well, we were sort of taking advantage in a way. Using the idea that, if he moved a muscle he would ruin the state. But it actually was a back door way of getting him to relax at a level that he ordinarily didn't relax at. He's very high-strung, and we needed to unstring him somewhat. [they laugh]

R: Well, it works very well; that's just an observation.

Alternate Realities

R: All right, I have one more question here, and I must say, I don't understand the question. I can read the words, and maybe you understand it. This gentleman says: "I would like to encourage folks to explore the notion of alternate realities as convergent, this juxtaposed to the notion of alternate realities as divergent. It is also significant to incorporate the notion of duration or extent – e.g. is the duration of a divergent alternate reality finite, i.e. does coherence/cohesion diminish through divergence."

TGU: Well, we understand the question, but it's based in a misunderstanding of what we're saying. Let's see if we can explain this.

That question is rooted in the assumption that you begin with one unit, and it splits, and splits, and splits. And his question is, do they then converge and become one unit again, or do they diverge continually and more so. You see? And we would say that's a misunderstanding. It appears to your consciousness that things split, but in actual fact all possible paths exist. It isn't like they only exist at the time – well, wait a minute.

Again, it's a matter of viewpoint. You could look at it this way and say, "all paths exist before anybody has to make any choices, in the way that the background for a video game is all on the CD ROM before anybody puts it in the machine." Or, you could say, "you exist in a wilderness of choices and every choice you make takes you to another place that may or may not have been in existence before the combination of choices created it."

We know those sound like radically different situations, but actually they're meaningless differences. Because, the center of creation is not material, but consciousness, so it's more a question of "which way are you going to see it" than it is of "which way is it really that you're finally seeing."

Perhaps we didn't say that clearly. We could do it again. It isn't a question of which of those two realities is correct, it's more a question of which way do you prefer to see it. Because it's the consciousness that's central, not the seeming reality. So this rather intelligent question comes from a point of view that assumes movement, whereas in fact the movement is actually a movement of consciousness among places, rather than a movement of things on which consciousness rides. That being so, the answer is, "sure they diverge!" and the answer is also "no, of course they don't diverge!" All possibilities exist.

Did that clarify the question for you, by the way?

R: Yes it did. Very much so. There's a continuation here, which I think is another question.

"Does the notion of consensus reality mean 'we all agree' or does it mean 'our views integrate'? Are alternate realities a field of possibilities from which a time-space stream arises? When a view concedes to integration, manifestation is possible. Again, consider the notion of alternate realities as convergent."

TGU: Well, again we would say it's still based on a misunderstanding. [pause] Let's take it piece by piece. Read the first sentence of that?

R: "Does the notion of consensus reality mean 'we all agree' or does it mean 'our views integrate'?"

TGU: Okay, that's enough. You should see by now that that is based entirely on your side. And a good exercise for him and for you and for others would be, rephrase that question seeing from our side. When you do that you'll see that it's not the question that it appears to be, and the answer of course is, yes and no. Because it's not a real choice. It's not a real "it has to be either/or"; it's a choice of consciousness, is all.

R: All right, and this continued, "Are alternate realities a field of possibilities from which a time-space stream arises?"

TGU: You see again, it's based in the idea of movement. He's clever about the duration, but it's based on the idea of movement rather than on universal pre-existence, or universal creation on the moment. See, it's not an important distinction, although it seems like it, but once you move your center to the consciousness rather than to what the consciousness is perceiving, you see that it's strictly a matter of individual choice.

All right. You should tell them that of course we're willing to go more about any of these questions if they have supplementaries.

R: That's all the questions I have.

TGU: Well that's good, because we're billing you for overtime.

R: We still haven't run out of the second side of the tape, but we're probably pretty close.

TGU: All right. Well, this is always a pleasure.

R: Indeed. Very much so.

TGU: And we'll see you in a week.

Session Nine
October 9, 2001

R: Maybe this is me nit-picking, and we can turn off my nit-picking at any time, but I tend to get caught up in things like definitions, and making sure I understand what we're talking about, and –

TGU: Could we re-phrase that? We would say you tend to get caught up in trying to get clarity! That's what you're supposed to do! [they laugh]

R: Oh good.

TGU: [laughs]

Channeling

R: All right, I think the first one will be easily taken care of. It has to do with the word "channeling." Frank has not used that word for what's going on here, on the grounds that he is present. To me that doesn't exclude that definition at all. Being present or not present is a matter of whether the consciousness can tolerate being present or not. So when someone asks "is this channeling?" I hate to say no because I think it is. Do you have any suggestions around that word?

TGU: Well, five or six years ago we suggest the term ILC – Intuitive Linked Communication – as a term that will indicate what we're doing as opposed to trance channeling. The concern on Frank's part is almost an editor's concern, not wanting to leave the initial wrong impression that then has to be corrected. So in avoiding the word channeling, he was avoiding [comparison to] Ramtha and even Jane Roberts, you know, because he felt there was a significant difference between what he was doing and what they're doing, and at the same time there's a large unacknowledged gap in your language. There *is* no real word for what you're doing. You know how Eskimos may have 57 words for ice, depending on various qualities of ice that *you* can't even see, because you don't live in that environment. Well, the English language lumps so many different variants of communication under the word "channeling" that the word channeling has very little meaning beyond "someone who is still in the body communicating with something by non-sensory means." And that's a very vague and unhelpful definition.

So we sympathize with the attempt to get away from the word channeling, for fear of the unexamined assumptions that people put around the word. We invented ILC because we thought it was catchy enough that people might take to using the initials, and because intuitive linked communication does express pretty well what's going on.

Now, just as a sidelight, of course ILC happens between people in bodies all the time. And that's another plus for using it, because again we're stressing that the difference between us and you is the turf we're on, rather than the being that we are. We don't care, though. Use what you want.

R: I've done quite a bit of work in this arena, and I haven't had the experience of exactly what's going on here. So I can easily feel that we need other language. Maybe we have to use several concepts to describe it, but it is quite different from the experiences I've worked with, in which people are channeling or in which people are doing several other variations of this same getting information from a non-physical source.

TGU: Well of course, as pioneers, one of your jobs is to hack paths through the forest. Linguistic differentiations are both the product and the source of better understanding of distinctions.

R: This could be a very helpful part of the book, I think, too. Say some more about those issues.

TGU: Well we don't know anything about those issues. [they laugh] We'll be glad to, any time you want. You know it as individuals, but you don't always know it in the moment when you're thinking about a different subject. It's always true that *your language shapes your perceptions.* Your language embodies so many understandings of the world that you could almost say it becomes necessary to speak incorrectly if you're going to get any new understanding. Not quite, but almost. And in the absence of that, you have to do what *we* have always done: which is, look at it from one point of view, and then another, and then another and then another, to try to triangulate it, because you can't really describe it, you have to sort of look at the view from different viewpoints and hope that it comes across.

R: All right. [pause] I think that's also going to be a continuing topic here.

Definitions of Consciousness

R: Another definitional issue here. Last week, you differentiated between consciousness, awareness, and focus of consciousness. And you also differentiated between full consciousness and effective consciousness. I struggled with all of these, and I came out thinking that we could say that effective consciousness and awareness are the same thing in your definitions, and that they are both the same thing as focus of consciousness and the flashlight.

TGU: Correct with the minor caveat that the word "awareness" actually folds in several different kinds of awareness that vary. Let's just bookmark that for the future. But yes, that's exactly right.

R: That is confusing, and we'll have to spend some time thinking about how to best deal with that. Because often people think of overall consciousness and aware-ness as the same thing.

TGU: We think that if you will begin to explore this with us – you, Rita – from the unusual and quite unorthodox perspective of regarding what you commonly call your subconscious as part of the background consciousness, we think – if you'll pardon the play on words – it'll illuminate the whole subject.

There is no such thing as a subconscious different from a conscious, except situ-ationally. There's not one piece here and another piece over here and they're sepa-rate but they sometimes communicate. The areas of your full consciousness that aren't lit up are what you're considering subconscious. And that starts off looking like a quibble, but as you look at it more, you'll see, it will illustrate more.

R: I have more than a quibble about the word subconscious, because that has specific meanings in the field of psychology, and particularly psychoanalysis. And so I think we have to be very careful how we use that word.

TGU: Well, bear in mind, if we're going to do this, we're doing it for an audi-ence whose familiarity with all these terms is not predictable. Therefore, the very things that you're worried about are the things that will tease out the meanings. So as we come out with the words unconscious, and subconscious, and shadow and full consciousness and all that – how *we* see all of that, as opposed to how *you* see it – will be more clearly laid out by your laying out the way you see it, and it just so happens [chuckles] that you happen to be knowledgeable about that subject. What a coincidence.

R: [chuckles]

TGU: There's method to our madness.

R: There are big chunks of things we have to deal with. And one thing we can do is simply say that, "for the purposes of this book, this is what this means." So that we don't have to use a language that's acceptable to a whole body of –

TGU: Oh no. No, no, we're going to be extremely politically incorrect. [chuckles] We meant, you have the ability to set out the way that it's commonly accepted, at least in Jungian terms. *We* have the ability to pick that apart and say "if you take this term which you use for that, and realize that this term and this term are actually looking at the same thing in two different ways and thinking they're two different things..." You see? That process will tease out a tremendous amount of meaning and even if your readers don't know where they're left, it will still be worthwhile because they will begin to effectively think about something that at most they've only read about and passed on. It will give them a place to stand on the subject.

Intelligence Inherent in Universe

R: Another phrase you used was "the intelligence of the universe," and although I thought I understood what you were saying in context, is there some more you can say about that? [pause] I mean, I know there's some more you can say about that: Would you say some more about that? What do you mean by the intelligence of the universe?

TGU: We don't know in context either.

R: Okay, I could easily find that section. Fortunately I've marked the page and part. But let's not bother to do that now and waste our time. I can run it down later.

Frank: Well, see – now, this is Frank again. This is exactly what I wondered would happen. When you asked them a question and nothing happened, I'm going, "okay, how come they don't have an answer for that?" I don't know the answer, but – [laughs]

R: It would probably be helpful to get that reference.

Frank: Yeah, but why shouldn't they know? Anyway, all right, we won't worry about that. We'll go back in.

R: Well, it's interesting because it suggests an intelligence inherent in the universe. Not all people would subscribe to that idea. I think that's a very interesting idea.

Frank: It's self-evident!

R: Well in a way it seems self-evident, and yet what does that really mean?

Frank: Well, I'll tell you exactly what it means. [Sliding back into TGU's "voice," their "feel," in the next few words.] Anyone who could believe that the universe is not intelligent, could only do so by believing that at least part of the universe is *dead*, is *matter*, is something other than the great thought. That's the only way that one could force oneself to believe that the universe or any part of the universe is *not* intelligent. Starting with the universe as consciousness, as – for lack of a better word – spirit, it's by definition impossible for it *not* to be intelligent. This is the way we see it, anyway.

R: All right. So there are all of those assumptions in it, that are important –

TGU: Well, they *are* assumptions, aren't they, but it seems like just stating that the sky is blue.

R: And of course there's no reason to believe that the sky is blue. Analyze it –

TGU: Why bother? Just look! [they laugh]

R: Okay, you think that's self-evident also, huh? Let's move on.

Group Minds and Animal Minds

R: Another follow-up from last week. I asked about co-creation between you – the guys upstairs – and a life form, and you gave the example of a maple tree, and noted that it was better to think of one generic maple tree than to think of ten thousand maple trees.

TGU: We didn't say better, we just think it's more useful, more accurate.

R: So my question is, would you say that maple trees or other life forms such as whales, for example, have a group mind?

TGU: [pause] If you hadn't said whales, we would say yes, because everything has a group mind, including even things like clouds and rocks, even things that are quite ephemeral, because that kind of mind is fed directly from what you call the other side, rather than having to be passed on genetically. The reason we hesitate on whales is they have a group mind in the same way as you have a group mind, but they also have individuality in the way you have individuality. More so than, say, a maple tree. Their flashlight is a much brighter flashlight than maple trees.

R: And is the distinguishing point at the difference between plants and animals, or where is that?

TGU: Mmm. [long pause] You understand, any distinguishing point, by definition, is going to be arbitrary. Or we could put it this way, by definition it's going to be by definition. [they chuckle]

If we had to give you a rule of thumb, we would say that yes, you could make the limit between plants and animals. Animals have more ability, and therefore more responsibility, to take care of themselves as individual units. You know? A tree, being planted, granted it puts out chemicals and granted that it can defend itself in limited ways, still basically it is where it's planted, and that's its life, whereas a deer or a woodchuck or a mouse can enhance or detract from its own life by its own decisions.

Therefore the circumstances of animal life automatically imply a certain budding out from the common consciousness more into a consciousness of the individual.

However all of your animals obviously have instinct. What is that instinct? It's actually the group mind providing the underpinning of the life.

R: You could say, I guess, they have more choices.

TGU: They have more choices physically, and therefore they have to *make* more choices which makes them slightly more aware. They *have to be* more aware.

R: The reason I'm bringing this up is because I didn't understand why you felt it was more useful to think of a generic maple tree rather than a thousand individual trees.

TGU: Well, in fact, the maples are more like *a* maple sharing a group mind than they are like each individual maple being a part of a community. That's the distinction we were trying to draw. Again, as in most things, you could look at it the other way and there would be a certain justice to it. Things can always be seen more than one way.

R: Well, within the animal kingdom, is there just a gradually progressive, more and more individuality, or individual choices, or –

TGU: Along what scale?

R: Along the scale of the developmental complexity of animals.

TGU: [laughs] Well –

R: An amoeba presumably would have a different number of choices than an elephant.

TGU: Oh yes! Yes. We thought you were going to try to establish a hierarchy between cats, deer, and horses, say.

R: Not to establish the hierarchy, but to assume there is one.

TGU: Yes. Well, in general, the easiest way is to assume that as the abilities are greater and the environmental hazards-slash-opportunities – because they're the same thing – are greater, then the nature of that existence will call forth more separation from the herd.

R: And what does group mind mean when you get to the human being?

TGU: Well – look at it from our end. If *we* are in continual contact with each of *you*, as we are, and we are the same "we" on our end, then chances are the input that you're each getting has a lot of similarity that is not based on anything you're doing as individuals. So that it's again the nervous system down to the fingers, even though the fingers are in rubber gloves – you remember. Well, the nervous system is the same nervous system, so that will seem to you to function as a group mind. Most people are not even aware you *have* a group mind, if you want to look at it as a group mind. Since you're looking at it that way, well, let's back up a bit here.

From your end, it looks like you have individual consciously created consciousnesses, with subconsciouses and racial subconsciouses and human subconsciouses. All right? But from our end, that's a big confusion, because what you really have are you as individuals continuously and inevitably slopping over between yourselves at your own level, between other *levels* of yourself, between other *lifetimes* of yourself, between other *realities* of yourself, and in all of those cases, at the same time intercommunicating with us back and forth. Now, where is there room for individuality in that? There is, but – there isn't. You see?

There is – but individuality is not what you think it is. It's not as individual or isolated as it feels. You're always in communication with so much, but that communication is so constant, and in a sense it is at such a background level, that it is usually overlooked and not even considered.

So, in that respect you have a group mind because you're all in the same family, you're all in the same mental environment, and you react to things in the same way as others who seem to be individual react, for the very good reason that you and they are reacting to the same things *inside*, regardless what it's like *outside*. Is that too complicated?

Messages from the Other Side

R: No, that's all right. I'm thinking about what we're getting from the other side, because as current events are very clearly indicating, there's a very different message coming from the other side to some parts of the world than there are to other parts.

TGU: Oh, do you think so?

R: Well, it seems that way. What Allah insists on seems quite different from what some perspectives of God requires.

TGU: [chuckles] Oh yes, but Allah and God might have something to say about it if they were consulted! We'll back up here just a bit.

If we from our side pour forth the admonition "love your neighbor," and that admonition goes into a culture which is formed in such a way as to refuse to recognize as neighbors anyone who is not of the same race or class; and in another place goes into a culture where for one reason or another class and racial barriers are more or less irrelevant; and in a third instance goes into an area where it's only class, or only race, the same impulse sent forth will express in very different ways.

R: Be interpreted very differently.

TGU: [pause] Well now, that's an interesting word. Yes, *interpreted* differently, but – that's another way of saying it will be *experienced* differently. The people who get our impulses – which is to say, all of you – yes, it's absolutely true that they *interpret* the impulses, but they don't *think of it* as that, they think of it as "that's what it was." So, because the interpretation is cultural, and it is also (confusingly enough) personal, because it's running through the filters of that individual mind which is shaped by other lifetimes and other realities, blah blah blah, the potential for infinite division or infinite variance of interpretation – is infinite! There's no limit to it. We can send forth a very simple message and have it interpreted approximately six billion different ways! Because of the receiving sets.

Also, do remember, it's not necessarily in your interests that there be no conflict or that there be no progress in this drama. Remember that everyone in any situation is a volunteer, and some of those volunteers are playing heavies. Now, who's a heavy on one side looks different from the other side, but it is not our intent or our wish – even if we could do so – to come up with a conflict-free situation, given that the situation is so heavily toxic and needs to be cleaned.

The day before the airplanes hit the buildings, no one would have described the world situation as wonderful or as something where you would want to stay, or something where you would even expect to be able to stay. So what's different the day after? There are things that are having to be destroyed – and we don't necessarily mean buildings or cities or even civilizations – but there are attitudes, there are certainties, there are, let's say, comfortable assumptions; there are all sorts of things that need to be attacked and destroyed *in the best interests of all concerned.* Well, to do that, you can't have everybody thinking you are getting the same message, you know.

R: Or even thinking they're agreed on things.

TGU: If we were not fundamentally and primarily concerned with your free will, it would be easy. But in the absence of interfering with people's free will, we can only advise, and that advice or those promptings will be processed through the individual's filters, biases, experiences, hopes, dreams, fears, wishes... [pause]

R: All right. I'll leave us stuck there, with the free will.

TGU: It's the greatest gift in the universe, what are you complaining about?

R: [chuckles] I understand that that's true.

TGU: [chuckles] We just want you to grovel a little. [they laugh]

Looking at Seth

R: All right, last session, passing on someone else's questions, I asked about comparison of material that Frank brings forth and the Seth material brought forth by Jane Roberts. And you suggested that we practice looking at this question from your point of view.

TGU: Have you done so?

R: I tried to do that, and I didn't get any new insights, because I find myself going back to things that you have said, and it comes out something like this: From your perspective, you are seeing that we are all a totality that includes Frank and Jane, a totality that's not sliced into time and space segments, yet somehow Frank and Jane each have a collectivity that includes some aspects that are specific to the cores of themselves, so that Frank has The Gentlemen Upstairs, and Jane has a Seth, as well as possible overlapping aspects. And in your position, you could focus on Frank, and/or Jane, but in the two cases, the responding collectivity would be somewhat different in composition for the two of them. So, I don't think these interpretations are wrong, from what you said.

TGU: Well, that's an ingenious first attempt, but it underlines the vast distance we have to go. Very interesting. We had no idea that you'd come at it that way. It's very interesting.

We expected that you would try to imagine where Seth is coming from, from this side. You see? Knowing your Monroe background, we thought that you would say, "well possibly Seth was still in existence in 26. Or in 27." So we thought you were going to say that it would be the difference between us as a sort of collective affinity of Frank's, on the one hand, and Seth as an individual who had an affinity with Jane Roberts from past incarnations together, but was functioning as *an* individual. And instead, you were attempting – as you said – to summarize what we were saying of the difference. Let's pursue this a little, if you don't mind another homework assignment –

R: [chuckles]

TGU: Try this time to *intuit*, to *feel for*, where Seth is, and *what* Seth is on this side. Now *you* will remember, of course, but some of your readers may not, that Seth said specifically he came through this time *without* being in a body for the specific reason of *not being worshipped*, or running the risk of starting a new religion. And that in itself is a small clue. But if you don't mind, we would like you to try that experiment a second time, with the intent of imaginatively reconstructing where Seth is and what Seth does.

R: All right, this is saying it has something much more to do with Seth than the questions came out before.

TGU: Well, you can do the same assignment trying to envision us, but we've told you so much that it would be difficult. We've told you nothing about Seth, and if you *intuit* your way there – if you (so to speak) remote-view his location, in a way it's almost remote viewing – if you try to remote view where Seth is and where he's coming from, well, we'll see how much good that does. We can always try something else.

We're trying to show you that there is a real difference between us and Seth, and give you a sense of what that difference really is. We could say it, but it wouldn't have the texture or anything. It wouldn't lead to the depth of insight.

Crop Circles

R: Okay, I'm going to move to some of the questions that came from people who read this last session. There are a series of questions here about crop circles. Who makes them? How are they made? Why are they made? What are they trying to communicate?

TGU: [pause] The simplest answer – although not the most useful answer – is they're trying to communicate the magical, indivisible nature of the universe. In other words, these are signs coming forth in 3D without ostensible mechanical or physical means, which by definition tells people that they were made in some other way. So the meta-message is that there's more to physical life than physical things. Or a better way of looking at it is, physical matter has a seemingly non-physical component to it. You extend into other realms. Those realms in turn extend into yours, and so they can affect it. Your crop circle phenomenon is – how shall we call it? A prayer? A song? An instruction book? A greeting card? A little of each of those.

Suppose you had two groups of people, races of people, on opposite ends of an ocean, who never saw each other, and who never *could* see each other because for some reason they couldn't cross the ocean, and one found a way to communicate with the other, but they had no common language and no common traditions. How would you begin?

This is the situation of those on the other side – or no, let's clarify that. When we say "on the other side," they're in another dimension, they're not on our side in the way that we are. You know how we say we look at everything that's in the physical as earth, whether it's in Alpha Centauri or here? Well, it's also whether it's here in what you look at as four dimensions, or whether it's here in what they look at as five dimensions, or three dimensions, or six. In other words there's only one earth, but there are all kinds of earths superimposed at different frequencies.

This is another frequency of the earth. What they can do is manipulate the frequency of the wheat in *their* dimension, which has the effect of manipulating it in *this* dimension. You may have read how crop circles are partially formed by the grain growing parallel to the ground rather than at right angles. In other words, they make a right angle on their own stems, without being damaged, or injured.

Well, there's no way to do that in three dimensions. But in another dimension, you just turn it. And if you turn it in that dimension, that's what happens down in three. It's quite simple on their side. The [pause] message is that you will have these symbols appearing in more and more unlikely places including on the sides of cliffs. All right? And when they appear on the sides of cliffs it's going to be more difficult for guys to say it was two men and a board in the middle of the night.

That's one reason it will appear on the sides of cliffs. But they will appear and then disappear. And when crop circles appear, there's residue, you know. They don't go away exactly. But when people have gotten sufficiently accustomed to the crop circles that they actually forget that they were new and magical, then a *new* manifestation will appear, because one of the important things that's being said is that it's new and magical.

So that's the greeting card element. There is an attempt also to convey information, and some of the easiest ways to convey information is to say that "we are as intelligent as you are." So when you have a crop circle that looks like a Mandelbrot set, they're saying, "we know what Mandelbrot sets are"! This tells people on this end who are sufficiently mathematically advanced, "all right, these people must be at least this much advanced." They didn't write e=mc squared, or H2O, but they said "okay, we know this. So if you can recognize this, bingo, you know where *we* are."

Now you may very well ask where this is leading to. And the answer to that will seem to have nothing to do with crop circles, because the answer to that is again, the extension of your consciousness into other realms, into other parts of yourselves, to extend your effective consciousness further. When you do that, you'll be in contact with the people that are making the crop circles. The crop circles by themselves, although they're beautiful, are not the end result, they're the means. When a ship sends a semaphore signal, looking at the beauty of the flags fluttering in the wind is not the point of the exercise. It's okay, it doesn't hurt, but it would be better to read the signal. [laughs] And in this case, many people will believe that they're reading the meaning in the symbols themselves, and that's all right, but be skeptical of people's explanations. It's easier to come up with an explanation than to have the *right* explanation. But the underlying purpose should be self-evident now. They are designed to stretch your way of thinking so that they will stretch your effective consciousness so that you will become more aware of what you are, which, in its own turn, connects you with previously unsuspected facets of the universe.

If you're listening to that sentence carefully, you understand that "facets of the universe" is the same as saying "facets of yourself." Because at that point you're stretching over to our side of the equation, in which we're all one. The more you stretch your perceptions and your everyday consciousness, the more it leads you to see things more our way. That's the fundamental change that's happening in your time. And we will say this, somewhat flatly. *Every* mysterious circumstance that you see in your lives has that same purpose, to lead you to stretch your consciousness and to stretch your awareness, to bring you closer to experiencing and living being both an individual and part of one. It's never been done for a long, long time on earth.

R: I'm aware of this stretching dimension, but I'm finding that, although one can say "all right, I can stretch my imagination to the point where I can see something else in what seems like our space and time," I don't know what to do with that. It sounds like you're saying that the process itself is the achievement, not the interpretation of that phenomenon.

TGU: More or less. You build muscles and flex them, not for the sake of moving the barbells up and down, but for the sake of another purpose later. UFOs, or crop circles, or other things, stretch your ideas about the limits that you've set around your own universe, but then as you get a little familiar with that, the stretching goes further and further. The more you look at them, the more you question. So they remain mysterious, and they actually get *more* mysterious the more you know about them, because you have more detail, and that's part of their purpose. We don't mean to say that they have no purpose on their own and their only purpose is to confuse you into waking up. However, that is *a* purpose. *A* purpose.

But then, so was World War II, in a sense. Beyond the battle of free will that went on in terms of "were individuals going to continue to be encouraged or not," the entire war was, not a *wake up call*, it was a *waking up*. [pause] Digression.

R: Let me just ask if I understood that the energy that's making these crop circles is another form of the earth. A non-physical earth?

TGU: No, it's a physical earth, but it's not the same dimensions that you're in.

R: Another dimension, still physical.

TGU: Yes. That's right.

R: So that the energies from that world are still individual energies who are bringing this about? Or are we now talking about a completely different form of operation here?

TGU: Suppose we told you that it was yourselves?

R: [pause] Well, I would say how am I supposed to understand that?

TGU: It's an encouragement for you to consider that in this way as well, you extend far beyond what you are typically conscious of. You see?

R: To other dimensions?

TGU: Yes, exactly. After all, if from our point of view everything is one, when you carry it over on your end, there are analogies there. You might want to think about it. [pause] All right, how do we say this? Every identity depends upon the viewpoint. We could say that you and your neighbors are all Virginians; all Americans; all inhabitants of earth; all mammals. We could also make divisions at each of those levels, and the divisions would be as real as the unity; it just depends on which way you look.

Well, you that's here now, and you in other places, and you in other times, and you in other dimensions – your jobs, should you choose to accept them, are to pull together your awareness of your underlying unity in all this seeming diversity. Now, this is at least a two step process, because first you have to become aware of the diversity. But that's happening. The next step beyond awareness of the diversity is to become aware of the unity *within* the diversity. This does not have to be completed by next Wednesday.

R: [chuckles] Good. [they laugh] I don't know if I got an answer. Well, I did get an answer, when I was asking how these crop circles come about, what's the process. You're saying we're carrying out the process.

TGU: You could shine a light upon a surface, and something that lived on that surface would experience the light as something extraneous. That's a very rough analogy to what they're doing. They're manipulating one dimension of their own reality in such a way that it shows on your reality. It's a simple thing, but difficult to explain. None of the terms are here. If you will concentrate on the fact that the stalks grow at right angles more or less to what they should grow, without being in any way damaged, and take the implication that that means they were drawn through another dimension and turned – and that's all we can say about that – that'll give you as much sense as you need, because we can't explain it – I mean, if we said, "well the mesons interfered with the" you know. [they chuckle]

R: We wouldn't understand it any better.

TGU: No, that's right. And it's not a reflection of your intelligence; you don't have any of the experience. How would you explain to a fish a bicycle?

R: All right, one of the questions is, "why are they made," and I can understand what you've said about their being made with respect to our information, but what are those individuals who are making them trying to do?

TGU: Exactly what *you're* trying to do. It's a reciprocal process.

R: The being in touch with –?

TGU: Yes. Yes, exactly. And for *them* to be in touch with *you* is a stretch, and for *you* to be in touch with *them* is a stretch, but if you're each stretching, it helps. And if you're sort of touching fingers in the meantime by way of the crop circles, that helps too. Because it [pause] objectifies a possibility, sort of. Gives *you* something to look at, gives *them* something to do with their time [they laugh] and in both cases it focuses your attention. Once you get the idea that it is not the crop circle but the question of contacting the maker of the crop circle, then it focuses both of your attentions on something that will show you that it's not both of you at all. [pause] We could rename the book Paradoxes Are Us, if you wish. [they chuckle]

R: Well, we made a feeble attempt in this direction, I guess, when we first sent out satellites into outer space, to send along elements from our civilizations in hopes that we would communicate with someone out there who might find them.

TGU: But look at the difference in your civilization's assumptions. You sent out a mechanical object, with designs and equations sketched on to it, and thought, someone out there in a different body would look at this piece of information and possibly trace it back to the owner. All of those assumptions packed into that whole project! That it isn't *you* out there; that material objects are the only feasible way, or at least the *most* feasible way, to communicate; that technology is the desired or even the likely interface. You know, there's a lot of assumptions stacked one after another. That mechanistic approach is as far away from us as you can get, and crop circles are nearly as far away from it as you can get. We take your point. Somebody was thinking about contact. But you see, it isn't the same, because they were thinking about contacting *others*. But then, having said that, people who are trying to contact the makers of the crop circles will be thinking of them as other, as well, so, so it's –

R: Yes. And they were done by mechanical means, it looks like, at this end, and –

TGU: Well, we would have thought of it as organic rather than mechanical, but we can see that. All right. It is the manipulation of matter, after all. [yawns]

R: Mm-hmm. You up to another question, here?

TGU: Sure.

ETs?

R: This question is, are you extra-terrestrials? [chuckles]

TGU: [laughs] Are *you*? [they laugh] The question is rooted in some assumptions that we don't share. In the first place, there is no difference between you and extra-terrestrials except where you're living. And there's no difference between you and *us* except where you're living. So again, if you look at it all as one unity, the question falls down.

However, if you look at it from the point of view of diversity, then we would have to say the answer is "no because" – this is strictly looking at it as though diversity were the reality, rather than one way of looking at things – *we* are closer to *you* than anything else there is. And we are of course equally close to the extra-terrestrials than anything else there is. You know? The primary link is between the individual in the physical and us in the non-physical. So asking us if we're extra-terrestrials is putting us on the other side of the divide, so to speak. Now if they're asking are we weird, that's another question.

R: [chuckles] They're asking whether the extra-terrestrials are cooperating with you, and I guess the answer to that is – I don't know who's doing the cooperating, but there isn't the same interaction that you have with us.

TGU: There isn't?

R: There is.

TGU: Yes, there is. Absolutely. Yes, that's right. Well, [laughs] the level of cooperation is different not only between races but between civilizations and between cultures and between individuals, so – we don't know *how* to answer that question! It is unpredictably the same, let's put it that way.

R: Okay. Depends on the extra-terrestrial we're speaking about.

TGU: That's right.

R: Then he asks, what are the ETs doing?

TGU: Same thing the crop circles are doing, on one level. One level is they're stretching your definitions. Another level, [long pause] we hardly know whether to broach the subject. [pause] The ETs are taking huge amounts – well, it seems to you to be huge amounts – of tissue samples. In case you lose it all here, something will be saved. You're living in a society that is destroying your species at an unprecedented rate, and if no one saves the species, they're gone. Obviously.

R: So that is the purpose in what people experience as being taken in ships to some other –

TGU: Well, we were thinking more of the animal and plant samplings to preserve the gene pool. But the gene pool also describes humans. That's not *the* purpose, it's *a* purpose.

R: Okay. And then they ask, why does your side, as well as ETs, communicate with some people and not with others?

TGU: Ha ha ha ha. You know the answer to that question? We expect you do.

R: I assume it's the receivers' willingness and capacity that we're talking about here.

TGU: Yes. Yes. Yes. Not really the capacity, because you can all do it. The main thing is to be able to suspend your disbelief and to be willing to be fooled. If you're not willing to be fooled, you're not open enough. You see? If you're not willing to take the chance, you're not open enough to communicate. Doubt inhibits. That's an absolute flat statement.

And the more you doubt, the more you inhibit. Even if it comes through, then you look at it and you say, "well, I don't know about that." Frank's been through it. [pause] The process of him learning to do this has been one of his having to learn that it is not enough to doubt, it is equally important to be willing to believe, even if provisionally. So you know the old saying, "great doubt, great faith, great determination." This is the attitude that's required, and it takes a little bit of doing. We have no favorites, okay? We play no favorites.

R: [chuckles] You don't prefer Italians, or anything like that?

TGU: [chuckles] Don't give him an opportunity for good lines. [they chuckle] But if your questioner wishes us to speak to him, in fairness he must be willing to listen.

There is no one who cannot and should not – and will not, really, ultimately – engage in this, because, let's put it this way, the *only* point of this is to encourage people to do it themselves. Until they do it they will not have any *knowledge*, they will have *belief*. Now, belief's a good halfway house, but until they do it, they won't know. And once they know, then it's not just a question of knowing, but then it becomes a question of what they actually learn from it, and what it enables them to do, and how it enables them to grow in their own effective knowledge; effective consciousness. [pause] A very good question.

R: Yes, and the next part which seems as though it would already have been answered, is still a good question, and that is, why choose Frank? Why does this work well with Frank and is not working well for others?

TGU: More than any other thing is his willingness to be a fool if he has to be. [pause] If he can learn something, he'll try it. He'll try anything once, or twice, or three times. And he doesn't feel like anything is permanent. So that if he says, "I'm talking to the guys upstairs," and two weeks later, he decides, "you know, I've been making that up," he's willing to do that. And that leaves him free, you see? That leaves him free to jump in with both feet and experience it entirely, without having to say "now for the rest of my life I have to do this because I'm consistent." He has no interest in consistency; he has more interest in truth. So the short answer is, that quality made it attractive. However bear in mind that there are millions of people doing this, and you're only hearing about him because it's being transcribed. Which is another reason why we chose him, but – there are millions of others.

R: *Qualified by knowing how to type.*

TGU: Yes, and he learned how to type in order to be qualified. He knew what he was doing, coming in here!

R: *[chuckles]*

TGU: Not afterwards, but he knew it when he came in.

Exercises for Spiritual Advancement

R: *Well, here's an easy one. A question from the same person.*

TGU: We'd like to know what an easy question is. It'll be interesting to see this.

R: *[chuckles] What would you recommend as the five best exercises for spiritual advancement?*

TGU: [pause] Not an easy one, but it's an awfully good one. [pause] Well, he didn't ask for qualities, he asked for exercises.

Practice love every day. Find some object to love, whether it's a pet or a flower or an abstraction or a car. It would be better if it were a person. As you practice this day by day, raise the bar. So that practice loving something that's successively less lovable. Anyone can love a dog, because the dog thinks you're wonderful. It takes a little more to love a cat, because the cat thinks *it's* wonderful. It takes more to love a woodchuck, because a woodchuck doesn't care one way or the other. It takes more to love a rattlesnake, because you may be afraid of it. You see. So you could easily raise the bar a little bit every day. The practice of love is the practice of overcoming the illusion of distance.

That's really one through five, but another exercise? [pause] Well, this won't seem to have anything to do with the subject. Practice changing points of view. When you are in a dispute – or even if you are in a pleasant exchange with someone – try, every so often, changing into their point of view. Try to *really* see it as they see it, *as opposed* to the way you see it. All right? Swap back and forth. Now, that seems to have nothing to do with spiritual self-development, but you'll be astonished. If you're able to do it. Difficult exercise.

[pause, chuckles]Do we have to come up with five? Those are two very good exercises!

R: We don't, that's true, just because he asked.

TGU: Give us a moment here. [pause] Well, of course, a third one is, practice mindfulness, by which we mean do everything remembering that you are *doing* everything . In other words, don't let your attention flow outward to the object without also being internally lit in your own being. So when you look at the watch, remember that you're looking at the watch; don't only look at the time. When you're driving a car, remember that you're driving a car, don't just only drive the car. Again, this is the kind of exercise that can be scaled up as you get better at it. Although, it's not predictable what will be easy and what will be difficult. It will be different for different people.

So those are three exercises, anyway. You notice what they have in common is, the raising of *a certain kind* of consciousness. Because the giving of love is also an experience of love, it's a becoming familiar with love, so it is a form of consciousness raising, as well. We would leave it at that for now. [pause]

An excellent question.

Finding the Best Way to Spiritual Advancement

R: I think this is another form of the same question here. How can a human select the best way to its spiritual advancement.

TGU: Well, we would add, become on very good terms with your conscience. And we don't mean conscience in the sense of something that's constantly telling you that you did something wrong. We mean – stay on the beam. You know? There's a beam, and once you experience it, you can stay on the beam.

R: This is your conscious mind that you're in touch with.

TGU: Well –. The conscience that we're talking about seems to *you* to be external, seems to you to be not part of yourself, in a way. It is sometimes experienced as being carping. But we're talking about an internal compass –. And from our point of view, that really is you learning to intuitively stay in touch with our advice on our end. Again, ultimately aimed at stretching your awareness.

R: The reality we share, it sounds like.

TGU: There isn't any other.

How to Best Use TGU

R: The next question is, how would you suggest that we use you to get the most value from your wisdom?

TGU: It's actually very well stated in that question: *Use us.* Don't *read about* us, don't *theorize about* us – although there's nothing wrong with that – don't think about us as an abstract warm fuzzy idea. *Use us.* Extend your consciousness to us, extend your openness to us, and grow. It's not complicated, it's not difficult. It requires doing. It's a conscious freewill choice on your end.

R: And then he goes on to ask if it's just a matter of us coming up with questions we think up, and I think it's a good idea for him to do that, however –

TGU: That's right. That makes it almost an intellectual game. And the primary benefit of it is for you to really know that you're not alone, and that you're not accidental, and that you're not meaningless. Those are better rewards than just asking questions. [pause]

R: Well, speaking for the question askers, there's a lot of value in thinking of questions that would be meaningful to ask of such –

TGU: Oh, absolutely! We don't mean to discourage that of course, at all. We're just saying don't *limit* it to that. Knowledge is all well and good, but *living* is the most important thing. You can live without knowledge, but you can't know without – [pause]. Well, you could more or less say you can't know without living. [pause] Well, you *can't* know without being conscious. So again, creating and expanding your consciousness, which means living in love – and that's a major failing of your civilization, that it doesn't see that those two things are synonymous. But that's your task here. Which you can refuse to do; it's a free will universe. But you'll not find it any happier by refusing.

R: That sort of seems pointless.

TGU: [chuckles] "Sort of."

R: All right, here's a person who is asking about what Bob Monroe identified as Locale III.

TGU: It's too late in the evening. That's an easy question and it'll be a nice one, but he's getting tired; probably we should stop.

R: All right. Again we appreciate all the help we're getting.

TGU: Well, you know we do too. It helps us too. Till next week.

R: Till next week.

Session Ten
October 16, 2001

Performance Anxiety and Access

R: Frank seems to be worried that some time he or I or someone else will ask a question and there will be no answer. Would you comment on that?

TGU: [coughing] Well that's the symptom, but the actual worry is more like there will be no answer because we don't exist, [laughs] because he's making this up as we go along. We told him once, it's remarkable that on the one hand he thinks we know everything and on the other hand he's not sure we're here.

So when you ask a question and nothing comes up, he's failing to realize that what's happening is, he's clutching. He's so worried about us not performing that he's having our performance anxiety for us. And the access is closed and we couldn't go through with a sledge hammer. Which, by the way, totally parenthetically, is most people's problem with talking to their equivalent of us. They're so concerned about it that they clutch and the tube is sealed off. The answer is, play and pretend, and don't worry about what comes, and just make it up as you go along, and when you realize after a while that it's real, it will be too late to have performance anxiety. That's parenthetical. But that's his real problem, and that's our response. Our response to *him* is, "if you're so worried about it, why don't you just let us fall flat on our face, and then you'll know?"

R: This seems to have come up for him a couple of times. Since we've been doing these sessions I can remember I think twice when he opened his eyes very wide because he seemed not to have – there seemed not to be an answer there.

TGU: Once he was startled. [coughing]

R: Do you think there's anything else we could say about this that would help remove his doubt?

TGU: What will ultimately remove his doubts is if we come up with a scheme that he can logically accept as to *why* we don't immediately know everything. And in the meantime the only thing is for him to do what he's learned to do, and that is trust. [pause] He's willing. It's just, you all learn to live at a level of trust, and when something requires a little *more* trust, sometimes you fall back into older patterns. And sometimes you rise to the occasion.

173

R: Considering that those doubts are still there, we seem to be doing very well.

TGU: Well, you remember you asked why we chose him, and it's because he's willing to [pause] go out on *no* ice, let alone *thin* ice. And that's what he feels like he's doing.

Angels and Guides

R: I've been wanting to ask about angels, guides, guardians. Most people that we know seem to have some way of thinking about energies that are not in body and are helpful to them, some choosing one of these names or the other. Are these all equivalents of what you do, or is there something else going on there?

TGU: It's more like they're equivalents to what we *are*. Those of you in 3D Theater who are accustomed to defining yourself as your body plus your mind, not considering yourself to extend over to this side (our usual pedantic definition, you'll notice) when you first become aware that you have guidance, it becomes necessary for you to devise or accept some conceptual scheme for that guidance. If in your society you thought of voices in the air as extensions of the radio, say, a lot of people who first experience guidance would say, "okay I heard the voice from radio."

Often when people experience angels, guides – guidance in any form – they are actually experiencing an opening of their connection *to us*, which is to say *to themselves* on the other side. They have expanded their effective consciousness. And depending on their beliefs, and on external circumstances, it may come to them very strongly as "other." Someone else with slightly different beliefs might experience it as "kind of other," which would be "a guardian angel assigned only to me." And someone else might come to it as guidance in the sense that you and the Institute community have come to think of it, as a part of yourself. So we would say they're all more or less equivalent, the major differential coming on *your* end, in the form of your social concepts and your individual concepts – which sometimes cut against each other, by the way.

R: I'm not sure quite what you mean there.

TGU: Well, if you are living in the medieval Catholic society, and you're a medieval Catholic, your beliefs and your society's beliefs go the same way. But if, say, you're Jewish, or you're a quiet freethinker, your personal beliefs may cut against what the society believes. This may have the effect of leaving you freer, it may leave you totally disoriented, or anywhere in that spectrum. That's merely an aside.

R: And for some individuals this has a clear religious connection. Others, though, seem to accept the guidance without that religious component.

TGU: That's right. You all fit it into your pre-existing scheme, or you expand the scheme to fit the new experience. It's just common sense. A western Christian is unlikely to instinctively respond to the experience of guidance by bringing in some aspect of the Chinese Tao, or Buddhist or Muslim cosmologies.

R: Both of my children, without much in the way of religious training, say they knew when they were children that they had a guardian angel. [pause] I was surprised to hear that.

TGU: And the question is –?

R: Well, it related to what you were talking about being in a society or –

TGU: Ah, you mean why they chose that symbol, rather than another symbol. Now, bear in mind, they didn't come into this life *tabula rasa*. [pause] We could go look, if you wish.

R: That would be interesting.

TGU: All right. [long pause] It seems to us that although there may not have been conditioning in the home, there was conditioning in the society around them in such things as the surroundings of Christmas and other social surroundings that had angels as common assumptions. On a human level, you could expect that it would be easier for a child to think of an angel – either an angel or a playmate, a friend, a human-seeming friend – than a somewhat chilly abstraction like guidance, or a somewhat disrespectful appellation like The Gentlemen Upstairs. [they laugh]

R: It's true they both had invisible playmates when they were little, too.

TGU: Which is the same as saying, of course, that their connection was wide open. [pause] Well done. [Meaning – though I'm not sure Rita ever realized it – "well done" in her raising of her children, in that it left them open.]

R: "Well done." All right.

Earth Changes

R: We used to hear a lot about earth changes, and some people even moved here to the New Land [a community near the Monroe Institute] because they thought it might be safer here. In recent years we have had a lot of very powerful storms and floods, and this year more tornadoes than are usually present. These things seem to be happening at an exaggerated rate. Does that seem to you to be true, and if so, what's happening?

TGU: The two halves of your question don't quite seem to fit together, and we think we're missing some connector that's obvious to you. You said, first, that there was talk of earth changes, and people moved here to be safe; then you said, it seems as though weather and things are getting a lot more violent. What's the hidden connector that we're missing there? It's probably quite obvious to you.

R: Well, only that people are wondering if all these changes that are now occurring didn't seem to be occurring so much 20 years ago when people first moved here.

TGU: Ah! You're not asking, is this no longer a safe place? You're asking what's going on in general.

R: In general. The whole topic of earth changes. You have hinted sometimes in the past that there's some such process going on.

TGU: We have to smile at your saying "in the past." There's nothing wrong with it, but it shows how you all think, and can't help thinking. It's as though you entered a conversation with someone and 20 minutes later they said, "well, you know, we used to talk . . ." [they laugh] It's very pointed, on our end.

All right. This is something well worth talking about. We don't need to hint. But we do need, as always, to back up a bit.

You know now that human consciousness is fundamental in creating the world. Human consciousness is defined more widely than only people who are in bodies in the physical. There's a saying you have, that all politics are local? Well, that's true in this sense as well. Your interactions are somewhat localized.

Supposing there were people on Mars, Venus, and Earth. The people of each of those planets by their actions would be influencing what was going to happen on *their* planet, not on another planet. In other words, it's local. In a larger sense, it is true that they would all be interacting with everything, but – [pause]

A difficulty with explaining things to you is that we want to say everything precisely, which leads us farther and farther afield in terms of making every last qualifier. The qualifiers then unbalance the statement, and some of it gets lost. So do be aware that we're somewhat at a disadvantage in that we *almost entirely* have to make statements that are false. Because there's no way to make statements that are true without lasting till the end of time.

R: Because of all the qualifiers?

TGU: Well, not only because of the qualifiers, but because everything connects to everything else. So at some point we have to stop drawing the connections, and that point is always arbitrary. So from *our* point of view, what we're telling you is shockingly inaccurate, and superficial, and probably misleading. But it is the best we can do and it's still probably better than nothing.

So, let's drop back again. Forget about the fact – although it is true – that every-thing influences everything. Look at it only as it appears on your end, for the moment: that you as an individual certainly affect your own life. That is, you create your own mental, spiritual, and physical eco-system. Then, to a degree, you do the same with your family, your neighborhood, your larger community, your larger mental community if you have friends at a distance, your (shall we say) emotional community if, say you're a Democrat or an ecologist – you understand? And ulti-mately, the more advanced you are, the larger the group of people you can identify with, and there is not any shortage of people who can really identify, at least for moments, with the earth, with the people and the being that *is* the earth.

Your consciousness is central in the world; your consciousness is the world; mat-ter is the illusion produced by the consciousness. It's not a trick, and it's not a misunderstanding, but it is an illusion, it's a construct.

All right, now we have to put another qualifier in and then we're going to forget this qualifier. But we need to put it in just so that you know, later, that we know what we're leaving out. And that qualifier is, you *can* choose your own realities. Each of you. Out of the infinite number that are there. So, to that degree, since you can choose a reality in which others do whatever it is you want done, you can theoretically live irrespective of anyone else's choices. In actual practice it isn't so, but that's the theory. Now let's leave that. We don't want to pursue that line, we just want to mention it.

Let's go back. You're living in a world in which *you* choose and all your neighbors choose, and all your friends and enemies choose. All of those choices [pause] add up, shall we say. Ed Carter in his novel *Living Is Forever* talked about people "voting" by what they *are*. And that is a correct concept. Not voting in the sense of having this or that opinion; more like voting in the sense of *being*. If you *are* in hatred, if you're *choosing* hatred, that's a vote a certain way. If you're *choosing* love, that's a vote a certain way. If you are *choosing* to be lukewarm – *almost* but not quite a contradiction in terms – that's a vote, in a different way. Well, all of these votes change moment by moment as you all change and things move, but at some points there come decision nodes; these become moments in which things happen. (Don't know a better way to put that, at the moment.) And if enough have chosen one way, World War II starts. *But*, if enough have chosen one way, sometimes a volcano erupts. The intuition that said that the earth changes were a condition of mankind's choices was absolutely correct, if not inspired.

You've wondered why haven't the earth changes that were predicted come about, and it's strictly because of the saving remnant. The people who did change. Now, the things that cannot be averted but can be delayed have *been* delayed, and now you very well know in your bones that it is the time of – you could say "reckon-ing" if you feel grim, or you can say "harvest," if you feel hopeful. Both true, just two ways of looking at things. You don't need to be told by us, you *all* know. Anybody who's reading this knows, in your heart, that things are not the same as they were a month and a half ago. [i.e., before September 11, 2001.]

You know there's no going back. You know there's not even any standing where you are. You know that everything *is* changing, *will* change, and you know probably – you *should* be able to know – that it's going to change increasingly quickly. What you *don't* know and *can't* know is, which *way* its going to change, and that's because it's up to how you vote. All of you, that is. [pause]

You *know* that the violence of the weather is increasing, and that is certainly true, although perhaps it would be more accurate to say the violence of the weather is *shifting*. There are places that are experiencing more, which have in the past experienced less. Probably the net total isn't so much different. But if, say, the poles shift, if the ice slips off the Antarctic continent, if the water rises 300 feet – or, alternatively, (not necessarily alternatively) if volcanoes erupt, earthquakes happen, what you must realize is, all of those massive effects also preclude other effects. When you see what looks to you like a catastrophe, bear in mind, all that energy is energy that *didn't* go somewhere else. That may make it a little more bearable to you, because there will be great suffering here.

A volcano may be the equivalent of a major act of rage in the sense of a huge war, you know, or a genocide, that kind of thing. We're not making exactly a one to one correlation, but we're saying things aren't as disconnected as they appear, and they're not as simple as they appear. Does that answer what you asked?

R: [pause] Yes, I think that's helpful in thinking about that question.

A Hard Winter?

R: One of Frank's questioners wanted to know, is this going to be a hard winter? [they chuckle]

TGU: Did they mean climatologically?

R: I think so.

TGU: Or emotionally?

R: I think they meant what's the climate. And other people of course are looking at the caterpillars to see how fuzzy their coats are, to get this information.

TGU: Well, let's leave it at this. Remember how every time you ask us what's going to happen we say "yes"? [they laugh]

Yes it's going to be a hard winter; no it's not going to be a hard winter; yes it'll be an average winter; no it won't be an average winter. Depends on where you go!

Now, we'll qualify that. You'll notice we *didn't* say that about the increased level of earth activity, because it's well past the point where it could *not* be. The level of manifestation and the form and the variety of manifestation, and the time period over which it occurs, is all still subject to flux, but it has to happen. At some point that energy *must* be balanced. That's the best way we can put that. And the simplest, most effective way to balance it is the last one you as "people" will try. And that of course is, change of heart. The religious would say, repentance. Metanoia.

R: And you suggested that this had been in some way delayed, for a bit, but that the delay is not going to continue.

TGU: Well for it to continue, a tremendous amount of choices have to be made in the right direction. All we're saying is that based on people's track records, the odds are that it won't. But it could. And any one of you could have an unpredictably strong effect. You mustn't overlook that. You're not helpless victims here.

Suffering and Choice

R: [pause] While we're still in this territory, I'm going to move to a slightly different focus. You said that we're all volunteers for whatever experiences we're having, if I understood you correctly. But it still is such a difficult thing to believe that people would choose human suffering in the way that, for example, people in Africa are experiencing the AIDS epidemic, or people in Afghanistan are choosing starvation and war. I guess it's easy to understand the individual choices, or even small group choices, but when one talks about such immense problems of this sort – the same principles are still at work?

TGU: We think that the difficulty for you is the concept that these problems are immense – but what's a few million people? [pause] See, if it's true for an individual, it's true for a few million individuals. In the first place – there's only one individual! [laughs] You see? We understand and respect and honor that you don't want to see this kind of suffering on this widespread a scale. That's certainly honorable. But what is a little askew here is that – to put it in light a humorous way – it assumes the universe can only handle itself when it's in small limited numbers. You see? Do you remember the scriptural saying that no sparrow falls unnoticed? Literally true. Well, if it's true of sparrows, it's true of people, and that's what Jesus was attempting to get it across! *There are no accidents. There is no neglect.* Nobody dies of anything (or lives of anything, or lives in any circumstances) because the universe slipped up.

Now this is not to say that it's not worth your while to try to relieve that suffering. But it *is* to say that that suffering was *chosen*. Well, it is to say that that lifetime in that circumstance with the *possibility* of suffering was chosen. That doesn't mean

179

that person would necessarily be disappointed if instead they got fed, or got cured. You see? In fact the experience of mercy that they received might make a huge difference in that soul's existence. [pause] But, if they *don't* receive it, it isn't like they got cheated.

Also, there are some people who like to live on the edge. They like to go into hazardous situations for the fun of it, for the thrill of it – perhaps we should say, for the skill of it. [pause]

You're thinking, "this is so selfish of us to be living here in comfort and safety," and we're saying, your life's not any more easy than theirs, because theirs is simpler and yours is highly complex and highly divided. You're each specialized instruments; don't worry about it. Don't worry about your guilt, you see.

Locale III and Focus 23

R: All right, we'd had a leftover question last week that wanted us to look into this issue of what Bob Monroe in his first book called Locale III.

TGU: [pause] Bob Monroe as an honest reporter, and also as a man with a taste for drama, did his best in his first book to give a sampling of various perplexities that he had at the moment – including some which he later entirely forgot about, and are left as lacunae in his archipelago. When he talked about Locale III he did not at that time understand much at all, certainly not in terms of what he understood later. At that point he was still sort of quietly flabbergasted at the existence of the non-physical to begin with.

Later, when he came to define the various focus levels – somewhat arbitrarily, in terms of the numbers, but a good definition of what's there – he would have identified Locale III as most likely Focus 23, had he grown up in the tradition that he later founded. We need to say one more thing here, too: Even to the end of his life, he misunderstood the nature of Focus 23, which he took to be a land of people who are disoriented and desperate. He did not see it, as we explained it to you "a long time ago," that the difference between Focus 23 and consciousness one, C1, as you call it, is mostly a matter of your own personal choices as you walk along. The path you choose seems realer to you than the others. Monroe did not realize that Focus 23 is a vibration of unlived possibilities on earth. [pause] Neither of those is really the right way to look at this, but we don't have time to do that now, we'll do it another time.

Staying within the Monroe concept, we will say that he saw other lifetimes of himself in which he had taken other choices, and those other choices included winding up in societies that were significantly different. And he thought, you see, that Locale III was different from Locale II, because he experienced Locale II as having great freedom and fluidity, and in Locale III he experienced the same kind of constraints he was used to in ordinary life. He wasn't realizing that those constraints were part of that belief system. Let's put it that way.

R: It seems as he describes it just either a different lifetime, or a different dimension.

TGU: Well, how do we go about this? In a very real sense, it was a different earth. But for a better way of looking at it, which might make it clearer to you, take it out of Focus 23 entirely. Imagine it as a belief-system territory. Now imagine that in the earth, oh, 100,000 years ago – totally arbitrary, this is not meant as real – there was a society like that. And he existed in that society, and one day, in one of his excursions, he wound up in that belief system territory, attracted to the analog of himself, and found himself living that lifetime. You can see the potential for terminal confusion.

Now, we should say that neither 23 nor a belief system territory is really quite right, but it's good enough for the moment. We hope it's good enough for the moment; you tell us.

R: By saying it's good enough for the moment, you're saying it's –

TGU: Another long story. [laughs]

R: But it's approximately true, or something of that order.

TGU: It puts his experiences into a closer approximation to the truth than you've had. But your present understandings of Focus 23, -4, -5, -6, and -7 are vague and more tentative than you think they are. You think you know more than you do, or rather, you think you've explored further than you have. And if you don't think *this* is going to raise some anxiety [in Frank] as we go through it [laughs] you're wrong!

The Monroe System: An Exploration Just Beginning

R: All right, well let's say some more about that, because people who are Monroe students are being exposed to this. I'm sure there will be some questions around that.

TGU: Well, the first thing to remember is that you've just barely gotten Columbus ashore, or Cortez or somebody. You haven't even seen a whole city, let alone a whole continent, let alone the whole universe.

So that, for instance, Focus 22 is understood as the frequency level at which people who are still incarnate but are disoriented for one reason or another are liable to be encountered. And that's true enough. But Focus 23 was initially experienced as people who were dead and disoriented, totally lost, no idea what to do with themselves.

R: To some extent. There were other groups there.

TGU: Right. And that is natural. It's an accurate perception, but it's only a small part. There is beyond that all of the living out of this huge expanse of every possibility unlived in C1. And to talk about the difference between C1 and 23 is going to require more putting together than we've done yet. We can do it, and we probably will do it – but it will be a chore – because your questions will help us to sort it out.

So when you come to Focuses 24, -5 and -6, which he called the belief system territories, his initial assumptions were that these were basically societies that people had experienced on earth and re-created unconsciously, or gravitated into because they were still resonating to those belief systems. That's not exactly true.

There's nothing wrong with that explanation, but another explanation that will give you a different viewpoint on it is that the people in each of those various territories are there not because they have similar *beliefs* but because they have similar *vibration*. Their essence is similar to each other. A natural result of that is that they will have similar beliefs. In the experience that we gave to Frank with the old man, the father of Katrina, the important part of the experience was sending him to look for him, on the basis that he was Jewish, atheist, socialist, and scientific.

We told him – well, we didn't tell him, but he got the bright idea "all by himself" to go searching for the old man on the basis of those characteristics. We *didn't* send him to search for the old man on the basis of, "look somewhere in Poland or Switzerland," or "look for a re-creation of a synagogue." Of course he was an atheist, so it wouldn't have been a synagogue, but you get the idea. What we sent him for was *true defining characteristics of a person*, which is *what they vibrate to*.

Now, supposing that person is an atheist, socialistic, scientific Jew, and in the belief system territory, and let's suppose for the moment that it was possible for him to change on his own and that he retained his socialistic scientific views but decided that he realized for some reason that he wasn't in a body and he didn't have to be Jewish anymore. Let's suppose that. In that case, his essence would change vibration a little, and he would sort of settle out in a slightly different place. This sounds like quibbling, but it's not. A valuable resource to any of you, which Frank talks about but hasn't read yet, is Swedenborg. And that's because Swedenborg talks about heavens of similar souls.

(And it should be apparent to Frank, and it hasn't been until we say this now, that when he comes across an idea and the idea resonates deeply, to the point that he begins referencing it without having read about it, that is suspicious. And that ought to tell him that in fact we're giving him a little prodding there and saying "this is the way it is, here's an excuse for you to think it.")

So we say the Swedenborg explanation of "souls of a feather flocking together" – although that's Frank's terms and not Swedenborg's – is a good way for you to understand how things sort out. People are not in the same heaven because they're Presbyterian, they're in the same heaven because they are what they are, which made them more likely to be Presbyterian, if you follow that. That's a vast over-simplification, but you could have someone who's a Presbyterian in this life who resonates in the same way that an atheist or a Catholic or a Muslim or somebody resonates, so that once they shed the body and the external cultural features, they would wind up in the same place, more or less. In those cases, what are they?

Just for the sake of a thought experiment, suppose you had a Muslim and a Jew and a Christian and an atheist who for some reason or other had very similar vibrations. Maybe never met. They die, go back to the other side, and in the other side they find themselves drawn to each other, because they are more or less the same thing. How would you describe their situation? Are they in a Mosque? A temple? A church? [laughing through the three choices] Or – you know?

So the initial way that Monroe saw these things is inaccurate in that very subtle but important respect. The tendency is to think of them as being environments that have been determined for people, but it's a little more accurate to think of them as being people who are at the same electrical frequency and create around themselves something that is familiar or comfortable. Well, we say create around themselves; it's actually created *for* them, but they don't know this because they're not really thinking about these things.

R: Let me try as an example an experience I had when I went looking for a belief system group. I found a group of individuals who seemed to have in common the fact that they had all died for their country. Now, is this enough of a similar vibration that one could think in those kinds of very specific terms, or –?

TGU: Well, you see, it *was*. However, the only caveat we would add is that various people can do the same thing with very, very different feelings about it. If you die for your country resentfully, you're unlikely to be of the same vibration as the person who died for his country either gladly or with resignation or out of valor. But, sure, that's enough. And we would add, what you just described is *not* to be found in Monroe's literature, is it?

R: No. I just found that when I went into that space that he's describing.

TGU: Well, our point is that you're only beginning the explorations. In fact, you're missing tremendous amounts, although ultimately it won't matter, maybe. But it would be nice if more of this were recorded from the various people who do it in a program. The various program people hear about it, and it's forgotten about.

R: All right, several people are asking about out-of-body experiences and phasing that Bob talked about in his later years. Is there something worth commenting on here beyond what Frank has already put into writing?

TGU: The major focus of what we would like to get across to people is that you are all one huge being, seen from one point of view, and you all live as disconnected beings, seen from another point of view. It's very worthwhile to think in terms of phasing and not out-of-body, mainly because it reminds you that you haven't left home.

Seth and TGU

R: Yes. That distinction. All right, well how about the Seth question, then?

TGU: Who's that? [they chuckle]

R: I think the questions had to do with where is Seth, and what's he up to, and –

TGU: No, the questions really had to do with how are we different from Seth?

R: Yes, and that was a part of it too, yes. Well, what I thought is, if Seth's worst fears came about, he could be in the form of Rajneesh or Jim Jones or David Koresh or any of the individuals that Colin Wilson called Rogue Messiahs. Or if his worst fears didn't come about, he could be Bob Monroe – who also said he didn't want to be a guru.

TGU: [pause] Now this gives us a productive entry into Frank's fears about "are we real and do we know anything and why not, or do we know everything and why not." Because you're asking us something, referencing things that *we* don't know and *he* doesn't know. Now, if *he* knew, we would already know. You know, it's merely passed through. But if he doesn't know, we may know or we may not – and in this case we don't – and so what we *could* do is, so to speak, ask "okay, what's that all about?" of your angel, your equivalent of the guys upstairs. We, obviously, can establish diplomatic relations and swap notes. But it's roundabout, really, next to just asking. It's going to take a while to show you the everyday ways in which this works itself out, so we'll mention them as they come up.

About Seth. [coughing] [pause] It should strike you that Seth is an author without a body. And every author creates a persona in the writing of the book, whether he wants to or not. There's no real choice. The part of yourself that you put into a book that people read is the persona. You can't put everything about yourself in the book. For one thing it's not relevant, and for another thing it's not possible.

So the selective elements of yourself that you project become a persona and that's what people can react to. That's *all* that they can react to.

Seth has projected himself through Jane Roberts into print, but print isn't the distinction, it's that he has interacted with consciousnesses in your world. In so doing he has unavoidably presented himself as a persona; he has presented a portion of himself. Only because it *couldn't* be otherwise.

Now, is that what *we're* doing? [pause] You don't really know any more about us than she knew about Seth. You don't know whether we're one or multiple, but you also don't know whether *he* was one or multiple. *He* chose to present himself as he; supposing we said, "he/they chose to present him/them selves as he," or that "we/I chose to present ourselves/myself as we"?

Again, we're trying to gently remind you that our turf is different from yours, and the necessity for any individual to preserve that individuality against others, or in contradistinction to others, doesn't really exist. It is as though we are a reservoir with hoses leading from the reservoir, feeding you the waters of life. The difference in which hoses you receive or how many, is important on your end because that's how you receive it, but not on our end.

Well, it's an awkward analogy. Let's back it up and try again. If two rivers lead from the lake, it isn't like the waters of the lake divide themselves and say "I'm going this way" and "I'm going that way" and they're different. They appear different because they appear in different places. We're much less individualized than it appears.

However, having said all that, now we're going to contradict it entirely. [sigh] The chances of expressing this clearly are miniscule.

You accept that we have said that each of you is actually a part of a larger thing that appears to you inextricably as individual. And you realize that if your individual life is one finger, your other lives might be other fingers, but you're all part of one hand. And you realize that all of those hands in one dimension might be a part of something that has hands in other dimensions and other realities as well, so that you're really a vast being. And again, ultimately you come back to the fact that we are all one.

Well, the same thing is true on *our* side, *if* you're looking at it that way from your side. So, *if* you want to look at it and find Seth, you need to separate out and separate out and separate out so that you're only dealing with that part that you can think of as Seth. In other words, just because he's saying to you that he is Seth, you mustn't forget that he has other lives, other dimensions, other realities, all of which are just as real as Seth – and, all of which, is *us*.

So to make a distinction between him and us is valid enough and it's also nearly a *hypothetical* distinction. Individuality within total unity. It's absolutely contradictory, it's absolutely true both ways, and so it depends on what you look at.

In fact, to go a little further, when you're looking at your Monroe states, your various heavens and all that – after all, that, that's a matter of *how* you're looking. You're looking at *one* aspect of yourself, in *one* place in *one* non-time. But all the rest still exists, you're just not looking at it. So if you look at what you call the afterlife in one sense, you have all these individual pieces in various belief systems, or in Focus 27 so-called, and if you look at it in another sense, you are back to the source and you are all undivided. It isn't that one's right and one's wrong; it isn't that some go one way and some go another way, it's that it is the same ambiguous, shall we say, reality that is delineated more by your concepts than by anything inherent to itself.

Sorry that's a long answer, but –

Amoeba Analogy

R: You'd said to us before that we are in the all-one state and at the same time in the individual state. And if you think about the distinction which you mentioned here, that when we seem in Seth's case to be talking about the individual aspect, why would we be asking about him unless we were talking about the individual aspect? Of course he's part of the totality too, but –

TGU: Again, that's his persona, shall we say. [coughing]

R: Yes. The fact that he seemed to be coming from the same place you're coming from as he worked with Jane Roberts, and a few people afterwards who also said they were hearing from him in the same way Jane Roberts did, I can't remember from those books whether he was the kind of energy that might want to come into a physical body again or not. If he did, and set up the criteria that he had set up, he might have come into the kinds of individuals I was mentioning. In earthly form.

TGU: Well. [coughing] We do, we really do see how it looks like it to you, but it isn't really that he would take another life. This will seem a fine distinction to you. [pause] We need names for these things. Suppose we call your over-all self, that has all lives, all dimensions, all realities, let's call that the amoeba. [chuckles]

R: But this is still the individual part.

TGU: Yes. You. You yourself. Let's look at Rita's amoeba, which is vastly larger than she is, but still we're looking at it as if it were a separate thing not connected to everything else. *Seth* wouldn't be taking on another lifetime, it would be Seth's *amoeba* taking on another lifetime. Now, it sounds like a quibble, but it's important to avoid that.

R: No, I see what you're saying.

TGU: And the answer to that question, did he or did he not, is "sure he did, or sure he didn't." [they laugh] Could he or could he not? Sure he could, sure he couldn't. You'll get used to that answer. There are realities in which he did one and realities in which he did the other, or something else, sure.

Next Stage of Human Development

R: I have one more question, but I'm wondering if this is enough for tonight.

TGU: We're all right if you're all right.

R: I wanted to ask some more about the next stage of human development. You've suggested that on the way to that next stage of human development we might begin by seeing things from many points of view, including seeing things from your point of view, and that we might even be moving toward becoming like you. Now, is any of that what you said?

TGU: That's correct except for the last part, because you already are *like* us, in fact you *are* us, but we know what you meant, which is that you will develop habits of consciousness that will make you more aware of your connection with us on an ongoing basis. The ultimate is for all of us to be one again and to be functioning as one. The penultimate is for all of you to be still retaining your individuality with vast extensions of your psychic awareness (which implies awareness of all the rest of you) so that you will be meeting amoeba to amoeba, shall we say, rather than person to person. And, by the way, you'll notice already how valuable a word-shorthand is. We can start using that word amoeba and it will mean things now and it'll make possible much more complicated dialogue, because we'll each know what that means, and we can create an elaborate although hopefully not over-elaborate conversational structure. Beware lest you make it too whimsical, because you'll be stuck with it. [they chuckle]

R: Well, but to be clear then, what amoeba means is any one of us in individual form, but with all the lifetimes and experiences.

TGU: All the lifetimes, all the realities, all the dimensions, yes, that's right. The over-arching thing that's you, before it's Rita. It is your largest sense while you're still seen as separate. I think you would call it a monad. [pause] By the way, this ought to clarify [chuckles], eight or nine years later, something that bothered Frank a great deal, which is that occasionally we would say "I." [laughs] And when we would say "I mean" or something like this, he would go into paroxysms of worry [laughs] for fear that he was really making it up. [laughs] But –

R: A language problem.

TGU: Well, it's a form of integrity, but he worries a lot.

Maintaining Equanimity

R: All right, well, that's all I had on my list to ask about tonight. Is there anything you'd like to add?

TGU: Yes, this is just in the nature of an alert, for you? Watching Frank, if it's happening to him it's happening to you as well, you all. It's very possible to begin to shake yourselves to pieces by on the one hand attempting to remain in multiple viewpoints but on the other hand immersing yourself more and more in news and in the media as it portrays things. The inherent contradiction of the two activities is not necessarily bad, but when you notice that you are losing a little of your equanimity, then spend more time either meditating or in some way cooling down to remind yourself of who you really are. This is a widespread problem that will get wider, sooner.

Otherwise, we're enjoying the experience, and we trust you are too, and we'll see you next week.

Session Eleven
October 23, 2001

Choice, Here and There

R: Last week, you were talking about a belief system territory of the Monroe scale, and said that "people of the same electrical frequency create a comfortable environment around themselves." Then you corrected this to say that the environments were actually being created for them. How do those creations happen?

TGU: Bear in mind, as always, that this is an analogy.

It's rather like when you first go doing retrievals, and at first think you are thinking it up as you go along? And then with a little more introspection or sophistication you recognize that in fact the scenario is being created and you are being inserted into it. Well, this is true of your whole life, and by your whole life we mean not just between birth and death at a given time, but the whole life of the amoeba, shall we say. We are all – and this includes us, as you pointed out at one point – we are all under guidance. We are all under an over-arching intelligence that creates the whole thing. Although in practice we act or even almost *have to* act as though we were responsible for our lives and our surroundings, in actual fact the circumstances of our lives precede us, and they follow us.

R: This raises the "choice" question. And I'm clear about the choices here on this side. How about the choice on the other side?

TGU: A very interesting question. Since we're learning to look with suspicion [laughs] on things that we're taking for granted, give us a moment to think about that. [long pause]

One could say, superficially, that because we are conscious of our unity on this side, things emerge rather naturally. Your pointing of the question led us to realize that in fact that emergence was perhaps better stated as guidance, from a level of consciousness and sophistication perhaps greater than ours. It would be an interesting exercise to determine if that consciousness is also somewhat less *pointed* than ours, as ours is of you. However, that's not necessarily the case, because for it to be the case one would assume a difference in turf as that between us and you. The short answer to that is, "we don't *know* the answer to that question." But what we should look for is an opportunity for us to choose, one way or another, rather than doing what seems natural, which is the way it seems to us. On your side you are much more conscious of choice, and in fact are – okay, there's the answer:

You are able to choose primarily because you are suspended arbitrarily so that you *can* choose. That is, – [sighs]

This is *one* way to look at it. This is *one* approach to the situation. You could say, because you are in bodies, and because, being in bodies, you don't sort out according to what you *are* – to your specific gravity, or your electrical vibration, or your pH [three alternate analogies] – not only are you enabled to associate with others of an unlike nature, you are also able to *move,* to choose. You can *choose* because you don't have to stay at the same level. You see? If you were on *our* side, you only *associate* with people at your same level not only because that's where you are but because, if you looked at each of us as individuals over here, we can't step out of the vibration that we're in.

Take the guys that you're talking to as your usual thirty and five-tenths people. Now, we 30.5 people, let's say, have a specific gravity of 30. This means we cannot associate with others at 50 or others at 20, except through intermediaries. (This is rough, but it's more or less true.) They're just not in the same place.

Your situation is clearer to us than ours, now that we think of it. The ability to choose depends upon pointed consciousness and upon the ability to associate unlike elements. Since we *don't* have pointed consciousness, except in reflection to you, and since we don't mingle unequal or immiscible elements, our choices are much more subtle and much less extensive than yours. If we're floating in a frequency of 50, we can't have a choice between, say, 45 and 55, but we might have a choice between 49 and 51. They can be small variants, but not large. At least not large quickly. Now, perhaps if our choices consistently led us to 49, then perhaps we could choose between 48 and 50 and in that case, our situation would be different from yours primarily in speed and intensity and range. Interesting thought.

But you know, we're more like a school of fish, with fish on all sides of us, so it isn't easy for one of us or even several of us to go off in a direction, whereas you can go anywhere you want, within the physical, emotional, mental, limits.

R: But as you were describing the affinity connection with Frank or others in 3D Theater, it seems clearly not an assignment, but a collection by affinity. And it seems that there might be some choices in all this.

TGU: How do you see that involving a choice?

R: Well, your group is not assigned to Frank, it is somehow a matter of your feeling some connection with him.

TGU: We're on the same wave length, we should say. That's what we mean by affinity. Not fondness, but it's more like we can *resonate*, as you say, to him, and vice-versa. But you feel you're seeing choice patterns. Go on a little further. Perhaps we'll pick something up here. How do you see that involving choice on our end?

R: Well, if you feel it's just a matter of vibratory rate or something like that that's connecting you to Frank, then the others that you work with would represent patterns similar to Frank, and you would be relating with them? Or is there –

TGU: Ah! Well, now, remember, "a long time ago" [comic cough] [laughs]

R: All right, no making fun of the questioner. [they chuckle]

TGU: You will remember that we talked about how individuals come into the world? That an individual emerges onto your side by elements of this, that, and the other being drawn together from here? Do you remember that? That we pick certain characteristics and certain elements and sort of put them together and package them. Well, [pause] this is a crude way to look at it, but supposing you as an individual comprise 30 different elements from our side. Each of those 30 elements will have a somewhat different vibratory rate, to use that analogy, and will therefore have elements on our side that correlate to that. You see, that's how we would describe an affinity.

It isn't that we chose, exactly, but that, in you being chosen, we were chosen by default, in that we are the same kind of elements, you see.

R: I don't see, but I'll accept your word for it.

TGU: Well, if your frequencies ranged from one to 50 and we chose to use all the even numbered elements to create one given individual, then any of us who also were of those even-number elements would continue to correspond to those elements, even though they were in a body on your side. That's where the affinity would come from between one side and the other. If you wanted to look at those elements as a filament, say, stretched into 3D Theater from there, we would be on the other end of the filament. That's a way of looking at it. Not a very communicative one, though, huh? [laughs]

R: [pause] Someone moves over from this side and presumably goes to something like the belief territories. I assume that's a step in a process, is that true?

TGU: It *can* be.

R: "It can be." Or someone can stay there, is that what you mean?

TGU: No, it depends on the level of being that's created by the time they die. They may not have to go to a belief system.

R: Yes, I see.

TGU: And, the experiment may have been unsuccessful enough that nobody bothers to bring it to a belief system, and they cease to exist. Those elements being returned to the mix, you know.

R: Hmm. I haven't heard about that before.

TGU: Well, not every so-called individual, by the end of its life, is really individual, is by itself really a success. And if there's no advantage to having that individual continue, then – there's no advantage, and so the elements can just be re-mixed. That is, allowed to dissolve on this side. You know, nothing's lost, it's as though you were attempting to form an ice cube, and the water didn't get cold enough by the end of the time period. It would just be water; you'd pour the water back in with the water. An inelegant analogy, but perhaps it may serve. It isn't like anything was lost. It isn't even like it was necessarily "an unsuccessful experiment," whatever that means. It just means that the end result's not promising enough to be worth continuing. It happens a lot.

R: Well, I'm sure I'm going to have questions about that, but I have three different questions I want to ask you at the same time.

TGU: That's why we're here.

Belief System Territories

R: Let's go back to the person moving over –

TGU: Dropping the body.

R: Dropping the body. I understand from what you're saying that a number of different things could occur at that time. But suppose a person does go into the belief-systems territory. Is there a choice there?

TGU: Is there a choice of which belief system territory, you mean?

R: Yes.

TGU: Well, we need to back up a little bit. The first variable is, how old is this person? How large is their body of other lifetimes, other dimensions, other realities? If conceivably this were their first time through, they'd have a vastly more constricted full soul. The amoeba would be tiny. And if they'd been around a long time, done lots of things, the amoeba would be huge.

For the purpose of the exposition, let's say it's the person's very first incarnation.

They formed for the first time. They have *nothing* else they're part of. And they live a life, and it's an interesting enough and successful enough experiment that we decide to continue. Not "we" exactly, but *it is decided* to continue. They formed enough of a beginning of consciousness to keep going. And just to keep it simple, we'll assume they were human, and that they had beliefs. Because some don't! Supposing they came in as –. Well, we're having the same problem you are: You have lots of questions, we have lots of qualifiers.

R: [chuckles]

TGU: And the more we look at it, the more complicated the situation is. Supposing someone dies at the end of their first incarnation, and that incarnation was as a mental defective. That sometimes happens. Often happens, actually. It's a sort of a trial run, you know? Well, you *could* look at it that they go to a belief system, but really you have lots of levels that aren't exactly belief systems, they're just sorting-out stations. You know? This is where they sort vibratorally, and that's where they are. However, in the early stages, there's not much consciousness *there*, and it's mostly just a matter of waiting for another opportunity to get to earth, or some other earth, or some other system. Now, take someone who's been around the block a few times. When they drop the body, the part of themselves that just came out of a body could go to a belief system, or a sorting station, whatever you care to call them, depending on their consciousness level. Not just *consciousness* level, but their level of *being*.

But don't forget, they also have the rest of the amoeba to consider. When *you* drop *your* body, one *part* of you will drop the body, the rest of you won't. The connections between that "rest of you" and you are much stronger and more easily resonated to once you drop the body. The body really in a sense is your insulator from the rest of your amoeba. [sigh] You can see how it becomes nearly impossible to talk about all this, but it's a good exercise.

R: So is it the amoeba that is making choices at that point?

TGU: Well, you could look at it two ways. You could say the amoeba is part of your vibratory level, if you start from your end; you could say that your latest life that just dropped the body is part of the amoeba's vibratory level, if you start at *its* end, you see.

Although you're in the habit already of thinking that they're individuals who separately go off into belief systems and then somehow automatically get pitchforked somewhere else, it's a mistake, because they are still part of a larger being that never leaves and never *could* leave them unattended. Just because you can't *see* the rest of your being doesn't mean that you're not integrally *connected* with it. You *must be*, because you couldn't live without it.

Everything we've said has been for the sake of attempting to make a clearer statement, but in a way it's so wrong that it's almost not worth going into it. To say that you drop a body and go to a belief system makes a lot of sense as long as you're trying hard to forget about the amoeba! [they laugh] But when you realize that it's one aspect of your larger self –

Well, perhaps the easiest way to think of it is that it happens in that way, but that the things that are controlling it, the scenarios that are set up, are the work of the larger being. It feeds thoughts and ideas and urges and perceptions into the part of the being that just dropped the body. It is the usually unseen background. Does that make a little sense?

Who Sets up the Environment?

R: *I got into all of this because I was really asking who was setting up this environment that someone would be dropping into, and then the question of choice came up.*

TGU: Well, it all mingles in together, but we came to it through the back door. The answer is always "*you* are, because *we* are, and there's only one of us even though there's many of us." [they chuckle] Again, the exercise of changing viewpoints gives a little *hint* of clarity. Not *very* clear. We would give it to you in total clarity if we could.

We would say that it's worth your while to think in terms of the larger being behind you being the scene-setter, the power behind the throne. It isn't exactly true that it's done *to* you, but since there is a perceived difference between you and your larger being, it will *look* to you like it's being done to you, or, it will look like it's happening automatically. We would say the conclusion that most of the initial wave of Monroe people have jumped to is that it's being done automatically. As you look a little closer, you'll see there's much more going on behind the scenes than this. And of course Monroe himself jumped to that conclusion after it was held in front of him long enough.

R: *Someone has asked whether the amoeba could be defined as what Monroe described as the I-There.*

TGU: Well [pause] we would say his I-There is a *part* of his amoeba. Not the whole thing. But it depends on what he meant by that, and we think he changed his mind on what he meant by that, maybe from day to day, maybe from year to year.

R: It did seem to include other lives he had, picking up the lives and maybe other dimensions as well.

TGU: Yes, it did, although he didn't fully realize that. What he called Locale III in a lot of ways could be looked at as other dimensions. But our question is whether he saw that ultimately his amoeba and other amoebas are all part of a larger thing. We would say he mostly did. [pause] So if you had to have a yes/no answer, we'd say "well, more or less." [chuckles]

R: The question was also asked about Bruce Moen's disc; whether that's also the same – [Moen is the author of several books exploring the afterlife.]

TGU: Yes, it's much the same idea. Moen's ideas are a simplified form of Monroe's, actually. Monroe had many more years of experience than Moen has had, and he had the advantage – well, the disadvantage – of a lot of confusion and a lot of thought, plus he had a tremendous intensive tuition over many years that Moen does not have yet. So Moen's job is more acting as a popularizer, an intermediary to Monroe. In giving a somewhat simplified form of it, he gives something that people can grasp, which will bring them to the next level when they think of some perplexities that haven't been dealt with. We don't mean at all to say that he's inaccurate, but he is a simplifier.

Monroe's System

R: All right, now we also talked last time about stages 23 through 27. It seems as though you have accepted Monroe's stages of 23 through 27, although you might not define it in the way he defined it. Is that the case?

TGU: Well, let's recognize what we're doing here. We on our side are attempting to talk not only to the two of you but to anyone who may unpredictably read the material, in terms that will be comprehensible to them. And to do that, we're working through what Frank knows, because way too much distortion [would result from] the effort to put something through that he doesn't know. So if we need him to talk about quantum physics, he needs to study quantum physics first.

He has his own understanding of the Monroe terminology and the Monroe concepts. Whether they're exactly what others within the system would say doesn't really matter to us. *Because* everything has to be conveyed by analogy, one analogy may be better than another, but this is fine. Were we talking strictly to Christians, we could talk in Christian theology – as far as Frank knew the theology. Were we talking in terms of [pause] chemistry, he would not probably say a word, [they laugh] because he doesn't know anything about chemistry. But you see where we're going. So, yes. And after all, remember that much of the structuring that Monroe did around his experiences came from tuition in two different ways. One was directly, while he was what he called at the time out-of-body, another is through his various explorers bringing through people like Miranon – which is basically us! And a third is the most indirect, and yet in a way the most graspable of the three: reading and absorbing the systems that *others* have devised, and trying to see what analogies there would be with what he had experienced.

And there's another, the biggest reason of all: It is a flexible American vernacular in the 21st century, even though he himself never *saw* the 21st century. You see? It's in *your* language, not in terms of the words used, but in terms of the understanding of the universe. That is to say, if you'll pardon us saying it, it shares the same distortions that you all take as accuracy. The Christians in the 1500s saw the world through their own filters. You see the world through *your* own filters. This belief system shares your filters. That's why it's more useful to you. So, we're fine using that. So, proceed then with your questions. [pause] Which is to say, we've forgotten what the question was.

R: Yes, well, I was asking if you see those distinctions along that scale of 23, 24, 25, 26. You had some comments about the earlier sessions that suggested to me that they weren't exactly Bob's definitions that were being used to discuss the question.

TGU: Well, he got glimpses of things over a 30-year period, or whatever it was. He got glimpses of things and did his best to make sense of them, using his auxiliary resources such as reports from the other side and belief systems and, as we said, other people's reports. But he himself should have realized, and probably did, that they were only *provisional* reports; that he wasn't going to understand everything right away.

So a minute ago we said that an inexperienced life that came out of its initial life as a mental defective would sort out to a place, but it wouldn't exactly be a belief system. That's something he didn't happen to come across. That doesn't mean it doesn't fit into his system, it just means it's one of the many details – even though they're *huge* details – he never saw. That's all. It doesn't mean the system can't be used, it just means it's not complete and, like any system, it's only an analogy.

R: Well, as an example, Frank seems to have quite a different definition of Focus 23 than Bob did –

TGU: He has quite a different experience of it, yes.

R: – and I'm really seeing that some of the differences come from your coaching.

TGU: Well, a very productive analogy would be for you to imagine that Monroe and Frank were two explorers, among others, of a new planet, the planet being earth. And Monroe happened to land in the Sahara Desert, and Frank happened to land in – oh, in Virginia. So Monroe's initial description of Planet Earth would be hot, barren, inhospitable, and brown. And Frank's would be green, warm, and wonderful. It would seem as though they're absolutely contradicting each other. What they're actually doing, though, is each describing *one* facet of an extremely complicated and extensive system. Future explorers are going to bring back much more that will at first confuse and complicate, until people shake them the right way and realize "oh, well, this is what this means. This is how this fits with that."

If you have one exploration, it's real simple, you just report what you saw. But if you have five explorations, there will be seeming contradictions and there will be different experiences. When you have 50 or 100 or 500, the contradictions and the seeming contradictions will all be understood in their relationship to the overall pattern. You're just at the beginning.

R: Is it then a useful thing to start out with a scheme of this sort, or some sort, or better off everybody go exploring without such a map?

TGU: We would say it's best to start off with a *vague* scheme, much like Monroe has now when people begin a Lifeline. He knew more than he said, and it was just as well not to put it in there, and that's one reason why it wasn't [put there]. A major variable is the way people feel about the unknown or with their own attempt to find certainty. For some people, a very detailed map would be wonderful and they would give you great results. But for other people a very detailed map would just stifle their interest, let alone their ability to explore. So if you have to have only one kind of map, we would say a vague map is best. But there'll be a time in which that will no longer help. It's only because you're in the beginning.

R: But you see progress being made in the direction of being clearer about these things?

TGU: Yes it is, no it isn't. [laughs] Yes it will, no it won't.

R: [chuckles]

TGU: In most realities, some form or other of this mapping will be successfully done, but there are *huge* differences among those realities as to what it comes to. There are realities in which this will come to nothing, because it will be shut off. Stifled. Sent underground. Purged. Persecuted. Stopped. [pause] Nothing to worry about. If you don't like those realities, don't go there.

R: [chuckles] "Don't go there."

TGU: It's not meant as a joke.

R: I understand. [pause]

Spirit Possession

R: *The question has been raised about the concept of possession, in which an-other spirit takes over a body. Usually when that occurs the descriptions are of negative entities taking over a body. Is that something that occurs?*

TGU: You only have trivial questions. [chuckles] Deep waters here. [pause]

Well, as always, back up and look at it from unity and from multiplicity. From multiplicity, you have your amoeba. Part of that amoeba, that larger being, is the one part of it that is born when you are born, dies when you die and lives your life in the meantime. You. [pause]

That being makes choices its entire life. And the rest of the being almost invariably respects those choices, waiting to see what kind of flower is produced by the end of the experiment, by the end of the life.

Now, within the field of flowers that is the world – that is not just the earth, but all of reality – there are infinite numbers of infinite kinds of flowers, many of them hostile to each other, many representing antithetical qualities, which seems to them that they are good and the opposite is evil. That being so, unpredictably any of your energies, any of your beings, may find themselves in combat with others. That combat is not necessarily restricted to physical manifestation, and not necessarily restricted to one life at a time. So you may have your amoeba conflicting with others. In fact, not *may*, you *will*.

This is not to imply a state of constant warfare. It's to state that within totality, all possibilities exist, many of them seemingly incompatible. [pause] (Looking for a good example; it's not real obvious.) Well, matter and anti-matter within reality appear to annihilate each other. (What they actually do is move out of this reality and into another one. To re-form, you know, to combine. But that's another story.)

The short answer to your question would be, "yes, it happens," if that weren't such a misleading statement. Because if we say "yes, possession takes place," you will think one individual by him- or herself is possessed by another individual him- or herself, forgetting that both are part of a larger being. Possibly *the same* larger being. This might take a minute, let us sort this out a little. [pause]

All right, start at the human mundane level. You may have magicians on earth. That is, you may have people who use their psychic abilities to get what they want against others. Certainly that's well documented. This one individual fragment, one piece of a larger being, attacking other fragments for its own welfare, not even perhaps recognizing that it's part of a larger being, but knowing how to use these abilities to get what it wants. Well, there's no reason at all for you think this happens only among individual fragments.

In other words, just because the larger being is huge, and extends to other life-times and other dimensions and other realities, doesn't mean that it's necessarily wise, benevolent, or even particularly intelligent. So one way to look at this would be to say that indeed, you have good and bad spirits; you have malevolent and you have benevolent spirits; that is to say, larger beings, and their local representatives are just that, our local representatives.

If you're going to look at it that way, though, it's important to remember that they themselves are part of a larger balance that is the universe. You will remember that we said that the whole universe is and must be in balance; that you cannot have positive and no negative. You just can't. That negative will express, in some form. There's no reason for you to think that we on this side are uniformly positive *as seen by you.* Now bear in mind, too, that what appears quite evil to you will appear quite good to someone else, and not because that someone else is warped, but just because it's subjective. You don't see your own shadow, they don't see their shadow, and it could even be argued that it's not really a shadow except that it's not conscious.

R: But you mentioned that it was possible that two components of the same amoeba were involved –

TGU: Oh sure, because the amoeba can have elements that are relatively plus and relatively minus, you know. It just depends on how they sort out. They may sort out into two beings each of which is a mixture of plus and minus, which is of course usually the case, or theoretically it could sort out that one is overwhelmingly plus and one is overwhelmingly minus. The only really ultimate condition of the universe is that it all balances out ultimately, but that doesn't say anything predictive about what the local balance will be. [pause] How's that?

Walk-ins

R: I see what you're saying there. In the same context, I wanted to ask about what are called walk-ins, where there seems to be a total shift in a personality of a person at one time. And those may be positive changes, as well as negative.

TGU: [pause] Well –. We have quite a quarrel with the underlying thought there. Because it implies movement where there really isn't movement. Look at yourself, now. You are a creation of your larger being. Your body was created and is maintained over a certain period of time. And within the body is the mind and it's all motivated by the same spirit. Now, it's true that another part of your being could move in and you move out –. Actually this may be what they're talking about.

Supposing you had ten lifetimes and one of those lifetimes was a magician and one lifetime was a gardener. And you began this lifetime more like a gardener than a magician and then something shifted, and you began pulling more of the magician in and less of the gardener, you know? It might *look as though* you had been replaced.

Now, this is not commonly what they're talking about, by walk-ins, but it's worth looking at in that context, because – *where* are you to *go*? And where is the new person to come *from*, in this walk-in idea? Can it come from anywhere other than a part of yourself?

R: I wouldn't think so.

TGU: Well, you see, that's what's missing in that concept. It thinks of you as if there really were such a thing in the world as an individual, rather than a concept that's convenient but not real. If there really *were* individuals, and the individual spirit could leave and another spirit enter, then it would be a question of "well is that possible, or is it not?" But the whole groundwork is wrong because it's like the people who think that when you go out of body you're leaving your body empty and something else can come in and take it over! [laughs] But there's no *movement*! That's not what's happening. And so because it's not what's happening you can confidently say, "well, there's nobody going to take it over while you're gone, because there's no 'gone' to go to!" You know. We'd say the same with the walk-ins.

We will say, the apparent phenomenon is very interesting to look at, because it *does* show how one unsuspected part of yourself can move in, seemingly a stranger. It's a slight exaggeration, from our point of view, of a process that happens all the time anyway, which is that you all drop in and out of various parts of your lives. Kibitzing, you know? Putting in a little here and taking a little there. At first you don't realize it, and then after a while you do realize it, and then after a greater while, you begin to do it deliberately, so that not only are you *aware* of other lives, as you call them, but you're then *participating* in them. And they're participating in *you*, consciously rather than – from your point of view – unconsciously. And this becomes an exaggeration of that.

R: That's very interesting. That does explain some things that I –

TGU: The whole theme of our work here is how many pretty acute observations are being misunderstood because of the persistent illusion of individuality on our end – and even, if we may say it, on your end! You are not the individuals you think you are. [pause] Some of you call each life a "fragment" of the larger life, and of course it isn't really. It's like talking about your shoulder. Your shoulder is not a fragment of your body, it's just a part of your body that you're choosing to put a name to and treat as an individual thing. But it's actually seamless. If it isn't, it doesn't work very well as a shoulder.

R: But in the context of us in our other lifetimes, there's the matter of consciousness being here, and not elsewhere. Is this true?

TGU: Say that again?

R: Well, our consciousness seems to be totally consumed with this particular life.

TGU: Well, now, let's go back. Look at this in terms of the effective consciousness versus the full consciousness. Your flashlight is here, and your flashlight may get a bigger battery, or come under better circumstances, and be able to illumine more, or it may be aimed at something different, but the background light remains. You're just not always aware of it, because of the intensity of the flashlight.

R: Okay. Yes. Thanks for connecting those.

TGU: You will find, we hope, that these concepts gradually begin to illumine each other.

R: It's a task for us to bring them all together.

TGU: It is, and it's a good task. It's good for you, and it's good work. [pause] We're not exactly watching you squirm, with satisfaction. [they laugh] We are attempting to help.

Astrology and Correspondence

R: All right, now here's another question. Someone asks about the validity of astrology.

TGU: By which we assume they mean, is it a superstition? Is it a science? Is it an art? Is it somewhere in between.

R: Is it true. Is it a truth there to be discovered?

TGU: Well, as everything else, it depends on the definition. [pause] We would say that any form of divination is true in the sense that it may be used adequately and may be used with great profit by the intuitive person who's willing to use it. It doesn't necessarily mean that every concept that's spun within astrology is accurate. Let's back up just a hair here.

What you see as planets are actually alive. Your own planet is alive and you are a part of that planet as well as a part of us. And we are a part of the planet as well as we are a part of you. And we are also a part of Mars, and Jupiter, and Saturn, and Alpha Centauri, and everything else. The difficulty is that on the one hand everything is all one, but there's no point of application for you when you reach that kind of level, so what we are doing is systematically trying to broaden your concept of one, even though it's very much restricted, from our point of view.

So while *we're* aware that all the Milky Way is one, we don't talk of it that way; we talk of it as if all the earth is one, say, or all the solar system. Because they're monads, as we've said. They can all be looked at provisionally as a unit or as a totality – as long as you remember that it's only a relative viewpoint.

All right, having said that. Jupiter is alive. Jupiter is the embodiment of certain energies. And you could rightly ask, what difference does it make what part of the sky Jupiter is in when I'm born, or when an enterprise is born, or whatever the horoscope is used to delineate. Why should it make a difference if it's up in the top of the sky, or it's at the bottom, or it's out of sight? And the answer, in a way, is, it *doesn't* make a difference. But in a way it's, well, it's all part of the master chronometer. Give us a moment here. [long pause]

Any correspondence that's observed with sufficient precision over a long enough period of time has to be presumed to have validity, and astrology has been studied for several thousand years that you know of, and more before that. And what it shows is not really necessarily anything about the planets, although it *seems* to, or the stars behind them, although it *seems* to. What it shows is, when this and that are in relationship, the times will be such that this will be in effect. You see? It's a subtle difference from saying "Mars in the tenth house means this, especially if it's trine Jupiter in the sixth house." It isn't that it's *caused* by that, it's that when that situation arises, the emotional/physical/mental atmosphere is such. That sounds like a meaningless quibble, and it will take us a while to sort out why. Because to us that distinction's clear, but as we even say it, we can hear that there's *no* distinction to you.

R: *Well, the element of causality still seems to be in it when you say it.*

TGU: That's what we're hearing, yes. And that's not what we mean. [sigh] The fact that the minute hand on your watch reaches twelve o'clock doesn't *cause* it to be on the hour, it just *indicates* it. Do you see? It's twelve o' clock because it's twelve o'clock, not because the clock says so. But if you *have* a clock that will tell you when it is, that's valuable.

R: *Because it has certain correlates.*

TGU: Exactly. The distinction between the fact that you can see something which will tell you that something else is in being, and thinking that what you see *causes* the other thing, is important. Can astrology be used? Yes, it can be used. And the reason it can be used, or tarot can be used, or other things, is because everything is connected. [long pause]

Think of astrology as your internal weather report. It will not tell you whether you'll get wet or not, but it may tell you whether it will rain. If you're inside a house, you won't get wet. You see? If you learn the astrological system, and follow it, you'll find that it has great predictive value in reverse. That is, it will give you a good analysis of something that's already happened. It will probably *not* tell you what's *going to* happen, because there are too many ways in which it might express. What it *will* tell you is, whatever happens at that time will have this nature. The difficulty – and it's a fortunate difficulty – is that there are too many things that could happen for it usually to be able to tell you anything. But after it happens, then you can see, "oh yes, this took this, this and this characteristic, just as it should."

Now, that's not you projecting onto it backwards, it's an analysis of the characteristics of what happened to happen. Had something else happened, it *also* would have had those characteristics, but according to its *own* nature, rather than according to the nature of what *did* happen.

We would say, too, using astrology to try to predict things is perhaps not a good use of the tool. Use it to predict the kind of weather that will happen ahead of you, rather than how that weather will probably show. Had you looked at September 11th, you could have quite easily seen what the various cross-currents and all were, but you could not have quite easily seen people were going to run airplanes into buildings. Do you see? *After the fact*, when you know that the airplanes running into the buildings changed your whole world, you could look and say, "oh, well, this, this, and this were elements in that situation."

If you're looking for a road map that will help you to avoid things, there isn't a very good one. And you should rejoice in that. But if you're looking for something that will give you indicators – in other words, "I have to be careful this day because my temper might be on edge," you know, or "I have to be careful during this period of time because I'll be likely to be careless" – that's very possible, and that's a good use for it. If you're looking at it to say, "will a terrorist hold up a bank while I'm there," we suggest you're wasting your time.

R: And is part of the difficulty the time dimension itself?

TGU: Well no, the *whole* difficulty is freedom of choice, and that's your saving grace, as well. The astrological dimension might be said to delineate the boundaries of your freedoms of choice, at a given moment. But what actually *happens* will depend upon what millions of people do in their freedom of choice within those constraints.

R: It still seems odd to me that predictions of the kind you're talking about now seem to be successful. To link what look like such relatively minor things to some immense system that we talk about when we talk about astrology. If we look at how the people are reading physical data in the planets and their movement of bodies in the sky, that somehow this has some suggested correlate in what your mood is going to be.

TGU: But that's not trivial. At all! That's not trivial. You *are* the universe! And that's why it works, because all of us are, in a very real sense, *one thing*. Think of – this is *only* an analogy, but perhaps an illustrative one – think of reality as a hologram in which every fragment has the whole design, but in lesser intensity. Therefore, you reflect the entire cosmos. You can't help it. Well, this is a way of honing in on that. And to use that to describe your own moods so that you can make your own choices, is not a trivial use, at all. That's what you *should* be doing. Not that we're advocating using or not using astrology, but using anything to make better choices, *is* what you should be doing. You are responsible for *you*, and there's no one else responsible for you. So that's your major task! It doesn't sound like much, when you put it that way, but every other task is really kind of a shirking away from that task, unless it flows out of it. [pause]

You could pretend to worry about international affairs or something, but your real task is what you yourself do. Now, if your life has you making an impact on world events, all right. But, what people are thinking of as trivial, they're thinking of as trivial only because it's close to home. And yet that *ought to* tell them, that's vital, that first step. There's an old line of Emerson's, that fortunately we can dredge the old mill here and find, that says "should I raise my siege of a hencoop and march off to a pretended siege of Babylon?" And that's what you do if you don't run your own life and instead go off to do something else –.

R: The "big issues."

TGU: Exactly. So it's not a trivial use at all, it's a good use.

R: Okay. Should we move to another question, or is this about it for tonight? How's Frank doing?

TGU: He's fine. We're okay. [pause] That is, go ahead.

R: This may be a very short question, but –

TGU: Yes. [they chuckle]

World Religions and Truth

R: Which of the world's major religions comes closest to the truth?

TGU: [pause] All of them, none of them. A better question is, which interpretation by any given individual of his own religion, her own religion, comes closest to the truth?

A close analysis of all of the religions would show that they all have aspects of the truth, and no one can have *all* of the truth, not while you're in a body, not while you're in time-space slices. It can't be done. But you can have various *aspects* of the truth, and what one religion emphasizes, another one de-emphasizes. It's not so much a loss as it is different flowers. So that whereas one might emphasize nearness to the divine, and another one might emphasize submission to the overall divine, and a third might emphasize, oh, submission within rules. In other words, in Islam, the underlying idea is absolute willing submission to the Lord, whereas in Judaism it might be a little more flavored like, submission to the following laws. You see, it's a different flavor.

If you look at all the major religions, you'll find they all have different aspects of divinity and they're all accurate. They're all true. You can't say, this religion is wrong. But if you look at Zoroastrianism, with its right versus wrong, with its very much "the world is a battleground between good and evil," that may or may not be in favor at any given time, but it's an accurate aspect of things. It's only *one* aspect of things, but that aspect is there, and the aspect of Hinduism that says "all is one and there is no conflict" is no more and no less accurate than Zoroastrianism. It's just that they're choosing different attributes.

Within the overall unity of the world, there are no *ultimate* contradictions. But within the duality in which you live, there are many *seeming* contradictions, because it's a matter of picking and choosing what your emphasis is. Having said that, if you will worship us and send money on a regular basis...[they laugh]

R: It seems as though some religions are more [pause] sympathetic with the human condition, or more appropriate on this level of existence, this physical plane of existence –

TGU: No, we can't go along with that. No, your western viewpoint leads you to certain values, and religions that don't emphasize those values or that even oppose some of those values seem to you inhuman, but yours seems inhuman to them. There's just not an absolute standard. If there *were* an absolute standard, it would say something like "you're all right, but you're all incomplete." Well, you're all wrong, yeah. [they laugh] You know Frank always says that he thinks God looks down and goes, "you idiots, what are you up to now?" [laughs] But it's *not* that, it's that you're all different kinds of flowers, and to each its own nature. When you think of the vast variety of human psychology in the world, it would be ludicrous to think that one kind of religion would fit all. There are too many kinds of needs in the world for one religion to meet all the needs. One religion for people who have a strong emotional need, and another for people who need to be part of the same thing, another for people who need to be freethinkers, you see.

There are practically infinite varieties of religion, because there are infinite varieties of emotional and mental and spiritual needs. And, rather than – we're not saying that you yourself are doing this, of course – rather than *condemning* the various religions, it would be more appropriate and more fruitful to try to get inside of the mind of someone who would find that religion appropriate, and that will *teach* you lots. It will help you triangulate your *own* point of view by going to *someone else's* point of view.

That was a good question, by the way.

The Meaning of Dreams

R: Okay, I was going to ask about dream analysis. What is the meaning of dreams and how to think about them and interpret them in a way that's of best use to us. Starting with, what is that all about?

TGU: That will all depend entirely upon the starting point of the person. Dream analysis for a person in an Islamic society or in a communist society as it was, or in an African society or in an American Indian society would be vastly different, not because dreams are different, but because the standpoint from which the local individual attempts to make sense of them is different. Do you mean, from an American-European point of view? We'll do whatever you want, but we're just trying to get the sense of, where do you want us to begin the effort?

R: You're saying that dreams have different meanings for various parts of the population? Or are you saying that the way of going about analyzing them – ?

TGU: We're saying that the standing-place of the individual is so different, that they'll have to approach dreams in a different way. No, dreams are the same thing always. Dreams are your larger being communicating with you. But your *society's* beliefs, and your individual beliefs *within* your society's beliefs, will condition the way that you *experience* the dreams, and therefore what's appropriate for a college-educated Westerner in the 21st century, would not be appropriate for a – oh, say a Puritan in the 1700s in New England, just to make a neutral example. That's all we're saying. Dreams are serving the purposes, but the *recipients* of the dreams will experience them differently and therefore you need to know something about where they're starting from. Don't know a better way to put that.

R: When you say that dreams are messages from the total being – is that the way you said it?

TGU: From your larger being, sure. Your amoeba.

R: Why are they made so hard to interpret? Why aren't the messages more easily understood?

TGU: Well, [pause] well, a simple answer, and as usual a somewhat inaccurate *because it's a* simple answer, would be, that you're not all that familiar with the language of the dream. You, Rita, know Monroe's emphasis on non-verbal communication, and that language that *he* had to learn is your easiest approach with dreams, because your larger being doesn't usually speak to you in words, it speaks to you in NVC, or in symbols. So even if the symbols are strung together to make a story, it's a story that's primarily in experience and emotional *feel*, rather than in words or logical concepts. If you have been educated in such a way as to recognize logical concepts and words, but *not* recognize gesture, emotional symbolism – drama, in short – then it's going to be difficult for you to get to make sense of it.

When Frank began his own dream analysis, he had a very difficult time because, being so word-oriented and being so literal-oriented, he was continually attempting to correct the dream. He would say, "well, it was my father's house, but really my father's house didn't actually have this, that, and the other." And he had to learn that there were no accidents in the dream, that that particular symbol had been melded to another symbol in a way that was illogical but that was emotionally significant. Once he learned the language, he began to learn how to do it. But the basic answer to your question is, your society does not teach that language, either by example or certainly by general schooling. *You* had to learn it through *specific* schooling.

And in any case, it had only been rediscovered relatively recently. How long has it been rediscovered, that language? A hundred years. Basically nothing. In fact, if we may say so, you are about as far with dreams as you are with the Monroe symbolism. [they laugh] Which actually is a hopeful thing, if you stop and think about it. You have much more to learn.

R: I think we might come back to that subject later, but I'd like to have the question that Frank had asked me to ask.

TGU: This is a good one to stop with, too. Let's stop after this one.

R: Whether or not we should speed up our process here by having more sessions than we've been having. There are sub-questions to that, but that's one part of it.

TGU: No, we think not. We think you're doing fine, and it's well suited to your energies, and he's just getting a little impatient. However, it's a free will thing, and if you *want* to do more, we won't *not* show up.

R: I understand, you're available. Very reassuring.

TGU: [yawns] We would say that's about it for tonight, though.

Session Twelve
October 30, 2001

The Larger Being and God

R: Last week we were talking about what happens when we drop the body and move into your territory. You said a number of things I'd like to follow-up on. One is, "a scenario is being created and individuals dropping their body are being inserted into it." And another quote, "we are all under an over-arching intelligence that creates the whole thing." This suggests, certainly, a creator or a God or a plan developer of some kind –

TGU: Well, now, we would caution you on the first part. Remember, somewhere we said that the scenario that you walk into when you drop your body is actually planned around you and for you and partly built by you – by your larger being that you're a part of. And the awareness or non-awareness of a larger being determines whether or not you think that scenario either came into being by itself or that you made it up. Remember? So, your speculation is not necessarily wrong, but in that particular instance, you yourself – the larger you, the amoeba you – are crafting the conditions for your own future development.

R: All right. That makes sense. Now the other one, the "over-arching intelligence creates the whole thing."

TGU: We don't know any more than you know. We surmise. Something created this. We can't believe in the thing that created itself. Maybe at some point we'll be wise enough to know; at this point we don't know. It's clear to us that something intelligent devised it, and that's as far as we're going at the moment.

R: Do you have a preference for one term or another for that, like creator, or God, or something to use rather than use all those words to talk about what we're –

TGU: That's a very good problem to bring up. You know how picky we are about language, often. Our concern is always to try to be sure that undesired nuances are not incidentally carried along. So our preference will probably change in the context. In some contexts "God" might be perfectly acceptable, and in other contexts it might suggest attributes or other things that aren't appropriate; that will warp the understanding. So, pick whatever you feel like at the moment, and if it's carrying nuances that we want to correct, that after all may be useful. Trust your judgment.

R: One reason I raise this is that Frank has said at one time or another that he doesn't know if he believes in a God. That could be changing now. So I don't like using that word I guess, because of the possibility of transmission difficulties.

TGU: Well, that's his problem. [laughs] Don't misunderstand that to mean that he feels like he's an atheist. He's more or less where we are; he knows there was some kind of creator, but doesn't know beyond that. And so when people say "God," what they mean by it is usually so vague, that's more or less what he's responding to.

Well, we'll go a little further. If we remember the conversation – and we guarantee you that he does not – [laughs] it was in the context of someone –

[As Frank]: Now isn't that funny? Popped right out [of the altered state].Hang on a second. [pause]

[Resuming as TGU:] Here's the point that he's going to be moving toward. Having the experience of dealing with us, he has seen that nearly everything that people have described as God may be their descriptions of us, depending on what kind of reporters they were. So he doesn't know if the evidence describes such a thing. Beyond that, he's probably not willing to go.

Stretching to Other Layers

R: All right. Do you have a sense of a number of layers between you and whatever or whoever is in charge?

TGU: No more than you do.

R: Well, we have a sense of layers.

TGU: How many? [they laugh]

R: Well, we've only communicated with one, but that's to the point here. Is there some way, either by our words or anything else like a meditation process, that we can get in touch with the next layer, if there is one, to ask questions?

TGU: Well, here's your problem. You're already dealing in territory that you can scarcely see the outlines of, because you're just beginning. And to go beyond this territory into something else, you'll be even blinder than you are here. Unless you're dissatisfied with the service you've been receiving [they laugh] we don't quite see why you'd want to do that.

R: We're definitely not dissatisfied. Well, I guess the question behind that is, can you get in touch with the next layer?

TGU: Well, now, don't let spatial analogy get in your way too much here. You know, it sneaks into everything.

Let's take out the word "levels" if we can. Let's say there are aspects of The Great Everything that are closer to you from where you are. And the best way to find the other ones is to change what you are rather than to stretch to them. Do you see what we're saying? You're stretching a bit to see us, and we're stretching a bit to see you, to communicate. And that's fine, that's appropriate. But to try to reach beyond us at this point would be the equivalent of your trying to reach us had you been at a lower level. (The "level" sneaks right back in again.) Do you see what we're saying? The thing nearest to hand is always the thing that's most productive to do. But on the other hand, maybe you'll try it and something will happen.

Now, having said all that, let's put one little caveat in here. People have direct experiences of God. They don't have to go through us to God. And we don't know what that experience is, necessarily, and they don't necessarily know, but people recognize something that's real. Do you see?

R: Yes, I see that you're saying that. Now, I don't want my last question to get lost, which was, can you get in touch with the next layer or aspect or whatever is next? And I don't know why we should ask that of you, because if you don't want to do it, then –

TGU: Well, no, we didn't say any more about it because we thought we'd answered it. You already have put us on that track. It is by us following our guidance that we will, to the degree that we can, reach that way.

R: Okay, so you're already doing whatever you're going to do about that.

TGU: Well, let's say the concept's in the mind, anyway. And we don't know but that the other layer may have given you the idea to give to us. Things do work that way. Different fragments suggest things to each other, which is a way for any given fragment to become more conscious; that some other fragment gave him something. You see it in your own life all the time: Someone will say something to you, which has impact. Well, that saying may sometimes have been suggested to them, and run right through them without their thinking about it. You may be serving the same function with us, occasionally.

Becoming More Individual

R: Another thing came up in the last session, the idea that not every individual leads what we were calling a successful life, so that when they drop the body there may be no advantage to having that individual continue. Would we have any idea on this side what would constitute a successful life worth continuing?

TGU: Well let's quarrel with your definition. It is because they *don't* become sufficiently individual that it's not worth continuing. So to call them an individual brings in nuances through the back door that you probably don't mean. What we would regard as an unsuccessful life – or, not necessarily unsuccessful so much as not worth continuing – is one that's not very individual, not very – [pause] Searching for an analogy, here.

If you were trying to crystallize a chemical solution, you might seed it correctly and come up with a wonderful crystal. Or, another time, or another solution, nothing particular might happen. A couple little grains or something. And you just throw it out and start again. [chuckles] That seems a little harsh, but –

R: Yeah, it did seem a little harsh, but then as I thought about it and you pointed out, nothing's lost.

TGU: Pour the water back in the same pan.

R: Okay, so then the question that came out of that was, would we have any idea on this side what would constitute a life worth continuing?

TGU: Well, that's actually several questions, because if you keep changing the definition of "we," for instance, every one could be different. But the best way to say it is, many of your religious and philosophical traditions are devoted specifically toward helping you to become an individual. Gurdjieff in particular is concerned with helping people to crystallize their individuality, which will be preserved on the other side. This is not saying that's the only way to do that, of course, but it's saying that there is that train of thought. You won't nearly so likely notice the failures as you'll notice the occasional spectacular successes. They will have an aura, so to speak.

R: You see, I'm getting a very different idea about this tonight than I had last week, because you're talking in terms of becoming more an individual.

TGU: Well, remember we say "you're here to choose and choose and choose," and all that choosing is what makes you an individual. It sets the flower that you become.

R: But the notion I had going into it was that the consequence of those choices is somehow increasingly different from others.

TGU: Can't help it. That's what happens. But if you are in a situation that doesn't call for meaningful choices, you might wind up with 400,000 flowers that are more or less identical, and you only have a market for 200,000 of them. [they chuckle] Put it that way. It's not that simple, but that's the best we're going to do at the moment; maybe we'll come back to it.

R: Okay, well there's some thoughts in that one. [pause] We've been using the concept "vibratory level" a number of times, and I found I don't really know what that meant.

TGU: Well, good! [they laugh] Good. It's only an analogy. Remember, we tried several. We tried vibratory level, we tried specific gravity, we tried pH. They're all inadequate analogies, *necessarily inadequate* analogies, because if there were an adequate analogy, we could discard it as an analogy and just use it. [pause]

As a person develops their own force, their own being – as they crystallize, let's put it that way for the moment – they raise levels, so to speak. It's an increase in self-awareness and an increase in self-command. That is, not only does the flashlight have a good battery in it, but the person more and more knows where to shine the flashlight.

It depends on how you want to look at it. As a light analogy, you could say it is the flashlight getting more and more intensity and a wider scope, so that the person's consciousness – in all aspects of the word "consciousness," not just awareness – spreads to a larger part of itself and therefore becomes, effectively, larger. It was always larger *potentially*, but now *effectively* it becomes larger. Or, a different analogy, you could say the person lives at a more intense level and therefore crystallizes around its own seriousness, its own being. It becomes more fully and thoroughly what it potentially is. It's really the same statement two ways.

It's only an analogy, but when we say a higher vibratory level, typically we will mean the person is functioning at a more intense and a more self-aware level.

Monroe and Religious Systems

R: One of the things that gets connected with this in the Monroe programs is the concept of using certain kinds of tapes with certain kinds of vibratory levels built into the tape, and then increasing vibratory rates as one goes into certain kinds of tapes, and so on. And it seems as though this is trying to help us increase our vibratory level. Is there any relationship there?

TGU: Not the relationship they're implying, because it is only an analogy. And we'll be perfectly willing to use a different analogy if you wish to suggest one. One problem with the Monroe system is that the spatial analogy sneaks in. And the assumption is, the higher numbers are a higher, more intense state, whereas from our viewpoint, the higher numbers are just a little farther away from normality. That doesn't necessarily mean more intense. It may mean different. So, to imply that going to Focus 21 is more intense than going to Focus 12 is totally misleading. It's false. It may be more intense, it may not be more intense. It depends on the intensity of the person at the moment when they're in one of those states.

You could have a state of intensity in C1 that would far exceed anything in Focus 21, if it happened to be that way.

The thing is, when they're concentrating themselves on the exercises whether they're using tapes or not, they tend to be more concentrated, because they have their mind on it. But that's all that's going on there. Now, to the degree a person is more mindful, more self-aware, more intent on becoming more completely oneself, that person is going to be at a higher level of consciousness, regardless whether they use the tapes or ever hear the word Monroe. That in fact is part of the mystical core of religious systems, throughout the world. One of the goals.

R: Could you say a bit more about that?

TGU: We thought it was obvious.

R: [laughs] Well, you suddenly brought in another dimension.

TGU: Well, every religion has an esoteric and an exoteric segment. We are ignoring for the moment distortions caused by ambition or political considerations. Ignoring those, pretending that it's pure, the *exoteric* trappings of a religion are designed to provide a society that will support development in certain directions among people who do not develop themselves; that is, those who depend upon their environment. The *esoteric* core is designed for those who do, and this provides them with internal and external supports, goals, laid-out paths. It's basically a mystery school. So that in this case, the Monroe system is an esoteric core of a belief system that has no exoteric core yet, although it's forming. Okay?

R: [Doubtfully] Mmm.

TGU: We'll be glad to say more. Tell us what you want.

R: Well, if we were to take Jim Marion's developmental system, he describes [in his book called Putting On the Mind of Christ*] a developmental path that has nine or ten or eleven stages. Would you call that increasing individualizing?*

TGU: Certainly you could. That's one way to look at it.

R: I think I've said enough about that right now.

TGU: We'll be glad to go more on this at any time. Some things are so obvious to us that we forget they may not be obvious from your point of view, and this may be one of them, or may not. Just as for you. For you, it's obvious that you're right here, right now, but we have to sometimes look for you. [they laugh]

Intermediaries

R: Okay. [pause] I'm still involved in some follow-up here. Last time we talked about intermediaries needed on your side to bring about interactions between those of different vibratory levels. Still on the vibratory level analogy.

TGU: Well, again, it's a good analogy. We'll use it unless it gets in your way. We were only saying that while you're in the body, you have the ability to mingle with others of very vastly different vibratory levels, and we do not.

R: So intermediaries are needed on your side. Who are the intermediaries?

TGU: Well, it depends on who you're trying to deal with. If we're on level 30 and we want to talk to somebody at level 60, we need somebody between 30 and 60 who can reach in both directions. That's all that means. But if we're trying to talk to level 15, we need somebody who is between those levels. Sort of like passing a message down the line, in a sense.

Entering the Physical

[Sometimes, communication gets difficult! This section is an example of what can happen.]

R: Why would a person be formed for the first time and sent into a body?

TGU: [pause] We don't see any real way to answer that question. Remember, the person doesn't exist until it's formed, so you can't say the person did it. The person is formed out of certain elements that are part of a common mind, so to speak. Oh, your question probably means, do we do it or does a higher level do it?

R: Well, or is this part of the activity of the amoeba? I'm just really clueless as to how that process is. One hears all sorts of things like, "well, they're standing in line in heaven to try to get a body," and obviously there are all sorts of things wrong with that statement.

TGU: Oh but we thought you said one starting from the beginning.

R: Yeah. That's what I did.

TGU: Let's take a little detour here. If the amoeba already exists, then the forming of another sojourn, so to speak – you know, the putting together of elements to go into another lifetime – is done more or less by the amoeba in connection with the elements around it that are closest to it in sympathy. But if you're talking about forming an amoeba from the beginning, to make its first foray, that's what we thought you meant, and we haven't the slightest idea.

R: Okay, well let me either add to the confusion or whatever, but are you saying that every amoeba has had experiences here?

TGU: Well, no. We're saying that every amoeba that has a body in the physical has had the experiences, but we didn't think you would be talking about the ones who hadn't, because they wouldn't come into it.

R: Well they would come into it in the fact that they had never had a body.

TGU: Well, but you were asking specifically about a new body being formed in the physical. So to us the other ones wouldn't come into the equation at all.

Let's look at this again. Say we have 100 amoebae altogether in the whole works. And of those hundred, maybe 15 have part of themselves – have lifetimes – in the physical, on earth. At whatever time, it doesn't matter what time. The other 85 have no earth experience, no physical life experience. And so to us when we're talking about something in the physical, we wouldn't talk about the 85, unless you want to just note that in fact the vast majority don't have expression in the physical.

R: That's including elsewhere as well as here?

TGU: Correct. Remember how we say we often use "earth" meaning "in the physical"? Yes, that's the sense in which we mean it.

So – of those who do have one or more lives in the physical, when they want to go in again, as we say, the elements already mixed. Well – we'll think about this a minute. How to say this.

We haven't looked at this before, but bear in mind, each of the amoebae could be looked at in the same way that you look at each of you as individuals. They're all comprising the same materials, but all in a somewhat unique way. Just as you all have the same number of limbs and organs, but your faces are radically different and your general demeanor and your energy signature, so to speak, is different, so with the amoebae. There is the equivalent. The analogy is good enough, all right?

So, an amoeba [pause] choosing to enter into physical life again can do it in one of two ways. It can funnel through lives that have already been through the physical –

(This is going to be very confusing for the moment. This will take us a while, probably – and not tonight – to untangle this, but it will be worthwhile.)

It can choose to go through lives that have come before (before in its soul growth, not necessarily chronologically) and in that case you get people with a strong sense of reincarnation, because it's feeding through. They [amoebas] can also pull together a little of their mix and put it in to the physical without feeding through the ones who've already been through, and there you get people with a sense of not necessarily having reincarnation.

Now, as far as we know we have never talked about this, and Frank's never seen anybody talk about it as far as we've dredged the old data banks. Because people keep thinking in terms of individuals on this side, rather than seeing the difference in the way things are. But one amoeba may have, say, six lives that are chained, and so the awareness of one comes through the awareness of another, comes through the awareness of another, all right? As in his case with John Cotton, and Smallwood, and Katrina and those others that he's sort of plucked out of the air.

But the same amoeba not only *can* but almost always *will* have others that are either chained in different ways or not at all; and he [any given individual] may not have any inkling of connection with them until he gets to another level at which he sees the broader connections. At that level you get people who really begin to understand that all humanity is one family. They understand it at a visceral, emotional level.

So those are three possible results, psychologically, on your end, of the process that comes from our end. This is really more or less of a diversion from the question, but –

R: My question really was about the other 85 percent.

TGU: It wasn't originally. [laughs]

R: I'll read you the original question.

TGU: Originally you said coming in the first time.

R: Yes. Why would an amoeba decide to send a part of itself – whatever one thinks about that – for the first time into a body?

TGU: All right, let's just be clear here. You are not, then, talking about an amoeba being formed for the first time.

R: I want to ask that too. [they laugh] I realize there are two questions.

TGU: That's the one we said we don't know. The second one, "why," well, there are as many motives as you would have as an individual in doing something new. There could be curiosity – in fact, would be –

Do you remember the report that Monroe made in his second book – Frank can find it for you quite easily – about going into the physical? [*Far Journeys,* chapter 10, "Newfound Friend."] The tourist was getting ready to go into the physical for the first time. And Monroe very carefully put four examples of different reasons why people went into the physical. And if you'll look at it closely, it will be very illustrative. For instance, one said, going back for retraining. And another one said, "don't come back until you're well." [they chuckle] One said he was doing an academic experiment, something like that. Frank can find that without any trouble at all, and that will shed light on this.

But, having said that, there are as many reasons for doing it as there are for you doing anything.

The Lure of the Physical

R: Well there's apparently some lure on your side that says how great it is to be a human.

TGU: The major lure to us – the major benefit – is twofold. One, you do have the ability to mingle with those of other levels, which is very productive, and you have the law of delayed consequences, where, being enmeshed in time-slices, and space-slices, you make choices and watch them go forward. That is to say, it's slowed down enough that you experience them. Those are very powerful lures. That's why this was created, because it's a compressed learning system. And although we've said repeatedly that it's not a school, there is learning involved in the sense of forcing a flower in a hothouse. Perhaps you don't want to be a gladiola today.

R: [chuckles] Daisy, please.

TGU: A daisy, you can be a daisy. So –

However, it's also known to be extremely challenging. There are some people who just like to join the Marines.

R: Okay, so what about this notion that there are many souls looking to be in a body, and having to stand in line for that. Does that compute in any way?

TGU: Well, it conveys the sense that being in the physical is in a way a tremendous privilege. It perhaps is a bleed-through of human terms into the idea, because they may be thinking that people want to be born into 21st-century America which is to say, one of the richest people in the world. There's more of a waiting line for that than there is to be born a peasant in India – unless those are the particular choices that you want to be faced with.

R: And at some point there are presumably going to be a limitation on the number of bodies to be supported on this earth.

TGU: Although we almost always deal in probabilities and choices rather than predictions, we will say that we don't see any significant number of realities in which the population continues to grow and grow and grow, or even to maintain itself at your present unsustainable level. It could be done, and occasionally is done, but mostly not. No chance. Not even desirable. However, it was desirable to bring you up to this level as you know. When you succeed in getting to the next level of complexity, so that you are actually interacting with us all the time, then there will not be a need for so many people here. So many people here would actually be in the way, and being on the other side will be beneficial to them and the earth. And there'll be lots of people dying, and everybody will say what a tragedy it is.

R: Yes, it's hard for us not to think of it that way, but I hear you.

TGU: Get used to it.

R: [pause] Okay, and so on the question of the number of amoebae. Can we think about numbers of amoebas?

TGU: [laughs] 100.3.

R: I don't want to know how many. [they laugh] We got into this possibility of forming a new amoeba. I want to know – is there some limit to the number of amoebas?

TGU: Well, we don't really have any idea. It's not something we've observed. It isn't like new beings are created absolutely. Lives are created in the physical and go out again, but that's not the same as creating a life from our point of view. However, that doesn't mean it doesn't happen. We don't know. We'll look around.

R: You don't think a couple of amoebas get together and create a third?

TGU: [chuckles] You may be really disappointed in the other side. [they laugh]

However, it is an interesting question. This may be one more thing that we have to consider. If something comes up, we'll let you know. It isn't like we sit around and take censuses. But we haven't observed it. Well, we can't envision it, actually. We can't envision new things being created. We envision beings coming from one portion and going to somewhere else. The equivalent would be, they're born into one area and die from another area, but the total is presumably the same. If we come up with new information, we'll let you know. And if you want to ask it, in slightly different ways every so often, that would be fine too. That might help. Don't take that as an assignment, however. It's only if you want to do it.

Dreams, the Amoeba, and the Unconscious

R: Someone asked a number of questions that were follow-ons to the dream analysis questions we had last week. And the first question was, "does amoeba mean the same as unconscious?"

TGU: Hmm. Well, that depends on what either of those mean to you! [laughs] But to answer the question in the spirit that it's meant, the contents of the amoeba might be perceived by an individual as part of the unconscious.

R: Then he also asks whether we could equate amoeba and Jung's collective unconscious.

TGU: We would say rather that Jung was courageously pushing into territory that seemed occult to his contemporaries, and it was nearly totally unknown territory. Starting from the point of view that thought that individuals were real, as he did, that's how he experienced it. If you will think in the terms that we're encouraging you to think – that is, of all of us being one on this end, and you appearing to be separate on your end – a lot of what Carl Jung did accurately *report* will be seen to be very inaccurately *interpreted*. Or, let's say we can come up with a better interpretation. You can come up with it yourselves.

He was a wonderful trail breaker, and had he been more accurate, he probably would have been disregarded entirely, and could not have served as the halfway house. You see?

R: All right, this person is also asking you to differentiate between dreams and lucid dreams.

TGU: Well, in our view the most productive way of looking at it, is that a dream comes to you when your flashlight is either nearly off or dim, and a lucid dream comes when your flashlight has for one reason or another become more intense. So that really "lucid dream" and "unconsciousness" are a contradiction in terms, whereas a regular dream and unconsciousness are not quite a contradiction in terms. If that's not helpful, we'll go back over it again, or add more.

A regular dream comes, and your own ability to apprehend it and to participate in it is very limited. A lucid dream and a dream may be the exact same thing, but your ability to interact with a lucid dream is greater, because for some reason or other your energy of consciousness is greater, and that's what's the difference, it's not a difference in the incoming experience.

R: In a lucid dream you're more a participant.

TGU: That's right. It isn't that you're more a participant because something came along that you could participate in more, it's that you are in a condition of being able to do it. We're trying to underline that you don't control the dream in either sense. The dream is coming to you. But how you interact with it depends on your own ability at the moment, which among other things includes your energy and your awareness.

We're trying to de-emphasize the idea of a difference between a regular dream and a lucid dream, and strongly emphasize the difference between where you are yourself between the one and the other.

It's meant to encourage you to realize you can do much more. Even the people who will teach you how to do lucid dreaming – their techniques amount to increasing your consciousness of it. You see? To putting more mental energy in it. When you do that, then the *dream* doesn't change, *you* change. You experience it as a lucid dream. It's the same thing as what it was. Your experience changes because you've changed the amount of energy that you have at your command.

R: Well now, this same question includes asking the extent to which either dreaming or lucid dreaming are different from out-of-body experiences or phase shifts.

TGU: A phase shift *is* an out-of-body experience, and we prefer Monroe's term of phase shift, as we said before, only because it helps to eliminate that nuance of going somewhere, where there's nowhere to go. But if you will look at the previous answer, this should be obvious in that context. A phase shift is again a different level of energy from a lucid dream and from a dream, and it's well known that you can move from one to the other to the other if you can increase your energy.

The variable that's not commonly known is, your own ability to mobilize your energy and your consciousness, your psychic energy, varies for reasons that are obscure to you. Therefore, it appears to you as though sometimes a dream will come, sometimes a lucid dream, sometimes an OBE or a phase shift will come, or the opportunity for one. But what actually has varied is not the incoming experience. What's varied is your own mobilization of energy. [pause]

So people, in beginning to look at these things, are naming what they think are three different experiences. Those are shadows. It's the same experience; the differences are on the other end, which makes them seem like different experiences. Okay?

We've messed that up a little bit by using the word experience too much. The incoming data, the nature of the dream, is the same in three instances; it's what you can bring to it that varies. That's why the one unvaried incoming experience looks different.

[chuckles] We have a feeling that we could have said that much easier and much quicker, and now every word that we're adding to it is making it less clear.

R: I was just remembering how annoyed Bob Monroe was when he was told by the lucid dreamers that out-of-body experiences were nothing but lucid dreams. He felt really put down by that.

TGU: And rightly so, because they were not saying what we're saying! They were saying it was inaccurate observation on his part. [they laugh] Which is not what we're saying.

Creating Reality, Being Dreamed

R: All right, this is a continuation of questions by the same individual. He doesn't think he creates the realities he finds himself in, even though he can change some things about that realities.

TGU: If by "he," he means his conscious self, we entirely agree with him.

R: That sounds like what he meant. He does not create the realities.

TGU: By definition your conscious self does not create your dream.

R: Okay. I don't know if he's now talking about dreams or moving on. I think he is still talking about dreams. So you'd say the amoeba is possibly creating the reality.

TGU: We wouldn't say possibly.

R: Yes. But it's not conscious. Some aspect of the amoeba.

TGU: That's correct.

R: Okay. And he asks if he's dreaming now.

TGU: Ha, ha! Wonderful accurate perception. Although it might be slightly more accurate to say you are being dreamed.

R: By the amoeba?

TGU: [sigh] What you just said isn't wrong, but it's not complete either. Let's leave that for a while, and we'll tell you why. Were we to say more now, people would be inclined to take it as the final word, or to discard it, whereas if we just leave it like this now, some people will think about it, and ponder it, and it comes better when it comes to you rather than us giving it to you. It's stronger. We don't mean to be too mysterious about it, but sometimes mystery is a powerful teacher.

R: All right, then the final question he had is, who creates realities, and the entities in the dreams and phase shifts?

TGU: We would say, the shorthand is the amoeba creates them. Not a totally complete answer, but for now.

Conspiracies and Living in Faith

R: All right, we have another questioner here, and you're going to have to give me some feedback on how long you wish to go on.

TGU: This is the illuminati?

R: Yes.

TGU: That has bothered Frank quite a bit, all week. And is quite productive.

R: Okay, let me ask the question as it's posed here.

TGU: Um, ask it in sequence, if you would, and give us time each time, rather than read the whole thing, 'cause there's no way we could respond to it that way.

R: Okay, then, it's: What do you know of the reptilian agenda?

TGU: Nothing.

R: The 13 Illuminati bloodlines?

TGU: Um, we'd better answer what she means rather than what she says. Because to answer what she says, the answer would be "nothing." What she means we'll get to in a bit. Go ahead.

R: Control of the human race by chloride, chemtrails, using humans as puppets, as in the 9-11 disaster.

TGU: Nothing.

R: Injection of minute computer chips by a flu or other injections.

TGU: Less than nothing.

R: The building of prisons, concentration camps, throughout the United States for people after martial law is declared.

TGU: Nothing. Now –

R: And FEMA, she wanted to add. [FEMA, of course, is the Federal Emergency Management Agency, officially tasked with coordinating response to disasters such as hurricanes, but suspected by some of having another agenda. It wasn't quite as well known to the general public prior to Hurricane Katrina in 2005.]

TGU: Well we know plenty about FEMA, everyone does, but not what they mean, so the answer should be nothing in a sense.

R: Okay.

TGU: Now, let us really get down to this. This is going to take a little bit, but it's very worthwhile.

We began by telling you that this is quite disturbing material, and not many people are going to like it, necessarily. Which is bothering Frank, you see. [pause]

When a person who is idealistic, or even decent – using good and evil terms, but we need to use them for the moment – when a good and decent person sees what to them appears evil, it is very natural for them to oppose the evil. That's the nature of things.

When such a person gets into a state of fear, the fear conjures up the shadows in all directions, and if they are not careful they will wind up in a labyrinth of shadows that leaves them feeling powerless, threatened, oppressed – and they can wind up becoming some of the worst oppressors the world has ever seen. We'll give you specific examples, because Frank's got 'em in his data base. And the first one is something that was called the Great Terror.

Back in the 1700s, in France, when the French Revolution began, the peasantry and the lower middle classes overthrew the aristocracy, which had kept them very severely downtrodden. In their initial freedom, for the first time in recorded Western history, the great terror came, the great fear, because they began to fear that there were plots to re-deprive them of their freedom, you see. Having gained an amazing change in their lifetimes, they feared that that change would be overthrown, because they knew full well, and accurately, that the old order wasn't going to just throw up its hands, but would counter-attack them. Having no way of gauging what the counter-attack would be, having no experience of the aristocracy and what their limitations and abilities were, the minds of the people began generating more and more fears, and the fears became exaggerated. And the fears had no limits, because they had no data, you see.

Now, it's well known how rumor will exaggerate, and it's well known, or should be well known, how a mob will have a mentality lower than any of the individuals comprising the mob. Put those two things together, and you have the emotional beginnings of the Reign of Terror, that happened in France. The Reign of Terror was started by people who themselves were in terror, you see? They were fearing to lose what they had gained; they knew they had real enemies, but didn't know where they were; they knew they were facing real dangers but didn't know what they were, and they knew they had to take action, and the action took on a life of its own, as it always does.

The Russian Revolution [of 1917] happened in more or less the same way. The peasants freed themselves from a thousand years of oppression; they were being attacked by real forces from the West and also they were being opposed by forces of their own aristocracy, who were also of course being financed and supported by the West. And again, not knowing who the enemy was, not knowing what the enemy could do, not knowing the limits and nature of the threat, the terror that they were in created a terror that was aimed outwards. And to look at it from a point of view of good and evil, evil came directly from fear, and the fear came from people who were doing something that they regarded as good, countering something that was too vague for them to be able to attack.

And we're going to bring in an example that bears on it, although not directly, and that is the Luddites. You may have heard of people who in the early 1800s in England began smashing machinery – looms and things – because they recognized that even the limited kind of automation that was there then was going to put people out of work, and they knew there was no social support network (there wasn't even a word for such a thing), and they knew they were facing starvation and ruin. And so they began destroying the machinery, trying to protect what they knew against they knew not what. Now, that's not relevant to terror; it's relevant to the unknown that's going to transform their lives.

Now, let's come more directly to the question.

The people in America and certain countries in Western Europe have a great disadvantage in that they mostly believe that their government is good, whereas most of the rest of the world knows that their own governments are not good. Americans are beginning to realize that government is not good, and that realization leaves them somewhat at sea. When people are faced with realizations that they can't handle, and dangers that they can't weigh, one possible result is to follow people who say, "it is the Bilderberger group, it is the Illuminati, it is this, it is that, it is the Rockefellers, it is George Schultz, it is" – name something. Even though, or perhaps we should say *because*, they know there is a threat but they cannot judge the threat, they're willing to listen to someone who tells them with great confidence, "this is the threat, I know what it is, here's what you need to do."

Now, we're probably going to offend everyone in sight, but – that's the way it is. Government at all levels, top to bottom, is set up for one reason but actually functions at a day-to-day level for a different reason. A government functionary is in business primarily to protect his own function, and secondarily to profit from that function as he can, depending on his own level of what you might call corruption, and what he might call self-interest. There was a congressman who said that the motto of Congress is "nothing for nothing"; that is to say, having the ability to make a decision that will make major money for one sector, or cost money to another sector, they see no reason not to profit personally from that decision.

It's worse than that, though.

In your time, your governments have totally become captive of those who have the money. Money has always run politics, but in this case, you now have your criminals running your institutions. People know this, and are getting somewhat desperate about it, but they haven't thought it through to realize that it isn't a few criminals who threaten an otherwise good institution, and it isn't that some people are good and some are evil. It is that, inherent in the nature of your society as constituted is the predatory society that Bob Monroe talked about. Once organized criminals overcame the reluctance that they had to take over civil society – and they did have such a reluctance – there was nothing to stop them from doing it. And they have done it. You have things done in your name every day that would appall you, were you to be aware of it, and you have no more ability to stop it than you have to fly to the moon, in your body.

Now, when you watch people overseas cheering because Americans were killed, you are seeing those people reacting to what they know of what your government has done in your name. What they don't know, of course, and you do know, is what *their* government is doing in *their* name.

In such a predatory situation, predators rise to the top of the heap, in terms of power and influence, and for you to assume that your secret services, or your law enforcement officers, or your government officials of any kind, have anything that they hold higher than their own self-interest would be naïve to an almost unforgivable extent at this point, because there's too much evidence.

Very bleak picture that we've just painted here, but it's important for you to realize that we see this. Having said this, this is not the whole picture, and the people who are following the trails of the Illuminati and the other secret societies that they think are running things don't realize that they are making a behind-the-scenes assumption that government is usually good and is being threatened by a takeover by these people behind the scenes.

In actual fact, governments are always in one way or another a conspiracy. You have had the unusual experience of having governments that were more or less neutral, and in fact in the perspective of history almost startlingly idealistic, particularly the British Empire, the American and the Scandinavian governments. Well, we can't at all say they were corruption-free, but they did their jobs, and their ideal was to do the job, rather than the ideal and the necessity being "milk the job for what it's worth so that when you're out of office you won't be destitute." Okay?

Now, we want to change the point of view a little bit. Take a congressman, or a policeman on the take, or any corrupt individual anywhere, and you will find a person in a position who says, "I am here for now; I won't be here forever, and these people –"

For instance, a policeman guarding rich people doesn't regard rich people as being better than him because they have money, he regards them as having money because in one way or another the deck was rigged. We would not disagree with that. So it becomes harder and harder for a policeman to maintain social order –

which is what he's supposedly paid to do – when what it really means is, protect the privilege of people who he may not have any respect for at all.

If you have a civil servant who has to make a zoning decision, or a decision between contractors, the idealistic way of looking at it is to do what's in the public interest. What seems like realism to him is, "these people are going to make a fortune on this; there's no reason why I shouldn't have some of it myself. I would be a fool not to." And in fact, many of them [the contractors] would regard the situation in the same light.

So, you have a situation in which your average citizen is taught an entirely incorrect view of civics and politics, and is kept in the dark about the real way that your society is managed, because of course it is not in the interest of the people who own the media and who own the means of information to make those things known.

In that situation, which could be defined as a vacuum of information, people see with their eyes that things are rotten, but they don't know why, and they don't know how, and so there comes the great terror.

Now, the joker in the deck is this. That's the grim situation as it looks from a Downstairs perspective, but guess what. The deck can be stacked from the other side, and we're stacking it every day.

Does that adequately answer the question, do you think?

R: [pause] Well –

TGU: We sense "no." [they laugh]

R: You're stacking the deck.

TGU: Oh, sure. Remember, we said on 9-11 that all the people who were in the planes and the buildings, including the hijackers, were all volunteers? That's what we mean. We're inventing the scenarios as we go along. We on this side have our own game plan in order to move your society from where it is to where it will be more effective in bringing us to the next level that we're talking about. We don't really care so much, you know, who gets a sewer contract, and we don't care whether cocaine flows between countries or not. We do care whether we move more or less successfully toward the next level of being where you will all live more conscious of other aspects of yourself. That is to say, we will begin to create One World, all right, but it's going to be one world of people who are aware of their connection to us.

In other words, your next step is, you'll recognize yourselves as individuals, and you'll also recognize yourselves as part of us. And when that happens, the political problems, and the social injustices, that many of you are tempted to concentrate on, will fall off by themselves. You know, when people change their view of themselves to realize that it's not just a pretty fantasy to say that all men are brothers, but to realize that you're much closer than brothers, when people realize that they themselves are part of an immortal being, and their neighbors and friends and lovers and opponents and enemies are part of that same being, it changes everything. So, we're not concerned with politics or ideology, except in terms of pushing the society.

R: And so all is well.

TGU: All is always well. [pause] Now, let's go on – this is a little personal, but Frank doesn't care.

This is part of the struggle that he's having in terms of living in faith. One learns to live in faith by increments. And so, he learned to live in faith about his business years ago, and say, "well, I don't know where the money's coming from, I don't know where the customers are or what will happen, but my feeling is, it will be okay, I can live knowing that we'll be taken care of because we're doing good work."

But this level now is one he's still struggling with, because he knows enough of the seemingly invulnerable, sickening corruption of the whole thing. He loves his country, and he hates what it's becoming, and he hates the way it's been hijacked, and what's been done in its name, and he recognizes his own helplessness on a Downstairs level to do anything about it. And he's had to learn, as you all have to learn, to live in faith that in fact, all is well, all is always well. But that doesn't come easy. It *may* come easily, and if it does, you're fortunate. But it may be a struggle. It may be a very serious struggle.

An example. Just as many of you had a tremendous problem with the people who got killed in New York that day, he did not, because in his case he said, "okay, I can see that, that's part of the plan." But there are other things that he has to struggle with. That's all. The only way to learn to live in faith is to live in faith, and that implies a struggle, until you get past it at whatever particular issue is there.

Many people worry about their health, or about their life insurance; what's going to happen in their old age. Or they worry about crime or they worry about the million things people worry about. And many of those he doesn't worry about. But there are still things that concern him. [pause] We seriously doubt he wants us to say any more about that! [laugh]

R: I'd just like to ask, because of all of the suggestions being made about the Illuminati and all the others, what's an appropriate response for people to make to it?

TGU: Oh that's an excellent question! The appropriate response is what we just said; learn to live in faith. That doesn't mean to put blinders on and walk around saying "all is well." It means reaching within yourself and developing your own consciousness and getting a better relationship with us, and a wider and a deeper relationship with us, and at some point you'll *know* that all is well.

That says nothing about whether or not a person should get involved in politics or should get involved in civic affairs, or put on camouflage clothing and head for the hills. It doesn't say anything about that. But it says that one – and to our mind *the* one – effective response is to become more closely tied to your own Upstairs development, and to live your life according to your guidance. Everything else can be and often is only a distraction from your real task.

R: So even the notion of trying to be helpful to your fellow man in whatever way you can contribute –

TGU: Well, there's certainly no contradiction there. You yourself know, looking at yourself, as you increase your links to your higher self, to your larger being, to your unconscious self, you become more altruistic, you become more interested in doing good, which is the only useful thing you can do over there. So to our mind that takes care of itself. We can't imagine becoming in closer touch with their higher self and becoming more selfish, or becoming more interested in piling up goods and – you know, the stupidities of power and wealth.

R: Okay, I guess I am still wanting to speak to the people who are supporting these organizations that seem to me are so awash in fear.

TGU: Yes, well, we don't think there's really a rational counter to such fear, if it doesn't come out of a person's personal experience of knowing that they are pro-tected and that all is well. And we don't know any other way for them to get that experience except to deepen their relationship to their larger being. And then if that deeper relationship tells them there is a danger, that's well and good. But we think that many people fall into fear because they fear that they're on their own. That is to say, that there is nothing policing the universe except Downstairs.

And so they engage in romantic dreams, or in desperate dreams, of guerrilla war-fare against an all-encompassing state, or of political campaigns that will over-throw the corrupt, and all that. To our mind, that's escapism. And you'll notice, we have not said they've made up a threat that doesn't exist. We've said that they are being inappropriately concrete about the threat. They're thinking they know more about it than they do, and they're not addressing it in the most effective way, which is to strengthen themselves as individuals by connecting with their higher selves. That will seem to be nothing but quietism or escapism, but "seeming" doesn't have much to do with what really is.

R: This is so important, and so importantly said, that I would like to cut this off for tonight. More questions will be available next time.

TGU: All right, that's fine. Well, we thank you for your participation.

Session Thirteen
November 6, 2001

[Rita had given me, as a gag gift, a "laughing bag" – a sort of soft misshapen pyramid with a smiling face on it which, when squeezed, gives off maniacal laughter. Her label on the box said "to your amoeba from my amoeba." TGU had said, playfully, that they didn't think it was a very good image of them.]

The Concept of the Amoeba

R: *I'm going to go back to where we started, which is this criticism of the image that was presented tonight in a yellow triangular form. The response seemed to be that it wasn't a very good picture of you! And the fact is that I was thinking of it as not a very good picture of the amoebas, but still, a move in that direction.*

TGU: Well, this is a very productive – keep going.

R: *I'm aware as I read our notes that I'm not clear about whether the amoebas are something predominately on that side, with a little life popping out of it now and then to be lived on this side, or whether the amoebas are operating primarily from this side. I'm confused.*

TGU: It's not a meaningful distinction. What you could think of that would be more meaningful to you is that you, as an individual, are part of an amoeba that extends well beyond your one physical life and your one physical time and space-slice, wherever you happen to be at the moment. That larger being may have other life forms in the physical or it may not, and by definition it exists outside of time and space with one or more extensions of itself in time and space. Of course, there are also amoebas that don't extend into time-space, but we're not talking about them at the moment. So the question about whether it's primarily there or primarily here is a misunderstanding. There isn't any "there" there. The point is that you and we are parts of the same thing, and we exist within the amoeba. Now, remember we only invented that term as a convenience.

R: *Yes, I'm aware of that, and yet it seems to be individualized.*

TGU: Remember, though, that from the beginning we've told you that we on our side are individual but not individual. We are one thing, but not one thing. That is, we could be looked at as cells comprising one tissue, or we could be looked at as individuals cooperating closely. It's not at all the hard and fast division that it appears to be, to you, because you're living in time-slices.

R: Well, the amoeba takes time-slices out of it, doesn't it? I mean, when you talk about other dimensions, or –

TGU: You are part of that amoeba, now, remember.

R: Yes, I'm understanding that.

TGU: So part of *you* experiencing time-slices, means part of *it* is experiencing time-slices. But only that way.

R: But there are many other aspects to the amoeba.

TGU: That's right. If you've had ten other lives, those ten other lives are of course going to be part of the amoeba. But to say *you've* had them is from your point of view. From the amoeba's point of view, *it* has had them.

R: All right, but we're not only talking about lifetimes but we're talking about other realities, other dimensions, and all.

TGU: Sure. Anything that's possible. And, we have to perhaps point out that "amoeba" is also an artificial concept. Remember we said a while ago that we pretend somewhat that distinctions exist that really don't, but if you go too far, you always come back to saying "everything is part of one thing," which isn't helpful. So if we were describing the earth, we would talk about Europe and Asia as if they were different things, for the sake of keeping them clear, or we could talk about Eurasia as if it were a thing, but it's part of the whole globe. You see what we're saying, it's merely a matter of convenience, and it's important to remember that amoebas don't exist any more than France exists, or an individual exists. It's just in the concept that you wrapped around it.

R: This is a very helpful concept, however.

TGU: [comic cough] That's why we brought it in! [they chuckle]

R: We appreciate your bringing it in. As long as we don't carry it too far, we're okay.

TGU: Well, we know that was only an aside, but – you know, there's something to be said for carrying things too far. In fact, there's an old saying that you know very well, "the path to wisdom lies through excess." If you don't go too far, how do you know it's too far? And anyway, what's too far mean? But – when you do, we'll rein you in. [they laugh]

Individuality on the Other Side

R: All right, something from our last session. We were talking about the process of our choosing, and that that choosing led to increasing differentiation of us as individuals, and that individuality would be preserved on the other side. Now, what does that mean?

TGU: Well, it means that we're monads, as we said from the beginning. We're not an undifferentiated piece of jello over here. The flower that blossomed in your lifetime – that you were, that you are – remains a flower on our side; otherwise, what would be the point of it? That flower that blossomed in a certain area of time-space remains. So, look at it one way and it's an individual that retains its individuality. Look at it another way and it is one part of the brain cell that is everything.

R: I guess I had the impression, before this discussion, that when we move to the other side, we are moving toward much greater awareness of the all-is-one phenomena.

TGU: Well, but now bear in mind, who do you mean by "we"?

R: These little sub-aspects of the amoeba that have been over on this side for a while.

TGU: Yes, but you see, you are not who you are at the moment thinking you are. You are a part of your larger being that is encased in a body and a mind, in space-time-slices. Take away the casing, and your awareness expands, but –. A moment here; let's think about how to describe this.

You remember we said a while ago, you could have an effective consciousness of three out of a hundred, say. And your flashlight could illumine three and your background lighting would be the other 97. Well, maybe the amoeba is ten thousand. When you drop the body, in a way you could say you drop the flashlight. There's not the need, because the hundred units are no longer sealed off from the rest. Without it being constrained in that way, now you're part of the ten thousand, rather than seemingly only part of a hundred. You always were part of the ten thousand, but you didn't really have access to it; now you do. The hundred that was here is still the same hundred, but now the physical barriers between it and the rest of the ten thousand are gone.

So suppose you have ten lifetimes, each of them using a hundred out of the ten thousand. The proportions are wildly wrong, but it doesn't matter. Then you have one thousand units, in ten places, all of them seemingly connecting to each other and to everything else. We say seemingly only because it would depend on from which portion's point of view.

You're accustomed to thinking of each of them as individual, and you don't take away the individuality, you sort of flow into it. It's hard – your language isn't designed to say this. [pause]

You enter a highly cooperative arrangement in the way that the cells of your body are in a cooperative arrangement. The cells of your liver may be looked at as part of one thing, or they may be looked at as individual cells cooperating. Okay? It's much the same thing.

R: Okay then, back to this question of the individuality being preserved. Does that mean the sense of individuality is somehow preserved within the amoeba?

TGU: Mm-hmm. That's the flower, you know?

R: So that the sense of individuality of that aspect of the amoeba might continue, might be, as you say, ten of those or something.

TGU: It's not "might"; it *does*! Unless it's dissolved and found unnecessary, as we talked about once.

R: By the sense of individuality, are we including what we think of as our identity, our personality?

TGU: Well, it's a little more like you were an actor who had been playing Hamlet, looking at the movie of yourself playing Hamlet, and remembering what it was like and how you felt and all that, and at the same time seeing the effect; and it's frozen in time, so that you can always see yourself playing Hamlet the same way, but you don't identify with it in that moment any more. You can *allow* yourself to identify with it, but you don't *automatically*. Because you're not only more than your physical body, you're more than the role that you played, you're more than the costume you wore, and all that.

R: So that our identity might be more with the total amoeba.

TGU: Yes, that's what's hard for you to understand. It always is, but because within time-space you think of yourselves as being separate, and you experience yourself as coming into consciousness from childhood, and gradually watching the consciousness get larger – because that's the way you think that happens, you think this is going to be a change. But it's going to be the dissolving of the barriers that prevented you from seeing it in the first place. And in that context let us say that widening your own access to your guidance is an example of what will happen to you afterwards, do you see? You are being dreamed by the amoeba every second. You couldn't live without it. The breath of the eternal flows through you every second. And you think it's your own breath. And, it *is* your own breath. But it's the breath of the eternal.

You needn't fear death as a big change, because the only change is the melting away of the illusion of separation. *You* don't change, so much as your *perception of limitations* changes. Which of course changes you, but you understand what we're saying.

R: How about carrying on the memories from this lifetime?

TGU: Oh absolutely! Absolutely. [sputters, looking for words so fast] What would be the point of not –? But – but, you see, here's the thing. [pause]

What makes it difficult for you to understand this is that to say "carrying on the memories" seems to you to imply someone sitting there all the time, holding on to them. You find it hard to imagine a third position between someone always holding that memory and sense of that lifetime, or someone sort of dissolving in the whole thing and not particularly noticing it. But that's a false dichotomy. It's more like the cells of your body – this is probably going to be the easiest analogy for you to follow. If you were to experience the cells in your body on a cellular level, you would see that they experience themselves as cells but you could experience them as part of an organ, or part of the larger being.

You needn't fear that your individuality is going to be lost; that's the whole reason you were sent in here, or sent yourself in here, whichever way you want to look at it.

R: You attribute fear in a number of those questions, which is – I'm not experiencing it that way –

TGU: Not necessarily talking to you! [laughs]

R: Fear would hold it that way, yes.

TGU: Actually, though, we could eliminate the word "fear" and say, "it's wrong to anticipate that possibility. That possibility is not a possibility. That's really what we're trying to say. The only thing you came in here for was to choose and to create a flower, and they're not going to forget that when they pull you back over on the other side! [they chuckle]

Successful Lives and the Amoeba

R: I'm still somewhat caught up in this phenomenon we talked about last time, of some energy coming into physical existence here and not having what we call a successful life so that its parts were returned somehow to the total energy pool. I have no concept when we're talking like this whether we're talking about "this happens now and then," or "this is the major picture and those people who are really trying to stretch their consciousness and so on are the exceptions" –

TGU: You're making a wrong turn here. You're making a mental association that we do not mean, that in order to not be dissolved, you have to in some way "earn it." That's not at all what happens, it's just that some lives don't contain within them something interesting enough, or important enough, to be worth continuing, and so, just put it back in the mixture again.

If you were creating a field of grass, you might have 99 percent of that grass basically identical. That doesn't mean that that's not valuable. You need those 99 percent that are identical. So it is not a question of being unusual, but it's a question of being – [pause]

Well, [pause] we may have to put that in abeyance until we can think of a way to describe it differently. We know you don't think we have duration, but – we'll think about it. It's so simple – you put the stuff in the mix and it works or it doesn't work, and if it doesn't work, you put it back in again. But we realize that you don't know what we mean.

R: One more question about this and then I'll quit. When you say put it back in the mix, is this back in the mix of the amoeba? Or something beyond the amoeba?

TGU: [pause] Well, we know that sounds like a meaningful question to you, but we're having a little bit of difficulty with it. It's not –

You're saying *the* amoeba, and we think that means that you think that we mean that anything coming into the 3D Theater comes from an amoeba.

R: Yes, that's what I thought.

TGU: But not the same amoeba, but just any.

R: An amoeba.

TGU: Yes, okay, that's fine. We just wanted to be sure. [pause] Yes, where else would it come from? Oh! Okay, here's why we can't make sense of your question. There's a linguistic problem with the question, and we can't figure out how to untangle it. Your language makes it seem that if there's not whatever puts people into existence, that there would be something other than that. You see?

R: Yes.

TGU: And that's tangled in your language, it's not tangled in reality.

R: So there isn't anything –

TGU: It's not meaningful.

R: The sum of the amoebas is the sum of –

TGU: No, it's more like, by definition whatever puts something into the physical can be considered an amoeba. By definition, you see. And it would be like saying, "can I change without changing," or "can I have a life without living," or something. On our end, it's a contradiction in terms, but it's hidden by your language structure.

R: But that doesn't work the other way around?

TGU: Hmm?

R: I got lost in trying to straighten out the language there. But you were saying, by definition, anything that puts an energy into the physical is an amoeba. But an amoeba doesn't have to put someone into the physical.

TGU: That's correct.

R: Okay, so that's what I meant by the other way around.

TGU: We're beginning to wonder if we're going to regret having invented this concept, but we'll keep going with it for a while.

R: There's a temptation to concretize everything –

TGU: Exactly! Exactly!

R: – and I don't want to do that, but we'll see what happens. Okay, that was the last question in that frame.

TGU: We get paid by the hour, we don't care. [they chuckle]

Obtaining Psychic Abilities

R: Okay, here's one I wanted to ask. Does developing our psychic abilities increase our Upstairs development, or our moving closer to you?

TGU: When you say your Upstairs development, you mean – ? Here's what that sounded like, to us. It sounded like you're asking, do you, in increasing your own development, increase our development. Is that what you meant?

R: Hmm. No. No.

TGU: Okay, good. Because the answer would be no.

R: No, what I meant was, one of our goals on this side, as we understand it, is to become more like you.

TGU: Well –

R: To move closer to you.

TGU: To broaden your access to us, is what we would say. There's a difference.

R: All right. Let's use that then and ask, does developing our psychic abilities on this side increase our chances of doing that?

TGU: We would put it just the other way around. The easiest way for you to develop your psychic abilities is to increase your access to us first. To broaden your channel, to extend your willingness to say "your will, not mine." Not in the religious sense, exactly. An example from Bob Monroe would be when he said his total self should do the driving when he went out of body – not necessarily his idea, by the way, although he thought it was – and the minute he did that then everything changed for him, because he had increased his access by handing over the reins.

If you want to increase your psychic abilities, the easiest, simplest way to do it is to broaden the channel from which they flow. Anything else is doing it the hard way. In fact, it may not even be possible. Since psychic abilities are inextricably connected with your ability to overcome the illusion of separation, and since that ability is always connected through the heart, whether consciously or unconsciously, and since the decision to flow through the heart can be taken consciously –

[interruption]

R: We were talking about psychic abilities and the best way to develop them is to –

TGU: Open your heart, open your channels. That is so simple. That's why people have it happen to them without intent, surprising themselves. Because they've had their mind on something else, when the heart opens. [pause]

Now let's flip the tape, because your next question takes a longer answer. [An interesting example of TGU knowing something that my conscious self did not. The tape was indeed near its end.]

R: Okay, I'm trying to take that in while I think about this process of what we do when we call psychic abilities. It seems such a wide range of things that we include in that. For example I wouldn't have thought of them all as coming through the heart, but you're saying that's the case.

TGU: Well, we're saying they come as a result of enlarged access between you and your larger being – between you and the amoeba – which, not coincidentally but by side-effect, results in your opening your channels to each other, by way of the larger being.

R: So a person who doesn't have this perspective, and is using their psychic abilities in some way or another, can we think about that as a way of their stretching their consciousness? Is this a help or an interference?

TGU: Well, it's true that for some personality types what we just said would be abhorrent and would actually interfere with their efforts. Some people might have such a need for perceived autonomy, and for control, that they would not allow themselves to realize what they're doing. [chuckles] They would still be opening the channel; but they wouldn't be thinking of it in those terms. For many people what happens to them is less important than the way they think about what happens. Suppose you had someone with a long-term bigotry against religious symbolism and anything that reminded them of religion. If you were then to quote to them the words of Jesus, they would be emotionally shut down from doing what it was, only because of all the associations that they consciously or unconsciously put with it. But that same person, if you put it in terms of "identify with all that is," or put it in some sanitized context, could do the exact same thing, but [chuckles] they'd have to see it differently before they'd be able to do it. That's all.

We can't think of any psychic ability that doesn't depend upon your connection with us, with the larger being, with the other side, by definition. And so expanded access has to make everything else easier.

Now, some of you will connect primarily through emotions, some through intellect, some through the heart. That's fine, it doesn't matter either way. But what you want to do is to open the access.

Now, that sounds like an absolute contradiction to what we just said, which is the heart is the only way, but it isn't really. Someone who is a thinking person *thinks* their way through to the idea of all things being connected, all things being one. To their way of perception, they've done something radically different from an emotional person who *feels* the unity. You see? But it's just your own invisible mental structures making distinctions for you that seem to you to be absolutely real. It's just your perceptions playing games with you.

R: It feels to me like I've seen individuals who went straight to the attempt to connect directly with you, and out of that process gained psychic abilities, and other individuals who seem to develop psychic abilities without that attempt to make a connection with you, and maybe out of that moved toward the connection with the other side.

TGU: The operative word here is "seemed."

R: Seemed. Okay. [chuckles]

TGU: It's just that you can't any of you see where the others are coming from, and half the time you can't see where you yourself are coming from, because there's so much going on that's in the background or in the shadow. [pause] Nothing wrong with it. That's the way it's set up, but – it's not an exact science. You're back again to whatever it was you said that time, "we can measure that it seems to be this." [they chuckle]

Duality

R: *Okay, I've been wanting to ask some more about duality. It's clear that our physical world seems to be wrapped in duality, and I have sometimes felt from your answers that duality exists on the other side as well, but I'm not clear about that.*

TGU: Oh, I think you're very clear about that. It's always a mistake to assume that the other side, as it looks to you, is perfect, or completed. When creation split things into duality, in order to create something, it didn't only happen on the material realm. If you'll look at your Bible, you have the good and the bad angels, or at any rate the angels that fought. Well, that's a duality well beyond the physical. And don't get your hopes up, once you go over to the other side it's not all over. [chuckles]

R: *I though it was all going to be love, because love has no opposite!*

TGU: Uh huh.

R: *[pause] You don't want to respond to that?*

TGU: Oh, well, we will if you want! It didn't sound like a question!

R: *[laughs]*

TGU: Well, why isn't that true for where you are?

R: *Well that is true –*

TGU: All right.

R: *– but there are a couple of concepts that seem like they don't have a dual aspect. Love is one of them.*

TGU: Well, now, Frank and Charles [a neighbor and close friend] were just this Sunday talking about perfect moments, and we managed to get clear to both of them, very clearly, that all moments are perfect, but they're not all fun, they're not all desirable, they're not all pleasant. The universe is created in love and is enfolded in love, and cannot exist without love, but it's not all pleasant or fun either, because – if you'll remember what we said "a long time ago" – the pluses and the minuses balance out. If you want to have a universe of all pluses and no minuses, you can't do it. It just can't be done, not as it's set up. Therefore you're going to have either mild polarity widely spread or sometimes really sharp polarities, where the pluses gather in one place and the minuses gather in another. And you may experience that as strife, or as complementarity, or as pleasing diversity. You could experience it in different ways, but it's a great mistake to think that "all will be nice and love and light." You'd be bored! We would too.

R: So a state in which duality does not exist wouldn't be a state to be desired at all?

TGU: Well as far as we know, the only state that doesn't involve dualities is beyond creation, and we don't know what's beyond creation. We said a while ago, all creation could be looked at as comprising pluses and minuses in equal amounts. Now, we may have said that in such a way that you took that to mean physical reality, but we didn't mean that. We meant all creation. We don't think it's possible to have anything else. So. This actually should explain to you why there's so much flux and change and play in the entire universe, not just in physical matter reality. You know, we have our pluses and minuses going on too. [pause]

The difference may be that we're not seeing them in time-slices as you are, and so to us it looks much more like a kaleidoscope with patterns to be enjoyed than it does like warfare, with victory to be won. You see? Once you fully know that you cannot have more pluses than minuses or more minuses than pluses, except locally, it takes the desperation out of things and it adds a certain amount of aesthetic satisfaction, shall we say. Then, you don't mind playing the villain in the movie, either. Because you haven't created the villainy, you see. All you've done is localize some minuses. And that enables someone else, somewhere else, to localize some pluses. We *know* this is going to seem cynical to your readers [chuckles] – but it'll be good for them.

R: No, that's all very interesting to me. I think I've been making the assumption that dualities are of this physical realm.

TGU: Yes, many people are making the same assumption. Now, you have dualities in the physical realm that don't exist in the non-physical, strictly because they're local to material. But there are other dualities, as we just said, that extend beyond the physical. And, may we say, if you'll hark back a hundred years or so to the religious dogma of the Christians in your country, the unthinking ones thought of endless singing and playing harps in heaven? And Mark Twain made fun of the whole concept and pointed out how hideous it would be. They were trying to envision all pluses and no minuses. And he was pointing out that would not even be aesthetically pleasing.

And in fact the concept of heaven and hell assumes a geographical split, although the spatial analogy is somewhat hidden, but there it is; it assumes a geographical split between all the pluses in one place and all the minuses in the other place. And that assumes that there wouldn't be any interplay between them, they wouldn't be swapping places. So it's kind of a boring idea. [laughs]

Now – sorry to complicate it – we want you to remember that "souls of a feather flock together," and people at a certain vibratory level (which implies a certain mixture of pluses and minuses within them) do segregate out. So we're just going to leave that in there for you to think about a little bit. On the one hand, we're saying there are pluses and minuses and there's movement all the time; it's like a kaleidoscope. On the other hand, we're saying, souls, people, monads, whatever, of a certain composition not only *want to* flock together, but really have no realistic choice, because they're held there as though their specific gravity is holding them. We're deliberately building in a contradiction for you to think about.

R: Thank you. [they laugh] Very much.

TGU: Well, we can talk about angels and harps! [they chuckle] If you prefer.

R: Well I don't know whether to go on with that or not.

TGU: We'll tell you this. It's far preferable for people to be thinking about stuff even in getting so-called wrong answers, than to think they know when in fact they haven't really thought about it. It's better to be in perplexity than to be in a false satisfaction. Because the perplexity won't last. At some point you'll make sense of it. [pause] Maybe.

R: I was thinking that a resolution to the dualities is often to take the positives and negatives off the duality.

TGU: Well – thank you for mentioning this – we are using plus and minus in the electrical sense, only. We're not meaning good or bad. We're only trying to come up with a neutral description of polarity, that's all – and perhaps your language isn't neutral enough about plus and minus. [pause] Perhaps we could use blue and orange as colors on opposite ends of the scale. We would use red and green, except that wouldn't work in your society [because people would make analogies to stoplights]. But we could say blue and orange instead of plus and minus if you wish.

Earth's Other Inhabitants

R: All right, now there are a number of questions that keep coming up from Frank's friends out there about the earth and earth inhabitants and so on. Our early sessions spoke to this issue to some extent, but there are specifics that are being asked, and I think Frank feels okay either way about including these.

TGU: We would say, follow your own impulse as to whether to ask or not, judging that it won't just be only your own impulse. Be irresponsible about it. [chuckles]

R: Okay, we had talked in other sessions about all the inhabitants not being visible to us, and so I don't know whether visibility is what's coming up, but people are asking about fairies and elves, the little people, about non-humans in bodies like Bigfoot, the possibility that there is a group of energies living within a hollow earth, werewolves –

TGU: Well, we think we can handle that whole subject in one over-arching paragraph, if you want us to.

R: Yes, please.

TGU: We would say, whenever a phenomenon has been described by a society or a part of a society over a period of time, it would be extremely unwise to disregard that testimony. Elves, fairies, gnomes, exist and are perceived by cultures as well as individuals whose mental structures do not prohibit them from seeing them. Cultures that you call "primitive" describe them. They're describing, they're not inventing. Now, in your own time you have a variant of that, and that is, in a literate society there is something of a chance that someone's imagination can create something and in such a persuasive way that others will then perpetuate that creation deliberately. The Lovecraft stories are an example. Lovecraft in his imagination developed a whole mythology of beings within the earth, and of a sort of proto-history of the earth, which has had a profound impact on many people over three generations. There are people taking those mythologies seriously. And we say to you that the reason why some people will come up with something like that that will have such an effect has to do with a question of definition. Whose imagination? Where did it come from?

Do you see what we're saying? You think when you sit down to write that it is you making something up out of whole cloth. But in fact, sometimes – often – if not most times – you are receiving a transmission.

Now, when you speak of beings in a hollow earth, what we see is a fallacy of misplaced concreteness. There are people who think that the earth is a hollow sphere with actual hollowness inside! And that isn't what it is! But what they're perceiving or what some have perceived is that the interior of the earth is inhabited by beings that are intelligent. But that doesn't mean they have bodies like yours or they're wandering around under a blue sky like you. And that is a translation error, you see?

Now as to Bigfoot and Sasquatch and – you know, the Loch Ness monster; all the kinds of teasers to science. They are much like UFOs; they are phenomena that have been deliberately constructed to be just beyond reality, to stretch you. We'll say nothing about who's constructing them. We do not mean individuals hoaxing. So, you have crop circles, you have UFOs, you have Bigfoot, you have Loch Ness, you have gnomes, fairies – well, no, actually they're in a different – [pause]

R: How about werewolves?

TGU: They're ordinarily in a different category. They're in the same category now because they're having the same effect. Werewolves are actually a special case of shape-shifting, and that's a special case of people moving from their one body to their second body, and creating a – well, a simulacrum, but it looks like a real body, and functions like one. Those are just facts, but they're facts that your science refuses to admit, because it doesn't even deal with the energy body. It'll be obvious enough, once the actual plodding everyday scientists begin to deal with the world as primarily thought, rather than primarily object. Their view of what is possible and what isn't possible will be unrecognizably transformed. And they could save themselves a tremendous amount of false starts if they would go first – first, not last – to the folklore of all the societies of earth – because that's where your historical records are. These are the historical records of "what is."

Not quite one paragraph, but it's shorter than we usually are. [they chuckle]

R: In the same group of things, people are including something that is somewhat different, asking about the dolphins and whales, since they've been described as having great intelligence, and perhaps more intelligence than human beings.

TGU: We will suppress several sarcastic comments that come to mind! [they laugh] Such as: How hard would that be? Yes, you're right, they are a different category of things. We once told you that all maple trees could be considered extensions of the prime maple tree. And we said that animals are sort of like that, and yet a little more autonomous, because they have more responsibilities. That is to say, they have movement, and more possibilities. Your beautiful sea-borne mammals are humans without the necessity of work. They are one thing with very active consciousness of every single one of them as a node of consciousness.

Your cetaceans spread a net around the entire planet, not just physically in that they can whistle for thousands of miles, but metaphysically, because they're all one thing. The fact that they're being systematically and ruthlessly destroyed, and the fact that some of them are voluntarily leaving, is changing the plus and minus equation on the planet, but it need not be looked on as a tragedy. It's a change. There is reasons for this. It's a sacrifice, perhaps you should say.

But yes, the whales, the dolphins. But, see – sharks are as intelligent as dolphins; you just tend not to like them! [they laugh] They have a purpose, but you tend not to like the purpose. They are one of the longest-lived species on earth [not a clear way to have said this: They meant sharks had been here a long time, not that they have long individual lifetimes] and they are fabulously efficient killing-machines. Well, you don't like to hear it, but the earth needs killing-machines, the same as the earth needs scavengers. Without scavengers you'd be awash in corpses. Without killing machines, you'd be awash in live bodies. Now, if that's all you had, you'd have death. It's all a matter of balance. Again, the pluses and the minuses.

You're attributing to the shark your own malevolent impulses, and you decide that it's evil. By looking at the whale and projecting onto it your own impulses toward play and toward community –

R: Benevolence.

TGU: Benevolence, exactly. Then you say, "oh, they're good." Well, we say to you that there's nothing in creation that's good or bad, but that thinking makes it so. You may have heard that before.

R: Well, what's the relationship between all of the things we've been talking about here, and the concept of the amoeba?

TGU: [sigh] It's hard for you to remember, but it will help you to remember, that everything is part of one thing. Killer whales, and dolphins, and sharks, and you, possibly in descending order [humorous cough], are all part of the same thing that's on the other side of the time-space slices. You're not separate. And also, people on Alpha Centauri. You know what we're saying.

Therefore you mustn't necessarily assume a difference in kind between the whale intelligence or the whale spirit, shall we say, that goes back to the other side, and yours. They may well be part of the same larger being, or they may be part of different larger beings. That's not predictable, it could be either.

R: I see. It could be either.

TGU: Sure. Sure, you see, your larger being could express partly as a whale, partly as a tree, partly as a person.

And, again, we'll say to you, go back to your native traditions and see! There have often been traditions that talked about souls migrating from one to the other. Well, we don't see it as migrating, but we see it as a valuable clue. Or, look at it a different way, we'll give you the clue, and much that's been said that hasn't seemed to make sense will make sense in a different sense. Too many uses of the same word, but you understand.

R: So that the concept of the amoeba is growing a bit, to include other forms of being on this earth as well as other forms of being not on this earth, in other dimensions. You've already said all this, I'm just repeating it to myself.

TGU: No, you're clarifying it for others as well. And we'll say to you, if you'll make a habit of trying to see your world as a great thought rather than as a great thing, or a great machine, or a great being, it will clarify to you some of the fluidity underneath the seeming rigidity of structures. If you will start from the amoeba and say the amoeba thinks into being a Rita, and a whale, and a blade of grass, and a tree – it's a sort of halfway house between what conventional religious might say, God created all those, or a pantheist might say, God *is* all those. It's a new way of thinking, because it's a very old way of thinking. But neither is Western civilization a detour.

Instead, by your coming through this entirely unprecedented path to a re-understanding of what the natives understood all along, you actually add sophistication to the concepts, strictly because you came at it from another point of view. That's the value.

The West and the World

TGU: Now, the West's sin has been to hold in contempt what you didn't understand, which is most things. Your redemption will be to not only learn to hold them in reverence, but to offer to them a new understanding that they don't have. Because the native traditions around the world – the native religious traditions, you might almost say – are disconnected. They can't speak one to the other. The West was created to create a global civilization that could then translate to everyone, so that your tower of Babel can be reassembled. Not that you need to speak the same language like English, French, Persian, but that you need to speak the same language in terms of how you see the world.

R: *Overwhelming.*

TGU: Well, you want to be bored?

R: *[laughs]*

TGU: It's a great task! It's a great joy!

R: *A great task.*

TGU: You see, the Tahitians understand something of the world that you do not. And so do the Peruvians. But only through the West can the Tahitians and the Peruvians communicate and be part of a large global culture. That's the West's chore and task and joy – *if* it loses that initial, provincial, somewhat juvenile assumption that it is right, and everybody else is ignorant.

Half of your society is very arrogant, and the other half has almost an inverse arrogance, which says anything the West does is wrong. And both aspects are well beyond incomplete. They're sort of silly. A sophisticated view will say, "the West was created for its own view; let's find out what that was. And each of these other civilizations was created to create its own view, let's find out what that was. Now, how can we and they put it together, so that we can recognize different ways of viewing the same reality?"

You see, it's the same process that we're talking about here. Only it's a much larger process because it's global, and it will take you more than a little longer than [learning as individuals to do] this. Probably three days instead of two.

R: And we're going to be around long enough to make a dent in that?

TGU: Well who's we?

R: We all.

TGU: Who's we all? You in your body?

R: The human race on the earth?

TGU: Well what difference would it make? We'll say yes you will, no you won't.

R: All right. I think that's enough for tonight.

TGU: Always a pleasure.

Session Fourteen
November 13, 2001

The Nature of the Amoeba

R: We still have questions around the concept of the amoeba. We want to make sure that our understanding is as complete as we can get it, and I'll have some questions about that.

TGU: We'll be glad to ask you questions if you like.

R: [chuckles] Frank noted, the other day, that maybe everyone he's ever been close to was part of his amoeba. Is that a possibility?

TGU: Well you know, we've been listening to your conversation, by definition. You and your readers are going to have very different ideas, and we want to express things in a way that will have the least chance of being misunderstood, which is difficult.

You could conceivably have all the inhabitants of the earth in one amoeba. We never meant to imply one amoeba to one person or one amoeba to a few people. But at the same time – it isn't the case, but it could be the case. As far as we know, there's no theoretical limit to the number of space-time lives one amoeba could generate. You mustn't think of us as being bound in bodies the way you are. At the same time – [pause] we'll back up a little more.

Remember our discussion about pluses and minuses, or blue and orange. And how everything is a combination of blue and orange, and that if there's more blue in one place, that frees room for oranges somewhere else. But that blue can't overcome orange, and orange can't overcome blue, except locally, which could be locally in time.

Well, one way of clustering blues and oranges is to make them into teams, so to speak. And you can have amoebas that are orange amoebas and blue amoebas, more or less.

We're going to go back to plus and minuses, because blue and orange starts sounding like football teams, and we don't want to give you that sense. But you could have one amoeba that was 78 percent pluses and another amoeba that was 60 percent pluses and a third that was 23 percent pluses. The overall flavor of the various amoebas varies, just as the overall flavor of various individuals varies, and for the same reason.

So, when you, in your Downstairs lives, meet people that you have no affinity for, many times this is because they are not of your amoeba, but more than that, because that amoeba is of a different specific gravity, so to speak. So that you and this other individual, were you out of the bodies, would never mix, because –

Oh, that's one more thing we need to tell you. Here's something that's really going to make a problem. [pause] If Frank is any example, you are thinking of the amoebas as a relatively shapeless bag that contains things in it. But that would imply that two bags next to each other had surfaces that they didn't intermingle, and that's a spatial analogy. It's *only* a spatial analogy, and if you have within the amoeba an individual who is 17 pluses and three minuses, and you have within another amoeba another individual that's 17 pluses and three minuses, they are going to be at the same level of being, regardless of their life experiences or their beliefs or anything else. They're going to sort out to the same place once there's no body holding them separate.

Now, they're from different amoebas, but at the same time they are of similar composition which brings them to the same level. You could look at it as saying this is as close as different amoebas come to interacting with each other. [pause] Time out.

We're going to restate the way we think you see it, and then try and restate the way we think it is. We think you see it as maybe ten amoebas sitting together, each of them looking like a bag full of peas, each pea being an individual life-time. We would see it as perhaps ten different clouds, and the layers of the clouds intermingle without the clouds losing what they have in common. That is to say, each cloud maintains its own self, even though it's intermingled with others. And the levels of the cloud have different gravities, and the various levels sort out together. That should be pretty well incomprehensible to you.

R: [laughs] Well, I haven't been seeing it the way you've described us as seeing it.

TGU: So how have you seen it?

R: First of all, in your description I thought we had one amoeba per person, so to speak, although there might be two lifetimes going on in the same time-space that belong to the same amoeba, but a single amoeba would include an individual who's living a lifetime but also includes all the lifetimes that person has ever lived, and all of the dimensions in which they've existed, and so on.

TGU: Yes, we described all that, but we didn't mean to imply that's all there was.

R: So I was thinking of that as one individual, or as perhaps that same amoeba having the possibility of several lives even at the same time. So you change it as soon as you put other individuals into it. I hadn't quite caught up with that until Frank asked his questions about maybe everyone he's close to is in the same amoeba. Can you start from that point now?

TGU: Sure. We think the easiest way is to start with Bob Monroe's description of the INSPEC, because it was really very acute. That is, a being outside of time-space, that inserts itself into time-space to experience time-space, and does so with multiple extensions in time-space. You were thinking of them somewhat locally, and we are thinking of it much more globally. You, Rita, were thinking you are one of 15 lives led by your amoeba. And that's true, as far as it goes. But it doesn't go very far, as far as the amoeba is concerned, because remember we said that a new being from the amoeba might be drawn through the other lives, or it might be drawn separate from them? And if it was drawn through them they would experience the idea of reincarnation, or they might? And if it was drawn separate they probably would not, because it wouldn't resonate? Well, that's true, but that was an example based on one person. We never meant that to be the extent of the amoeba, though. The amoeba may have millions of the same thing. As far as we know, there are no theoretical limits to how many lives at various times, or even together, one amoeba may have.

If you wish, you might think of the amoeba, as you have been thinking of it, as one cell of a larger amoeba, and that works okay. In fact, there's something to be said for that. It's sort of true that you could have the amoeba be various lives that this small portion has put together, and then that small portion together with other small portions, make a larger amoeba. But don't think that it's all concrete differences. It's more like viewpoint. Again, it's a cell if you look at it one way, it's an individual if you look at it another.

It's true, the super-amoeba, shall we call it, that deals with people on earth, is not undifferentiated between it and the people. It isn't like on the one end there's the whole amoeba and on the other end there are all these tiny little particles. It sort of is organized by its own affinity. So that if one part of yourself is five pluses, and another part of yourself is ten pluses, and another 15 and 20 and 25, each of those will develop into the physical world according to what it is, so you could look at it as those various sections being individual amoebas or portions.

Again, we always come back to the fact that individuals of any kind are really literally not possible, so when you're talking about anything being "an individual," it's only an approximation. It's only a convenience.

R: And that's true when you're talking about amoebae.

TGU: Sure. You could look at it like there are x numbers of amoebas, or you could look at it like there's only one. The difference is a matter of viewpoint. From your point of view it would be probably more productive to think of the amoebas as being vastly larger than one individual or group of individuals, because if you start thinking that your individual amoeba is different from Frank's individual amoeba, and different from Marilyn's individual amoeba, it will slide you back in your mind toward thinking of us as individuals again. It isn't exactly that it's wrong, but it leads in an unhelpful direction.

R: Is there any advantage to thinking about an organizing principle that would pull individual components together into a larger unit? You used the word affinity there – does it have to do with the proportion of pluses and minuses?

TGU: Yes, exactly. We thought that wasn't going to work for you, but that's the only analogy we can think of. Proportions.

R: You used the words "specific gravity" at one time.

TGU: Just trying to give you a physical analogy. Because if we say specific gravity, and you can imagine a bunch of potatoes or something in various depths of the water, there's no connotation of right or wrong, or positive or negative in the moral sense that way. That's what we were trying to avoid. It's just convenience. We know that this became an unsuspected can of worms for you tonight, but – that's just as well. [they chuckle]

R: Well, each time we've talked about it has led to further questions.

TGU: We congratulate you.

R: [chuckles]

TGU: It's not meant as a joke.

R: Well, could you say that everyone has an amoeba, or everyone is part of an amoeba, but not everyone's in touch with a concept like the guys upstairs.

TGU: Well, now remember, we've answered part of this before. By definition, everyone is part of an amoeba, because it is the amoeba that puts you into physical time-space. There's no other way. Remember we had that problem with your language, and how your language made it look like there could be that or not? But just say by definition you are all part of something outside time and space that inserts you into time and space.

The other is just a question of access. Some people don't have any realistic possibility of developing conscious access during a lifetime, because that's how they've set it up; others have no realistic possibility of *not* having that access, because *that's* how *they've* set it up. You're a standard bell curve: Most people are in the middle, and depending on the choices that they make, and depending on the circumstances in which they put themselves – or as they would say, find themselves – they will to a larger or a lesser extent open those channels.

Now, sometimes the plot of their life is that they will be surprised by it opening – in other words, that it will open from the other side – but that's no more accidental than anything else in life. If you look at the whole pattern of Bob Monroe's life, as he could not (because he was in the middle of it), you see how perfectly it was done to insert this surprise into his life, from his point of view at the time. He had no clue what was going on! But Upstairs and in the overall purpose of his life – the Worm Monroe – knew full well.

So that's a long-winded answer to your question. There is a bell curve as to whether people will or won't develop that access. Most people are in the middle and have the ability to greatly increase it, but it's a matter of choice-slash-circumstance. We're talking here only of conscious access. You always have unconscious access.

The Amoeba and Crystallized Beings

R: *[pause] I think this question would change, now that we've had this discussion tonight, but the question I have written here is that you said earlier that you have some responsibility for, or sort of an affinity for, looking after others besides Frank. Does that mean others within the same amoeba that he's in, or others in other amoebas, or is that a meaningful distinction?*

TGU: [pause] Well, it's a meaningful distinction, but not an easy one while you're in the body, exactly. We would say, there's no real access between ourselves on this side and those who aren't of the same amoeba that we're of. That's the easiest answer. There is an indirect access, which means someone speaking to someone, rather than us thinking through them, or giving them hunches, or whatever. That's one of the major functions of your culture, to provide the ability to talk between amoebas.

R: *Via us.*

TGU: Sure. By you, by your cultural concepts, by your constructs like books or movies or whatever, by someone in the body expressing something, which affects someone else in a body who's of a different amoeba. Take that and churn it about a million times, and you can begin to see the beautiful complexity of it. It's a kaleidoscope, it's wonderful.

R: Okay. The package that is any one of us is created by the amoeba. At death we rejoin our amoeba, but if all works well we may have a crystallized soul, or may become individualized. So when we drop the body, do the crystallized souls become part of the amoeba?

TGU: [Sigh] We're getting really tired of the English language. It makes a lot of trouble. We really would like it if you could find a way around this!

It's a mistake to say that you're away from the amoeba and then you rejoin it. You've never left it. The only thing that's happened is, there have been barriers to your awareness of it, and the removal of barriers to your awareness of it. That's the only change. All the time that you're developing your flower, the stem connects to the amoeba which is the ground. The flower may think it's just a flower out there by itself, but it's still part of us. When the flower withers into the ground at the wintertime, it may remember then that it's always been a part of the earth, but whether it realized it or not, it has always been a part of the earth. (Taking us to be the earth, for the moment.)

So we're going to come back to that every time you say something that implies something other, because everyone who reads this will need that reminder. The way the Christians look at it is a very good hint: There's never any separation between yourselves and God. There's never any separation between you and us, except in your awareness of it. The Christians would say, "God never turns his back on you, but you can turn your back on him." We would say, "we're always aware of you, you may not be aware of us." It's the same thing, only without the overlay of guilt. [laughs]

Now, perhaps saying "crystallized" gave a misleading impression. Although, it really is a very good way of stating it. But let's change the analogy and say that you were a new kind of tulip; you somehow developed new colors that had never been seen in tulips before. You're still a tulip; you're still a flower; you're still connected to the earth, but you have added something a little more complex. Now you're a special tulip. It's true that everything is special, but when everything is special, the special-ness can be taken for granted and they're *not* special, in a sense. Sorry to do that to you, but that's the way it is.

Let's go back to crystallizing. We really like the word crystallizing, because it implies several things. Perhaps this will shed light on the other thing, which seemed to perplex you. If you crystallize elements, they're permanent, and it (it's no longer a "they," you see; it has crystallized) has its own center of being. If it doesn't crystallize, you could look at it as being thrown back into the water, in the way that we were talking about before; the ice cube that didn't gel. Most of the time the ice doesn't gel, and when it does, those cubes are permanent. We're saying few, it's just relative. But – you understand what we're saying? Don't think of the ones that don't become permanent as a tragedy, so much as think of the ones that do become permanent as an achievement.

Now when they do, then you have a nucleus, you have a seed – shattering the metaphor – that crystal is a seed from which new tendencies can develop. It opens new lines of endeavor.

Radical change of metaphor here. A musician might come up with a phrase which could be elaborated, and elaborated and elaborated and he winds up with a sonata or a symphony or whatever he winds up with. A crystallized person, a crystallized being, could be considered to be the equivalent of a phrase that could be elaborated and elaborated and elaborated upon. One that doesn't crystallize doesn't give you that possibility, and so you just keep going until it does. That is to say, it's back in the pot; the pot manifests others, some of which crystallize and some don't. And the ones that do, offer the ability for specialized manifestations. That's really what we need to say. Not specialized in the sense of division of labor, so much as just specialized as precious and different and individual.

R: And does this manifestation occur within the amoeba when the body is released, or are you talking about the implications for another lifetime?

TGU: Well, there's not much difference, really. Remember, when you created this crystallization, it doesn't matter whether it's in a body or not, because when the body falls away, it'll still be there. Well, you might look at it this way, which is slightly misleading. The amoeba projects another lifetime through that crystal, which polarizes the light, so to speak – which, you see, systematically warps the energies to produce a certain bias. It acts as a polarizing filter to produce a certain shape, a certain pattern. We're stumbling looking for a metaphor that will say that the crystallized being acts to give shape to the energies flowing through it, without those energies duplicating it. It's somewhat of a catalyst. It catalyzes new developments. That might be a way to look at it.

R: And does it matter whether we're catalyzing new developments in that same individual in that lifetime, or a further lifetime, or in the amoeba on the other side?

TGU: It would be the amoeba's energies flowing through that pattern to create a new pattern. It wouldn't be in the same lifetime. It's not worth going into, but theoretically it could happen while the person was still alive, we suppose. It's too long a detour, but take it as given that the energies of the amoeba are establishing a pattern, and channeling something, and molding it. Here's an example. If you project light through a slide, the picture appears on the screen. That's sort of the way that the crystallized being is functioning, as a slide. Energies go through it, and are patterned by it, only the difference in the analogy is that they become something quite different from it. Does that help at all?

R: I think I understand that as a theory. [laughs] I'm having a little trouble thinking what that would be like in manifestation.

TGU: You ought to see the trouble Frank's having with it!

R: [laughs] Yes. Well, I don't know if these are worthwhile distinctions, but we have a great need to know, for some reason.

TGU: Well, we would say, you will come up with more interesting questions when you allow what happens to flow through you, rather than depending on notes. Just like him speaking.

R: Well I was wanting to make sure I got in the questions that had come up in me since our last talk.

TGU: We understand. We don't have any problem with you doing it, we just see you as a more versatile tool than you perhaps see yourself.

Of God and Satan and Polarities

R: Okay. We've talked about all sorts of phenomena like fairies and elves and werewolves as phenomena that have been part of our cultural observations over the years, and one additional concept, even more powerful, is that of Satan. And we have satanic cults operating. I guess you could say we have god cults operating, too, as churches.

TGU: Mm-hmm. And the symmetry is not accidental.

R: So we have issues like God versus the dark angels in the last chapter of the Bible. And I wonder if you could comment some on these concepts.

TGU: Well, we've given you all the clues you need. If you go back to the concept that an imbalance of pluses or minuses is impossible, that there have to be as many pluses as minuses – what are God and Satan, after all, but the localized congregation of pluses on one side and minuses on another side? Now, in so saying, we're talking in terms of good versus evil, dark angels versus good angels – well, Good versus Evil, not about "God" meaning the ultimate source of life or what is above creation, because you don't have any first-hand knowledge of that. Neither do we.

Now, we need to say this carefully. It could happen that as your pluses congregate, your minuses congregate, and you wind up with a more and more clear-cut antagonism, civil war down the middle. However, it could happen that on one side they will congregate whereas the others remain diffuse. Remember, we said the totals are always going to balance, but some could be real intensely gathered and others cover a more widespread space, but not as intense. And we said that some could congregate at some times, and others at other times. So that things could get worse and worse and worse from one point of view because the opposite ones are congregated at other times.

Both the pluses and minuses in your time are feeling the tension of the opposites getting more intense. Your god-cult and your devil-cult each have lots of energy being given to them, particularly because they feed each other. Each fears the other, and the fear adds the emotional fuel to the fire, and they watch each other's excesses and that fuels them to do prosetlyzing. We said there's no good, there's no evil, ultimately, but locally there certainly is. The difficulty is, what's good and evil to you is different to someone else. You will therefore wind up congregating with people who think that good is the same thing that you do, and that evil is the same thing that you do. And if you don't, you'll be uncomfortable, and you'll move until you are if you can.

Now, granted, in the earth, in physical matter, you could live your whole life in psychologically, physically uncomfortable territory, living your life among people whose beliefs are radically different. But that's only geography, because you'll also be living among people whose beliefs are the same as yours, even if they don't live near you. That's not obvious to you in bodies, but someone in China and someone in Virginia with the same feel for things are together in ways that those in a body don't understand. You're together spiritually. It sounds airy-fairy but it isn't, at all, it's just practical, but it's not provable; it's not even observable. (Nor is it necessary to prove or observe it; we're just saying that for completeness.)

R: Well, when we talked about elves and fairies and so on, you said that we ought not to dismiss anything that had been so often observed in our culture over many years. And certainly the concept of the God and the Satan energies have been most extreme in this regard.

TGU: That's right. And good and bad angels, same way.

R: Yes. So I'm asking, are there those forces that operate, aside from whatever we're doing with our definitions of good and evil?

TGU: Well, we thought we had said that, yes, there are. That is...the forces that cluster because they're negative, that are at the extreme, may be 99 or almost 100 percent negatives. And on the other side, 99 or maybe almost 100 percent positives. Those are the respective commanders of the army, shall we say. And they have around them some that are 80 percent, and some that are 60 percent. And the two fight over the ones that are 50 percent. Just to give you a rough idea.

There's no reason not to see them as sentient forces. There's no reason not to see them at war, if you care to. But we would say, when you get to something that's all negatives, probably it will be evil to everyone. But when you get to something that's a mixture, it will strike you differently depending on what you are, and you might be more struck by the pluses in that mixture than you are by the minuses in that mixture.

That's very vague, but it's difficult to make a non-distracting and non-misleading analogy here. Overall, good and evil, pluses and minuses, must balance. There's no way out of that. But in any given time and in any given place, no formula says that the balance must be within x range. So you might live in evil times, say if you're in Central Europe in 1942. Even if you are a fanatical Nazi soldier, you're still living among negatives, so to speak.

We don't want to go too much further, because the difficulty is, people immediately begin placing examples, as we're drifting into doing too, where they say, "see, well that one really was evil." But take the Kaiser's troops fighting in World War I, and the French troops fighting in World War I. Which of those were good and which were bad? All the ministers were fighting for their own country and their own interests. And one side wasn't angels and one side devils, although each side saw the other that way. So perhaps Hitler is a bad example, but we could give you Japan in the same war. Viewed from America, Japan's actions were evil. Viewed from the colonies which were freed forever from the Europeans by the Japanese actions, it's a mixture. They don't see the Japanese as good, necessarily, but they don't see that action as necessarily bad either.

R: There's a tendency to think that the definitions of good and evil forces simply come out of our definitions. And I'm saying do those forces exist in nature aside from our interpretations of things?

TGU: Well, the pluses and the minuses exist. And on the one hand you'll have, let's say, the forces of good, and on the other the forces of evil. Probably it would be better to say the forces of attraction and the forces of repulsion, or perhaps the forces of optimism and the forces of pessimism, or the forces of hope and the forces of despair. We're trying hard to avoid making it just good and evil, but really that's what it amounts to.

What makes it difficult is to try to make a statement while looking over our own shoulder trying to see the ways people will distort this. And that makes it quite difficult. So we'll just state it frankly.

There is the positive, which is hope and love; there is the negative, which is basically *lack of* hope and *lack of* love; and there is the middle, those elements mixed. Those at either pole could be considered to be dark angels and light angels, and they have their followers in various mixtures of the pluses and minuses. They are at war in the way that matter and anti-matter might be considered to be at war, or two electrical particles of opposite charge. They are contending in the only place where they can really contend, and that is in matter, because it is in matter that you have people of various specific gravities *interacting* (because they're in bodies); you have them *choosing*, because they're in bodies seeing things in time-slices; and you have them *experiencing the consequences over time*, and therefore those choices will affect what those individuals go back to.

Now to show you how things loop back and shed light on each other, look at it this way. You, Rita, are here choosing. As you choose, you add or subtract pluses to your full being. As you're doing that, you are by definition, and necessarily, changing the composition of the amoeba in which you are a part. Now, it might only be a tiny change.

You, Rita, are a mixture. Let's say you're 73 percent plus and 27 percent minus, when you come in. By diligent choosing throughout your lifetime, you become only 25 percent plus [they laugh] and 75 percent minus. Or, you become 90 percent plus, and ten percent minus. Whatever.

Now, we said percent; let's take "percent" out and let's just say 97. You become 97 one and three the other. Now, you're added back, and your total alters the total of the amoeba, and maybe the amoeba is numbered in the billions, or the millions. Nonetheless, you've changed the equation slightly. There are millions of people living, all voting [by what they choose to be], all having their cumulative effect on the amoeba. That amoeba changes. It experiences life in various bodies, all of those lives choosing and becoming a part of it, particularly those that crystallize and become more, shall we say, influential, the ones that are going to be the slide through which the energies are projected, which means that the new energies will reflect them, to some degree. This is how the dark and light forces, or the positive and minus forces, contend. They can contend on earth – in earth – and remember by "in earth" we mean physical matter, not just one planet. They can contend in physical matter for the reasons we've said, and they can't contend very well outside of physical matter because we are what we are.

So physical matter could be considered to be a flank attack on outside-of-physical-matter. Remember we said we could maybe go between 51 and 49, but you could go between zero and a hundred, so to speak. It isn't one versus the other; we're just concentrating this time on how you, as an individual choosing, affect the overall design and how you really do affect this contention between pluses and minuses. From your point of view, minuses are always going to be evil, but anything that's a mixture will depend on where you are as to how you see that mixture. It will depend on your compassion, on your insight, on your – well, on your point of view.

So there's two things going on. We'll summarize this again, just for clarity. We are, shall we say, diehard moral relativists in the sense that we don't believe in any firm code of ethics that's absolutely right. We don't believe in any firm set of individual values that is absolutely right, because everything is a mixture, and in different circumstances different things are right and wrong. You can't just say you shan't kill, and have that be an absolute, because sometimes killing is in the service of life, or in the service of the good. It's obvious enough.

Now, having said that, on the other hand we also recognize that there will, ultimately, be some resolution of the tension between pluses and minuses. [pause] Well, we're getting into something entirely different here, actually, and that is – remember we've always said that pluses and minuses balance out in all of creation; they don't necessarily balance out in any given part of creation.

R: So what part of creation are you meaning? Time spans, or space dimensions, or –?

TGU: That's right. Or anything. Any way you care to slice it, it's up for grabs. Ultimately it's all going to balance out, but ultimately doesn't help because you don't live in "ultimately" any more than we do. If there's a time-space at one point where all the pluses are clustered, that means it's going to be grim somewhere else. But if it's grim somewhere else, that means it's going to be less grim some other somewhere else.

So on the one hand we say, you can't make the pluses overwhelm the minuses except locally; but on the other hand, you might as well try it locally. But on the other hand while you're trying it locally, recognize that what you're doing is forcing minuses to cluster somewhere else.

This is why, you see, you can have Zoroastrians who see the world as a fight between good and evil; you can have Buddhists who see the whole thing as being not reality; you can have Christians who see it as a battle between the good and the bad in a different sense, where God is the ultimate victor but first he has to fight, you see. (That's different from the Zoroastrian.) You can have all these endless permutations because it's people picking up a certain portion – but *only* a portion – of the reality and building a logical structure around only that portion. Just as we're doing. It can't be helped.

R: [pause] Okay. I think I understand your talking in terms of the pluses and minuses and forces that get attached to those. I started the question out with the elves and the fairies, and the way I'm understanding our discussion tonight, it feels to me like somebody is going to misunderstand what we have to say about elves and fairies.

TGU: [chuckles] We guarantee they'll misunderstand everything we say!

R: When I asked about elves and fairies, you said by implication "well, they're there, of course. People are seeing them."

TGU: Oh yes. We don't mean to take that back. They are. Just as they see people.

R: Yeah, but I'm asking about God and Satan and we're balancing positive and negative forces here.

TGU: Well now, bear in mind, no one has ever claimed to see God and Satan as bodily beings. That's the difference between that on the one hand and elves and fairies and trolls on the other hand.

R: Well, in the art world they certainly are very real figures.

TGU: Well, now, wait a minute. The art world is representing for the senses something which is understood to not be a sensory reality. But people who see fairies and elves and trolls do see them as sensory realities, but just not quite on the same frequency that you live. To our mind those are entirely different realms of being. If you were to see an angel – well...if you see angels, you see them. There's no difference, really, between seeing an angel and seeing a fairy, or a troll. All right, we'll concede that. And if you can see an angel, you can see a devil. Many people have seen what they think to be God, and perhaps we shouldn't say that they don't. We would incline to say they've seen representations, but we may be wrong.

Where does this leave us? Do you feel that we've contradicted ourselves at some point? Not impossible, of course.

R: Not really, I just needed to clear that up because I think people need to be able to understand the extent to which we're personifying things, and the extent to which we're describing things.

TGU: Given that we've told you that there aren't any such things as individuals, if you find a way to make that distinction, do let us know! [they laugh]

About This Book

R: All right, I think the only other question we would have tonight still had to do with our thinking about the book.

TGU: Well, let's do that off the record, so to speak. We'll tape it, but you don't have to disseminate it.

R: Did you have some reaction to our discussion earlier tonight that made some paths seem better than others?

TGU: [exaggerated, amused snort] And where pray tell do you think you got your ideas? [laughs]

R: *Well, if we're just quoting you, that seems like a simpler way to go, but somehow it doesn't feel like that takes the work out of it for us.*

TGU: Well, now, we didn't say it wouldn't be any work. We said it would be easy and fun. [pause] We think that you have the idea of it, easily enough. You each know what your strengths are. Just do only what your strengths are. Just do what came already. This means you don't have to bother to go back and re-organize it. Just take it as it comes. And what you will see, as you get to our second pass on it is, that with a few bridge transitions, you'll make it quite clear to people, and it will flow for them as it has flowed for you. We think. And we'll stack the deck that way.

R: *That's good.*

TGU: Have you noticed? Well, you *have* noticed, as you read the transcripts, how you start with increased clarity each time.

R: *That's true.*

TGU: This will work for them too; that's why it's coming out this way. However, you could ask entirely different questions – or you could ask the same questions in an entirely different order – and it could still come out in a way of increasing clarity. So there's not just one way to write a book. There's not just one way that a book can be written, is what we mean. The same book can make the same point by going different ways.

Session Fifteen
November 20, 2001

Lessons from Frank's Experiences

R: Frank seems to have had a really good time at this conference he's been to [Prophets Conference, held in the Florida keys].

TGU: As we did too.

R: Is there anything that occurred that he didn't take note of that would be worth mentioning?

TGU: Good question. Very good question. The kind of question you might ask every so often. We've encouraged him to say "what am I forgetting to ask," you know.

Actually, not a whole lot, because he lived very nearly all of the time consciously connected to us. Which is one of the reasons for the euphoria, if we may say so. If there were anything that we would call his attention to, it would be that there was still in him the tension between "what should I do, what could I do." "What's desirable, what's possible," that kind of thing. But actually that's really not worth mentioning, because every time the temptation came up he made the decision to say, "no, no I'll trust." And it's not the first time, but it's the first time that he's ever done it for such an extended period of time. There's nothing he didn't see that's worth talking about. The question will be more in his living what he knows now.

R: Sounds really good.

TGU: It was very good. [pause] You see, to him it was a homecoming. At the end, he looked around and – well, how do we say this? He has said already that this is a time that you all came here for, but it was at a different level of knowing this time. And now to see himself as one of the players; not as a *potential* player but to realize that he as Hampton Roads [Publishing Company] is already a player, was very validating. *And* [chuckles] we've been telling him for years, "if you want to be a writer, be a writer, but that's not as important as what you came here to do, which is Hampton Roads." And he's had serious resistance to that message! [laughs]

R: But he's now heard that.

TGU: He heard it. [pause] And appreciated it.

R: That doesn't mean he can't also be a writer.

TGU: Well, we never said he couldn't be. In fact, this might be worth a word, because it has its instructive quality for others. One writes out of what one knows, and what one knows is partly one's internal experience and partly external. And although it's not obvious, partly what one knows internally comes from other lifetimes, other experiences, other dimensions. (And, in the case of genius, other things from the larger being are channeling through them.)

So what a writer *is* flows out of what a writer's *life* is. It's not like a writer has to have an interesting set of external experiences in order to write about something that's important. But the internal experiences are not divorced from the external life either. So in his case, he has been led, kicked, forced, prodded, encouraged into a life that he never would have chosen by himself, and he chose this life seemingly for other reasons.

He often thought that he was in business in order to support himself and not have to work at a different kind of job, you see. But what was really going on was, this was a part of his contribution toward providing a major axis of realignment for the world. Hampton Roads as a company and Hampton Roads' books as product, and Hampton Roads' relationships among its authors and customers, and readers and investors and all, itself provides part of the way for people. This is not what he set out to do, consciously. And often he would have gladly given it up save there was no way out.

And had he had the opportunity to write in those ways (and we wouldn't have had any objection) it wouldn't have been much more than the exercise of a skill. Whereas now, by what he has become and experienced and where he is and who he knows, the writing will be more than that; it will be in service.

You asked, "was there anything he didn't realize, that we'd want to say," and the answer more or less was no. But – it occurs to us now – had the question been, "was there anything he realized that he hasn't realized in this context," the answer would have been yes. Let's tell it as a story.

He told you about Ilona Selke, and what a great impact she made on him. What he didn't happen to tell you, only for lack of time, was that he'd spent time in the mornings watching the dolphins in this penned enclosure. Even though it interacts with the waters right outside of it, it's still penned off. And someone mentioned that Ilona had told them that she didn't like communicating with those dolphins, it made her too sad, because they were captives, as opposed to the ones that she's used to dealing with, which are in the open oceans.

And although he saw that point of view, his immediate response was, "no, these dolphins are not having their lives wasted. They are in service. Many, many more people will see dolphins in captivity than would ever see them in the wild, and those who see them can be changed. And so therefore, their life is a dedicated life of service." And he specifically made the connection to the people who were working at the hotel, who weren't necessarily thought of by the participants, you see, because they were background. But they were in a life of service as well. Regardless of their intent. They may have been just there for a job. But the effect was a life of service.

The realization that he came to is just that: that the important tasks are tasks of service, not of an attempt to gain notoriety or money or satisfaction or the exercise of skill or anything like that. So it'll show you how important your questions have been, that a slight nuance in the question elicits an entirely different – sometimes seemingly contradictory – response. We've said that you point the question and we sort of coalesce around the point. And so this is an example of that.

R: It's interesting that I had thought first about asking it in the terms that turned out to be the alternative question, and then changed.

TGU: Yes, and had you done that originally, we wouldn't have come with this explanation. Well done.

Geniuses, Perception, and Potential

R: You mentioned in passing something about geniuses bringing forth parts of the amoeba that are not connected to other lives? Is that what you were saying?

TGU: Let's look at it by analogy. A person who has muddy perceptions knows only a little bit about their own life and could draw on that if they were writing. Someone with clearer perceptions could draw upon psychological insights, memories, inferred connections, you see. They would have a much bigger portion of their own life to draw on in writing. Someone who was connected Upstairs to other lifetimes – as one example – might be able to draw on that, perhaps not consciously. And by extension, someone who for instance went, by way of the larger being, to another part of the larger being that had expressed as a dolphin, might be able to seemingly fictionally, seemingly through imagination, express a dolphin's world, you see.

This is what we're getting at. The larger the access, the clearer the channel, the more there is to draw on. Then it becomes a matter of a combination of the clear access plus the technical ability to do the writing, which involves several skills that have to be all together: vocabulary, perceptual strategies, that kind of thing.

R: And then what determines the amount of the amoeba available to a person living this physical life?

TGU: Let's just for the purpose of clarification point out that you and we made a distinction a while ago, that level after level after level of seemingly separate things become a part of a larger thing which becomes a part of a larger thing. You know, that there are chains of monads. So that when we talk of the amoeba, we don't want people to accidentally slide into thinking of it sort of as one amoeba per one person. Or one amoeba, one person and the person's other lifetimes. By extension, you could say all sentient life is one amoeba, with various subdivisions.

We want to keep that not only in your mind but in the readers' minds, because there's always a temptation to concretize things at the level of an individual, rather than remembering that everything is a two-sided monad. It's individual at one level, but it looks upward to being part of a larger thing.

That's a detour – not really a detour. There's not really an easy answer that we know of to what you said, because we don't know any theoretical rules. If you have someone – just as an example – on the level of a van der Post or a Shakespeare, their range of sympathy and their range of suffering-driven empathy, shall we say, is so great that it's kind of meaningless to try to say what made that possible. Do you see? You are all theoretically capable of accessing everything in the universe. It's only theoretical, but it is there. Do you follow?

R: Well, I'm following, except that I had understood that in setting things in motion, you were making a lot of the decisions in this regard. And I guess I would assume that one major factor would be the extent to which a multitude of things are available to the individual.

TGU: Well now, [pause] it may be that we misunderstand you, but what we think you're saying is, that we in creating an individual in space-time make a mixture of a series of attributes and abilities and what-all and put them into one package, so to speak. Is this what you mean?

R: Yes, and within that framework, lots of choice possibilities –

TGU: Exactly. That's where we're going. If a person is created who naturally has a lot of abilities in a certain line, by their choices to consistently maximize their potential – their exploring potential, their loving potential, their access-to-Upstairs potential, if you want to put it in those terms – they could, if they consistently move in those directions, unpredictably widely extend their abilities to access. Does that sound circular?

R: Well, except I guess that I felt that you were putting emphasis on the plan for a particular lifetime coming about through decisions made by you and the individual involved.

TGU: That's true, but some people's plan is to be the eyes and ears of the species, so to speak. Some people's plan *is* to grow as much as they can, given their own decisions and given the circumstances in a given lifetime. In other words, one person may be entering a life in which they need a life of emotional discipline, and so their externals are severely constricted. Another person might need a life where the physical constrictions are such that it moves them spiritually. And so perhaps they are imprisoned for life unjustly or something. You see what we're saying. We may plan a life in which we say, "let's see how far you can go with this."

R: That could be done from a range of abilities.

TGU: Absolutely. Can be and is. It's not a rare thing. What *has been* rare, due to the difficulties of your circumstances in matter, is people maximizing their opportunities for growth. Fear and losing the way, getting off the beam, happens a lot, and it's relatively rare for someone not to have one of those problems stunt their potential somewhat. When you see one whose potential hasn't been stunted, such as Jesus, then you look and you just say, "my God, the rest of us are just wasting our time here!" [laughs] You aren't, of course. The difference between his actuality and your potential is a measure of how much room there is for you to grow, if you wish. In other words, it can be looked at as a hopeful sign.

R: It's suddenly occurred to me to wonder, what about the other end of that scale? People who seem to have very low desire to exploit any of their potential experiences.

TGU: Well, there is that, but we would also point out your very advised use of the word "seem." You made Frank struggle tonight, and we were delighted to see it, with the idea of judging other people's lives. It's always a temptation to judge people's lives, and you never have the data to do it. I mean, on the one hand you do need to do it, provisionally. On the other hand you need to keep in mind you can never really do it. So, yes, there are people who make little use of their opportunities. On the other hand, that itself can be used to fuel an opportunity at another time, for them. And also, that's a flower in itself. If we can use the drunk who dies in the gutter, we can also use the person who just floats by and doesn't have what seems to you much of a life. But you know the old poetic line from Blake: "How do you know but the bird that cleaves the air is a world of delight, closed to your senses five?" It's difficult for you to judge, and it's more difficult for you to remember that you *can't* judge. Although, as we say, you do have to judge provisionally. Modes of understanding, on either side

R: All right. I was going back over some of our work, this week, and ran into a couple of things where we said we needed to return. I'd like to mention two of those, and see if this is a good time to continue those discussions or not.

TGU: Frank would say, "see if we've arranged our cover story yet." [they chuckle]

Relative Advantages, There and Here

R: In one instance – this will be familiar – you said that we have the advantage over you in perception because we have the focus, and that you have the advantage in perspective, because you see wider and broader. And then I asked you whether it was just a situation where you simply understood more. And you said it was an interesting question, and we'd return to it.

TGU: Okay, this is a good enough time. [pause] Probably what will bring more clarity to the issue than anything else is to remember that when we said we have advantages and you have advantages, we're talking about the same being.

R: Yes.

TGU: It's like we're a two-ended wrench here. [laughs] If you have a box-end wrench, you use a box-end wrench on one side for some things, but in a restricted space you use the open-end wrench for other things. Same wrench, but different applications. And it's *because* you have no difficulty focusing on the moment – well, when you're *in* the moment – that that's your specialty! That's relatively more difficult for us, because as we once told you, we have to sort of scan around to find where you are at the moment. Because to us we see it not in slices. Well, given that reality, how would you answer that question?

R: Well, when I asked the question, I guess I was assuming that you understand more because you always seem to be answering the questions that we have, as opposed to your questioning and our answering. So the understanding is implied in answering the question.

TGU: Well what's shaping the dialogue is the fact that by necessity it has to take place in time-slices, in 3D Theater. Therefore you're asking and being answered in time-slices, therefore it looks to you like you can only ask and we answer. If we were doing it on our side, we could ask and you answer. And in fact in a sense you could say that that *does* happen, not only when you're in the body but also when you come back, when the barriers are lifted.

We find it works well if we have a physical analogy. People will remember the analogy, and it will help them to hold the concept. Just as the leaves of grass, or the flowers. People can hold that. Well, you point a question and we coalesce around the point, and that's why you ask a question and we answer it. But when we ask you a question, it's more like you live the answer.

R: I don't really understand what you mean by that.

TGU: We, on our side – which is also you, but it's the aspect of you that's on this side – say "what would it be like if you lived as an academic and then retired and went to work at the Monroe Institute as a volunteer and got involved with very interesting stuff, which brought you away from the original but you still had the training, and then, 20 years later, you came and sat down and talked to us this way?" That's a form of a question, you see. And your answer is what you live! But it doesn't appear to you as question and answer, because it's not in time-slices.

Your lives are answers to our questions. It could be looked at that way, without a lot of distortion. It isn't the only thing you're doing, but in a sense, your lives have posed a question, and you're exploring the answers. And no matter what choices you make, they're the right choices, because that's one answer to the question. Do you see?

So your lives are like an algebraic problem that's been set – No! No, that's a mistake. No, because an algebraic problem would have only one answer. Your lives are a blank canvas. No, that's not quite right either. When we find the RIGHT analogy, you'll be amazed how it will open up. But the wrong analogies always – well, they at least don't help, and sometimes they hinder. A moment here. What's a good analogy? [pause]

You know what it's like, more than any other thing? [chuckles] It's like, when we send you into life, we're firing up into the sky a firecracker, and the firework goes off and we see what we have. Now, we knew we sent up a big purple flower, but every purple flower that we send up will form differently. Will be different. It's also beautiful. It's also evanescent, from our point of view. Doesn't last very long. Pretty to look at. Interesting to watch. And in fact, if you add the factor that the firework itself is choosing how it will go off, so that if it really wants to, it won't be a flower at all, it'll be a fireball, or a dud, or whatever, you know. That's not a bad analogy. And in fact, we're rather proud of it. [they chuckle]

You see the point, though. Looking at it that way, we are asking questions and you are living the answers to those questions. Bearing in mind that the we that's asking and the we that's answering are the same we.

R: But looked at from two perspectives, which you have taught us to do.

TGU: I *know* that we are driving you crazy with that, but it doesn't –

R: No, not at all.

TGU: Okay, good.

R: That's the whole essence of the book, right?

TGU: Absolutely. Well, it's much more important than the book. It's the essence of your ability to get free of the singular point of view habit of mind which holds you to a lower state of consciousness than you need to be held to, because you're way above that. That is –

Well, this isn't anything you asked, but we'll go on, since it started.

All the preparation work has been done so that you're now – we're now – as a species, ready to move to the next level. This doesn't just include humans. And as you do that, some things are holding you back, and one of them would be a clinging to a familiar but now constricting mental series of habits, the worst of which is the thing of "good and evil, my viewpoint only." So we're attempting to help release that little distortion.

If you had a balloon that was trying to inflate, and someone had accidentally tangled a string around it or something, it couldn't inflate past a certain point without bulging out in certain places. But if we removed the string or cut the string or did whatever we had to do, then the balloon could assume its natural potential shape.

R: There are several things that came up there, and I'm trying to –

TGU: We often have this feeling we're not answering your questions at all, we're just using them as excuses. [chuckles]

R: Well, but isn't that wonderful.

TGU: Thank you.

R: It is. Wonderful. I was thinking that you said one of the tasks was to see the variety of perspectives available. And I was thinking about doing some work as a graduate student in which I would ask people to arrange a number of things in what seemed to be an appropriate order. And some people could hardly wait till they finished one order before they had another one in mind, and another and another. But most people had a "right" way to do it. And it was a sort of a discouraging thing, it seemed, that even people who should have known better were kind of stuck in this one perspective.

TGU: We'll make a suggestion to you. If you'd like to. Go back to that younger self of yours, and suggest to it that it's a simple trick that can be taught to them. Just as you talked to Frank about expressing his emotions, that it's not a matter of intense study and all that, it's just not even a trick or a knack, it's just a learned skill, and an easy one. If you will have your younger self go back to them and set it up so that they're told from the onset "there are three ways to order these," and see if they can order them three ways. By the fact that they know there are three ways, they won't be limiting it to one. And then, when they do that, say to them, "well actually there are five." And if they do five, then say there are seven. You see what you're doing, because each time they will think "we've got what can be done," and then they'll realize "oh, there was more there all along that we did not see." You might enjoy that, if you can go back. And therefore it won't be frustrating and you won't have wasted your time.

R: [chuckles]

TGU: And you see, this will be an example of you moving across time to influence another part of yourself. You'll go by way of the larger being down to the other person – that is to say, the younger you – and she will get this *bright* idea out of nowhere. Relieve a lot of frustration. And we won't even require a footnote.

Looking for the Footprints of Guidance

R: Okay, this is another "return to" question. You said that you were about to get into deep water because you were looking for footprints of guidance and we were helping you do that. You said you found this puzzling and interesting. I'm not sure if the puzzle and interest were because we were helping you do it or because you were on your own, looking for footprints.

TGU: No, it wasn't because you were helping us do it. We were very glad of that. It was puzzling and interesting because it was a degree of introspection that we're not accustomed to exercising, and weren't aware that we weren't accustomed to exercising. And our own thinking has clarified as we've engaged in this process. It's really a wonderful thing. It's remarkable to have the fireworks answering you.

At this point it's almost inconceivable that we didn't always see it this way. The answer presumably is that lots of other parts of us did, but that this particular cluster did not. But it's so obvious now that we are monads, and as monads obviously there's another level of complexity which would by nature not even be able to *not* direct us, guide us, impel us.

That is, just as there are individuals at your level who do no introspecting and are therefore unaware of the guidance that comes to them even from their own conscience, let alone other levels of their being, it is still relatively rare for people to be aware that they are interacting with other levels of themselves in other lifetimes. It is somewhat less rare for people to be aware that they are interacting with a form of guidance, whether they call it God or guardian angels or their higher self. But probably a majority of people in the West are unaware of this. And this is of course what makes their life so difficult.

Well, we locally were kind of in that unreflective position, and it's a little puzzling as to why we should have been, in retrospect, because it's so blindingly obvious, once we looked at it reflectively. We may be the cells in the liver of some larger object, so to speak, but the cells in your own liver know... We don't mean that as a biology lesson: What we're saying is, now it's staringly obvious to us that we as an organized part of something larger obviously receive direction. Now whether we're receiving direction from the equivalent of hormones or electrical impulses, or chemical tracers, something on that level, or whether it's something on the order of intelligence guidance saying "okay now do this, okay now do that" – although there's less difference between the two than might be thought – we don't really have a firm opinion.

But it's remarkable! It's just a little astonishing. It is as though we were functioning, thinking ourselves more individual than we – no, not that. It is as though we were functioning [pause]

Ah. We were always well aware of the difference between us and you. What we weren't aware of was the degree to which we at our level were functioning in a degree of ignorance common to your level. In other words, thinking of ourselves as more individual than we are, thinking of ourselves as more isolated than we are. So it's quite productive. And we suspect, that like yourselves, we are flowers of another level and perhaps someone posed this question to us: What would it be like to operate this way? We don't claim that; it's just speculation.

R: As you're describing this, it almost seems like it's a kind of a matter of logic to figure this out, rather than some experiential thing, for you.

TGU: Well that's exactly the borderline there. That's what's so puzzling. The logic is so obvious now, and we just described it, in fact, in terms of logic.

The experience was there all along, but the experience in the absence of the logic was not noticed. It's strange, really. You may remember, when we talked about this, that we first realized that we had probably been under the influence of something that wanted us to do something. And that was sort of a new thought to us. The logic followed the experience, it doesn't contradict it or supersede it.

R: It's a way of making sense of things.

TGU: Exactly. That's exactly it. And perhaps not the only way to make sense of it. We may be totally wrong in the logic, but the logic seems blindingly obvious. That's an implied question. As to the experience, we have no experience at this point – although of course it could change at a moment's notice – of a consciously expressed guidance in the way that Frank might experience us as consciously expressed guidance. We're beginning to recognize the experience of guidance in the form of a sort of a continued bias in a certain direction.

R: You called it "footprints," before.

TGU: What we meant by that was signs that something was around that we hadn't suspected. That's all we meant by that.

R: Well, but that is the experience, I guess. Observing footprints.

TGU: Well, it's the process of going from thinking "what a bright idea I just had" to saying "I wonder who gave me that idea," and beginning to find their telephone messages to themselves around the house.

R: So is there any more you can say about the process of that awareness emerging?

TGU: Well, point us a good question, and we'll see. [pause] Can be later, if it doesn't come to mind. We're not going anywhere. As far as we know! [pause] We can say this: The experiences that Bob Monroe reported in *Far Journeys*, the second book, will be suggestive to you of things that we can't actually predict, but you must bear in mind that everything there is reported from the point of view of an individual, rather than from our point of view. There's nothing wrong with that, just bear in mind that it was from one perspective, not two.

People's Awareness of Manipulation

R: All right, I don't have too much more tonight. Another question that came up when we were talking about your suggestion that you had manipulated the "disaster" scenarios, trying to move us in what you called a good direction. I was wondering whether there are people on earth who are aware of this kind of phenomenon, and who they would be.

TGU: Tell us first what you mean when you say "this kind of phenomenon."

R: The fact that you are manipulating our scenarios in order to move us into a direction.

TGU: Oh, sure. Certainly there are. And the difficulty is, the interpretation that they place on it. Let us say that you yourself were someone who is firmly stuck at a level where they only see one viewpoint. That immediately leads them, almost inexorably, to good versus evil. And that tells them the devil's doing it. They jump to that conclusion, and they have enough emotional evidence, and they have enough psychic hints, that it persuades them that this is exactly what's going on. And there's no way out of that for them until they can raise their psychic level – we don't mean psychic abilities, we mean the level of their psyche. If they can raise that to the point of seeing more than one viewpoint, that will automatically get them out of the "good and evil" trap, and then they'll begin to say "well, maybe this was orchestrated from the other side for some reason that is considered beneficial."

But the most likely people to see this are people who are stuck in that level and cannot and will not see it any other way than the devil doing it – just as, had it been something approved of, they would not and could not have seen it any other way other than God doing it. You see. They would make a firm dichotomy in motives and in agents, based strictly upon their own approval or disapproval of what they thought they understood of what they thought had happened.

We seriously doubt they would put it that way.

Now, we don't think that's the question you were asking, but it does clarify something, we think. You're asking more like, "do people have their access wide enough open that they can sense this?" And our answer to that would be, well, you did. Frank did. It isn't difficult. The main variant there is trust, and if your emotional dial is set on trust, so to speak, then you find reasons to trust. And if your emotional dial is set on distrust, on fear, on hatred, on separation, on accident, on coincidence, on chance, that's what you'll find. The setting precedes the interpretation of the data. Precedes and determines, mostly.

R: We just had a recent example of this in one of the ministers, attributing the disasters to God's getting even with us for all sorts of in his view negative things like homosexuality and –

TGU: No, we don't think so. You're talking of Jerry Falwell? No, that's different.

R: All right. You think that's another scenario?

TGU: What's happening with Falwell is different. He is not intuiting at all. Falwell is applying his logic to what he thinks the situation is. Do you see the distinction there? Falwell is saying, "this disaster happened. Therefore it is because the vengeful god that I believe in is taking vengeance." That's not the same thing at all as the scenario you set up, in which people intuit – they sort of hear – what's going on. We don't believe that in his case it was a matter of him having his channels open and realizing that this had been set up. We think in his case it was a matter of his applying his own predetermined logic to the situation.

Now, we will also say to you there is a third category of people. There are those who – you might call them religious, but some of them are devil worshippers, after all. They see it only one way; they decided that the devil did it, unless of course they're Muslims, in which case they decide that Allah made it possible, but it's psychologically identical. Then there are those like yourselves, who say, "all right, this has been sent forth as a drama for our own, shall we say, edification."

There are a third category who recognize that it happened but tend to put it in terms of chance. It is difficult to put a logic into it, because they're mixing things that are really incompatible, but don't seem incompatible to them. It is as though they're saying, "the other side is deliberately sending a pattern of chaos, and therefore we can't trust anything." That's a clumsy way to put it, but that's very clumsy thinking, too, on their part. Those people are almost not known; that's why we mention them. That is to say, you could have your organized religious, you could have your metaphysicians, but these people are more like, oh, lost sheep in the hills. They have the perception, they don't have any categories to put the perceptions in, and it leaves them more lost than if they were blind. Temporarily. Doesn't mean that's where they'll wind up.

Monads and Biospheres

R: All right, let me ask another question and we can decide to talk about it or not tonight.

We were talking about prayer in an earlier session. You mentioned among a list of things electromagnetic fields. And this has been something that I've thought about asking about before, because apparently it's one of the physical properties of the earth's atmosphere – in the sense that people can measure it and so on – that seems to have some major impact beyond other physical dimensions on human beings.

TGU: [pause] The question is –?

R: Is that true, that electromagnetic properties have major consequences for human beings? Or is this among just a list of things that includes temperature, and rainfall, and everything else.

TGU: Well, we're trying to be sure we understand the sense of your question, rather than the specific of it, but here's what we would say. All of your environmental factors – internal as well as external – have their own particular given sphere of influence. Your heart's pulse doesn't particularly affect rainfall, to make an absurd example.

Electromagnetic properties by their nature are fully physical and they're also beyond mechanical or chemical. Therefore they extend wider and they're more evanescent. On the other hand, although they're seemingly evanescent, they're also in a way more permanent, because you live in a sphere of that. At least, until the earth stops you will.

So this is very difficult for us to answer not so much because we couldn't arbitrarily answer it in a way that would be absolutely true within the arbitrariness of it, but because it's one of those questions that's very meaningful to you from your side and nearly incomprehensible to us from our side. And since we play both sides of the fence, we really do know what we're talking about here!

From our side, a question of importance would be like ranking leaves on a tree, or flowers in a field. If you had electromagnetic forces and didn't have the chemical or the hormonal forces or the blood coursing through your veins or all – what good would it do? You couldn't live. So which one is more important? You see? You know how children at a certain stage in development will rank their friends and it will be very important to them? And to any adult it's not only obviously nonsensical, but it changes by the second and the child hardly notices. You're doing the same things! [laughs] If we may say so.

The electromagnetic field has, as one of its major functions, the interconnection of individuals on earth, in earth, in a totally unconscious way which can unpredictably become fully conscious. It is a way to facilitate mental, spiritual contact between people in two different bodies. It's not the only way, but it's a very good physical way. In fact, you can't avoid it. Frank heard at the conference that your electromagnetic field extends as much as ten feet outside of your body, you know. So it is a natural harmonizing mechanism between individuals.

But how could we say it's more or less important than the flow of serotonin, or the function of the pituitary gland? We can't rank things that way. We could if we wanted to, but it would be just so arbitrary it's silly.

R: But you're comparing it there with other properties of the physical body.

TGU: Perhaps we misunderstood the question.

R: Well, the electromagnetic force compared with other physical forces operating in the environment seems to have more impact on human beings than other elements in the physical environment.

TGU: What does "more important" mean?

R: Well, you've just talked about the way in which the electromagnetic field has an impact on relationships between individuals, for instance. Rarely is this true with other physical forces in the environment.

TGU: Well, that's true. But if you were to ask us, "is the electromagnetic force more important than other forces in harmonizing relationships between individuals," we might be able to give you a reasonable answer. But that's not the question you asked. You said is it more important than other forces, and those other forces have so many other properties –

R: I did mean other environmental types of forces; other things we experience.

TGU: Well, for instance take humidity. Certainly seems innocuous enough. But given that the humidity interacting with other factors affects your ability to think – it may not be obvious, but it does – it affects your level of functioning.

Well, we don't know anything to say except that everything operates within its own sphere, and within its own sphere it is crucially important. Humidity, temperature, astrology, electromagnetic forces, the absence or presence of other beings in your life sphere – that is to say the animals and plants around you – affect your own being. You're a part of them even though you don't seem to be. That's just one more element.

So given all of those things, it's still hard to answer your question in any way that doesn't seem arbitrary. But that's not a bad answer in itself, actually, the fact that in fact they all deal within their own spheres. There's nothing on earth that is not on earth for your well being. Doesn't mean it's the only reason it's there, but among other things for your well being. When you have a functioning system that is a self-regulating system, and all parts function to the good of the whole, all parts are essential to the whole, therefore all parts are important to you. And you, to it.

R: Okay, now if we think about the distance of seemingly individual energies on other planets, is it also necessary to have these same –

TGU: Ah. Do they have to have the same kind of climate and forces and things?

R: Right.

TGU: Well, no, but they need to have whatever comprises their own biosphere. So that if you have a planet in which there are silicon creatures, in an environment adapted to dealing with silicon creatures, those factors may not be the same as your factors, but they will need everything in that biosphere. It's really almost by definition.

R: And this would be in part to do with why we find different kinds of creatures on different planets, presumably.

TGU: Also it has to do with why you find it relatively more difficult to interact with those even if they're part of the same larger being that you're part of, because they're farther away emotionally or rather in your expectations. You have less in common, and so it requires more effort, or a little more advantageous situation, to build the bridge. Or someone loading the dice, which may be the same thing.

R: So we've been talking about the totality of ourselves including energies from other realties, other dimensions.

TGU: That's right. And remember, just to throw this into a little different perspective, just as you in planet Earth are part of a biosphere, when you cast your net wider you realize that that biosphere also consists of the entire solar system – because you live in the sun's atmosphere – and the earth, as a functioning biosphere, cannot live for a second without being in the sun, and without being affected by the sun which in turn is affected by all the other planets. Which makes your whole solar system part of your immediate environment. You can immediately and intuitively see that the entire universe is one, just as you've been told. By extension of that same principle it really is all interconnected, because it all is one thing, although it can be seen, and perceived, and experienced, separately.

Your sun does not live in isolation in the middle of nowhere, so to speak. Your sun lives within the atmospheres of other suns. We don't mean that quite literally, but you know what we mean.

R: It's part of a galaxy, which is then part of a –

TGU: Yes, but that's not just a physical collection of things; it is a unit in the same way that the solar system is a unit; that your biosphere is a unit; that your body is a unit. Well, now, go on one more step. Just as that's all true – that all of physical reality is one functioning biosphere – well, other physical realities, as well as your own, are all part of one biosphere. In other words, it goes on forever. It really is literally true, that it's all one thing. And it's also of course literally true that it's a million different things. Trillions of different things. Quadrillions of quadrillions of quadrillions of different things. But it's all one thing.

R: But one of the –

TGU: *"But"!?* How can you possibly put "but" to that sentence? [they laugh]

R: I didn't mean to put "but." [they laugh] One of the levels of that oneness is what people have thought of resulting from the Big Bang, or some other –

TGU: We remind you we don't believe in the Big Bang any more than you do.

R: But, I say, or some other form of a creation of an immensity that has to do with physical bodies.

TGU: What's the implication there? What's the question?

R: You were enumerating the onenesses. We got through galaxy and then I don't know where we went next, but I guess we were going in terms of what looks to us in space like size dimension.

TGU: We're saying that everything is all one thing, and what appears to you to be creation and destruction of stars, of universes, or galaxies, whatever, is very similar to what appears to you to be births and deaths into and out of 3D Theater. And within your own body there are trillions of births and deaths of cells, you know, and – at any given level it looks like there are things being added and subtracted, and at any given larger level it just looks like maintenance.

R: And are you saying that there's no end to this increasing size?

TGU: We were just saying that a solar system, a galaxy, a universe, a nebula, anything, is not single as it appears to be but is in fact a monad. Part of a larger –

R: I'm trying to find the end of that scale.

TGU: Everything.

R: Everything.

TGU: We don't know any other end to the scale. Beyond creation, we can't answer you. You'll have to talk to someone a little better! [laughs]

R: See, I was trying to, at that next designation, say everything that seemed to be created by the Big Bang – you don't buy the Big Bang, but it's somehow created at that point.

TGU: We do buy creation. Okay, yes, if you mean, do we take as the ultimate monad everything that was created –

R: Yes. That's my question.

TGU: Well – how do we answer that? We take it as the ultimate monad that we know of, but only because that's what we know. For all we know, there might be scads of creations. But we don't know, and there's no point in our speculating and pretending we know. Although if it will help sell the book, we will. [they chuckle]

R: All right, I think that's all the questions I want to ask tonight. Is there anything you would like to add?

TGU: Well, there is, a little. We continue to be delighted by the process because, not only are you doing good work, and not only are you enjoying it, and not only is it affecting your own lives, but it's affecting our lives on this end too, whether you can accept that or not. Which in turn affects – well, again, it's all one thing. So it ripples unpredictably in all directions. You're not the only people doing good work, but it's good work, and we just –

We're delighted with that firecracker analogy, just as you are!

You might say, in fact – you might look at it in either of two ways. You might say that fireworks analogy did not exist and we created it tonight together. Or you might say that fireworks analogy always existed, and we discovered it tonight together. Of course, you could also say [chuckles] that we went to the reality in which we discovered it, which would equally be true.

But we think you will agree, it's a pleasurable, and an interesting, and, we think, an important exercise. It's good work. Onward and upward!

Session Sixteen
November 29, 2001

Definition of Now

R: I've got a couple of questions this evening. One refers to a couple of ideas that have come up in previous sessions. First is that "all the preparation work has been done, so that you're now as a species ready to move to the next level." And then a discussion about how few people are aware of interactions with guidance and even fewer aware of connections to other lifetimes. A woman asks whether there is a contradiction here.

TGU: We see why she thinks so. It's the same old story of seeing it in time-slices. What is "now" to us is not exactly "now" to you. It's the difference between taking ten years as now and taking only this afternoon as now. We mean by the first statement that you're ready to take the leap. That doesn't mean you're in the air. It doesn't even mean you have one foot off the ground exactly. But you're ready to take the leap right now.

But if you're *ready to* take the leap, that means you haven't *taken* the leap. And where you are now is that most people are not in connection with guidance. As they get in connection with guidance, they'll be taking the leap. So if you look at humanity over the course of a million years and you say, "okay, now you're in the last hundred years, ten years, thousand years," you know – it would depend on your scale, what "now" is. To us, "now" is the moment of application. This particular time-slice where you are is your moment of application. Of course, even this is almost incommunicable because *every* time-slice is your moment of application and you're *in* every time-slice, but it doesn't seem like it to you. So that makes it a little difficult to talk about it.

Looking at it from your point of view, we're saying that in your particular time-slices, as you're marching along now day by day, you are right at the point where the transformation is happening around you, whether you're in the front of the parade or the back or you're not even on the road, it's still happening. Now, maybe it won't finish happening for another 27 minutes or maybe for another 27 years or another 270 years, but it's still happening.

R: The process has started, somehow.

TGU: More than any other thing, this illustrates one of the different ways *we* see time and *you* see time. It's interesting, though, she put her finger exactly on the necessity. That's one thing that you can do with this project, show people that getting in touch with their guidance, hooking up and extending their own range – getting an extra battery in their flashlight, is *exactly* the operative thing to do right now, to help everybody make that transition.

Making the Transition

R: And what's the best way for us to think about what the transition is?

TGU: Remember, we discussed this at one point. The next step for humans is to be fully aware of yourselves and – boy, this is so funny because everything we just said is wrong. Even the words "as humans," that's what stuck us there for a moment. But let's continue.

Every one of you living your ordinary life, so-called, remembering all your past lives and all your other connections, still thinking of yourselves as separate, but seeing all that connection: That's your next step. That is, we think, the penultimate step towards leaving, because you all will be living fully, rather than thinking of yourselves only as the Downstairs individuals. Frank's bright idea about the Copernican shift *may* have been suggested to him over a thirty-year period.

R: So people are getting ready for this at different rates. And there is, as you said, a beginning of the parade and the end, and so on.

TGU: Some people have already done it, of course.

R: And is it necessary, for humanity to make this major step, for everyone in the parade to have the ability to connect with –

TGU: Sure. Sure. But that's not as difficult as you think. The difficulty is to be the first one. When you get the first sheep out of the herd and move them across the river, that's difficult, but as a majority of the sheep are across the river, the other ones are actually hurrying to catch up. Group energy always makes something easier, and as more and more people do it, that bridgehead gets widened more and more naturally, and there comes a point toward the end where, to change the analogy, the gravity is overwhelming, and the people who haven't yet done it are helped by *all* of the rest. *You* are not at the beginning stages, but those who *were* at the beginning stages were very lonely. They were – oh, pick your analogies. Swimming against the tide, single-handedly achieving escape velocity, you know, whatever your analogy. It's easier for each of you as more of you get there. When the time comes that the last ones are there, it'll be easier for them to do that than to stay. But, yes, you all have to go, because *we* all have to go. You're not going to leave something behind. You couldn't. Does that answer the question?

R: Well, that answers the question of getting ready for the transition. Can you say some more about what the transition is?

TGU: Sure. We each do our own work and the easy part is, your own work is always right in front of you and you just do that. You don't have to go across the ocean and count the cats in Zanzibar. You just do your work that's right there for you. When we each do that, then we begin to speed up the process a little bit and in a way you could look at what we're doing as changing our definition of home. So that instead of you thinking of yourself primarily or entirely as the part of you that's in 3-D Theater, the more you change your awareness, and the more directions that you change what you are actually living… Let's see, let's find an analogy. Can't use the flowers and the fireworks to any advantage on this one although we're very fond of that.

We're looking for an analogy that will indicate the access of power that will come to you as you connect the dots, as you live more connected. We like analogies, as we've said, because people can *picture* them and the picture is important.

Let's think about this a little.

All right. An analogy. Supposing someone discovers a talent previously unsuspected. The talent was always there, but unsuspected. When the talent is discovered and then fostered, they turn more of their potential into actuality. So it's fun, it's fulfilling, it's challenging. It could even be a little bit threatening, because it changes their self-definition, you know, which is a form of dying in a way. That's not a bad analogy. It's a question of growing into realization that you're much more than you thought you were. That's a familiar message to *you*. Bob Monroe, after all.

R: At the transition point, will there still be some difference in the stage where you exist and where we exist?

TGU: Well, that's a funny question because you're *at* the transition point and there is the difference because of the nature of the turf, but you're becoming aware that we and you are the same thing. And so, *you* tell *us*. Do you see what we're saying? You're already experiencing it.

R: Well, yes. We're experiencing it, but you say the transition doesn't occur until everyone has experienced it.

TGU: Oh, oh, oh! We misunderstood. Well, let's look at that misunderstanding, too. The transition is person by person. And then ultimately it adds up to a full transition. So, all right. We see. *You* are experiencing the transition now. Others will not experience it until later, or at least not at this level. Then ultimately when everybody has experienced it – you want to know where you go from there?

R: Yes.

TGU: Okay. Well, it will be akin to us in that the interaction will be complete, the identifying-with-all will be complete rather than thinking of yourself as a fragment, but the interesting nuance is, you'll still be experiencing in time-slices, but you'll know better. You see?

R: We'll understand another perspective.

TGU: You'll *experience* another perspective. You'll be able to *shift* back and forth between time-slices, *in a sense*. Now, your body – well, let's see – let's see how you want to…How about if we just leave that alone? [they laugh] Because your body is…Well, no. This is worth pursuing.

Your body is already in every time-slice in which your life exists. Rita exists between a beginning point and an end point and Rita exists in 3-D Theater *only* between those points, but exists in every point between those points. Every point between those points is a present. That is to say, it's a point of power. But you, right now, are being carried along by your physical body, time-slice by time-slice. That's what your physical body is doing. It's carrying you. It's holding the place, so to speak, and moving you forward one card at a time through the deck.

But when you get to the point that you are –. It's too much to say. All right. Let's look at this. One deck of cards is Rita. The bottom card, Rita is born and the top card, Rita is born into the next world. Rita is in every card in that deck. Now, there's another deck over there and this is the person who is born on Mars. Born into the world is the bottom card, born out of the world is the top card. All right? Same thing.

Now, the person who connects the two – your amoeba, that larger being in which both of them have their own being – can read *all* those cards. Supposing you were living today (as if you're not) after the transition has been made. You could live day by day, slice by slice, card by card, but you could also sort of remember or foresee, whichever. Neither of those words is right, but you get what we're saying, you could also move up and down through the card decks, and other card decks.

In other words, your physical body would still hold your space, but given that your mind would then –. Let me think about it. Gosh. [pause] It's so difficult because the language twists it as we try and say it. We'll go through it again.

You have the Rita card deck and you have the Martian card deck. Let's just use those two. You have the card *dealer*, which is the amoeba. And there's a hundred cards to a deck, so everybody lives to be a hundred years old, and each card represents a year. Of course, every single instant is a card, but forget about that. Every card is a year and there's a hundred cards to the deck and you are at presently on card number 63, or 35 or 90, it doesn't matter.

The way you're living now, it's very difficult and usually impossible for you to move from your card somewhere else, because your physical body carries you along from card to card and your mind follows where the body is. There will come a time – elsewhere there already *has come* a time, of course – when *all* of those cards are available to you on an active basis, no matter *where* your physical body is carrying you, because your physical body is *in* every card. It's just a matter of moving your consciousness to it.

Except it's not so much a *moving* as it is an activating. And the reason we're making that strange distinction is because "moving" always implies that you aren't there, or you wouldn't be moving. But you really *are* everywhere and so it only becomes a question of what you want to focus on, once you get to that point. Now, that was very clumsy and very difficult to get across. Imagine that now you have three million people on the planet, and let's even assume that each of those three million people have different amoebas.

So now you've got three million people walking around aware of all the rest of themselves. And not only *aware* of it, but continually *accessing* it. In the first place, you've eliminated your fear of death, you've eliminated the illusion of separation, you have opened up the vast fascination of –

Just think of the possibilities alone. That is to say, just think of active contemplation or actually active experiencing of every alternate choice. You see? Endlessly amusing. And that's really what we see here, the kaleidoscope. Now, take all of that and move your awareness up a couple of monads, so that you realize that all those amoebas are actually part of the same functioning organism and you begin to get the sense that the mystics get of the unity of all being and the beauty and the complexity and the purpose of the whole thing. Now, you've got a whole planet full of practical, loving mystics, because really it is true, love is the opposite of fear and then there *won't* be any fear. What are you going to be afraid of?

So that's a preview of coming attractions. It's not the ultimate either.

R: Well, yes. Because, the ultimate would include those of us who've moved out of the physical body in the –

TGU: Well, now wait a minute. You've already *been* included in the previous definition, because you no longer feel like "you" are confined to the card deck. So the people who are on the planet – or *in* the earth, as we would say – are fully conversant with all the other parts of themselves that aren't, and when you move up a couple of monads, that's everybody, and everything. So, in other words, that's *us*.

R: But you're saying that that's a possible stage to reach while still in physical bodies, so some of these three million or whatever you mentioned are in that state, have those abilities, but are still in the physical body.

TGU: That wouldn't be terribly wrong to say that, but we don't want to go along with it because of one thing. It implies movement, again. It's very hard, given the structure of language, to avoid that implication of movement, and we just want to be sure that that's not in there. While you're in the physical body, you're also *out of the* physical body. If we could do nothing more than help blur, if not destroy, the idea of individual fragmentation, we would be very happy. There's nothing wrong with seeing it that way, but it's important to be able to at least sense that it's really all connected.

After the Transition

R: Okay. Now, earlier you said that people become more and more individual through their choices. That the system works that way. And so, some of those energies are still in the physical body at this ultimate point of transition. They have seen and understood the whole concept of the amoeba, and all the things you are describing as part of this transition. At that point, have we all joined or do they continue in their —

TGU: What's bringing your confusion here is that you're looking at it from time-slices, which won't be nearly as important then. When your mystics say there will be a time when time is no more, what they really mean (but they may not understand it the same way) is that if you are living outside of time because you're in all time-slices, you no longer see it as slices, so it no longer seems the absolute that it seems to you. Implied in your question *is* an absolute about the time, you see?

R: Well, my intent was to ask a question about — there seems to be still a distinguishing between where you are and people operating in the physical.

TGU: We don't really mean to imply that, because given that we are part of you and you have expanded your awareness to all parts of yourself, the definitions will break down. It'll be — even more than it is now — a question of how you want to look at it. You could still look at it from unity or you could look at it from diversity. It's just that it'll be harder to fully believe in the absolute of the time-slices as you do now. Do you see what we're saying?

If you remember all your lives and all your possibilities and all of your dimensions and all that, you will be remembering that you're part of us. Right now, you're struggling to make it real to yourselves. And when you have accomplished that, there will still come a time when all of a sudden it's more than *real*, it's *experienced*. And the *living* won't be much different, but the *consciousness* will be vastly different, you see? Right now you already are a part of us, but you're not conscious of it on a day-to-day basis.

R: Okay. What I'm struggling with is, at that stage, is there still some need to be in the physical bodies, the three million? If a person who is in the physical is able to make all of these connections, understand itself to be the amoeba or whatever – what's the distinguishing feature between those who are in the physical and those who aren't?

TGU: Well, you still have the one big thing that you can experience in the physical: choices with delayed results. You will remember that we keep saying "in earth," but we mean "in the physical." Well, there could be a time when the earth is no longer needed as the garden that it is, but other places might be used, still in the physical. And so to that degree, you could say that there is never going to be time when the physical ceases to exist, unless for some reason it becomes unnecessary. But it's as real as anything else and, therefore, why should it cease to exist? Why should we cease to employ it?

We know that people think that the physical is either a prison or a school, but really it's just a place to experience. It's a canvas to be painted on, it's a kaleidoscope to be shaken, just as the non-physical is. We know that most people tend to think that the distinction is physical and non-physical, with the non-physical not having gradations. And it isn't so. Just as you have gradations in the physical, you have gradations in the non-physical, but –

Oh, an analogy that might help is in physics. If you have four dimensions, you *have to* exist in all four if you exist in any. If there are four that you realize, but six more that you *don't* realize, you *still* have to *exist* in those other six whether you realize it or not, because you can't *not* exist. Those dimensions pinpoint you. That's only an analogy, but do you see what we're saying about the physical and the non-physical? You wouldn't *not* exist here either. Or that is to say, the physical would not exist in all dimensions. Do you want to put a hole in the fabric of everything? [they laugh]

R: I'm really caught up in the concept that at some point individuals in the physical are, in fact, in touch with the whole amoeba.

TGU: Well, don't you think it will be interesting to be choosing, moment by moment, and watching the results of the choice, even though the results are slowed down at the same time? Do you see? It'll be different. It'll be fun. (We say it *will be* as if it wasn't already, but you understand.) We really are playing on your turf and this means that we're lying to you all the time without the slightest intention of it, but everything comes out as half truths or misleading analogies. It's difficult. It's pleasant and it's useful, but it's difficult. (This is our way of saying if you don't get it, it's *your* fault, not *our* fault.) [they laugh] By all means, pursue that if you wish.

TGU after the Transition

R: I'm wondering, at some point that we could define as the end of the transition, what's happening with you?

TGU: Well, you remember, we told in the first place, we don't know. We know that *something* happens. We know it's the next thing. It's the same thing Bob Monroe talked about, winking out. And he had a very strong and a correct (*we* think) intuition that what happened is they all completed. *Having* all completed, *that* game's over. Now, we don't mean "game" in the sense that it's meaningless or just trivial. But at the same time, we don't want to make it like you've learned your lesson and gone to the next grade. So what we're saying is whatever *was* going on is completed, and *when* it's completed, you don't keep doing it, you go on to do something else. But it *may* be that there's no fun in knowing what's going to come next.

R: Well, but, you know, we have this notion that at the end of the physical life here we move over with you somehow. We move back to the amoeba.

TGU: You don't *move* anywhere, in the first place.

R: Okay. Take "move" out of it.

TGU: And in the second place, that has built in the time analogy, and we know you can't help it, but we're going to keep coming back to it. At the end of this physical life, you are what you are, and the part of you that was in your physical life, moment by moment, is still in those moments of time, but what happens is, the barrier between your consciousness in the body and the rest of you, is removed. That is to say, you drop the body, the barrier drops, and you then have it all accessible to you. Now, even there, even the word "then" –

R: Yes. It's very difficult to think without that time and space language. But I understood from something you had said in another session that you or most of you had kind of finished experimenting with physical existences. Is that true?

TGU: It's a little misleading, only because of this. [pause] The center of gravity of our consciousness is over here, but as you know, we have probes over there. So are we or are we not in the physical? But the center of gravity of our consciousness is not in Frank. *His* center of gravity is. However, he's part of us and when he comes out of there – go out of your time-slice analogy if you can and realize that when his card deck is over and he's born back over here, *he* becomes a TGU that somebody can talk to over there, so to speak. Except it isn't "becomes," it's just *is*, you know. So that question is rooted in time, and we know you can't help it and we can't do any better. But – you see? How does he answer the question? If somebody asks him, are you finished with physical matter and he says, "well, yes," except he's still *here* at a different time, which is equally existent. So it just becomes difficult.

R: All right. But I was asking if at this point, which we're thinking of as the end of the transition period or something like that, are you moving to yet another state?

TGU: You mean, when the whole transition is completed for everybody?

R: Yes.

TGU: Well, yes. We think so. We'll let you know. [laughs] We won't *have to* let you know!

R: So that's what you're saying, you think something happens, but you don't know what?

TGU: We *know* that *something* happens. We don't know *what* the something is, but you'll know as well as we will because we'll all be in intimate connection, as far as we can tell. That is to say, the barriers between and among us will be gone and, therefore, we'll all experience it at the same time, whatever "it" is. A better way to look at it might be that, by itself, the elimination of the barriers will change us into something else, which will have its own momentum or dynamic. That's certainly true enough.

Communicating with the Next Level

R: As we're in the process of being in touch with you, isn't there some way that you can get in touch with the next level?

TGU: Well, yes. We've been looking at that, and you mean, we take it, ask *them* questions the way *you're* asking *us* questions. [long pause] We were just attempting to do that. It would be funny if we have to piggyback all the way down from where you are, through us, to them, but we could try that. Do you want to ask them a question?

R: Yes. I'm not sure if I can do that.

TGU: What we expect will happen is, *if* it works, we'll get a knowing and we'll tell you.

R: Well, I guess the first question is, is it possible for you to communicate with the next level and to get information from them?

TGU: Well, we're doing that all the time and mistaking it for our own selves, just as in your case. It's just a definitional thing. That came through very clearly.

R: And is there some merit in your becoming more conscious and doing it?

TGU: That *is* the value of it, becoming more conscious of what already happens. Because it opens more possibilities by opening the channels. The content may be competitively trivial, but the practice in opening the channel will, itself, transform as it does between us and you.

R: When you're able to ask those questions and get responses, does it seem that it changes some of the information you have? Are you now saying things to us that will no longer be the correct answers as you channel through from still another level?

TGU: This will give *them* a chance to insult *us*. Let's see. [pause] No, there's not the distinction between us and them that there is between us and you because the major significant distorting influence, which is the proceeding from time-slices, is not between us and them. So it's more a matter of, you could look at it as a federation almost. We are the locals and they are the next wider level up. That's interesting. That's where we would go to get information we ourselves don't have. But it's not a difference between us in the terrain. We and the next levels up are on the same terrain. Therefore, we don't have to translate across differences and perceptions caused by that time-space illusion as Monroe called it. Very durable illusion.

R: And is there some way of identifying the difference in intent or characteristics between your level and the next?

TGU: [pause] You could say a wider view, more than any other single thing. That is, let's say we are 14 and they are 28, but their 28 is more tightly knit than our 14. Therefore, they see more broadly and draw connections easier. Obviously, the numbers are ridiculous, but the idea is there.

R: And are their perceptions focused on your level, or the totality?

TGU: Well, you know what's going on here? This makes a lot of sense. We don't know whether *you're* suggesting it or *they're* suggesting it, but you could look at it as us being – just as an example – a halfway house between a time-space interface and them. And *they* are a halfway house between us and something that's *more* broad and more tightly knit and more of a unit. So that conceptually you could say that at the center of the whole thing is one active, widely extended consciousness that experiences itself as one. And as you go toward the periphery – bearing in mind this is only a spatial analogy – the associations are looser, the specific gravity is a little denser and it keeps on going down until you get to us, who are really in a unique position because we're on the interface between the time-space and the not time-space.

Now, the only thing is, with that analogy, you have to at the same time remember the contradictory data that we are all one. So, therefore, this means the being that is at the beginning of things and the cloud of individuals that are at the end of things, so to speak, are all one, and they are experiencing themselves, to some degree or other, as all one and as not all one, simultaneously, depending on their awareness. On our end, it's real easy to do. On your end, it's very difficult.

Huh! And *that* implies specialization of function. Now, this isn't the only thing we're doing, but to this degree it implies specialization of function. And thus, well, you know, you've heard people say they leave the earth, they're born into this side and for a while they can still interact and then after a while they can't because it's too far away. What's going on is, they're moving to higher levels of complexity and a lower level of density, a higher level of vibration, which makes it (a) harder to bridge the gap and (b) harder to even remember what they were doing down here. They are more interested in other things. They have other games to play, new games. Carry that through and in the middle you should see clouds of angels, and in the middle of the clouds of angels, the one being, the God, the creator, the center of everything.

We're saying "should" because this seems logical to us, but it's not . . .Well, it does seem logical to us.

Consciousness Levels and Focus Levels

R: Well, this fits into the questions that were being raised by people who were talking about level 50 and level 54 and level 99 and all these things. Maybe we're talking about actual levels. Are we doing that? Are we talking about four levels, five levels, something comprehensible to us?

TGU: Well, we would say they're mixing two concepts. They're mixing the Monroe focus level concept, which does *not* imply that each different, higher number is necessarily a different level of vibration. It's more like your numbers are farther away from normal everyday consciousness, and that would be about the only distinction we would draw among the Monroe system. Again, even the word vibratory level is only an analogy, but we think they're intuiting that, as you go higher, it's different. As you expand your range – well, they're all spatial analogies. They're right, there are gradations. But people would be confusing themselves were they to think that the Monroe numbering system, which is of convenience, is an absolute, or is a direct correlation there. Focus 12 is not significantly lower than Focus 21 in terms of going towards higher levels of awareness and higher levels of vibration. It's that it's easier to get to Focus 12 than 21 from normal consciousness. But see, all of that is within the same...(Do you really want to hear all of this?)

All the early focus numbers are within the same time-space interface and, therefore, you're not *climbing* anything, all right? And the numbers from 21 on are still within the time-space interface, but you are, shall we say, flirting with the other side. Obviously, you're only flirting with it because you're still in bodies, but you *can* experience them. We're not saying it's not a real experience, but it's more like flirting with it than living there, obviously.

R: I bring this up because one of the individuals who channeled an energy that Bob was quite interested in, called Miranon, presented itself as being at Level 49 or Focus 49 or something of that sort.

TGU: We would doubt that it presented itself as *Focus* 49. But maybe it did.

R: I'm not sure.

TGU: Well, you see, what we suspect is happening is that confusion of thought that we mentioned, because spatial analogies slide into everything just as easily as the assumption that a time-slice is an absolute. It's so difficult to keep out of it, even trying as hard and as carefully as we are. With our attention on it, we can hardly do it. And to try to explain something else without going back and saying, "but, but, but, but, but," it's very easy for these things to creep in because, you see, it's relatively unimportant next to what they're really trying to get across. And so they sort of give up – perhaps we should say *we* sort of give up – and say, "well, a lot of this is going to be inaccurate. Let's hope we can get across what we're trying to get across." It would be like judging the content of Focus 27 by the fact that some people think there's actually rock houses there, okay? [pause]

Although, in a way there are. Really in a way there are. You get to the point you can't say anything. The difference between a house created by consciousness *there* and a house created by consciousness *here* is really – the difference is the consciousness. Your houses are created by your consciousness here, too, the same as they are there, obviously.

R: Yes. Well I don't see the advantage of going on with that.

TGU: Okay. We won't get our feelings hurt.

R: [laughs] It's probably because I am remembering more about that Level 49 now and remembering that it had a scheme that went up by seven levels at a time.

TGU: We would say to you that it might actually be worth your while to put that into writing because you may be the one who remembers those distinctions better than nearly anyone left. Not absolutely, but nearly. In other words, of those who remember the distinctions, you may be the one most likely to write it. It doesn't matter now, but in 15, 20, 30, 50, 100 years, it may matter a lot in terms of reducing the distortion level.

R: I think that's something we could look into to. I think there are people around who would have some specific memories of that.

TGU: That might be very good work. [Never happened, though.]

R: I don't think I have any more questions right now. Do you have some other things you would like to suggest?

TGU: Oh, we think you had a couple of questions about Frank, actually. [pause] If we're wrong, that's fine.

R: I had some more questions about the book and proceeding with that. Frank didn't clue us in on anything else we should be asking about.

TGU: Well, on the book, just proceed in the least disruptive manner possible. That is, follow the line of least resistance. That's our recommendation. Otherwise, you have our continued blessings.

R: I really appreciate that in this session as we usually do. Very interesting content in there.

TGU: Thank you very much. Same time, same place.

TGU: [Yawns]

R: You're getting very relaxed, I see. Very good.

TGU: Someday you're going to turn on the radio and there'll be no show. [they laugh]

Multiple Perspectives

R: One thing that's already come up this evening is a concern Frank has about an over-focus on the individuality of perspectives rather than backing-and-forthing between that and the oneness perspective. Is that it?

TGU: He is occasionally suffused in one viewpoint and finds it persuasive enough that he finds it difficult to remember the other viewpoint. You might not think he would, after this time, but when he looks at the complexity of the systems that have been worked out from the assumption of individuality, and sees these elaborate systems involving reincarnation and judgment and karma and apparent progressions of individuals, then harks back to our explanation of all of those individuals as being part of larger beings that are also monads, he finds himself at sea as to how both can be so. He sees nothing in our explanation that shows the other ways of seeing things from a different point of view. In other words, it somewhat seems to him that our unitary description doesn't exactly *contradict* the multiple description, but goes off in another direction entirely. He sees little overlap. That's what's distressing. And he merely points out a gap that remains to be filled. There are many things to be said, and that's one of them.

For instance, we lightly touched on how a larger being, an amoeba, might create a new life in space-time either using part of its essence that hadn't been before, or chaining it through another life that *had* been before. That gives a misleading impression, because it sounds like life that hadn't lived before would make it kind of isolated and solitary. But that overlooks the fact that that life, even if it had never been on earth before, still connects with us, which connects with everything that's been on earth before. And that's perhaps not obvious. We thought it would be, but we still forget how easily things are seen as separate rather than connected, just from your mental habits. It's not meant as a criticism, it's meant as a description of the state in which you find yourself, the mental environment.

So, we would advise that he just cool it, that it's very good to ask those questions and bring up the perplexities. But it is needless friction to worry about it quite so much. It's easier just to ask the question and see what happens than to worry, "what if they don't have an answer," or, "what if it doesn't work?" You see? That's all. The long and the short of it is, anything you can ask us we can answer, and supposing our answer was, "we don't know," it'd still be better than you sitting around wondering, "oh, God, do I dare ask a question," which he tends to do somewhat. If he'll come loaded for bear next time with some specific questions about ways in which he thinks that our scheme doesn't overlap with what he sees, we'd be delighted to answer. That means that that will have come to the top of the stack, and there can't be a wrong time for a question.

R: All right. This will be depend on Frank trying to pose those kinds of questions that will fill in that gap.

TGU: That's right. And tell him there's only one way to do it right. [they laugh] There's only one path that's good.

Both Sides Work Together

R: I've been reworking some of the first chapters, and am very aware there that we're talking about the whole point of this being to look at things from the two perspectives, but I can see that it would have been very easy for us to slip into language that's a bit more familiar to us, and concepts based on an individual.

TGU: Remember, too, that we said that sometimes perplexities would arise in you, or fears or doubts or whatever, for seemingly no reason; that our dealing with them will prove very helpful for people who will read this. So sometimes, the deck's being stacked in a different sense. There's your alibi.

R: So I assume you're planning this all along.

TGU: Well, the straightforward answer to that – you may have heard this before – is yes and no. Yes, we have a sense of how to shape this in such a way as to make it the most useful and accessible to the people who will follow it. But no, it isn't planned *without* you, it's planned *with* you. You see? We're going to continually repeat, it isn't a question of *us* manipulating *you*, it's a question of *us* manipulating *us*. You don't remember the planning in your daytime phases perhaps, but you're in on the planning all the time, you're willing participants, and that takes away the element of manipulation, although to the degree that you can't remember your participation on this side, it can only be seen as manipulation. There's enough suspicion of manipulation going around in your culture now that we think it's worthwhile to remark on this. If we were only dealing with you and Frank, we wouldn't bother.

R: Well, one thing I've noticed is that the humor takes that form, that when we say we had thought of something, you suggest perhaps that we hadn't thought of it, so that adds to our perspective that we have only some minor part in this, somehow.

TGU: Well, you *can't* have a minor part in it. You are as much a part of it as we are. If you were writing with a pen, it'd be like saying your third finger had a minor part in writing. Do you see what we're saying? Even though it seems separate to you, you're as much a part of it as we are because you have to be. We is we.

R: Yes. I was just speaking about the humor, I assume, as meaning that, and somehow it often takes that form.

TGU: Well – besides the fact that we find it entertaining – we're trying to emphasize that what you think is not local to yourselves, any more than what we think is local to ourselves. We're all the same thing, thinking together.

Let's see if we can come up with a fireworks-quality analogy, because it would be very well if we could come up with a nice visual image you could remember. [pause] Well, supposing – it's difficult. The analogy hasn't come yet. Well, wait a minute.

We're looking for an analogy which would show that we're still all together, but that some pieces of us are separated by something which makes those pieces not aware that they're part of it. But we would need an analogy that didn't imply separation or space or an actual barrier rather than a relative one. And the closest analogy we can think of is actually an osmotic filter, where you have saltwater one side and plain water on the other side. Perhaps if you look at the veil between us as a filter – but not a very good analogy. [pause] In fact, it's a downright terrible analogy. [laughs] We'll think about it and let you know.

We're looking for something to give the analogy of a massive unit, one part of which doesn't recognize its unity, for a physical objective reason, but it's not really obvious. [pause] It may come to me in the middle of your asking a different question.

R: I am interested in what we were just talking about, though. Because you suggested that we have given you some ideas – one or two – whereas you've been giving us lots of ideas all along, some of which we thought were our ideas, true enough.

TGU: Well, for all you know, we stole your ideas and called them ours.

R: Well, that's a possibility. [they chuckle] But since we've been focused on this individuality – and Frank feels, uncomfortably so – that suggests that it's more apt to be coming from us.

TGU: That *what* is more apt to be coming from you?

Essence and Personality

R: The kinds of questions that we raise that represent our topics here. Frank's uncomfortable that those are too focused on our individual perception, a perception of us as individuals.

TGU: No. That's not what he meant. He's uncomfortable with our explanation. He doesn't think our explanation takes into account the evidence of things that happen to people that they've reported individually. He's not concerned with your questions at all. He's concerned with our answers! You may know that his bias is that if anything has been believed over a long period of time by a lot of people of a serious nature, there's something to it. It may be distorted or incomplete, but there's something to it. So coming from that point of view, from that emotional mindset – which is not a contradiction, although it sounds like one – he looks at our explanation and says, "well, what does this have to do with repetitive reincarnations, leading a person to grow and to work out their salvations?"

Most anything you can read, study, hear about, or even experience comes in a container of "individual," coming out of time-space. Even if that individual, based in time-space, then goes to the other side and is no longer in time-space, it's still perceived as an individual and still perceived as returning on this side again, you know, being born *from* one side and then being born *to* one side. And so within all of that, he feels it's way too much elaborated to be a misunderstanding from your side, and he doesn't quite see how our exposition from our side can be accurate in light of all that experience.

R: Well, let's go back over some of this material that we've talked about, and see if that brings any light into the subject. We've talked about how, as we spend our lives here making choices, we've become increasingly individualized. And at some point we move across with this – now representing this individual who has made all these choices and has somehow sharpened the focus of who they are, become more crystallized. I don't know if that's right.

TGU: That's good. And let us interrupt you for a moment. Now, he sees that as the end of the story as far as we've gone, and how does that tie in. He can see that being one of the pieces of grass in the field. The question that rises, although he hasn't put it as clearly as you've just put it, is, "well, then what," you see. Because from our way of describing things, he can't quite see how that same individual can then come back into this side again without –

Oh, we just found out how to answer it, too. You could look at our side and your side being divided by a veil or, you know, a divider, and being stitched. And the thread that stitches from one side to the other is the individuals coming back and forth. [chuckles] It's not at all necessary for us to say, "you, Rita, when you come over to our side and give us the flower that was Rita . . ." Ah! That's where he's –. Okay. Well, we just found something interesting.

You see, he sees that the flower that is Rita *is* here from our point of view, [but] *will be* when you get here, from your point of view. He's saying that that's not compatible with your going back again. But, of course, your underlying *energy* is not the same thing as your *personality* expressed in your life. The *energy* goes back, the *personality* doesn't go back. But that's not been clear to him. You see it?

R: No. We've said that personality does go back, but my understanding was that it joined the amoeba and in that sense became part of this overall energy.

TGU: Let's call your side the individual side, and we'll call ours the unitary side. The personality dying from the individual side and being born into the unitary side has an underlying essence, an underlying energy that came, of course, from us. It went into your side. Let's pretend it was the first time through. The energy left the unitary side, dressed itself in a personality on the individual side, and returned from the individual side to the unitary side dressed in the personality that it acquired and polished during that lifetime. When it reaches the unitary side, that personality is completed. That personality is then a part of us.

The underlying energy from that personality can then stitch through again over to the individual side and obviously – or perhaps not obviously to you, if not let us know – it will have a different personality rather than the same one. It will have been born at a different time in a different place with a different set of attributes. That's the whole point of it.

Now, the *Division of Consciousness* book [by Peter Novak, an examination of views of the afterlife] should explicate this for him, actually. The human personality in any given lifetime is here as part of the field of grass. You don't recycle Rita. The *personality* Rita will not become part of something else in another time and space on the individual side. The *essence* Rita, either mixed or unmixed, will come over to the individual side again and pick up another personality as it has before. The person living on Mars is *not* Rita.

The essence of Rita and the person living on Mars may be the same essence, you see. Now, everything coming from us could be considered the same essence, but we're pretending [for the moment] that different parts of ourselves are a little more individual. There's nothing wrong with subdividing our self into selves. Let's do it that way and say that your self picks up a personality, develops it, leaves it off, goes back in, picks up another one – not necessarily always in the physical, not necessarily always on earth. Does that aid the situation at all?

R: Well, yes. It does. But when you say "ourselves," how does this relate to the amoeba?

TGU: We're referring to the unitary side. Any of you, any of your individual essences, that is to say that the essence that right now is Rita, the essence that right now is Frank, any of those *may be*, for the focus of convenience, considered one cell of the unitary body. And that cell can come in, pick up a personality, drop a personality, pick up another personality, that kind of thing.

R: Okay. Well, we've talked about that before, we've said when that cell returns, it moves back into the amoeba.

TGU: Yes. And see, the cell, the energy, the essence –

Okay. How do we – we need to think about this a little bit. A moment here.

There's not a real good analogy, but supposing you, Rita, learned French. The essence of you has nothing to do with whether you learned French. The personality learned French. The acquisition of the skill is at a different level than the maintenance of your being. In other words, what you *are* remains unchanged no matter what happens to you, in a way. It's not literally true, but it's close. So that if you get sixteen academic degrees and pile up three fortunes and get on the cover of *Time* magazine, it doesn't really affect your essence directly. It will in the sense of perhaps affecting the choices you make, but we're trying to make a distinction between the essence that is at the base of your life and all of the personality-oriented superstructure, that is acquired.

We are attempting to come up with a distinction between what is almost an artifact – that is to say, that personality and that lifetime pattern – and the underlying energy that was responsible for *creating* the artifact. The life that became Franklin Roosevelt is the artifact. The individual part of ourselves that went in and stoked the boilers and ran the ship during the creation of that life is not the same as the artifact. Without it there could have been no artifact, but it was not the same. So the Franklin Roosevelt lifetime, which includes the mind, the spirit, the body, the acquisitions, the character problems and all that, that's not the same as the essence.

Accounting

TGU: But here, again, we'll take a little bit of a turn. Here we've found another problem that's bothering him, and that is that if one looks at Franklin Roosevelt – to give a neutral example – as a person who came into this existence on your side with potential problems to deal with, as we've said, dealt with those problems well or badly, and went back on our side again, the assumption is, "okay, that underlying energy has to come in and deal with those remaining distortions."

In other words, supposing it came into this life with sixteen issues and left on the other side with ten issues, or twenty issues, the question is, what happens to the accounting system? If the artifact that is the life of Franklin Roosevelt is not the same as the energy, where's the accounting? Wouldn't you say that's sort of a problem?

R: Well, let me ask this. The actual energy that comes into this side from the amoeba. That basic energy, the essence, through the choices that it makes on this side, becomes an essence with a lot of attributes added, situations met and solved or not solved. It returns to the other side, returns to the amoeba, with a lot of components that weren't there initially.

TGU: That's right. That's the flower that it brings back, or the gift.

R: Okay. Then if we think of the essence being again represented in another life-time, coming forth again there so to speak, I'm not sure what Frank's problem is with that.

TGU: Well, his problem would be that most people would describe it as "he came in empty the first time, at the end he came in maybe at minus four" or whatever. In other words, they're keeping a score. The assumption is, then, that something has to carry that score back into your side, into the individual side, and make it all come out even.

R: Karma?

TGU: That would be their description, yes. They're trying to make it all come out even at the end.

R: And "even" means an equal number of positives and negative –

TGU: Or smoothed out, anyway, yes, depending on points of view.

R: Except where you said that in any one person, that doesn't have to balance out.

TGU: Not only that.

R: You can have an excess of positives or negatives.

TGU: That's right. And not only that, the whole accounting system is skewed by your culture's inclination to look at everything as individual at a time when that's not appropriate. So supposing you're talking about carrying ice cubes – I don't know why this analogy came, but let's see if it works. Supposing you're talking about carrying ice cubes over to our side from your side, and you, when you come over with the rest of Rita, bring fourteen ice cubes and Frank brings twelve ice cubes, of a slightly different flavor. Okay. And someone else ten, and blah blah

blah. And we've got to get those ice cubes over on the individual side again. In other words, people have a sense that if you make bad choices, so-called, you have character warping and you need to un-warp that character in order to get perfection. So they think that it's an endless accounting system until you get it even, until you get it all screwed down and right. This what we've seen repeatedly.

R: And the assumption is that it has to be done within one individual.

TGU: Exactly! And that's the bad assumption. So that, in other words, Hitler has to go through another fourteen lifetimes of presumably being a saint until he expunges the last of his guilt for what he did. But it isn't personal that way at all. The *essence* underneath the Hitler personality isn't guilty of *anything*.

R: Yes. So I'm not sure how this balancing leads from...I'm stuck.

TGU: [chuckles] Because it's true that we tend to balance it out, over time, but it isn't true that one piece of essence –

Suppose you were players in a repertory theater, and each actor takes a different role. There's no necessity for one actor to take as many good roles as bad roles. And there's certainly no necessity after he took a role as a selfish person to take a role as an unselfish person. As complex as it is, you would never have it come out even. You see, people are getting glimpses, but because they are inappropriately putting them into individual analogies, not even thinking they're analogies, but thinking it's accurate, they're drawing the wrong conclusions. So that, for one thing, many of these [conclusions] have as a silent, sometimes not even noticed, assumption that the whole purpose of all of this is to lead people to be moral and good, and that enlightenment equals being "good." (Put good in quotes.) But in actual fact, it doesn't have a thing to do with that.

R: At the individual level or –

TGU: Well –

R: There's apparently group karma as well as individual karma. The Buddhists talk about it.

TGU: But is the group any realer than the individual? That would be the point we would make. It's real from a certain point of view, that's what we would say. But – all right. Let's look at this a little bit. Take as a group karma, the United States. And say that in the United States they put all races of people in slavery. They exterminated or persecuted other races and, you know, got them out of the way. They systematically exploited whole classes of people to keep them poor and out of the way. And when they fought wars, they occasionally had their own atrocities, as everyone does. So take all that. Now, does this mean that that group is going to have to suffer the equivalent of that? Or that it's going to have to, at least, fully understand where it went wrong and resolve not to do it again? Or – if one is identifying at the moment with the victim of any of these things – does that mean that that victim was being paid back for something they had done earlier, or will be paid back in the future? You see what we're saying, the same dilemmas that come when you look at it individually are even more so in group senses.

However, it isn't exactly wrong. There *is* a tendency to balance things out, but it isn't "this must balance the last jot and tittle" kind of thing, and it isn't a thing of getting even. And it isn't even a thing of making the scales balance. It's more like it just tends to balance out because things tend to balance and don't tend to imbalance.

So, every country does good and does bad. And, of course, what's good and what's bad depends on the actions of 50 million observers, internal and external. How can anybody try to make that scale balance? It's just that things are followed by other things. People as individuals – that's what we'll call them – affect each other because they're all one thing – well, okay. Let's look at this for a little bit, if you're interested in this.

As people in bodies, you're individuals. As people in groups, you are not necessarily really individual because you interact with each other so, and you're so intertwined, even physically, that you can't consider yourself an individual really except by not looking, and then, that doesn't even take into account the fact that on our side you're all connected through us. Well, the airplane attacks in September led people to react, everybody out of their own backgrounds. To the degree that you in the same society share the same media, share the same understanding of history, the same habits, your things that are taken for granted, that pushed you toward reacting more or less the same way. Someone in Peru would react quite differently from someone in Canada to the same given event because you react *against* something, you don't react in a vacuum. And what you react against is what you have become, which is shaped by your history. It has a lot less to do with balancing the scales than it does with "every action has an equal and opposite reaction," although we're not saying that literally, of course. [pause] Have we lost anybody in the thickets here?

R: [chuckles] Well, I'm trying to figure out whether this was a treatise on why our original concepts are wrong or why they're right.

Water and Ice Cubes

TGU: It's more like, all the concepts that have ever been formed are very, very valuable clues. And Frank's got the direct intuition on this one, you know, even if he doesn't know how to pursue it. You take those clues and you run them through a new way of viewing, and it gives you tremendous data. So that if you could start

THE SPHERE AND THE HOLOGRAM

with a different point of view and go through all of your scriptures, you would find the sophistication and the precision would be vastly enhanced, because it's already been worked out for you. All you have to do is correct for the biases. Now, of course, that means you're putting your own bias in, but that's the only way you can come up with a concept, about the only way you can explicate one.

We still haven't quite found a way to make that analogy. If you had a bag of potato chips and a few of the potato chips were individually wrapped, but they were still in the bag...But it's not an obvious – it has to do with a phase...Well, okay. There we go. There's your analogy, a phase shift. That's where we started, with ice cubes, isn't it?

If you had water at 32 degrees more or less, and some of the water had become ice cubes, those ice cubes might not think they had much in common with the water, and, in fact, if they were only acclimated to recognize ice cubes, they wouldn't even know they were *in* the water. If you will look at the unitary side as the water and the individual side as ice cubes, you can see that here you have something that's identical in nature but in a different physical state, which makes them look very *un*-identical. (It's also possible, if the water had mentality, the water might not recognize the ice cube as water. We'll leave that for another day. What we just said is revolutionary when you think about it. The water might not recognize the ice cubes.)

R: That's very good.

TGU: So it took a bit of work, but we came up with an analogy. We knew we could do it. But if you can take those ice cubes and turn them into fireworks – [they laugh]

R: Well, do you want to leave that that way? The water might not recognize the ice cubes?

TGU: For the moment, we do, actually. Mainly because some people will wonder "what in the world can that possibly imply?" And as we said before, it's better to puzzle out something yourself than to be given it to you, because the teasing it out on your own is valuable, even if you get the wrong answer, whatever a "wrong" answer is.

Notes on Prep Sessions

R: Frank's been working on the information from the sessions in the lab with Skip [10 black-box sessions in the fall of 2000], and has come up with what he believes is an essay based on those.

TGU: He's *hoping* that he's going to come up with an essay. What he's come up with so far is three pages of typed notes. But he will.

R: And the thought is to keep those sessions separate from these sessions.

TGU: Well, the thought is that the reporting of the surround of those sessions and the content of the sessions can be done in a pretty concise manner, which will sort of set the stage for the next stage, which is yours. Even though it included visions and really going off into new territory and being given stuff, rather than responding to questions, it can be described more simply and quickly, so it should really be the porch to the house. It should be relatively short. Not over 500 pages. [chuckles]

Those sessions were very, very important in turning him to this work. And they have very important clues in them as to what people can do to tune themselves. And the main value *he's* going to get out of it is to remember what was in there, because he's really ignored and forgotten it. And so now, as today and yesterday, he's beginning to remember to *do* some of the things that he learned to do and forgot, you see.

R: But it is all available to him.

TGU: Oh, sure. The transcripts were there, he made the notes on the transcripts. It's just, the immediacy of later work took him away from what he learned there. Every week, you know, was a new nail driving out the old nail. And now it's very much the process of collecting them and looking at them and saying what they mean. And then, putting them into words.

R: So is that something that should have been done before this?

TGU: Oh, no. No. It's perfect timing. Perfect timing because that won't take long at all, just as yours isn't going to take long. And then you go on to the next part which is this sequentially. We told you, you can do it easily. Just be irresponsible.

R: It's sort of fun sometimes.

TGU: It's *supposed to be* fun. Imagine what *we're* doing.

Difference in Consciousness

R: My Buddhist daughter was asking us to bring a question in.

TGU: We suggest you check the tape.

Frank: We'll check the tape. I don't remember them doing that before. Let's see how far we are. [changes sides of tape] All right. Go ahead and ask that question again.

R: I don't know exactly how she asked it, but I know the meaning. The concept is that while we respect and honor all sentient beings, we note that there seems to be a difference that exists between human consciousness and the consciousness of other sentient beings. And the question is, is that so, then if so, can you speak about what the difference is?

TGU: [teasing]: Like mother, like daughter. Notice that the sentence depends on the word "seems" – and that's exactly true. The difference between humans and others *seems* to be absolute – that animals don't have self-awareness, that plants don't think, that rocks are not even sentient beings. And we would say the difference is more *seems* than *is*. There *is* an absolute difference, and we'll tell you what that is, but it's not in absence of –. Well, let's just examine this a little bit.

You've heard the concept that animals have group souls. And you remember that a while ago when we discussed the difference between plants and rocks and animals and humans, we described it as a difference in freedom, and you remember that we described everything as alive, even rocks, but that as living beings acquired greater degrees of freedom, they required a greater degree of local mind to, shall we say, manage the equipment.

Perhaps we should start with that definition, although we won't finish there. The flower needs enough locally oriented intelligence to find the sun, to face the sun, to close up and open up when it needs to, to extend its roots into the ground and to feel its way toward minerals, that kind of thing. A rock doesn't need any of that. A rock's sentience has nothing to do with motion at all. It has to do with an entirely different thing and that is to feel itself within the matrix of everything that is. We'll leave that alone for the moment.

When you go beyond plants, the next step is animals, roughly – there's an intermediate step, but we're not going to bother with that. The animal has needs beyond what flowers or plants do. It also has the ability to move. Having the ability to move adds the necessary of another dimension of awareness. How should we define sexual procreation? It has the ability to procreate by coming together with another of its own kind, physically, that is to say, to merge motions, to interact deliberately with another of its kind, with all the consequences that follow, including kittens or puppies or whatever, and the care of them. All of that requires higher and higher amounts of intelligence.

Now, people are sometimes surprised at how intelligent a given breed of dog becomes, or appears, as though it were trained above a dog level of intelligence.

It has been given new requirements, and the abilities expand to meet the requirement.

Humans expand beyond animals in that they have the ability to use tools, to use hands. And we're not quite talking about technology, although it sounds like we are, but humans modify their environment more than any other being. And this is not by accident – the humans are *required* to modify their environment in order to survive and to flourish and thrive. And once it got to a certain level, that just took over and now they're modifying it just because that's what they do, what they've become. Well, all of that requires greater and greater and greater adaptively, and requires greater presence of mind in ways that are being granted because they're needed.

You've now so modified your environment that you couldn't survive if you remained at this level and therefore, another level of intelligence has been required and therefore, is being supplied. And now you're beginning to come across the group mind, you see. Not only your intuitions and what you call your extrasensory perceptions. You are growing into the next stage, *because* you need to.

So the simple answer to your question is, the difference between humans and others is a difference in the necessary faculties resulting from the additional abilities. Now, as a sidelight, if you will look at your cetaceans, the cetaceans are as intelligent as humans, but they don't have the same requirements, because they can't modify their environment and they don't need to modify their environment, and, yet, look what's happening. Because of that they're now in serious danger. Do you think that that will mean that they will be exterminated? That is to say, choose not to live here? Or do you think that that perhaps is leading to a radical redefinition of what they can do because of what they *need* to be able to do? That's what we, in the trade, refer to as a broad hint. [they laugh]

It's a mistake to think there's a difference in souls between humans and other species in the sense of "humans are more precious than others" or "humans are later in the developmental scheme" or anything like that. It's more a specialization of function. And we would remind you, at the same time we're saying all this, that the same larger being extrudes rocks, plants, animals, people, and cetaceans. In other words, there's not an absolute difference between them from *our* side at all. The absolute difference is only on *your* side, and there are no absolutes.

Freedom and Intelligence

R: The question was, does the difference in human consciousness offer anything that you –

TGU: Well, that's what we were saying, that humans, because they *need* more consciousness, *have* it. And because now that they're altering their environment enough, that forces them to have a new kind of consciousness that is being developed. But it's not a question of them having been a different order of being, so to speak, from everything else. It's difficult because you don't have the words to make the distinction, but some people think animals are here without the rights people have.

[Terrific, inexplicable, audible interference on tape, obscuring whatever was said. We heard none of it at the time.]

TGU: That's right.

R: They have different needs for freedom.

TGU: That's right.

R: And so, it doesn't essentially explain anything, it's just that's part of the plan.

TGU: What's to be explained?

R: Well, someone decided that we need to be set up on gradations of freedom.

TGU: Say that's true. Then what?

R: Well, it seems from your description that having decided the basic dimension, you have different characteristics based on how much freedom that you have.

TGU: That's right. And the freedom is neither a gift, nor the lack of freedom a punishment. It's just, a rock doesn't need those kinds of freedom, and it has its own life. Or a cloud. Now, you'd never think of a cloud as having intelligence, but the intelligence comes from the other side as a totally different kind of intelligence. It has no sexuality, it has no reproduction, it has no development over time. A cloud is and then it isn't. But that doesn't mean it's not intelligent while it's there. It doesn't mean it's not reporting to central control, so to speak. Not the kind of intelligence you could realize, and it can't count two and two is four, but it's still alive as everything else is alive. And alive implies sentient, although that doesn't appear obvious to people. There's no – you know what? We'll go back a way.

We talked one time about how everything in your ecology is necessary. Remember that? We said that no matter what your ecology was, whether you're on Alpha Centauri with a totally different life system or you're on earth, whatever the ecology is, everything in it is needed, and if something leaves, it'll change the whole thing. It won't change just one part of it, it'll change all of it. It has to.

Well, perhaps we don't quite understand your perplexity. Perhaps it'll clarify it just to say that you *need* plants, the animals need the plants to live. The air needs the plants to help regenerate itself. The plant doesn't need, and couldn't abide, being able to walk around. Therefore, it doesn't need the localized focus of intelligence that follows the ability to walk around.

Forms and Development

R: All right. Now, since you said that all of these forms are in the amoeba, is there some developmental scheme here at work at all?

TGU: No. That's a mistake. You don't start off as a plant, and by being a good boy or by learning your lessons, then move on to being an animal. Well, you could almost say that, if you choose to look at each bit of essence being an individual piece that retains its individuality – which is not very accurate. If you looked at it that way, we suppose you could then see it as, "okay, it came over again, it had learned a little bit, and could in turn do more," but that's not an accurate picture. That's based on the idea of going in and learning and developing and then coming in and learning more and developing and finally, you'll be a star, my boy. But there are so many wrong definitions involved in that, including the idea that it starts ignorant.

R: Okay. But – maybe I'm inferring this – you've said that the human being has ways of becoming increasingly individualized in ways that a rock does not, and therefore what we take back to your side is bound to be somewhat different than what a rock takes back.

TGU: Well, let's say this, although this will sound strange to you. You may regard the rock as the personality, and the essence underneath the rock as essence in the same way that *your* essence is other than *your* personality. Perhaps that will either clarify or make it more obscure.

R: Is it so, as I just assumed here, that a human being has more ways of becoming individualized than a rock?

TGU: Wow! Even to explain why we're having a hard time explaining that, must be a major explanation. Okay. We'll try. We take a little of our essence and extrude it as a rock. Let's forget about the rock. Let's make it a plant because it'll be much easier for you to visualize it being born and dying. So we decide to be a daffodil. The piece of essence of us – really, it would be more accurate to say that piece of essence becomes *all* daffodils than to say it becomes *a* daffodil, but leaving that to the side – the piece of us that becomes a flower does the flowering, returns, and the flower is the flower. What the flower's life was is the gift, just as what your life is, is the gift.

Now, the essence that returns, if you want to keep it separate, has learned how to be a good flower. It has had first hand the experience of germinating and growing and dying down. Not a big lesson, but it has had that lesson. And perhaps, being a very intelligent piece of essence, after it's done that a few times with different plants, it generalizes it and says, "well, okay, I got the whole concept down." And then it moves on to animals. And after it does enough animals, then it moves on to humans. I think a lot of people think that way.

The trouble is, this assumes the essence began as ignorant, and it assumes that the essence is here to learn. What the essence *hasn't* done is learn. What the essence *has* done is *chosen*. And even a daffodil is choosing this and that. You might not think a daffodil's choices mean much, and perhaps they don't, from your complicated point of view. But if you choose to continue to regard that piece of essence as separate and say that that essence then went back in and learned other things, its underlying awareness was never ignorant. Just as *your* underlying awareness is never ignorant.

You know how we've said that when you move into your life, it's almost as though a barrier drops, and it's hard for you, in your life, to remember our end? Well, nevertheless, there's that part of you that knows all of that, even if you don't have good access to it. And that part is in the flower, too, and the rock, and the plant. So it isn't a question of an ignorant little bunny *learning* to do things, nearly as much as it is a very wise-as-anything-else piece of myself, coming in and enjoying the experience of being a flower, and enjoying the experience of being a bunny, or whatever. Now, it's true, you can't have an experience without learning from the experience, probably, but the emphasis is not on the learning but on the experiencing.

R: We think of plants as directly inheriting their characteristics, much more than the human being does. Not that the human being doesn't inherit all sorts of things, but the change possibilities are so much greater.

TGU: Yes. You have more degrees of freedom. But the plant's life is a little more complicated than you think it is. They share emotions. You know that plants use their own chemical extrusions to war against things they don't like and to protect themselves. You know all that.

R: And respond well to kinds of atmospheres around them.

TGU: Yes. And the main atmosphere they respond to is love, which should tell you how the difference between you and them is mainly in the degree of freedom. Now, it may occur to you that a degree of external freedom may involve servitude to the things that you're free to do, and the degree of external constraint may give you much greater freedom because there are things you don't have to think about. No flower spends its time making a living. No person can be free of the ideas of self-protection and of self-development and planning and those kind of things that surround you. Or, if they *are* free of it, it's because they are incapable of functioning at your level when they are in institutions or their families are pro-tective of them, like someone with Down's Syndrome or someone who's retarded or someone who's profoundly what you call handicapped. What this may be and often is, is a greater level of internal freedom because they are bound from other things. Okay?

Now, this is slightly fanciful, but you might, just for the purposes of thinking about it, consider that everything has the exact same degree of freedom, and if they are constrained externally, it may be an outside sign of greater internal free-dom. A cetacean has great freedom. They are, perhaps, the most fortunate people on your planet because they have great internal and external freedom. They can't affect their environment, and they don't really have to worry much about that. They have to worry about protecting themselves and protecting their young and all that, but that's really about the end of it, whereas you have so many cares.

And, that very difficulty is your biggest gift, you see. That very difficulty provides the *need* for you to grow, which allows you to grow. It's obvious to us. We know it's not obvious to you.

R: And so that the freedom implies the need to handle the resulting problems.

TGU: Yes. And sometimes it's a great freedom to be unable to move. A rock that has absolutely zero external freedom has 100 percent total *internal* freedom. Now, you'll never interface with that. Well, you *could* interface with the rock, once you get past, "am I making this up?" [chuckles] And we will tell you that if you ever do, the way you interface with a rock will very much surprise you, although Frank has already learned this, and forgotten it twice. (Crystal is a rock, after all.) That is, you interface with them through emotion. And to interface with them you need to somehow, the best you can, go through, go around, destroy, dismantle, evade, your own mental structure that tells you it's only a rock. If you will perceive the rock heart to heart without preconceptions, you'll surprise yourself, because the rock has absolute internal freedom, you just don't see it. Your internal freedom is probably less than a rock's, although your external freedom is more. We're not saying any of that is hard and fast. It's just for the sake of your seeing the variable in play.

R: Well, I had the experience of feeling that I was communicating with the mist, and feeling quite successful at being able to communicate, interact, and so I'm feeling like perhaps a lot of human beings can choose some form of, what seem like inanimate –

TGU: [laughs] Inanimate?

R: Oh, yes. [laughs]

TGU: Now, we would suggest to you that if you'll cast yourself back to when the Germans used to worship in oak groves back in Caesar's time, they were very close to that same sense. To go from communicating with mist to communicating with the unseen spirits – which you also do – is a very small step. And what you're doing, in a way, is closing the circle. You've come the very, very long way around to be able to do what the rocks can do, only you can also do what they can't do. In a sense this is what your Bible means when it talks about angels being more restricted than humans, that the humans are going to be placed above the angels. They weren't exactly *placed* above them, but you *grew* above them because of the various ways you've developed. Not finished yet.

R: Okay. I have run out of the things I wanted to ask about. Is there anything that you would like to add to this discussion?

TGU: Only to suggest that you might have a question or two about the book, and if you don't that's fine. And we have great confidence in the project. We don't think we're going to have near the trouble you think you are. But if you had any questions, we would be glad to make something up.

R: I don't have any specific questions about that right now.

TGU: Okay. [yawn] We will see you next time.

Session Eighteen
PREP Session
January 11, 2002

[Frank inside the Monroe Institute's black box, "the booth," with Rita Warren communicating via the monitor's microphone in the control room, and Skip Atwater monitoring the instruments.]

R: Are you totally comfortable in there?

Frank: Yes, indeed.

R: Okay. Just relax and go to a place where you're comfortable and can report, and let us know when you are there.

Frank: All right, how about if we just go up to 21. That feels like the flavor *du jour*.

R: All right, just taking your time, move up to 21, and us know when you're there.

Frank: Okay. [Long pause] All right, that feels pretty good.

R: All right. Very good. Can you tell me what you're experiencing right now?

Frank: Just very calm. I used the energy conversion box [a Monroe technique designed to encourage concentration on the moment at hand, eliminating distracting thoughts], which I don't always use. I've got the beginnings of a crystal building around my feet, which are quite cold. And I'm encouraging that to happen. [The sensation of a crystal being grown around me, encompassing me, had happened in several of the 2000 black-box sessions.]

R: Are you aware of the guys being with you?

Frank: Well, not any more or less than ever. They're just always there. I mean, you can talk to them if you want and we'll see what happens.

R: I was wondering if they are aware of the difference in their experience of being in the booth, or being outside.

Frank: Hmm. What say you to that, my friends? Well, the first thing is that they get that I'm more concentrated here, that I'm more "here." That's interesting. Wait a minute. The crystal's up to my thigh. Let's wait a little bit before we go into that question. Give me just a moment until it gets up over my waist, and then we'll see.

R: All right, very good. Just let us know.

Frank: It's building nicely, and it's amazing. Because the bottom of my body is quite warm with the waterbed, and then there's this [laughs] unbelievable cold. [In the sessions in 2000, cold had become associated with close contact with the other side.] [pause]

The answer to your question is, it has something to do with outside cues, that in the absence of them I'm actually more concentrated. So that when there are no flowers to look at, or windows to look outside, or things to flick my eyes from one thing to another without even knowing I'm doing it, I'm more in one place. [laughs] They have a problem holding me in one place.

R: I'm not sure what that means, "holding you in one place."

Frank: I think it means my attention. That I flit from this to that to the other.

R: But you're able to concentrate more on the situation where you're in now?

Frank: Mm-hmm.

Meaning of Crystallization

R: I'd like to ask a question around this crystallizing. In one of our sessions, the guys were noting that when we drop the body, if we've crystallized our soul during our lifetime, we will remain crystallized as we move over, and be able to carry that back into another lifetime. I'm wondering if there's a relationship between that idea and the phenomenon of finding yourself surrounded by crystals in the booth.

[As TGU]: Well yes. In both cases, it's an analogy, but a pretty useful one. When we say "having crystallized an essence of yourself" it isn't that that crystallized essence then goes on to take another lifetime –

Okay, we have to back up. Remember, that from your point of view you're always looking at things as individuals. Perhaps connected individuals, but individuals. You should put more attention on the connection, and less attention on the individuals. The sense of which we mean you crystallize your personality is, that then when you have dropped your body and your attention is back here, what you have been can be used as a lens to send another excursion out into matter. In other words, you say "when I have a past life," and "when I have a future life," and that's in a way true, but it's truer to say that the whole being has lives, some of which are focused through previous lenses, in the sense of taking certain tendencies or certain patterns in the energy field. Visualizing of a body within a crystal is just a form of exteriorizing an image to remind you of the communication that is always possible. Okay, so Frank now has the idea that "okay, inside a crystal I can contact the Egyptian, or the Norman." Which is true enough. At the same time, it isn't so much communication, which implies overcoming distance, as it is identifying, that's all. You see, they're holding the frequency and he's holding the frequency, so they're in the same place.

R: If I understood that, there's not necessarily any relationship between your having this experience in the booth and the notion of crystallizing the soul.

TGU: That's right. It's just a convenient analogy. [pause] Sorry. You mean can the crystal be only held in the booth, or more conveniently held in the booth? And the answer to that is no, it could be held anywhere, and in fact it would be pretty useless if it could only be held here, but this is a good place to inculcate the habit, because there's no distraction.

We can go a little further with that. When he is lying on the bed talking to you, or we're talking to you, or whatever it is that is happening, there is not the physical isolation that there is here. [pause] You could do all the same things at high noon on Broadway, if you happened to be of a mind to, and already knew how to do it, and in fact that's the idea. It's just that here, all the physical surroundings act as subliminal clues saying "concentrate on the internal." That's perhaps the best way to put it.

R: All right, I think I can understand that. So that one wouldn't think of this is any kind of practice for the process of moving to the other side?

TGU: More like practice in redefining yourself so that you'll know a little more of the extent that you extend to. And it's true that a part of it is on the other side, but we wouldn't put the emphasis on that as much as expanding yourselves in all directions.

Memory

R: All right. I'd like to go on to another question, unless you have something more to say about that.

TGU: No, at your service.

R: I've been wanting to ask the guys about this. We understand that there's now quite good scientific evidence that our consciousness does not seem to reside in the brain or in the physical body. There's now interest in the same question with respect to memory. Do you have any comment you'd like to make about that?

TGU: Well it's all the same thing. You're looking in matter for things that are not material, and you're not going to find them. Given that the organizing principle for the whole body is outside of the physical, and the physical is laid down on energy patterns that are set from beyond the physical, it would be foolish for us to then entrust a vital part of the mechanism to a physical place, when it's already in a nonphysical place.

The circulation of your blood is a physical function. The storing of your memories is not *entirely* a physical function. The accessing of the memories is more physical than anything else, but the actual storing of them is not. Just as with your consciousness, the accessing of your consciousness is *partly* physical. If you have a brain injury (even though that's also an energetic injury), you could look at it as a physical injury that may make it impossible for you to access memories or abilities that you had prior to the injury. But when you drop the body you'll find that all of those abilities and memories are still there on call, because they weren't destroyed. They were never in the physical in the first place. Your *access* to them was destroyed, or damaged, but not the actual abilities or memories. This is why some of you have been surprised that people with extensive head injuries who were given sympathetic and loving attention over long periods of time regained abilities that had been thought to be lost. They learned new pathways to something which was invulnerable because it wasn't in the physical.

R: All right, can you talk about the process – it's important to some of us, these days – about losing memories as we age.

TGU: Well again, you aren't losing the memories, you're losing the access to the memories. The memories are as they are, as you would find were you to have an operation and have them open your brain and touch portions of the brain with the needles. They've done that for years, they know that they are there. But it isn't that that particular piece of the brain is exactly the memory, it's more like that particular piece of the brain is the doorkeeper to the memory. A subtle difference, but it is a big one.

R: So something has happened with respect to the antenna that picks up the external information?

TGU: The switching mechanism, we would say. Like a telephone exchange. It could be that portions of the lobes that are the gateways no longer function, and it's as if the memories are gone. But ordinarily it's that the switching function is inhibited, and can be restored sometimes, and when the switching function is restored, it's found that, lo and behold, the memories were there all along. You see, there are two things going on. The switching function on the one hand, that enables you to access the places in the physical gateways, which then access the memories, and on the other hand the gateways themselves.

So if the gateway cell, shall we say, is destroyed, then there may not be any access to memory, although perhaps another one can be developed. Or, if the switching system fails to access the cell that's perfectly good, still you've lost your access. In neither case has the memory been lost absolutely, it's all there, as you would say, in the Akashic record – which ought to tell you that it's there in the first place. It hasn't been so much transferred from the physical as stored, in the first place, in the nonphysical.

R: So this is sometimes a matter of choice on the person's part?

TGU: Well, as always we're going to ask you, what you mean by the person? Which level of person? It's sometimes a level of choice Upstairs. Partly you could look at it as a result of habit. A person who does crossword puzzles every day is going to have a more active switching mechanism than someone who doesn't do anything to keep the little mental muscles limber. However, that statement is "other things being equal," and of course between people they are never equal.

R: I'm wondering about this in part because Frank feels he has a memory problem.

TGU: He has an access problem.

R: Yes, an access problem. Is that a physiological state?

TGU: [pause] Well, we would say it's a switching systems problem. Which only backs the question up as to why that problem is there. He has a pretty large vocabulary, and perhaps it's just as well that he is humbled every so often at being unable to find words that he wants. It's not a progressive disease, or disability, if that's what you're worried about.

R: Well, it was more his worry than mine, obviously.

TGU: [laughs] Well to us it's all you. [laughs]

R: Does the Free Cell activity help this? [Free Cell is the addictive computerized solitaire game that comes loaded onto computers.]

TGU: That's actually a very astute question. It's a matter of seeing patterns nearly unconsciously – that is to say, such rapid recognition of sequential possibilities as to become nearly automatic. Actually though, whether he knows it or not, he thinks on an emotional level while he is playing Free Cell. A stream, a sort of a flavor of consciousness and subject matter will flow through in almost a daydream kind of a way, while his surface attention is concentrated on the Free Cell. And were it not, he would never put the surface attention on that, and put it front and center. So this way it gets tended to, sort of. That's not your question, but we thought you'd be interested.

R: Skip has a question here for me to ask. He's asking, what is the equivalent of the switching system when you leave the body?

TGU: Well, you see, when you leave the body, you don't need that switching system in just that way, because that switching system is necessary because you're living in time-slices. You're going blip, blip, blip, blip, and so there is a sequence. There's a limitation on your consciousness, which is that it can only hold so many things in consciousness at the same time, and your consciousness really does sort of have to move moment to moment, to stay in the same place. Once you're outside of the time-slice problem, and once you're outside of moving, moment to moment, to stay with a sliding present, you don't have that same situation, and then it's more like the crystal analogy that we gave you a long time ago, in which we said that the volume of the crystal has innumerable places in it, all of which interconnect. They don't move, it just depends on which way you shine your flashlight.

Did that answer the question? Your switching system is because your consciousness is required to hold things together while you're moving from moment to moment in the present. That is to say, while the present is moving around you and you were staying up with it.

R: Yes, that does answer the question, but takes me back to the question about Free Cell activity and what's going on underneath it. How is that working with the attention in two places?

TGU: You all work with your attention in many places, whether you know it or not. When you drive a car, your primary attention is on the driving, and then occasionally your primary attention is on the conversation you're having, or the radio that you're also playing, or a daydream that may sort of overwhelm your physical presence at the moment, and they all go on at the same time, and they mix back and forth in various proportions. So you all think and experience on many levels at the same time. In fact, we doubt it would be possible for you to experience on one level only a given time. It would be probably painful, if even possible.

R: Yes, that sounds right. So all these activities, the daydreaming and the attention to all the things we're doing, are something we should think of as being part of the field rather than part of the physical apparatus?

TGU: Hmm. It's difficult to see why that's an important distinction, really, but yes you could. You have to look at it that you in the body are an interface between systems anyway, and so in a way you could say it's meaningless to say that something is physical or not physical, because if it involves you by definition it has to involve both. You can't move a muscle strictly through physical activity, and you can't move a muscle without physical activity. Everything you do has to be a mixture. Not even a mixture, it's just integrally connected. You know how people say "flesh and blood" as a saying, but in actuality you couldn't have flesh without blood or blood without flesh and have it function. You see?

We're suggesting that the distinction about "is a daydream a physical process or a metaphysical process" – we know why you're asking the question and we know that your science has been tied up in knots over this for years, but rather than say "well yes, it's primarily a nonphysical function," we would prefer to take it out of that either/or situation at all, because either end of the either/or is equally misleading. We'd rather you thought of it a different way. Actually, we'd rather you thought of *yourselves* a different way.

R: Yes, well this comes up because of the resistance of science to move outside the body at all. So this is important to us.

TGU: But, you see, by definition they won't listen to this anyway so –

R: [laughs] Well, someday.

TGU: But we do want to say that, as little as Frank is inclined toward their point of view, still theirs is one end of a polarity, and the truth is in both ends of the polarity, not either end.

R: In other words in this movement toward recognition of external dimensions, we're kind of trying to take the physical out of it to more of an extent than is appropriate.

TGU: Well he certainly has. We've been correcting that. With some success, finally.

The Sphere and the Hologram

R: All right, I'd like to ask another question if you're ready for that. Frank, you will remember that we talked to the guys about their awareness that there is some energy beyond them that perhaps acts as guidance for them. I want to see if from where you are now you can make some contact with that energy. See if you can call on that energy to make some kind of communication contact with you. And see what happens.

TGU: Well, it would probably be easier if we function toward it as you function toward us, which implies a question. Do you have a question that we can relay? [laughs]

R: OK, I was taking into consideration the possibility that it might not be a verbal communication, that there might be some energy contact you could become aware of that might or might not have a communication capacity. Could you try it without verbalization first, and see what happens?

[As Frank]: All right. [pause] Hmm. [pause] Well, I don't know how they are doing, but I'm getting an image that's kind of perplexing. It's like, if I'm at the bottom, and they are above it and there's something above them, that above them is actually circular and comes back through me. It's as though you kept looking in a microscope at something smaller and smaller, and you realize that it's actually bigger than the microscope. Or the other way around with a telescope. Let's see what more we get here. It's got to do with a hologram. [pause]

Well, it's like a sphere. Seems to be more or less featureless. What are they –? Using the sphere as a symbol – well – [pause] the sphere is a symbol of everything that exists, not just physical but otherwise. And the sense of it is – oh, again it's a matter of viewpoint, as to whether to look at it as an individual or as part of a thing. And in that sense, that's why they mention a hologram, that sense of guidance that they have outside them is in fact *larger* than them, *smaller* than them, and *them*. And larger than *me*, smaller than *me*, and *me*. We just keep coming back to the same clichés. It's all one thing.

R: Would it be helpful to think of it in terms of a series of concentric circles, where you represent the most dense point in the center?

Frank: No, that's not what they're getting at. They mean that all of us interpenetrate the whole thing all the time. We talk about levels, which is a spatial analogy, but there aren't really levels that separate things or people or whatever. We're all everywhere, just like a hologram. So I guess that means – well let's see what it means. [pause]

[As TGU]: That was a pretty good explanation, and probably as good as you're going to get for the moment. The totality of things is not bigger or smaller than the biggest or the smallest part of the thing. It's all one thing, except it's not a "thing" at all, but you understand.

So you don't have to be able to comprehend larger levels to be able to see those larger levels in miniature, right in your hand, so to speak. And you don't need to be able to comprehend smaller levels to see them in magnification in your own hand, so to speak. The fact that we can't necessarily be conscious of other levels of being that we have been thinking of as above us, or larger than us, or as more extensive, doesn't mean that they are not in fact in evidence at every moment, because we're all one thing. It's really almost too simple to explain, and too complicated to begin to explain.

The only things that come to mind now that are going to help are the sphere and the hologram, those two concepts. If you see yourselves as holographically part of the entirety of the universe, this doesn't mean that you're a tiny part of something huge, it means you're an integral part of the whole thing, and size is not relevant. It's just really not relevant. And the sphere, again, is only used as an analogy of completion, of totality. It doesn't mean that reality is literally a sphere.

R: All right, I think I understand that. It seemed though that the guys, as representing a different level than you as an individual, seemed to see things from a different perspective than you do, and they're trying to teach us on this level to understand their perspective, but we don't in fact see without the time and space dimensions. So I'm wondering that about another level, that would be different from the first two layers here.

TGU: Well, in fact it isn't an "us" and a "you," and it isn't a "they" and an "us," it's all one thing and these distinctions – we go along with your making them, but you have to remember that they're not real distinctions. It isn't Frank on one end, the guys on the other end, even though it's convenient to look at it that way. You are seeing a part of a being and trying to understand what you're seeing. You are dissecting the parts, but don't lose sight of the fact that the parts are parts of one thing, and this goes all the way up and all the way down. We do know that you know that, but we need to continually reemphasize it, because your spatial analogies by their very nature separate things into here and there. And your time analogy separates into now and then and when. But the separation is not real, it's just convenient. We understand your question. Is there a difference beyond us that is as noticeable as the difference beyond us in your dimension where everything is compressed into matter. But we have to say, one world at a time.

R: OK, we're ready to release that for now unless you have something else to say about that.

TGU: No, just that if you would magnify pictures of the ganglia of the brain, and think of that as a miniature picture of the way reality is, and don't look at it logically but as a picture (in other words analyze it by your spatial appreciation), it may give you some sense of the holographic nature of things.

Suggestions for TMI

R: All right, I can get the image so I'll think about that. I would like to ask the guys today whether they have a message for the Monroe Institute. What's the most important information that you could give to the Institute at this point in time?

TGU: The message to the Institute is very simple, and that is that your time is now. Everything that you've done to now is only the preparation. It's been good preparation, but it's only the preparation. Now you are able to, and it will be in your interest to, spread the magical technology throughout the world to various other seeding centers.

You might look at yourselves as monasteries at the decline of the Roman Empire, where each little enclave saved a little piece. They didn't necessarily coordinate with each other, or even necessarily have anything to do with anything. They didn't necessarily know that they were doing that, cosmically. They were saying, "we will live this way. We will preserve these values. We will do this."

Well, you can do the same things now, and the people are now open to this. It means, not encouraging a million people to come and do programs at the Institute: just the opposite. It means encouraging the development of other institutes at convenient locations throughout the world. Particularly throughout the English-speaking world. No one asked us, but we would advocate that this be more like a friendly confederation than any formal control or formal articulation of structures.

[interruption in tape]

. . . and go on from there. There'd be something in it for the people who are setting it up, and there would still only be one original Institute. A very big opportunity. It's what you really came for, it's what you set up for. And the time is now.

R: This seems like an issue at the organizational level that would require the Institute to give up some of the controls they have tried to impose on people for teaching this kind of material.

TGU: Well, what the Institute was set up for from our point of view, and what it was set up for from its own point of view, may not look the same.

R: Okay, do you have any kind of suggestions about the programs itself that the Institute offers?

TGU: Rather than answer that question, we'll say that Laurie and Skip and others traveling the land as prophets is a good thing. That's what will spread the word in time. And that's what will, on the one hand, defuse a lot of potential opposition, on the second hand create people with a willingness to experiment, and on the third hand, so to speak, insure that people will still want to come to the original. In other words, it won't damage their financial or economic position.

As to the programs, they don't need advice on their programs. The only thing that we would say is to have the people sit in a circle during debriefing, not in rows. It's a seemingly tiny little thing, but [people sitting in rows] is reducing feedback, it's damping the energy. If they would sit in circles and actually be able to see each other more, the energy would ramp up, and much more important and productive interactions would take place, many of them nonverbal. Tiny thing, but, important.

R: All right. Interesting. How about in research areas? Do you have any specific suggestions there?

TGU: Well, in that you have thousands of people going through these programs, there is your research base, and if you remember, that's how it was initially.

[interruptions in tape]

. . . What you might do, if you wished, would be to extend the program to Friday afternoon. And everything from the breakfast morning to whenever they broke up on Friday afternoon, maybe say 3:00, would be devoted specifically to people expressing what had happened to them that may not have gotten expressed in debriefing circles, with the idea of it being recorded by the Institute, for being noted and looked at.

That's not the kind of research you had in mind, we think, but actually that kind of experiential reporting is more persuasive to the people who will come than a statistical correlation would be. The statistical correlation would have scientific validity, but it doesn't have the emotional warmth, whereas testimony will have the warmth, and will attract the people who already – after all, they're going to be prodded from the other side, too. But that might be the final thing they need, and then it will help them to decide to come. Just as Frank's book [*Muddy Tracks*] does that. His book has no statistics and correlations at all, it just says "this is how it changed my life." And people have read the book and said, "I hope that something like this can happen, I'm willing to take the chance," you see? In other words, it acts not so much on a rational basis as on a rational and emotional basis.

That kind of thing can be gathered at a final session in which the participants are told that it is for that kind of purpose. And some very interesting correlations can come. If you had participants from 14 programs talk about their initial experience in Focus 12, say, in the context of stories that they were telling, then when someone gathered them all up the cumulative effect could be very persuasive to people. And very exciting, too. Small thing, but it could be done.

R: Thank you for that.

TGU: Besides, it also then bonds the participants even more to the Institute, even more than their experiences already have. Because now they've given, and people like to give. You see?

Information for Frank and Rita

R: That's true. [pause] I have one more question that I wanted to ask, and that is, what's the most important information to come through for Frank right now?

TGU: [pause] Well, you know he's having his difficulties, and we would just say that it's just important not to give up, and not to give in to the luxury of despair, you know. Despair just means, "well I don't feel like doing this anymore," whereas some hope is a concomitant of courage. And it's important that he not give up. He knows it, but it doesn't hurt to hear it.

R: That's very good. Thank you for that.

TGU: And for you?

R: You have some information for me?

TGU: Do you have a question? For you?

R: Well I can ask the same question for me, is there some information that's important for me to hear right now?

TGU: [pause] You're getting that information all the time, just don't close off from it. Not that you would, but in other words, you already have the access open. Just keep the access open. All is well.

Well, we could throw one other thing in, for what it's worth, and that is, you might ramp up your hope just a little bit more, about your own physical situation, rather than settling, and saying, "well, this hurts but at my age I've got to expect it." You might tend more to go, "this hurts and I'm going to stack the deck so it doesn't." Because you have those abilities. You know it, and you sort of put it off to the side sometimes. Not meant as chastisement, just as a suggestion.

R: Okay. I hear that. [pause] Can we just relax now into wherever you are, and just experience for a moment, and then if you can talk about it a little bit, we'd like to hear.

[As Frank]: I'd like to go up to 27 actually.

Egyptian Experience

R: Okay. Very good.

Frank: [very long pause] My elbows are pushing against wood, very uncomfortable. My hands are on that chair again, the Egyptian chair again.

R: Okay. Go along with the experience.

Frank: It feels like I'm wearing some kind of a constricting helmet, only not in front of my face, but around the back. Got a headache, too, and I've had it for a while.

R: Check out that feeling.

Frank: A sense of a hawk, seen sideways. Head of a hawk. It's connected some-how with the headache. Or it is more something heavy on my head, I think. It's a funny feeling. This thing goes from, I don't know, about in front of my ears all the way around the back of my head – up sort of straight. Feels like it's metal, but it might not be. And it's got this constricting band around my temples. And then this weight. But the feeling of weight is not on the top of my head, the weight is around the sides of my head.

R: Is there some meaning there for you?

Frank: Well it has to do with Egypt somehow. The position of my hands, and the feeling behind my elbows, I know – because I very carefully haven't moved my hands since I've been in here – I know that they're not in the position that they're reporting. But, doesn't matter. A sharp pain on the inside of my elbows too, like it's being forced. Inside and outside. Yet my lower body has no sense of being seated. [pause]It's hardly there. [pause]

R: You're saying you're having a sense of being held in a fixed position?

Frank: Holding myself in a fixed position, I think. In fact I'm going to move my physical arms, because this is painful. Actually was cramping up my shoulders even. Gentlemen, you have a message about all this? Or is this just amusement here?

R: Tell us what's going on.

Frank: Well, moving my arms parallel to my body again changed the nature of it somehow. There's this calm majesty, I mean it's just really magisterial. And has to do with – well I don't know, it might be a ceremony or something, it feels like my arms are being held parallel to the ground while I'm upright. They're out straight, resting on this maybe padded surface, each arm. But they are held straight out. And I think I'm standing. Pretty sure I am. It's something ceremonial. A sense of the river, but that could be overlay of course. [i.e., thoughts of Egypt lead natu-rally to thought of the Nile.]

R: Can you tell what this figure is thinking?

Frank: Huh. Well, let's see. Let's see if I can. I actually forgot I'm in 27. I wonder if I am, or if I wandered over there. Well let's see. [pause]Well, for what it's worth, he's thinking, "this is my land and these are my people and I'm responsible for them." And it's not a big crisis thing, it's just a calm "this is the way it is."

And he's looking at the city by the river, which seems more like a lake almost, because it's very prominent in their consciousness. And we would hardly call it a city, it looks more like a suburb, because the buildings are small with lots of greenery amongst them, it's not all just urban stone. But I think he's up in the air some. That is to say, he's on some elevated thing, because he's looking down at it. But that's the sense of it. And he's holding his arms out in something between a blessing and an administering thing. "These are my people, this is my land, this is my responsibility."

And I know that he's facing south. And it's daytime. And that's the river on the right, which makes sense. Okay so he's on the east side of the Nile. I want to say he's up on a pyramid or something, but I don't really think that's true. I think it's a temple of some kind. If not a temple – yes, it's a temple because he's in his – oh, is he? – he's in his role as high priest of some kind. May not be the high priest, you know; some kind of priest's role. But it's not – oh! And this may not be a political leader. It may be that he's leading in a non-physical way, but nonetheless it's just the same, "these are my people, this is my land, this is my responsibility."

Yes I don't think he's a political leader. Well, there's not the difference that we would have. Well, wait a minute, let's look at this a little bit. [pause]

Your political leader, like the pharaoh or anybody underneath him, would be concerned with the external adjustments of society, making the machine run smoothly. It's not politics the way we think of it, because everyone has the same vision of it, and they just administer. But the spiritual leader is doing the same kind of administering, but on the non-physical level. Again it's more like being a doctor than being a pope –

And the pharaoh is more like a streets commissioner than like a king. I guess what I mean is, the levels of problems are entirely different from ours. There are whole kinds of problems that we have that don't even enter into it for them, because they are a unitary society that shares the same vision, and therefore it becomes a matter of rather routine things, and you certainly don't have or need a house of Parliament to argue about whether they should follow this or that tack.

Similarly, the spiritual leader, if you wish to call him that, is not involved in making people believe or questioning their orthodoxy or anything like that. It's more like a doctor, adjusting to the spiritual needs of individuals who may be tempted to lose a frequency, shall we say.

It's a simpler world than ours. One reason it is simpler is because they're more on the beam. And they live in an oasis, which helps. They have long, harsh surroundings to protect them. As America did when it had its oceans.

R: How is this person feeling about the way in which he is doing his job?

Frank: [pause] Well I don't get any sense of pride or self-criticism. It's very matter-of-fact. [pause] It's certainly not "oh my God, this job is to big for me," or "I'm bigger than this job, I can do better things," you know. In fact I don't think there was that anywhere. That sense of "this is my land, these are my people, this is our responsibility"; it's like when you put on an old coat and it fits comfortably. It's a comfortable fit for him, not a stretch. It's not a stretch and it's not a burden, it's just an indirect way of saying who he is really to himself.

R: Do you have the sense that this is a picture of you in another time and place?

Frank: [laughs] If I had that sense, there would be the guys ready to say, "no, you don't get it." [laughs] But I think there's a resonance.

R: Okay, they would accept that. The resonance feeling.

Frank: I really don't know, but my understanding of what they say is that when we go back to them [on the other side], something else comes out, but it isn't exactly us coming out, it's shining through what we were. I don't know. If someone were to say this was a past life of mine, I'd say "well, I'm losing ground, but that's wonderful."

R: Well they have suggested a thread connecting some various experiences.

Frank: A resonance, for sure.

R: Do you have a sense of that? Does this figure have anything important to say to you?

Frank: He's the one who's often in the crystal, you see. He's the one who holds the frequency. He's one of us who holds a frequency.

R: So there's no particular message from him today, other than what he's contributing?

Frank: I think the message actually is in the widening of the channel of communication. It will be easier next time and next time, you know. In other words, I won't have to come into the black box to do this. I think.

R: The connection's somehow stronger?

Frank: Yeah, we widened the channel. I want to see if I can see Bertram here. This would be a good time for it. Bertram being the Norman Monk [in medieval England]. [pause] It's funny. Kelly says he was a bishop later, but I've never seen him as a bishop, I always see him as a young man. [long pause]

R: Are you still getting some impressions?

Frank: Well, actually I'm just getting impressions of the [Salisbury] cathedral, because I've physically been there this time. Not *him* particularly. We can go on if you want to do something else.

R: I think we're about coming to the end of the session.

Frank: Another ten-minute session, huh? It doesn't feel like a long time.

R: Is there anything else you'd like to do before we start coming back?

Frank: Anything for Skip?

R: Skip says you've only been in there nine minutes and you've got one more minute.

Frank: [laughs] Well he can forget getting messages from heaven by way of me then. [laughs] No, whatever you want is all right.

R: All right, Skip has a suggestion that you return to [Focus] 25, the belief system territory, and see if there's any information there for you.

Priestly Image

Frank: Well that's interesting. [long pause] My eyes opened up right away. I wouldn't be surprised if there's something here. I feel like I've waked up in the dark and am looking around. [pause] Is there somebody here I should meet or would like to talk to me? [pause] Man, there's this big heavy weight like on top of my stomach as if I were standing up. Like a big metal box or something or a wooden box. [sigh]

R: Can you identify what's in the box? Or what the box is?

Frank: [pause] No, not really. I think it's more like whoever it is carrying the box, maybe on a chain around his neck or something. [pause] Or maybe it's a priest. I don't know what they would carry there. Cross maybe, or something, I don't know. [pause] My right shoulder suddenly hurts for no physical reason and that sense of – Skip did you have a reason for suggesting this? Some thought?

Skip: No, not particularly.

Frank: Looking for a clue here. There's something going on here but I can't figure it out.

Skip: Ask guidance.

Frank: There's a thought. You know, I get a real sense of "to be continued." Like, we'll do this later. Or come back to this. Maybe not even in here. Maybe on my own.

R: You want to move back then through Focus 23 and then to Focus 21?

Frank: Sure. [pause, sigh] All right, you can take me back.

R: You mean you're ready to move all the way back?

Frank: Yeah, you can take me back when you want. [sigh] You can go back to 10, that's all right.

R: All right, all the way back to 10.

Session Nineteen
January 29, 2002

Consciousness of Other Lives

R: We had some questions occur to us around the issue of other lives we wanted to bring up and try to get a few things straightened out about it.

TGU: You won't mind if we snicker at the idea of "occur to us."

R: That's all right. We don't feel personally attached to being responsible for all the good things in life like questions.

How useful is it for us or for you to have us try to bring into consciousness other lifetimes in order to integrate them?

TGU: Leaving aside, for the moment, "integrate them" because there's many things that might mean, we feel it's very important, because it's your stretching to redefine yourself in a somewhat larger fashion than you did before. From our point of view, it isn't so much your *stretching* as that you're *ceasing to limit yourselves* to that degree. When you habitually are in contact with parts of yourself in other times, other spaces, other dimensions, you cannot see yourself in quite the same smaller way that you had before. And this is in itself valuable, for a couple of reasons. You can't increase contact with another part of yourself without in the very same motion, by definition, increasing the contact that other part of yourself has with you. You see? So, this good work works both ways. You in the year 2002 naturally look at your own personal self as the center of your larger self. There's no other way for you to see it. But another part of you that's in the year 2102 sees itself as the center of the whole extended self, of course. That's how it's supposed to be. Well, if you, from your end, widen the communication, the one on the opposite end also gains. From its point of view, it's an unexpected grace, like the grace of God. Very good work.

Now, in terms of integrating. If by integration one were to mean only the melding together of parts that had previously functioned separately without awareness of each other's identity, that by itself would be good work. But if, in addition to that, one is creating a larger consciousness, of which each individual node is a part, but neither of which is the center, nor perceived as the center, that's a greater work. And you could argue – to move forward to the real thing that's bothering you both – that since ultimately we're all one thing, *the whole process* is a matter of integration. As each autonomous, relatively unaware portion extends bridges to other portions, or has bridges extended to it, and becomes equally autonomous but less isolated, then it moves closer toward the goal of full integration, which means all of us functioning without the barriers between us. Does this answer what you wanted?

Importance of Separateness of Lives

R: Yes. *An additional theme has to do with the feeling I've had that it was important for each life to emphasize its separateness.*

TGU: That's right. In fact – and not for you so much as for others who may come across this record – we'd like to say a little more about that. Supposing you were born into a Cherokee Indian family in the 1800s. It would not in the slightest aid your integration into that lifetime if you came into that lifetime remembering a lifetime as a white American in the 20th and 21st centuries. In other words, to that perplexed question, "why don't we remember other lives," the answer is, because to the degree that you did, it would interfere with your assuming the point of view of only that one time and place. However, during the course of the lifetime, depending on your life plan, you could – as is happening to both of you – integrate more of other lifetimes. But you're *integrating* it into a base that's already been established. That is to say, Frank didn't in 1946 conceive of himself –

Well, we have to stop this. Let's back this up. We always know that it's a good explanation when we have to start it three times, because we keep thinking of new things. Here's what we were going to say, but we will disown it in advance. [laughs]

We were going to pick a given age and say that at that point it wouldn't have done good, and would have been confusing, to have specific vivid memories of other times coming through. But there's no such rule that can be given, because some people are born knowing other lives, for a very good reason. Other people go through their whole life and never come to conscious awareness of other lives, for a very good reason. And everything in between those two, okay? So there's not really a rule that can be given.

It isn't that any of you ever do this without having input coming in and out of your mind, but it is rare for you to recognize that it comes from another lifetime. You think it's your own, you see. So you'll come up with natural predilections, and the others in your family will be scratching their heads, saying where did that come from? Well, anyone who's had more than one child knows that those two children – or three or four or five or six – can be each totally different from the others, in terms of not only their personality behaviors, but their predilections in general. So that one is a born aristocrat, and another is a born peasant, and a third is a born soldier, and a fourth is a born courtesan, or whatever.

Well, all that coming in and out happens. The awareness of it happening varies radically because of people's life plans.

R: I'm not sure what we mean there.

TGU: By life plans we mean, when you come into the world, your freedom is constrained specifically in order to set you on the path you wanted to be on when you were on the other side. If you are born a woman, you can't be a man. If you are born in the 20th century, you can't be the same person born in the 19th century. Those constraints are to set up a situation, and then the freedom within the situation is what you make of it. So, if someone's life is aimed at experiencing material success in non-reflective manner, everything will conspire that they will not have consciousness of other lifetimes, you see. Someone – and we mention no names, but he's lying here – whose life is set to try to live it as intuitively as possible, with almost no grounding in ordinary social reality, will have an entirely different set of seemingly fortuitous external and internal circumstances that will push him in that direction, because that is what he wanted in the beginning. That's all. That's what we mean by life path.

Now, that doesn't mean that you are not free at every moment, but you're free only within those constraints that we set up right at the beginning. "We," meaning "you and we," you know. It isn't done *to* you, you do it yourself and then step into it.

R: Our plan that would have already established a challenge.

TGU: Mm-hmm. And you can change that plan anytime you want, and often do, but you don't start from scratch when you do that. If you go 35 years down one road, and then decide to change the plan, nobody will stop you from doing that, but you are starting from the place 35 years down the road. You're not starting from scratch, that's all.

We do want to emphasize your freedom. Nobody's forcing anybody. Circumstances constrain you, but that's why you're there, to struggle against circumstance, or *with* circumstance, however you wish. Is that still vague? Or is that more confusing?

Resonances

R: No, I can understand that. We have been struggling with the idea of all these lifetimes that Frank seems to be able to remember, and because they take on a reality in his mind, we have trouble integrating that idea with the whole idea of operating in something going on in a non-space-time arena.

TGU: Can we rephrase that? We think your dilemma is that you can't quite see how you can seem to experience a continuity of incarnations if in fact on our side we're putting out a new pseudopod each time, that may or may not use elements of the previous pseudopod. We are calling you pseudopods now instead of worms. You're working your way up.

R: [laughs] That sounds much better.

TGU: That's a fair assessment of your quandary?

R: Well I think we have a number of questions about it, and I'm not really on top of them all, but as we talk about it I hope to be.

TGU: Okay. As we've said, the better the questions, the better the answers. That puts all the onus on you, you see, if you get bad answers.

R: I understand that. [they laugh]

TGU: All right. We're going to surprise you somewhat. Both of you. Presumably all of you, if others hear.

What would you say if we told you that the number of incarnations that you are aware of had less to do with the number of times you had been on earth than it has to do with the degree to which your consciousness extends? It is the same thing from our side as it is on your side as we just described. Does that take your breath away? Or does it make sense?

R: I'm not sure if I understand what you're saying. It's been my assumption that we remember very little, and that it's a rare event when particular information comes to us about what seems like another lifetime,

TGU: Well, let's put that off to the side just for a minute, let's go a different way first. We'll answer anything, but let's go a different way first.

Here's what we're suggesting that you look at. From our point of view, we're all one thing, and we're all these different pseudopods that are set out. Now for you, inside the body, inside space-time, that barrier more or less cuts you off from active participation with the rest of us. That barrier is another way of saying that there is a sort of self-imposed isolation from the rest of what you are. But within that isolation, you have the ability to extend, and the more you extend, the more of the rest of us you can sense. Now, the reason that nobody in your scriptures or otherwise has ever been able to conclusively decide whether or not reincarnation is real or a figurative statement is because it's totally – you may have heard this before – a matter of point of view.

If you in the 21st century resonate to someone in the 18th century, you are resonating to another part of yourself, because *everything* is another part of yourself. And the question then becomes, why that one? And it looks to you like it's an inherited character flaw, or an inherited talent, or an inherited emotional link, or something like that. In other words, "I met this person, and we had a past life connection, and that's why we were attracted to each other, or repelled from each other." And that's not exactly an invalid way of looking at it, but it's equally valid to say, "I met this person and that person's make-up and my make-up, looking at it in electrical analogy, were such that we were pulled together or we were repelled."

And memories could be memories of – how do we say this? You in the 21st century meet another person in the 21st century, and you feel this past life pull. And let's say that there are two people in the 18th century. Those two people may have the same electrical vibration, so to speak, the same dynamic relationship, between the two.

R: Some kind of energy pull.

TGU: Yes, it's like a multiplier, you know, but we can't find the right words. He's not very good about technical stuff. [pause] Nor does he need to be. [laughs] It's just that we find it hard to use scientific or mathematical analogies.

The resonance between you two in the 21st century and you two in the 18th century may be exactly similar, and so you feel the human warmth, so to speak. Or you feel the human coldness, if it's a repulsive thing. But to say you had *been* them, or even *will be* them, in a future life that will happen in the past – which some people say – is just sort of a way of looking at it, because you're connected with everybody. But your awareness has opened up to those two particular connections.

And we have pointed out, whether or not Frank's really noticed it, he became aware of other lifetimes first from the most familiar. First the modern American and British, and then the internal, shall we say the spiritual side, going again from the very familiar to the less familiar. So that he is not particularly attuned to an atheistic scientist in the early Enlightenment, or something like that. There would be a lot of repulsion there. If he has a lot of plusses, that would have a lot of negatives, or the other way around. So, do you see? We know that to you it looks like you're born, you die, and you yourself come back and are born again, and then you die and you yourself – and that's true, but it's equally true that the whole mix is doing that, and it's *all* you. And it's just a matter of where you put your attention.

R: One of the things that seems to complicate that is that these come along as memories, and so there's a certain set of specific memories that seem to occur when you have these connections, and they may be a short time period.

TGU: We're not saying the memories aren't real, we're saying your *access* to the memories doesn't say a thing about you having lived that life; they just say that you have access to the memories because you are resonating to that lifetime. They are real memories, and they are real emotional behaviors, and real scars. We don't want this to seem inflated beyond its importance, but you all bear all of the sorrows, and the guilt, and the woundedness, of everybody, depending on how far you extend your awareness of it. And of course you also bear the accomplishments and the genius and the love and the positive things. It's all potentially there as your inalienable inheritance. Because we're all one thing.

Now we know that from your point of view it looks like you inherit certain tendencies from other times. It can look that way. And when you drop the body now, you leave the mathematical equation unbalanced in one way or another, and so you come in again and work on it from there. There's nothing wrong with looking at it that way, but, we want you to think of it at least another way. Well, it's just too simple to say. It's all one thing. We're all one thing. All of the play of various parts of us –

Well we'll try this analogy out, we don't know how this will work. Suppose you had a repertory theatre, and supposing the play went on for five nights in a row. A different person might take the same part on different nights. Or – a better one – supposing in a movie they are giving you the life story of someone from the time they were a baby to the time they're grown-up. They may have five different actors play different ages. Well, that mathematical problem we were talking about that has to be worked out, can be dealt with five different actors, it doesn't have to be the same actor. (Except that ultimately we're all the same actor.) [laughs]

All we can suggest is that you keep changing viewpoint, because you know there's a saying Frank likes a lot, "what can't be said, can't be said, and it can't be whistled either." [they laugh]

The Question of God

R: *This is a puzzlement, because when we think in those terms, that ultimately all of these interactions are part of ourselves, once you've said that, where do you go from there? That being true, why are we bothering with the rest of this?*

TGU: You have major religious and philosophical systems that say just that, because this is the aspect that they noticed.

R: *Well, [pause] but –*

TGU: Ah, you want an answer! [they laugh] All right. We can only give you suggestions, we can't give you an answer but here's our suggestion. If we extend ourselves into time-space and give ourselves the disconnected experience that you are currently living, there might be a reason for it. Now, many people say it's just that God is playing, as though God would be bored otherwise, you see, and the play doesn't mean anything.

R: *Isn't God part of this whole oneness?*

TGU: There's nothing else. God's not separate from anything. The question of God is a big complicater, because it has so many emotional aspects, it often stops people from thinking, because the emotional aspect is too overwhelming. A pious person fears blasphemy. An agnostic person or a rebellious person fears superstition, and in any case, since you're in the habit of thinking of God as having ultimate attributes – all-knowing, all-seeing, all-powerful – there's no modulation to it, and it's difficult to do anything with the concept. So if you can limit it somehow, we can talk about it. If you mean whatever created us – and we don't know either – that's one thing. If you mean something with specific attributes that has been created by religion, that's something else.

R: *I don't mean that of course, and if you think of God as creator, there seem to be two basic perspectives. One is that we and God are all one. And on the other hand, we're all one except God, and God somehow created this other energy which is the rest of us.*

TGU: Well we would suggest to you that the answer to that dilemma is the same answer. Just change viewpoints back and forth. From one viewpoint, yes, God took part of himself and created you, and that part is still part of himself, which means you are God.

From another point of view – and yes, we hear you saying "or herself" but we're not going to pursue that – [they chuckle] one could say that God, seeing everything undifferentiated, wanted something different and withdrew himself – herself – itself – themselves – from the other, so that it could have an otherness. But it's really more a playing with logic than is real. The two statements don't seem to have anything in common at all, and yet we would say they're just two different points of view.

Now, the thing is, it's very tricky using the word "God," because you could use the word "creator" in the sense that Bob Monroe used the word creator in one of his books – you know, he called him Someone and he said that Someone created these things as an experiment. By doing that, it left out all of the overwhelming numerous qualities of the Deity, the ultimate creator, and it allowed you to think of it in a more emotionally neutral way, because you're not required to adore the creator if the creator is just an experimenter. (And we would argue that that adoration, when it's imposed by belief, is always negative. The only time adoration is a positive is when, having had the experience, you're left with your jaw hanging down, and all of your being responds in this joyous loving embrace. But anything that's imposed is – imposed. It's not organic.)

Long detour there.

R: I wish my memory were better, but one of the Irish poets talks about God's loneliness and therefore his need to create the rest of us. Some of us.

TGU: Well, the same can be said humans, and so it may be true that humans are part of God, right? That is to say, sharing that creator aspect of God. You need to create or you are unfilled. Perhaps God did too. But we still argue you would be better off putting the word God on the shelf a bit. However, do what you want.

R: Usually I do that, but right now I'm feeling like arguing with you a bit. [laughs] It's not so much argument as…One way of thinking about all of this is that, yes there's a creator that created what we know of the universe. But he has brothers who've created something else.

TGU: Possibly sisters.

R: Or sisters – that we're not as familiar with. And so you get into this kind of hierarchical thinking of, if these are siblings who are creating different worlds, then they must have parents. You know, some level beyond – that's another way that has been thought about to somehow explain –

TGU: That may be less hierarchical thinking than it is anthropomorphic thinking. After all, clouds don't have parents. Nor mountains. We would remind you that we tried to give you an example using the hologram and the sphere to say that the spatial analogies of size and distance are quite misleading. If you can imagine a marble cake, or you can imagine that picture of the neurons, as we suggested, you can see that there aren't levels as much as there are, shall we say, joyous interpenetrations. There is a part of you that is in a star and part of you that's in a molecule and it's not a metaphor. It doesn't make physical sense –

R: It does make physical sense to me. It doesn't make sense beyond the physical, I guess, necessarily. I can believe that we're all made of stardust.

TGU: Well, can you believe also then, that there is only one of us? And if there is only one of us, you're right back to being part of stardust. You see, the difficulty is still – well, in this instance it's the difficulty but really it's the asset that you used in order to have your experience – and that is, that you still have that barrier between you and the rest of us, so that although you are presently peeking over the barrier, or sort of burrowing through it, you're having to do that because the everyday moment to moment reality is that you are separate because of the barrier. That's what the barrier is there for, and it does perfectly well. Just as we said that a person being born into a Cherokee family in the 1830s would not profit by having active memories of living in 21st century America, so you, coming into earth anywhere, would not necessarily actively profit by having full access to all what we are on the other side.

Remembering Past and Future

R: Well, go with an example there for moment. Just that part of it. That really imposes a time dimension. It's as though somehow in any lifetime there's a time span which makes it useful for you to "remember" what would seem like previous lifetimes. It seems that that's what we do when we think about other lives, but by and large though we stretch our minds and try to create something like a future event –

TGU: You remember one.

R: I wouldn't use the word remember, though I wouldn't reject it either.

TGU: [laughs] What else would you use?

R: Create, I guess.

TGU: Oh, but now would you say you created memory of the past?

R: No.

TGU: Then why would you say create a memory of the future?

R: Well because memory seems to be defined as an event concerned with the past.

TGU: All right, well, this is worth touching on. This is just simply the same problem: Your language was structured around an understanding of the way the world is. And that understanding being implicit in the language, the language makes you tempted to think that it describes the way reality really is, rather than the way reality has been perceived till now. If you want to come up with a new word for "remember" that's okay. But we don't see any difference between remembering the past and remembering the future. If that hurts, so to speak, you might say "stretch to the past," or "stretch to the future," or "communicate with," or something. You know. Something neutral.

R: It seems, to the extent that one is telling oneself a story about other lives, when one thinks about that in the future sense, there's a lot more freedom there to create.

TGU: Well, as we often say, supposing you're imagining it, why are you imagining that and not something else? You're not necessarily as free in your imagination as you think. We suspect that you'd find it difficult to change that remembered lifetime and then find the changes equally compelling. You might experiment with this. A man instead of a woman, a family of six instead of a family of two, you see what we're getting at. In fact, that's not a bad way to test these things, to try to change them. And you'll find that like a rubber band, it'll sort of pull back to the right one as you try to change it. Same thing with the past. It's not any different.

R: Well when we think in terms of other lives set in the past, we have a lot of information about what that time period might be like. At least we have some information. Whereas for future events we have a freedom to put the dimensions in as we wish.

TGU: What you say is theoretically true, and it's sometimes true, but it's not absolutely true, and it's not always true. You don't know a thing about ancient Egypt, although you may think you know some things. You know, there are x number of dynasties, and this happens then, and there was Cleopatra and that – but what you really know about Egypt is basically nothing. What you know about Atlantis is more than basically nothing, it's nothing nothing. And what you think is your degree of freedom at making up the future isn't really that so much as it's looking in alternate place in the future. You're not as likely to look in alternate places in the past because you settle easier.

If you were to find a past in which Mexico won the Mexican war, you wouldn't be inclined to say, "oh, that's an interesting past, I'll look there," you'd be more inclined to say, "boy did I mess that one up." So what you're doing, automatically, is self-selecting the past that to you appear to be accurate. But – and obviously we don't mean you only as an individual, we mean all you – what you know about England in the 1800s, or France in the 1600s, or Rome as an empire, or China or Peru – is nothing, it's really nothing. You have what you think is an outline of things but it's all based – and we don't mean us contemptuously, although it's soon going to seem so – but it's all based in your starting place in 20th or 21st century America, or, for those who are reading is elsewhere, wherever you are.

So a Japanese doing this exercise in 1953, and envisioning ancient Peru – you can see how much different from the real ancient Peru it's likely to be, from the Japanese beginning from his or her point of view. Well, you're not any less biased than the Japanese is. You're extending, but you're extending over barriers of culture and time, so although it seems to you that you have degrees of freedom in the future that you don't in the past (and we know you do experience it that way), we would argue that really you're automatically rejecting anything that doesn't seem to you to fit into that scenario. And you are casting about for a future, and because you don't feel the future is fixed, you are free to go here or there or there or there, and you don't really know from one moment to the next where you are. It doesn't feel solid, it feels fluid. We would say to you that the past would feel equally fluid if you approached it the same way, because there are of course infinite number of pasts, as well as infinite number of futures.

Okay? Is any of that persuasive, or do we need to –

R: Well when I tried to record this "memory" of the future, I was extremely careful to say nothing that went beyond the bounds of what I had pretty good evidence were scientifically correct assumptions. Which is really kind of ridiculous as I think about it, but that's what I did. I said nothing about transportation, about how we got where we were, what the lifestyle was like, all of that that I couldn't find a reference for –

TGU: Very scientific of you.

R: Yes, that's what I did. Because, I guess, those were the rules I was imposing.

TGU: And how could you do it more productively? Because you still could, of course. It would be actually very amusing to you.

R: As you were talking about the things that we have to know about the past, that we don't know, and so on, my experience when I think about a life time in Egypt is totally a felt response.

TGU: Bingo! Because why?

R: Because I don't have any information about the external events –

TGU: Well, well, no, that's not why. [laughs] The reason why is because you're feeling what's *real*. What was your phone number three moves and 17 years ago? Who cares? But somebody who slighted you, or somebody who did you kindness 43 years ago is as alive as yesterday. You see? So of course you picked up the feelings. That's what was *real* about the life. As now.

R: And that's harder to get for me, feelings about the future.

TGU: Well if you want them, it's very simple, just imagine. Just fantasize, and go with it. And you'll fantasize awhile, and then you'll find yourself sort of editing your fantasies, you'll find yourself tending a certain way. You are dousing with your feelings. And your feelings will lead you a certain way. "We used to get to town on pogo sticks, there were these pogo sticks with some kind of external power source that allowed us just to sit on them casually, there were pogo sticks with a chair," you see. And then your mind will be going "well no, that's not right you have to put something in there." Try not to let it do that.

Your friend Joe McMoneagle can tell you how to do this. It's a form of remote viewing because what you're doing is trying to get the feeling without the overlay. The feelings are there, the information is there, it isn't necessarily important for you to get it, but if it will amuse you to get it, you can. But the first thing to do is, you have to try your best to neutralize your 21st century bias. And the way to do that is not to insist that the future follow your logic, because it won't. If you had been trying that in 1878, we don't think you'd have got the Concorde, not logically, not technically.

Searching for an Analogy

R: *Okay, well I feel we got off topic there, it was very interesting, but I don't know, do we need to go back and catch up with what we're talking about –*

TGU: You've just defined life. [they chuckle] Well, your question – we fully realize we haven't solved your dilemma, because you're trying to find a way to get a handle around the idea that you as an individual essence either do or do not reincarnate again and again. And the problem with that is that you're seeing yourselves as individuals, but once that barrier's down, when you drop the body, if you haven't crystallized, you're back in the mixture, and you're sort of like raw materials, so to speak. If you *have* crystallized, then you're a lens that we could use to –

Well, you didn't get much out of that lens analogy, let's find another one. Hold on.

What we wanted to say with the lens analogy was, we could shine it through the lens, which would shape the materials going into the physical next time around. But that's kind of meaningless to you, so let's – give us a moment here.

[As Frank]: Rita, this is the funniest feeling. I'm sitting here waiting for something to come.

R: *Mm. That's all right.*

Frank: Mm-hmm. But it's really funny, because I'm not doing anything to make it happen, but I just sit here and wait. Lie here and wait. [pause]

[As TGU]: All right. You have a sense of your own individuality, and you are both crystallized so that when you go on the other side, there will still be a Rita personality, there will be a Frank personality. Those personalities are not your essence. It's as though your essence was a sculptor and that's what you've sculpted this time. So you have these living sculptures, back on the other side, or rather you have movies, or holograms, of these living structures. Or perhaps you could – well, we'll try that analogy.

Anybody who goes back to the other side and has firmed up, has crystallized, has formed themselves; that's the best we can do. There is this living structure that is a part of all of us but is of course a separate part of us. Your knuckle is part of your total body, but it's still a knuckle if you want to look at it as a knuckle.

When it comes time to form an individual, it may be instructive and may be useful to take that structure that was already there – [pause]

We need an analogy that's a little more alive to you than that. All right, supposing you think of yourselves as computer programs. Supposing that you are down here as a programmer, and the whole life that you lead is a software program. [pause] Nope, that's not going to work either. [laughs] It's very difficult. Now you might think that we'd have this right on the tip of our tongue and we should be able to give it to you, but – we don't.

R: Okay, we've dropped the body and we're back. And there's what seems like a time period.

TGU: Well we said there'd be duration on our side, you know.

R: So this form, whenever it is, that represents a crystallization of some of us, is in some space we're unfamiliar with, or maybe very familiar with but different from now. And we're spending some time there, in that state, awaiting the development of a plan, or awaiting the –

TGU: No, no, no, no.

R: We're not awaiting.

TGU: No, not in that sense, no. Planning goes on all the time. It's a continual ballet.

R: Yes, you've told us that we're participating in that and that even as we speak, we're doing it –

TGU: Right. But if you die on Dec. 31st, 2000, and you're not reborn until oh, June 30th, 3000, there's not any elapsed time as far as we're concerned, it's just, that's the next place you're inserted into.

R: OK, so that's what I'm asking about. It's not elapsed time.

TGU: Not in that sense.

Lifetimes As Experiment – Analogy

R: Is there a time period in which we somehow exist in some form on the other side before we get it together for another –

TGU: Well, you see, that's a good question but the problem with the question is the assumption that there's a "you" that's separate, and that's what we're trying to get across, and failing miserably. Let's try one more possible analogy. We can use the net result of one lifetime to set up a series of emotional and mental reactions for another lifetime. That is, we use the results of the previous experiment to set up the next experiment. In fact, that's not a bad way to look at it. And so, from the point of view of the second experiment, it had a previous lifetime as the first experiment. And from the point of view of the first experiment, yes their unfinished algebra went into the next experiment, and so that algebraic process continues, and this is why people can remember – or conceptualize – a process of going lifetime after lifetime after lifetime improving, losing ground, improving, losing ground, whenever.

But from our point of view, it is not the case that one person has gone in, come back, gone in, come back, gone in, come back, although it looks like that to you. From our point of view, that experiment came back, it's a part of us, we use that to set up another one, which is also part of us. It's only a difference in point of view, but neither point of view is quite the way any of you think of it, because you're not used to swapping points of view. And that's why we were smiling in the beginning of this, because we wanted this discussion, because we realized that all this has been left very inchoate. That's why we were bugging both of you emotionally.

Personalities Alive over There

R: *All right, I want to go on with that, but I still want to go back, because we've recently received a report of someone having an experience with [our deceased friend] Dave Wallis, on the other side, doing a whenever he's doing. And at a party we had here on Sunday, several people have called to tell me how much they were aware of Martin's presence. [Rita's husband Martin had moved over to the other side in April, 2000.] And last night in an exercise my daughter was doing, the presence of Martin was very real. Very specific things that came back into memories about him. I'm saying, is there some state like that that we can characterize in any way that's part of this process?*

TGU: No, you all made it up. [laughs]

R: *Well, that's – [they chuckle]*

TGU: See, here's the thing. Remember how we just said that the one experiment that came out can be used to set up the next experiment. But it wasn't used up, it didn't go anywhere, it's still with us. And so, Martin, when he dropped the body and came over here, or Dave, when he dropped the body and came over here, are available to work here, they're available to visit you. They are still alive and kicking, so to speak, in that sense.

R: Well I'm more with Martin than with Dave, but experiencing them as part of the larger self. I can do that with Martin. I can feel that it isn't just the Martin I knew here in the physical, but a larger Martin who encompasses that and much more. That isn't the way people usually think about that, though. They think about it much more in the way that they were thinking about Dave, moving around and taking care of things in very efficient form.

TGU: [laughs] We cannot be responsible for what other people think. [they laugh] People think things, drawing analogies to what they're familiar with, and these are totally unfamiliar circumstances.

R: But thinking that about this person who we've been familiar with here who's dropped the body and is now part of the larger sense. Probably you're saying there isn't any waiting period from your point of view, but in preparation for going into another lifetime –

TGU: No, you're...No, no, no, no, no, no, no. No. No. [pause] No. [they laugh]

R: I can see I've got that wrong, because what would be going into another life-time is of course not that identity –

TGU: Exactly! Exactly!

R: But some small aspect of that –

TGU: Well, even the whole aspect of it, it doesn't matter. In this case you can go and stay at the same time.

R: Yes that's what I'm saying, so a small aspect of that energy might be coming back into another lifetime.

TGU: *All of it* could be going into another lifetime – but it's still here. Your experience of Martin: There would be no point in your trying to explain it away. It's there. You could persuade yourself you were wrong, but in fact, you've had the experience. And it isn't so much that when you drop the body you go back to us, it's that when you drop the body you are able to remember that you *are* us, because you are us right now, but you can't remember it in that way that makes it real because of the barrier that was put there specifically to make it hard to do just that! [they chuckle]

Now, the people who are experiencing Dave's presence – we would argue to you that people experience anyone from this side more according to what they are, than according to any difference over here. So that someone with very sophisticated perceptions will perceive Martin differently from someone whose perceptions have been somewhat channeled by their own expectations or their mental structures. If they're expecting to see Martin in a certain way –

R: In physical form almost, or whatever.

TGU: Whenever it is, yes, that's right. Or they might bound him by what he was in life. And they might bound Dave by what he was in life. And, you know, people over here are pretty good-natured, they might show you that way. [they laugh]

R: But that still sounds like such a very strange phenomenon, that someone not familiar with a particular individual comes up with a series of images that seem so connected to the person as we knew him.

TGU: We weren't saying that's not true, at all. They connected with Dave.

R: It seems strange to us.

TGU: [chuckles] You know why? Because of your preconceptions that say that that person didn't know Dave in the body. So what? [laughs] And we suspect that they might be part of the same overall total thing. [laughs] You see?

To see it as strange is a leftover of the old view that sees you as disconnected. They had to be able to resonate to Dave closely enough to get the thing. You know we said Frank would have a hard time resonating with an atheist scientist? Well, they had to be close enough to Dave's vibratory level to be able to perceive it. And they did very well. The fact that they didn't know him in the body is why it was valuable. If they had known him in the body, everybody would shrug and say, "well sure I remember Dave that way too." We know your ways. [laughs] We hope this is helpful. This is really good work, to try to sort all this out.

Both Sides Equally Important

R: You just said, we know your ways, and that brings me back to one of the sayings that's not very convincing, when you say, "we are all one, just you're playing a different function than we are right now, so you bring this to our interaction, and we bring this to the interaction." It seems to us always you're coming from a perspective of greater knowledge, greater perspective, and so I find the other not very convincing.

TGU: That's because you've forgotten our fireworks analogy, which we were very proud of.

R: [whispers] That's true.

TGU: [laughs]

R: How did that go again? [they laugh]

TGU: The reason that we seem to you to be of so much more knowledge and so much more access is because we're not bounded in time-space, and we are more interconnected – but not centered in one moment, except when we're talking to you. And our questions to you, you will remember – you live those questions. Remember the fireworks? You are the fireworks that we send out. And – hey, it could have been sludge, you know? [they laugh] You find it not convincing because you have emotional barriers against the idea of how grand you all are.

R: Why do we have emotional barriers against that?

TGU: Well, why shouldn't you? You've got this barrier before you, that leaves you feeling alone and unconnected to the rest of us, and now we're here saying to you, "oh no, we're really together, it's just this barrier you can't get across." Why shouldn't you doubt it? It's perfectly natural.

Ordinarily there's no way that one will be able to actually feel that oneness, outside of certain mystics and certain very simple people. The rest of you are constrained to believe it, at best, or even to know it but know it at a remove. But, you know, it's only a temporary problem. When you drop the body you'll know. [Rita chuckles] No, seriously. It's only a temporary problem. And it's not exactly a problem, except in the sense of a mathematical problem. It's an exercise. Your whole life could be looked at as an exercise. Exercise in more ways than one, too. Exercise like moving your muscles and enjoying yourself, that kind of thing.

You'll notice – it used to disturb Frank a lot – we sometimes slip between I and you, and I and we – it's because it's just totally a matter of convenience. We say "you" because we're talking about that part of ourselves that's on the other side of the barrier, or we try to. And you say "you" for the same reasons. But occasionally we say "we" meaning the part of us that's on your side. And of course there's no side, but it's understood.

R: We have to keep reminding ourselves. It's not so understood that we don't have to keep reminding ourselves.

TGU: Well, that's right, but don't underestimate what you're doing. You are redefining yourselves. That's very difficult. It's a form of death, in a sense, a form of death and rebirth at the same time. A very big deal. Not something minor.

R: It's very enjoyable.

TGU: Well, it would be more enjoyable if you remembered our analogies about fireworks! [they laugh]

R: Sometimes we seem like very slow –

TGU: Nope. That's not how we see it at all. What astonishes us – we know why, but it still astonishes us – is that you can't remember things from one moment to the next, because for you it's three months later. And for us it's, "we just said that!" [chuckles]

Session Twenty
February 9, 2002
(PREP Session)

[Rita and Skip monitoring, Frank in the black box.]

R: We want an especially good contact today to get some questions answered that have been bothering us.

Frank: Give me just a minute, and you can start. [pause] If we can get supporting tones for 21, I think a lot of the session will be in 21 today.

R: All right, Skip has that underway.

Frank: All right, you can go ahead when you want, Rita. [long pause] Ah, that feels good. [long pause]

R: Without pulling yourself out of the state, can you tell us what is happening?

Frank: Well, I've been extending my awareness beyond the booth and beyond the building, and I just went back to connect with Bertram, and I had this sense of St. Ambrosius, and I have no idea what that's about yet. And I thought to rebuild the crystal, which it is doing nicely.

R: Very good. Let us know what you are experiencing from time to time.

Frank: Okay. Basically, I was just waiting for you to start with the questions and then, while I was waiting, I drifted, it was nice. Is nice.

R: I would like to have you just stay within the range of my voice.

Frank: That's up to the microphone. [long pause] Such a clear sense of the red hills on the other side of the river from the Egyptian. Had a warm feeling of affection toward them [the hills]. Not a color you would ever see here. [pause]

R: We have some choices here. We can let you just continue with your experiences, and let us know what's happening, or at some point if you're ready for questions we could do that.

Frank: Well, let's do the questions. I was just speculating about Iona, just sort of getting a feel of it, trying to. I'm ready for the questions.

Aligning Physical Energy

R: Well, ask the guys what they think about a trip there, whether that would be useful to you and in what way.

Frank: [pause] I always underestimate the physical. And to actually get in the physical proximity of a place helps by aligning the body energy, the physical energy – with the internal energy, the spiritual energy. So that the actual going to Machu Picchu and Avebury and Salisbury and Monticello helped align the crystal, so to speak. Whether I did or didn't know anything about it mentally, or did or didn't know what I was doing, you don't even need to know what you're doing, in a way, to go to a sacred site in the right attitude of receptiveness. Yes, it would be very helpful. You know, that's where the idea came from anyway. Or let's put it a different way. Sometimes we get ideas, and they are waiting for us to get the ideas, and the resonance means, "yes, you got it."

R: Is there something specific about Iona that is important to you?

Frank: Yes, the ability to be in a place where the veil is thin, to help consciously be able to wield the particular tool that is me, that is able to be here and there at the same time. When "here" and "there" are closer, it'll be more easy to observe the interaction, and therefore to fine-tune it later. [pause] Internally.

R: Very good. Very useful.

Frank: The temptation for me would be to spend my whole life in a place like that. And that's what it would be, a temptation. Because it would make me irrelevant.

R: What would it make irrelevant?

Frank: Me. My function – however much I fight it – is to be somebody at Hampton Roads who can resonate to certain things as being true and needing to be published, even if I don't understand them. And if I were in Iona enjoying myself, I couldn't be *away from* Iona doing that. You see? There is an advantage to functioning from a distance, in other words.

R: But a temporary stop in Iona, you are saying, would help you bring the layers together.

Frank: Experiencing living with the layers together will help me to sort out the differences. I'm accustomed to functioning a little in each place, but this will help me to recognize which is one place and which is the other place, and how I can shift the balance appropriately. It's almost like learning to skate or to ski or something. It's a question of shifting my balance to help *preserve* my balance, to be able to shift to circumstance more adroitly. They are sharpening their tool.

R: And you wouldn't be tempted to just move to the other state?

Frank: [laughs] Oh, you mean just go over? They're not going to allow that to happen anyway. But I might be tempted to live in a place, that would be all – to have it so close. [pause] But, as I say, it would only be a temptation. It wouldn't be something I should do.

R: Is there any information there about how to organize this trip with or without others, or is that for a later discussion? [pause]

[As TGU]: We can adapt to whatever happens externally. In fact, that's what we do all your lives. If the trip shapes up in a certain way, with a lot of people, then you can learn certain things. And if it were to shape up alone or with only a couple of people, you would learn other things. We can always take advantage. So that's really a matter of several people making decisions, and going with whatever happens. One trip might be a very contemplative trip, with great time spent silently in nature. Another might be a much more boisterous trip, but we could get just as much out of it. That's our dance. We do it all the time.

R: All right, very good. I feel like I'm talking to The Gentlemen Upstairs now.

[As Frank]: Well, a little of each.

Reincarnation Questions

R: I want to ask further questions – I know you're not surprised – about our understanding of reincarnation ideas.

TGU: Not surprised, and not displeased either. This is still good work. We keep saying that. We don't feel put on the spot, you know.

R: All right very good, I want to say just a few things before we start, to make sure that someone who's listening to this will understand where we are. We have understood you to say that following a pre-established plan, a part of the totality comes through the barrier into the 3-D Theater, lives a life, returns through the veil. However, during that lifetime, plans are being made for another lifetime that will involve the same process. And the individual will be working on that plan during the lifetime with your help.

TGU: Sort of.

R: Is there something that you want to correct about that idea?

TGU: Well, finish first.

R: All right. Frank says, "well, why can't it be that simple?" But you have said a number of things that indicate it's not that simple. For one thing, what comes through the veil the second time, so to speak, is not the same package of energy that came through the first time. So that when we have "memories" of "other lives," it isn't the same energy at the two time-slices. Can I stop there to see how we're doing?

TGU: Pretty well, actually. We would say that it's not necessarily the same energy the second time. It theoretically could be. We pick the things that show in your side as traits and characteristics for a given bundle. We might conceivably pick the same bundle twice, you see, if we wanted to. We are only making a small footnote there, that it doesn't have to be different energies, it's just that it usually is. But, okay, so far, so good.

R: Okay, when you say it could be the same or it could be different, are you talking about to quantities of various dimensions that go into that bundle?

TGU: Well – we're fishing around for an analogy here. It's not a good analogy, but suppose you had a sackful of marbles, and you took a fistful of marbles each time. If you wanted to, presumably you could pick the exact same marbles twice a row. It's just, you usually don't. It's not a good analogy because marbles don't have the differences that we're talking about, but we are trying to put a little more emphasis on the fact that it's all one thing on this side, and not individuals being sort of taken apart and reassembled. We know that's difficult.

R: Yes, we are assuming that when we come back through the veil, that we are joining with the totality of ourselves, or the totality of everything –

TGU: Well of course we know the question about, "if that's true what about all these belief system levels and what about the people that are stuck" and all, and we'll talk about that if you want. [The concept of people being "stuck" will become clearer, below.]

R: Okay, I'm still trying to go at this piece by piece, and I'm asking about the issue of the memories of other lives that a person seems to have. You suggested that there may be a certain resonance there, but that the person seeing what seems to be a past life, may not be seeing part of the picture.

TGU: Well, they are perhaps putting an inappropriate level of definiteness into that one way of seeing the picture. That's what we really would be trying to say, that you can see things as, "you go into a life and you come back and then you go into another life and you come back and then you go into another life and come back," and we know that many of you do. But it's only one way of looking at it, and we are trying always to give you alternative ways that are equally accurate, to get you in the habit of seeing things as approximations of the truth, or as one viewpoint of the truth. The difference from your point of view between a memory and a resonance is probably impossible to tell one from the other. So, when Frank picks up the Egyptian, or the other monks – he's had lots of monks in there – in a way you could say those are past lives, and in a way you could say those are the –

Individuals and Threads

TGU: Oh, all right well here's – [pause] Now, you will have to bear with us, because we don't know how to express this. Do you remember how we once said to you that minutes go by and you're watching the minutes, and we are watching maybe a gold thread in the tapestry? Well, a kind of person could be considered a thread. That is, a monkish or a bookish or a womanizing or a drunkard or – you know, any of the things that you regard as characteristics, could actually be regarded as a thread that has its own being, regardless of the individuals that it visits. Do you see that?

That's a very strange way to look at things, we know, but for instance, if you took drunkenness as a character, and you said, "Okay, drunkenness is this one gold thread that goes through our tapestry, and it sometimes hits this person or that person, or the other." Do you see? You are accustomed to looking at people as individuals, and you would say "one of their characteristics was, they liked to drink a lot." But you could also look at it like, one of the characteristics of drinking-ness, shall we say, was that "in one case it was George over here, that lived in 1740." It's no more arbitrary or mistaken to look at a characteristic as an individual, than it is to look at a person in a body as an individual. It's looking at it sideways rather than up and down. Does that make any sense all?

R: That's helpful.

TGU: So that for instance a scholar or an author have in common that scholar-ness, or that author-ness, and we could look at it sideways, and watch that author-thread, whereas you would look at it up and down and look at the author. That is to say, to you, one of their traits is that they're an author. To us, they're one example of the author-thread. You see?

R: That's very helpful.

TGU: Well, given that it's just as valid to look at things that way from our side, you can see that we don't want you fixating on the idea that things can only be crystallized around the idea of an individual. There are other ways to do it, equally valid.

Lifetimes and Time and Causality

R: That's very interesting. Another issue we have is the issue of time periods. If we look at this in the sense that there is no time, and all of the lives that seem to be related are happening concurrently, that gives us another problem with the notion of one life following another in time-slices.

TGU: Well, that's because of your language. Your language is messing you up in a way. Just because times are going on concurrently – and of course concurrently is a misnomer, but we'll use it – doesn't mean anything. Hmm. Hold on a minute.

Your geographical life right now is going on concurrently, so there are people living in Egypt, and in India, and in South America, and in North America, and you're not bumping into each other, and getting in each other's way, because you are spread geographically. Well, you don't bump into each other temporally either. What's hard for you is that you think that the initial part has to precede the following part. Your language all but forces you to think that.

R: That's right.

TGU: But supposing you could envision it as all popping into existence at the same moment, all of it, first to last, sideways to sideways, up to down. And then it's a matter of playing out, and you see –

All right, we need to find a way to make that more plausible to you. Let's say that when the world is created, all possibilities immediately exist. All alternative universes, infinite possibilities, all exist at the time of the creation. Therefore nothing is dependent on something previous before it can come into existence. It all exists. Much of it may exist, so to speak, empty, as far as you can see, because you haven't gone there. Napoleon didn't win the Napoleonic wars in your existence, and therefore all the things that potentially followed from it aren't open to you. Napoleon didn't win, the Kaiser didn't win, Hitler didn't win, Lyndon Johnson didn't win. So in all those cases, huge amounts of the infinite possibilities are closed to you. But they *weren't not created*, and they weren't dependent on those reactions whether they would be created or not. Your future lives are – from your point of view – potentially being lived right now with all potential avenues taken. That is to say, the entire game on the CD-ROM is there, and it only depends on which particular incidence of the game you're going to play.

R: All right, but then when we have these experiences of feeling that we're in touch with major aspects of ourselves in another lifetime which seems to have occurred earlier, and those memories exist, this is still some kind of interconnection among those energies, the energies that those lives represented.

TGU: Remember we said, you remembered a life on Mars. To us, it's the same, it's equivalent, because the same process is going on. You connected out to it, just as you might connect out to another one. Now, you could look at it as your life, or as a life that you resonate to, neither one is the full picture. But we don't see a difference between what's called a past life and what's called a future life. That just depends on where you stand.

R: But the experience – whether future or past – seems to be one of where we seem to be identifying certain characteristics in that energy bundle that relate to us in this current life. And it seems like we're picking up specific bundles, not just recognizing certain characteristics in a lot of bundles.

TGU: Can you say something more specific about that, to show just where you are on that?

R: Going back to our concept of the one person coming through the barrier, and then another: You're saying that the one coming through the second time has some of the characteristics of the first bundle. Others are not in the second bundle. Have I got that right?

TGU: But you see, the distortion that's contained here is embedded in your language. Things like "then." And we use your language because there's nothing else to use, but to say you go into, come back, and then come in and go back again is a linguistic convention but it's not –

R: Sounds like it isn't very precise.

TGU: Well, it's, shall we say, falsely precise. It's putting a precision on it that isn't really there. Let's say, somebody went into a life and learned discipline. And so – looking at it from the conventional way your side often looks at it – "in their next life" they were more disciplined, because of the past life experience they had. Or they were hurt emotionally, and they walked into their next life with that hurt to be dealt with. That's how it seems to you.

We would say, in all those lives you're sort of voting as to how you are going to respond to things. And it's the voting that makes what you are, and sort of moves you around the various possibilities. And all that interconnects, and so although logically to you it seems inescapable that the future is built on the past, we would say nothing is built on anything, there's not one moment that's real and all the other moments aren't real. They're all real and they are all choosing. And it changes all the time. Nothing is ever fixed the way you think it is. You think, "okay, there was the battle of the Marne and one side won and one side lost." Well, yeah, in a lot of realities; but in other realities it was different. And just think, for every person killed in the battle of the Marne, there is a reality in which the person wasn't killed. That's an exaggeration, but you understand what we're saying. There are billions of alterations all the time. And so the next time through, that person zigs instead of zags, and gets killed or doesn't get killed. All of which has implications, or doesn't, you see?

What we're trying to do is to sort of throw a hand grenade into your concept of causality and past/future relationships.

R: Okay, I'm getting that impact. [laughs]

TGU: Oh good, we're not wasting our time.

TGU As Monad, As Intermediary

R: I want to go back and try one more time on my question. I'm obviously not communicating it very well. Go back to a person coming through the barrier one time and then another time. Somewhat different set of energies the second time, because some decisions have been made about the plan; the plan calls for that. Maybe half the characteristics coming through, and some not. Now we're all in this space of all possible realities, and somehow a person coming through links up emotionally with another set of energies that we're calling another life. Why that connection, rather than to all the other possible ones?

TGU: Remember a while ago – not this session, another time – we said that one could look at one's life as a mathematical problem, and the unfinished problem could be finished another time, and it wouldn't necessarily imply it was you finishing it, just because you started it.

R: I had forgotten that last part.

TGU: See, we're oversimplifying this too, because it's true that there are intermediates between everybody-as-an-individual and everybody-all-one. It's even true here. Remember, a long time ago we were saying not only the I/we stuff, but "this particular group of energies talking to you." By implication there's a difference between us in our local part of the whole thing, and other parts of the whole thing.

Well, what we've been sort of slurring over is that in fact, just as the ultimate crystal is made up of all the smaller crystals within it, locked together, and all of those crystals are made up of smaller crystalline particles locked together, and all the way up and all the way down – so on this side, it is true that ultimately everything is all one, but it's also true that intermediately, so to speak, we function as relative individuals, as monads. So that we on our side can be looked at as individuals or looked at as part of the organism.

Well, hold that in your mind. Supposing you could look at a part of the crystal putting forth repeated entry excursions into space-time. One of your most valuable concepts will be Monroe's INSPEC, because there's a sense there of a cluster that is less than the whole but far more than an individual. In other words, you could look at it (regardless whether *he* did) as a monad, that INSPEC he was talking about. And we could be regarded as part of that monad, that among millions of others, has certain individuals. Those individuals come in and out, and all of that experience shapes what we are. How we change from moment to moment also shapes what is larger than us, but enough is enough at the moment, okay? Does that –

R: Then we think of you as the intermediary for Frank? Between him and some larger component of the totality.

TGU: You could look at us as the liver of a larger being, and he's a cell in the liver, if you wanted. That idea.

R: Okay, that's helpful.

TGU: It gives a slightly more specialized flavor than perhaps is warranted, but it might give you the sense. It's not just jello over here, but it's not trade unions either.

R: [pause] All right, you've said it's a good thing that we stretch ourselves to become aware of these other bundles that seem like other lives, and that even if they aren't our other lives, this is useful to us to stretch ourselves to enlarge our current sense of understanding. Am I closer?

TGU: Mm-hmm. You're shining your flashlight in a wider area, so to speak.

R: Okay. And, are you part of the process through which that occurs?

TGU: Why, sure. We're doing it right now. We're helping on our end and you have to help on your end. And it is helpful to us by definition, because if it helps you it helps us. There is identity of interest here, after all.

R: Okay very good. Now those were questions that I had, more than that Frank had. But he does have some questions, too.

Reincarnation Questions

TGU: Well we know them very well. Let's look at that a little bit. He has had the liberating experience, mostly connected with Monroe programs as initiators, of experiencing these lifetimes. John Cotton first of all of course, and Katrina, and others. So he is saying to himself, "how can this that I have experienced be true, and how can what I feel I have experienced in Focus 23 and 25 be true, and yet, not have the continuity of experience implied by reincarnation as is conventionally understood?"

And it hasn't struck him yet – it will now, as we say it – that he was given an unusual experience of Focus 23 at the very beginning of his experiences, partly so that he would keep his eyes open and not just think that he is going to experience whatever he's been told he will experience. (Not that he's very likely to do that.) But partly also because Focus 23 is very important. He has an importance in clarifying Focus 23 for people, because it is more important than is realized, and

Bob only touched a small part of it, and people have a tendency to sort of deify or reify what Monroe said, which is the last thing Monroe would have wanted. He would have continued to explore, given time, but he was sort of deliberately distracted away from that, because there were other things to be done. The point is, emotionally he would have been in favor of exploring.

If you now chew on this idea of functions and characteristics and traits being threads in a tapestry, as individual as individuals appear to you to be individual, some of your questions will be seen in a different light. We would just as soon give you a little time to think about that, and we'll talk about it anytime you want to.

His question for instance about Katrina, the eight-year-old. Is that the whole story, or can she go somewhere and live out her life? Well, a truer way to look at it would be that, given that there is an infinity of worlds, it's obvious that every possible thing happened to her, from being miscarried, through living 100 years and having grandchildren, you see? The fact that you experience one iteration of the game means on the one hand that you're going to have things like truncated lives, because it's only that iteration. But it doesn't mean that that's the only way that life is experienced. The life is experienced in all possible ways, because everything is. So to answer his question specifically – you didn't ask it but he's been asking it, somewhat clamorously – you might look at it like this. If there's a truncated life, you can be sure that life was lived out to the full, all the way through, in various realities. By the same token, there are lots of realities in which Winston Churchill was miscarried or died as a child, or died as a young man, or died as a middle-aged man, or died as a slightly older man, you see? All possibilities exist, and they're lived somewhere. But in any given iteration of the game, you're going to have this mixture. There's not only no way around it, there's no reason to have any way around it. It's fine.

If your filters would not be overwhelmed by it, which without preparation they probably would, it would be possible for you to contact an increasing number of those alternate lives. But then there's hardly a need to do that, you would be overwhelmed with just the alternative numbers of the lives you're living already. But still, it's all possible, it all could be experienced.

If you ask, does Katrina feel like she's an eight-year-old – well...[pause]. We can't think how to cram it into your ideas about how time and space is. We'll tell you, but it won't seem right. To us, it's as though every single moment of your life is a snapshot that can be played. This runs against your idea of time, so it's very difficult for you to get that, if you can get it at all.

You could play July the 12th when you were 14 years old. You could play 10:35 in the morning July the 12th when you were that age, but you have to be outside of time to do it.

R: It seemed like that was what Bob was trying to do with Focus 15, is to take you out of that time lock –

TGU: That's right, except of course, your body is still carrying you along. But that can't be avoided until you drop it. We're saying it's as though you were in an airplane or a balloon or something, trying to fly formation with a cloud. Your body is moving you through time all the time, and so you can't stay still, so in order to stay still at one time, you have to actually go relatively backwards to what your body is doing. You know how we talked about the switching system? This is an equivalent problem. It's a clever thing to do, and it's not a worthless thing to do at all, but it's just you can't entirely do it while you're in the body because a part of you is being dragged into the future. That's the way it would look to you.

"Stuck"ness As Habit of Mind

R: Mm-hmm. Let me ask about another one of the energies that Frank has dealt with, Joyce, who I think was suffering when she died. He has had the experience of going through the Monroe process, of moving her to Focus 27 and releasing her because of the sense he had that she was stuck somewhere along the line. Now, how does this sort of thinking sit with you?

TGU: You mean how does it square with what we're telling you?

R: Yes.

TGU: Well, just parenthetically, it isn't that she was suffering, it's that her suffering combined with the painkiller she was using disoriented her so that she didn't notice when she moved over. Okay, it's a big question, a worthwhile question. We'll chip away at it.

You have such things as ghosts, and presences, that sensitive people can feel. Patrick, for instance, from the famous Patrick tape [in which a channeled experience gave Bob Monroe the idea of training people to "retrieve" souls that had gotten "stuck" in transition]. We remember the question that you raised: When you dropped the body the barrier dissolved, so how can anybody get stuck? And the best way to put it might be to say that it's a habit of mind. The answer will be a little circular but bear with us. Patrick, because he wasn't aware that he had died and therefore had dropped the body and therefore was available to flow back into what was, *had* flowed back on our side, but was not at all aware of it. His attention was focused on earth. All we accomplished was to re-direct his attention.

It's not question of movement. The spatial analogy sneaks into Focus 27 as it sneaks into everything else in your lives, but it's not question of movement. Patrick was where Patrick always had been. He always lived and moved and had his being in us even while he had a body. When he dropped the body, though, his habit of attention was so fixed that he wasn't aware of it, and he was running a tape loop, as you say, just playing the same movie to himself all the time. The only thing that was accomplished in retrieving Patrick was a redirection of his attention.

You all visualize it in a bodily way as escorting someone somewhere. But it isn't movement or close to movement, it's just a movement of consciousness. It's a shining of the flashlight in the opposite direction, rather than toward the earth.

Any of the lives that you're referring to, including your own, have a preferred method, an habitual method, of looking. Now, if someone is already spiritually inclined, or they are for some reason aware that there's something beneath and underlying the earth, and they are conscious when they die, it isn't a problem. In whatever way they cognize the situation, they say to themselves, "I'm no longer in a body, now I'm on the other side." [That word "cognize" is TGU's way of saying, to employ cognition, to conceptualize or think about.]

But if someone has a firm belief there is nothing on the other side, or for some reason is unaware that they have gone, there is a problem. But in no case is it a matter of movement. So all of the people that you're thinking of – again, in a spatial analogy – as being in Focus 24, 25, 26, 23 – your default position is to think of them as spatially separated and being moved "up to 27," as you usually put it. At which time, you're not really sure what happens but you know they're taken care of. There's no movement there at all, the only movement is in their mental structure. They suddenly realize, "oh, I'm not stuck here, things are not what I thought they were."

How much does that help and how much does that hinder?

R: I think that helps. Skip wonders what is the whole purpose of the idea of rescuing someone, then?

TGU: Well, you are accomplishing a task. You are helping them to redirect their attention inward, toward us, rather than outward toward the material world. We don't care which direction they look at, what we care about is their freedom. If someone is looking toward the earth and is still fixed on it because they're unaware there's anything else, they're not as free as they are if they're looking down to the earth because they're interested. You are freeing them, literally, to be more themselves, because they won't have this tunnel vision that will eliminate all other possibilities.

So – to tie this with Dave that you talked of the other day – Dave was perceived in one of the focus levels, but only because he wants to be. He's fully aware that he can do what he wants. He's not fixated on the earth, he's where he is. That's the difference between someone needing rescuing, and someone playing. We have no objection to playing.

R: Well then, it isn't that the Monroe process isn't on target, in a way, but it sounds like it would help to use a somewhat different language.

TGU: Well, there's no reason to use a different language. It was, after all, an inspired program. You don't think it was an accident that Rosie McKnight and the Patrick tape came along and had the result that Bob set up Lifeline? That was needed and it is very helpful. Rather than change the metaphors, we would rather make people aware that they *are* metaphors. Our metaphor is no more correct than theirs. It's not literally a crystal over here. A metaphor is a metaphor because, looking straight at it, you can't describe it. All we are trying to do is remind people that is a metaphor, and that reality is always a little between the lines. What Monroe is doing is fine.

R: That's very helpful, thank you very much.

TGU: We are sorry to spoil our record. [they chuckle]

Monroe System Questions

R: I want to ask about the compatibility between the Monroe system and our thinking here. What about the vision of Focus 27, a park-like place that energies can go when they're on their way out of the body. Does that compute at all for you?

TGU: If you would say a non-threatening, attractive, tranquil place – as long as you understood that "place" is a metaphor also – we would have no problem with it. If you say a park, it might be Central Park, or some park in Illinois somewhere. We're only complaining about the misplaced concreteness. Focus 27 does track your conscious existence, in a way that the present does not, and it certainly is accessible, and you've experienced it yourselves, but it doesn't have furniture, it doesn't have paved roads, it doesn't have all of the misplaced concreteness that people give it.

Well, except that it does in a way. Hmm. A moment here. We have to think about this.

R: I have another question, if that will help.

TGU: No, just give us a moment here. Well, here's the thing. From where you are, it's not concrete. When you come here, it'll be certainly concrete. But it won't be

Portland concrete, you know. [chuckles] It won't be what you expect. We don't know a better way to put that. Okay, your other question was?

R: Bob seemed to feel that what had happened to make that Focus 27 more concrete is that the thousands and thousands of people had come through that experience, and the people themselves had in the process of doing that made a more concrete setting that was what people now found.

TGU: Yes, but, you see, your language is misleading you. You surely don't envision that a Peruvian, and a Chinese, and a South African, and a Lithuanian would all have the same vision of what a park would be. That's misplaced concreteness, you see? If you say a place where people will be comfortable and at rest, and non-threatened, yes. And you are right, it's been placed there in that way. But it hasn't been placed by a landscape designer, that's what we are saying. There is a tendency to mistake vibrations for concrete. There's a tendency to mistake function for form. That's the only thing we are trying to correct a little bit. Yes it's concrete, psychologically. No it's not concrete physically, because it isn't physical. That's all we are saying.

R: Would you suggest a change in the way that Focus 27 is presented in the Monroe programs?

TGU: No, it's not important. It's a distortion, but it's a distortion that's in the language, and it's so unimportant next to what they get from it that's it's not worthwhile. The people who continually use Focus 27 won't be particularly distracted by the language, and the people who use it and don't know the difference, it won't make to any difference to them. No, it's not important.

Limits of Physical Reality

R: Let me then ask about the concept involved in Focus 35, where presumably humans, having moved over, are interacting with other life forms. Does that sound like it is part of the process?

TGU: Suppose you thought of reality as a bowl. Think of it as a wok, or a bowl that slants concentrically and regularly inward and down. The very center is C1, matter. And as you go out toward the edge, you reach toward Focus 10, 12, 15, 21, 35. All of those are part of your physical matter reality, although you tend to think of them as not. All these focus levels are part of a very localized portion of the universe. That is to say, when you're in Focus 27, you are still firmly in physical matter reality.

R: That's hard for us to...Obviously, we're doing it, taking ourselves to what seems like a physical reality in 27, that's right.

TGU: But see, even 34 and 35 and things beyond – again, it's a metaphor – you could look at as an ever more attenuated form of physical matter reality, with the most concrete and the most dense being in the middle, and then working its way out toward the edges, to where you are in an entirely different realm. The differences to you are so great between being in the body and sending your mind out to explore these other focus levels, that you tend to think of them as being differences in kind, but really, they're only differences in degree. So 34/35, there are, let's call them people, from what to you would look like other realities, and this is as close as they can get to watching the big show down in the middle of the bowl. They have their own shows, but if they want to watch this show, this is about as close as they can get. It is just a matter of not being sucked into the density.

It's a poor metaphor, but it's serviceable.

R: Yes, I could get a good image of that.

TGU: Be aware, now, that when we say matter is the thing in the center, we're not talking about the earth, we're talking about all physical matter. The galaxies, and the space between the galaxies, and all that are part of this thing in the center. We don't want misplaced concreteness to say the earth is there, and, you know, the moon is maybe the equivalent of Focus 10. [laugh] It's not true. All physical matter reality is that very dense thing in the bottom of the bowl, and the mental states and the spiritual freedom move outwards from that, but are a part of it.

R: Yes, certainly I have seen that temptation in 35, people describing things with the density of C1.

TGU: The translation error in 35 is going to be so great, that anything you bring home is a gift.

Time, There

R: [chuckles] Okay, that sounds good. This is a little specific, that I never have caught up with. You've made a distinction between time and duration on your side. I don't understand that.

TGU: Well, we're only doing that to try to defeat the ingrained bias of your language. Because if we say "there is no time," your language tempts you to think "everything happens at once, all piled up on each other." And unfortunately, in a way that's true. [laughs] But in a way it isn't true, and that's what we're trying to preserve here. We don't live in time in the way that you do, being dragged from moment to moment to moment, at predictable intervals, without any way to move forward or backwards. So we're calling that "time," and quite arbitrarily we're calling what's on our side of the line "duration." That is to say, you can talk to us one day – so to speak – and then talk to us another day, and something will be different. The fact that they're different shows you that it's not all one thing. But because you live in space-time, we don't think there's any way for you to envision that, except as a kind of a time. "They did think this, now they think that. They did say this, now they say that." So, we tortured this word "duration" into a different meaning because your language, otherwise, will do the same thing to you in terms of time that the spatial analogies always do in terms of space.

R: So the duration idea implies that there is a "before" and "after"?

TGU: It more implies there's a separation of states. If you had ice, steam, and water – three states of the same thing – and nobody gave you a crib sheet telling you whether the thing froze and then burned – you see what we're saying? If you didn't know which came first, there isn't any question of duration involved there. But there is a thing about different states. Ice is different from water is different from steam, even though they're chemically the same thing. So, we're trying to sneak this word duration in, and perhaps that's a mistake, perhaps we should call it something else. There are separations of our consciousness –

Hmm.

Well, you know how we've said that you have a switching system to allow you to hold things in your mind while you move, with time? Well, we don't have that necessity, and we don't have the switching system. But we have a –

Well, a division by function, but that won't tell you anything. A division by what we are, sort of. [pause] See, you are accustomed to thinking of yourself as one person. You're not accustomed to thinking of yourself as a different person on Wednesday, Thursday, and Friday, not to mention every moment of time in between. If you weren't in time, you could do that. Remember, we say that sometimes we have to go looking to see where you are in time? Well, it's the same thing for us on this side, and we have no way of even remotely figuring out how to tell you about it. Sorry. It's equivalent to that, but maybe something will come to us. Maybe if you ask the right question it'll come to us.

R: We don't like making you struggle.

TGU: [laughs] Haven't noticed that. We don't mind struggling, it's just that the concept is so firmly embedded in time in your mind and in your experience, and we can't make it a spatial analogy without doing even worse damage to it. Well, maybe someday we'll think of it. See, you heard that. "Maybe someday." In other words, –

R: That's a duration away.

TGU: [pause] The very concept of change implies some kind of duration, or implies some kind of alternate state, but it's not movement, and so, you look at change and you think, "aha! That went from being this to being that." And there's nothing wrong with thinking of it that way, but you could easily think of it as – this will sound like the same thing to you – "it ceased to be this and became that." [pause]

Frank and the Material

R: All right, I have another –

TGU: Good! [they laugh]

R: Another area of the same thing to ask about has to do with Frank's career around this kind of material. Can you talk some about his role in presenting this sort of idea to the world?

TGU: You mean beyond what you're doing right now?

R: Right.

TGU: Well, don't underestimate that. One level of his career is to hold it, because anything that one person holds inside themselves is available then to everyone. Anything one holds within oneself and then puts into some external form makes it easier for people to recognize that it's available to them. Anything that one holds within oneself, puts into external form, and then goes up and down the land speaking to people about it, brings it to their attention so that they can recognize that it's available for them. You see what we're saying? It becomes a matter of how much more immediate the results are. And of course everything is always under your choice. If he wants to just think about things, knowing that having put them together they're there for others, but in a relatively inchoate state, because they haven't been forged by talking about them, or meeting opposition, or even getting new points of view – any combination of those things is possible. If you ask us what he would enjoy doing, what would be fulfilling for him, we would say a combination of inner work and outer work is perfect; that's why he's on the boundary between the introvert and extrovert. Sometimes writing, sometimes speaking.

R: I'm asking about what he reports when he gives presentations. One way would be just to talk about his own experiences of this sort. The other would be to try to think about and somehow present the political and social implications of this kind of view of things.

TGU: Actually, that looks like a difference to you, but it's the same thing. The more he expresses who he is and what he is, the more those concerns of his come out, so it is the same thing. The preferred option is both, because they are actually one. Everything that he does will center on his own experience. Everything stems from his own center. His impact is from what he is, rather than necessarily what he thinks, does, or anything else. He absorbs and focuses the world through his own attention to himself. It's difficult to say. It's so simple, it's hard. So anyway, we're saying, he will speak, he will write – to the degree that he does – about his own experiences, starting from there and going outwards. There's no other way for him really.

R: All right, very good. Sometimes he has a sense of futility about things, and I don't know if that sense is related to this topic we've been on here, or not.

TGU: Well he doesn't know this, but he is about to find it out. The sense of futility has always been there because a part of him has always been elsewhere. So, a part of him has always been aware of how small a thing it is to be a particular human at a particular time. And the disproportion between what anyone could do, and what is, often seemed overwhelming, so that it was like, "why bother?" He doesn't know that. He knows it now, but he didn't know it two minutes ago.

Pursuing Proof

R: All right, that's very helpful. I just have one more question today, and that has to do with a thought we've had about trying to explore in more detail the lives of some of the others that he has thought of as past lives. For example, Smallwood came to mind as a possibility. Would that be a useful thing for him to do?

TGU: Even more useful will be for him to realize, as he will now, that as long as anyone attempts to obtain proof, it will be nearly impossible to pursue it, because pursuing proof holds you in a state of mind in which you try to come up with probable results. As long as he does that, he'll go up blind alleys. But if he will play and just be willing to make it up as he goes along – which is what he always advocates to people – he can pursue them as far as he wants. There's no inherent reason why he can't find that information, because the resonance is there. And it's useful, because any kind of extension is useful, in our opinion.

R: I don't know that the proof factor came into it, it certainly –

TGU: It did for him.

R: Oh, it did for him? Oh, that's interesting. It didn't for me. I was thinking more about your sense of the helpfulness of trying to integrate these into our present thought about who we are.

TGU: That's correct. Because you see it doesn't matter, was this a past life so-called, or was it a resonance? As far as we are concerned, it's a thread. And if you understand the thread, you understand yourself. And if you extend to another person, it's like – if you have a very close relationship with a friend, does it matter that they are not a blood relative? Ultimately, if you trace your family tree back far enough, they're going to be a blood relative, but – you see? To us, you all have an exaggerated idea of the importance of biological individuals, because to us we can't find any biological individuals, they're all one thing.

R: All right, very good. I'm going to stop asking questions then, and if there's something that you or Frank would like to bring up, to experience there while he's still in the booth –

Connecting with Smallwood

TGU: Yes, let's – let's see, what's the easiest way to do this? If you'll go to Focus 25 with the frequencies, we'll go looking for Smallwood; see if he can connect.

R: All right, Skip is taking care of moving you to Focus 25.

TGU: All right, and then we'll either report or won't, but whenever we need to, you just bring us back. [pause]

[As Frank]: Wow, quite a sense of compression, of my chest – like, caved in a little bit. I wonder if he was tubercular? Got a wheeze back right away. [pause] Tall and thin, I think. Maybe taller than Emerson. Which isn't all that tall. Maybe a little gangly. Soft-spoken. Very polite, very cultured person, but not class-manners, just naturally. I think he came off a farm, actually, or – yeah, I think a farm. [pause] Boy, going out to Michigan just seemed like going out forever. It just seemed like so far. Great sense of bursting all bounds, out of New England. Almost like going where no man had ever gone, or no New Englander. Great sense of liberation from previous constraints. Not that he was a hell-raiser, he just wanted to see something new.

He worked – I think he worked – I think he did know John Muir, just that one summer. I think he didn't go right there, either. He was in Ohio, maybe Pennsylvania. Well, let's see. I think he worked here and there, just either odd jobs or as the actual chore-man. We're talking about a young man now. Which is kind of unusual, because he was a graduate – he was either a Harvard graduate or he had been to – well wait, let's see. [pause]

Yeah, I think he was a Harvard graduate, and it was as unusual for him to do that as it was for Henry Thoreau to do the chores and stuff rather than be a teacher or a lawyer or a doctor or a clergyman. But this was freer. I think there was a little bit of guilt, for a while, about throwing away his opportunities. [However, official school records show no Joseph Smallwood as ever having attended Harvard College.]

Now the interesting thing is, just as I do with the Egyptian's where my hands surround that chair, this time they're around something entirely different. The right hand is around a square corner; it's not a chair, but it's a – something accustomed, anyway, whereas the left hand, well I can't place it, the hand is sort of cupped. But the surface is flat in both cases, don't know what it is yet.

He was just picking up a lot of curious information, like the Indian names to things. And I do believe he was fascinated by Lewis and Clark, and he did follow them across – of course, this was 40 years later –

I have this sense of him on a horse by himself in the middle of nowhere. The Dakotas, maybe, or might have been Nebraska, but I actually don't think he was on the Oregon trail. I think he was avoiding it. Wanted to be by himself. But a sense of this nature mysticism, just like in that movie that affected me, that – wolf movie. Wild Wolve, uh – *Dances with Wolves*. He had that same sense of the holiness of the whole thing. It was fabulous.

He had something he could give the Indians as he went across. I don't mean trinkets, there was something he could do that was of use to them. Plus they recognized in him that he wasn't just another crazy white man.

R: I wanted to let you know that we're out of recording tape now. So you could go ahead with this, or you could come back to it.

TGU: Let's keep going for a bit, if it's okay.

R: That's fine.

TGU: One of the things he gave them, actually, was respect. He wanted to learn all their stuff, and that was important but – there was something he could do for them. [pause]

Frank: I think my left hand is around the saddle horn! But what the right hand is on, I don't know. I want to say the stock of a rifle, but I don't believe that's true at all. [pause] No, actually, they may be holding reins in the buckboard? This is a later time; this is some other time. Wonder if they're moving me along? Well, maybe it's time to quit. [stretches]

R: All right then, just be relaxed there for a moment, and we'll be bringing you back with the sound.

Frank: Okay, you'll notice – just as you thought – that my lungs cleared up immediately. Basically immediately.

R: Good.

Frank: Except I think Smallwood might have had TB or something, because my chest just went inward! It was just amazing. [yawns]

I'll make a small bet we weren't anywhere near the null today. That is, we didn't go across it.

R: Well, we will see.

Frank: Yep. Because the only time it happened, I got lost. Couldn't remember anything. You know, like normal life. [chuckles]

Session Twenty-One
March 19, 2002

Interaction with the Other Side

R: All right, this time we have a tape recorder. Let's review some things we talked about last time. I asked about the notion of your planting an idea that leads to a question. What I remember about your response was that you talked quite a bit about the energy resonating together.

TGU: Let us repeat that while we have the tape recorder on. We were saying that the interaction between our side and your side goes on continually, and it's often not noticed on your side. You have what you think are hunches or ideas, or something that comes out of the blue, and often that's us prompting you and you don't really recognize it. It's not particularly important that you do. But, that's what goes on, so that when we say we planted that idea, that's not particularly unusual. And it doesn't even mean that it's particularly important. It isn't like 95 percent of your ideas are yours and the 5 percent that are ours are sparklers. It's more like, we're always doing it and you're sometimes picking it up. Also, ideas are just out there and sometimes you snag some.

The other major thing that we mentioned was that we use you to prompt each other. That is to say, if you think something, you may not even notice it, and if you notice it you might not pay attention to it. But if you hear someone *say* it to you, you'll pay more attention, because you're more accustomed to paying attention to what seems like the outside world. So, when we need to get someone's attention, one way to do it is to use others around them. And another way, as Carl Jung recognized long ago, is we use all kinds of coincidences, so-called: dreams, thoughts, people, seemingly external objects, all of those things.

R: And I asked, "is your energy system resonating with our energy system in these sessions," and I think what you said is, "what's the difference there? Why do you make that distinction?"

TGU: That's right. Because you and we are the same. Supposing you had a garden hose that reached from you to us. You could, for some purposes, distinguish between the ends of the garden hose. But for other purposes, that would be a mere distinction that would cause trouble rather than clarifying it, you see? The one way emphasizes the difference, the other way emphasizes the continuation. Both true, it just depends on what you're looking for.

R: It seems you call our attention to this a lot and I was wondering what your purpose is.

TGU: Merely to redress the balance. If you were continually aware of it, as some societies have been, will be, are, then we would be emphasizing the difference.

R: And I was asking about the many, many energy groups that exist: How much interaction is there at your level among the energy groups that are operating? How much interaction is there between those energy groups?

Interaction on the Other Side

TGU: Well, believe it or not, we've given quite a bit of thought as to how to try and explain this. And really, we go back to where we began. We think the easiest way, the most structured and textured and three dimensional way, is to make a direct analogy to your world. Just as it is with you, so it is with us – with the major exception that we are not divided into time-slices, and that we do not have delayed consequences. Now those are major differences, of course. But, it should also show you, if you look at your own world as an analogy, the breadth and depths of the various differences and distinctions. You have some people who are scientists and some who are academics and some who are policemen, and some who are criminals and some who are politicians, and some who are military, some who are farmers. All of those can also be cut different ways. Some who are parents, some who are grandparents, some who are children. And could be cut different ways. Some that are liberal, some that conservative, and some that are agnostic, and some that are religious. You see?

R: Yes.

TGU: You can cut all those innumerable distinctions. Some are Chinese, some are Caucasian, some Negro – you see? There's this tremendous diversity, just among the few billion people you have on earth, the same thing with us only even more so – *but* not in time-slices and not in delayed consequences. Therefore, the lack of delayed consequences means it would seem to you that we change constantly and continually.

We keep calling it a light show. You know, that's in reaction to each other. There's a simulation game that you sometimes play where the proximity of one kind of symbol will extinguish or generate more of another kind of symbol. So you have a constantly changing pattern on the screen, proceeding from the few simple rules. Well, our rules aren't simple and they're not necessarily rules, but the pattern changes in that same way. And because there's no time-slices, that means that our field of action is a lot wider than yours. And less concentrated.

R: Okay, now, if you think about the communication going on within your level, and the communication going on with our level, are you communicating with still other systems besides those that are on our level or your level?

TGU: [pause] Are you asking is there an equivalent system to the time-space, what you call 3-D Theater?

R: Maybe that, or anyhow, other dimensions or other realities that are not just the same thing that's going on here only in some different space-time situation.

Personalities Still Exist There

TGU: Well, the only thing we can tell you directly is that we're confident that everything is one, and so no matter what's going on anywhere, there's some part of us that knows some part that connects to it. But you mustn't think, as Frank always does, that we know everything and we are aware of everything.

For instance – it occurs to us that we've never said this to you – think of your friend Dave Wallis, who you think of sitting in his laboratory [on the other side]. A part of him *is* sitting in his laboratory. We can communicate to that particular energy system called Dave Wallis as a separate person. *Or* we can flow with him, sort of. We can resonate with him. We can emphasize the difference between us, which is often worthwhile, or can emphasize the sameness, the continuity, which is often worthwhile.

R: So, does that mean that there is a Dave Wallis that is functioning as part of what you are and a Dave Wallis that is functioning, as we were talking about before, in his laboratory or something like that?

TGU: No, no. It means that Dave functioning in his laboratory *is* part of what we are and part of what we are is Dave in the laboratory. Just as part of what we are is *you* in 3-D Theater, only there's the barrier between us and you that makes it hard for you to really make that real to yourself. For him where he is now, there is no such barrier. So, it *is* real. But, at the same time, he's not any less what he was. He was created out of the experience on your side. But, he didn't *cease* to be created when he ceased to *be* on your side. That's the point we've continually tried to get across. And failed, it sounds like. [they laugh]

R: Would you make that last point again?

TGU: Well, remember we've said, we put together some group of characteristics in there and put it into your side, creating an individual, so to speak. Remember we talked about crystals. If that personality crystallizes –

R: Yes, which I assume for Dave it did.

TGU: Sure, or he wouldn't be there. When it goes back on the other side, there's then this – you could look at it as a being, but we would look at it as part of *our* being. This is like a formed facet on our overall crystal, you see. So, the whole purpose of this is to get *more* individuality, and it would be silly to lose it once you would drop your body.

R: Is he more a part of your reality. [coughing] I'm sorry, I have to deal with this cough.

TGU: Bodies are great inconveniences.

R: I don't know if I can get this back. I was going to use your words. Did you say he's more a part of us now than he was?

TGU: No, no. We're saying you are as much a part of us as he is. But he's more aware of it now. He's aware of it, not as a theoretical or even as a belief system, but, just in his day-to-day existence he knows it. You are not any less a part of us than anything else. It's just that the illusion of your individuality is so hard for you to see as an illusion, that's all. [pause] Which is Frank's problem, whether he knows it or not.

R: Can you say some more about that? How is it Frank's problem?

The Benefit of Isolation

TGU: Well, he may never have put this together, but the reason he finds it so hard to live there is because he *knows* he's not an individual, but he's –. Let's see. [pause] The very reason why the barrier is there, is the reason why, in his case (since it's halfway *not* there) it makes his life so hard for him. Do you understand?

R: The fact that he's not altogether here, that's what makes it harder?

TGU: The fact that *the barrier's* not altogether here. Yes, because it makes him acutely homesick. He hasn't the fear of, "if I die what will happen?" He *knows* what will happen and he can't wait and so – that's why the barrier is *put there* for people, to help them not only to form a character around a certain time and place, but a subsidiary benefit is, it grounds you in Earth as well as in a particular time and space. It orients you to the body. He's half-oriented here and half-oriented on your side. And as the years go on, he's become even more so. There's a purpose to that, but it's not easy. So –

R: And so, is doing this kind of work making it harder?

TGU: Oh, no, it allows him to complain to us and that's okay. [laughs] We would just say, "feel free to complain but, you know what you're doing, and you're do-

ing it, so, what's the problem?" And he would then say, "oh you guys are so *cold*."
[they chuckle]

R: Is that why most of us are not more in touch with your side, because it would make our Earth experience harder?

TGU: [pause] Well, it's true that it would make your experience harder, initially, but, no we wouldn't say that's the reason. We would invert that and say, the reason why he's a little different is that he's breaking a trail, just as many of you are breaking the trail and the coming people will not have this barrier. But it has been necessary for a long time – as you see things – before this. You can never understand what it's like to be isolated unless you've been isolated. Then when you begin living in less isolation, you will not be taking it for granted, you'll be consciously aware of the differences.

R: So, the coming people won't be as uncomfortable with that because they'll understand this process better?

TGU: No, because there'll be more of them, just as you could look at Bob Monroe as a pioneer, very alone. And very alone in another sense, because he was doing something without seeing where it had already gone. You all can see where it went, and therefore you see everything differently than he did, because you can see it point backwards. So, the interest and the use of skill of being a pioneer is at the same time the difficulty. Not much fun being a pioneer if you've got a four-lane highway going where it is that you're leading toward.

Work and Vocation

R: While we're on the subject, let me just ask about what Frank's going through now – feelings of depression or whatever. Is that related to this?

TGU: You mean to the work you're doing?

R: To the topic we're just been on –

TGU: Yes, very much related to the topic. *Not* related to the work you're doing. The work you're doing is an antidote. Because it has meaning, you see.

R: But the fact that he's relatively alone with the work he's doing is part of the thinking that goes with that.

TGU: Well, it's more like he's relatively alone, period. Whatever *work* he does makes him less alone, you see. Your society commonly doesn't necessarily realize that work is a connection. That's why it's so terrible to have *meaningless* work.

R: It's connection with others here and with the other side as well.

TGU: Well, yes. The medieval Catholics would have called it a vocation – not meaning *priestly* vocation, but one's calling, the thing that had called them, that person's part of the overall jigsaw puzzle. Now, you can have a 500,000-piece jigsaw puzzle, conceivably. And any one piece that wasn't there would make it an incomplete and less satisfying puzzle. So, there's no such thing in that concept as a meaningless job or a meaningless life. It's a concept that you find harder to *really* understand in your day than they would have five, six, seven hundred years before. You think of "important jobs" and "important people" and "unimportant jobs" and "unimportant people." And so [you may think] the person who cleans your house is not as important as the person who is a lawyer or public official or whatever. And yet, from our side, that's totally distorted.

Now, this is also not to say that the person who cleans your house is *more* important than the public official or whatever. What's most important is the person who is the most real and performs the function they came in to function as the flower they're creating. The better they do that, the more perfect the flower they are. We know this contradicts what we said about even the drunk lying in the gutter creates a flower, but let's leave that for the moment. That's true as well, but, since it distorts the point we're trying to make, we're going to ignore it. [they laugh]

R: *Well, do you have any suggestions for Frank in going through these experiences that we haven't already talked about? Or that you talked about with him?*

TGU: We've told him repeatedly, the only real thing is just a matter of courage and perseverance. We didn't say it was easy.

R: *And so, his expressions of wanting this all to be over are just part of his frustrations as he goes through this?*

TGU: Well, don't underestimate how therapeutic it is for him to be able to tell somebody that. It's a real feeling and it's a continual feeling, and it's as real as any other part of his life, and so, therefore, it deserves the respect that every other part of his life deserves – from him as well as from others. You all have a tendency, if we may say so, to *judge* everything in your lives and say "well, this is worthwhile and that's *not* worthwhile." And we want to know, if it's not worthwhile, how come it got into your life?

R: *Hmm.*

TGU: How do you like them apples? [laughs]

R: *Yes. Yes, I'm not going to take that one on. [chuckles]*

TGU: We'll come back to it sometime.

Two Kinds of UFOs

R: Is there anything else that comes up right now as we're thinking about it that happened last time while we weren't recording that we should mention?

TGU: Well, we'll mention, just for the record, the question was asked about UFO's and we said that there are two kinds of UFOs, ones created in your reality in your space-time by people, and others that come from another time and space, which get here by manipulating *time* as well as space. (Otherwise, it would take them too long.) And we said they come from seven different places. And Frank had a lot of trouble with overlay that night because he knows that people say they come from the Pleiades, they come from other places. *He* doesn't have the data and therefore, in a way, *we* don't have the data. We could probably go find out. But, we're not inclined to bother. Unless it becomes important to you.

The Value of Group Activity

Now, the *major* thing that we said of importance the other night, was in relation to the Jane Katra workshop. And that was that you all not allow that very worthwhile, and indeed almost a grace-filled experience, to be isolated in your lives as a one-time experience. That we strongly suggested that you find ways to incorporate it in your life on a daily basis. And we would wager that already you have forgotten to do that. And we know that he has. And this will make your lives richer and deeper.

R: Well I had thought about that. Mainly, I think of just pointing to the importance of mediation in our lives. But, Frank talked more about the possibility of some group activity around it.

TGU: Yes, and that's stemming directly from what we were giving him because – (you notice how we take credit for things that are pretty good?)

R: Even the questions.

TGU: Even the questions. Meditation is fine. And it absolutely is great and you can put that in your routine and there's nothing at all wrong with that. However, group activity is better, for two reason. One, it assures that you *keep* it on the schedule. And two, when you fall asleep, there are others there to wake you, and that's just as vitally important. There'll be a day, perhaps, when it is not. But, at your stage of life, it is, because none of you are – if we may say so – continually awake. Well, if you know you are going to meet on a regular basis, in one place or in a rotating place, with the same people or some subset of the same people, that *itself* is going to help you stay on the beam. And then beyond that, you will sometimes go, thinking that you're awake but not being awake, and the process of being there will wake you up. This difficulty is, after all, one of the underlying reasons for monasteries. Part of it was economic, part of it was convenience, but the largest part is to wake each other up. They may not have even always known that, but that's what happened – can happen.

So, in our love for all of you, we want you to live as rich and full an experience as you can, and one way to do that is to not take that kind of grace-filled experience and isolate it off from the rest of your life, but use it to connect to other parts of yourself Upstairs, and to connect with yourselves, person to person – which is another part of yourself. That, we would say, was the most important thing we said the other night. Much more important than UFOs.

Physical Contacts

R: Okay. You used the phrase, in an illustration last week [not in a transcribed session], of pulling Frank's ear.

TGU: No, that was – well, yes, it was an illustration, but it was literally true.

R: Well, I assumed it was. I heard it that way. Which emphasizes the question I'd already planned to ask last week and didn't, which is, what about these experiences we have of what seems like a physical contact with a non-embodied energy? What is happening there?

TGU: Well, first, let's describe more carefully than we did what happened. Now, here's the interesting thing. We're going to try and describe it as *he* saw it, and then describe the difference between what he *felt* and what he *described*. Not because he's a bad reporter – he's actually usually a pretty good reporter – but because it demonstrates the difficulty of the things. In other words, some things take so long to describe that are not intrinsically worth it, that they never get really adequately described, and therefore confusion enters.

He was sort of drifting a little and he felt something tweaking his ear, just pulling his right earlobe down. But he didn't feel it in his *first* [physical] body, he felt it in the *second* [energetic] body. It was more real than a dream, and not his actual physical ear. So, it took him a second to remember that he had felt it, if you can understand that. And then when he mentioned it – well, I mean he mentioned it through us – but he actually chose the words, you know? He did not – we did not – go to the extra effort of making clear that these things, which appear to you as a quasi-physical-body-experience, are usually a second body experience, as it was with him. In other words, we've gone over and tweaked his ear on the second body – energetic body – not on the physical body. And of course, your energetic body doesn't really have an ear, but it seems to you to. If you know what we're saying.

You know that when you are attempting to maintain your presence in an altered state, in an expanded state, it's easy to drift off. (That's how it seems to you.) It's easy to go beyond seeming continuity of consciousness. So, that you then "wake up" and say, "oh where was I?" If we're not mistaken, that's how you see it. We wouldn't see it that way.

We would say, you go into new territory and sort of attenuate the connection with your ordinary consciousness and the interpreter that's always there interpreting what you're seeing. Without the *interpretation*, you have pure *perception*. But, without an interpreter to compare perception to something, you don't bring anything home. Well, if in the middle of that process, you're interrupted, it will seem to you like you drifted a little bit and then came back. In other words, you still won't quite remember where you were, because you still don't have anything to compare it to. And so, there's no data there to bring back. You experience it as continuity of consciousness still, but you say to yourself, "well I was drifting."

You see, even the tweaking of the earlobe was more of a metaphor than an actual experience because, as we say, your second body doesn't *have* an earlobe. But, if you'll look at your life as a dream, it isn't any more of a dream to tweak your second body's earlobe, then it would be in physical matter to tweak your *regular* earlobe. They're both metaphors for calling your attention back to your body. And we know that sounds impossibly abstract, but that's really pretty accurate. We'll go through it again, if you want. Or, go on.

R: No, but I guess I'm saying, what happens from your end in that kind of event? Were you responsible for tweaking his ear?

TGU: Well…[pause]

We were about to say "the short answer is yes," but, actually – this is very confusing – we don't know. We could take credit for it and you could never prove it wasn't us. [laughs] But actually how can that be? That's very interesting. Actually it's as though there was an external agent operating and we didn't notice.

R: Let's see how to think about this. Is there some part of you that seems more embodied than other parts of you? At your level?

TGU: You mean part of us that's closer to your end and part of us that isn't? Yeah, but it's called *you*. [laughs] We know what you mean. No, if we had done it, we would know it. And the short answer to that is it was an external agent, that we weren't really even –

Well, you see, here it goes again. By your asking the right question, you made us conscious of something we weren't really conscious of. You've done this a couple times before. If you will go back to the rubber glove analogy, this is another one of the fingers in the rubber glove that came over and tweaked our rubber glove, so to speak. Apparently. We actually don't know. We can tell you that it was not us and it was not another level of him either. [pause] You might as well say it was a helper or an angel. Not so bad an idea either, really. See, we're not the only game in town.

R: Well the reason this is very important to me is because I have had the experience now, twice, of what seemed like physical contact with people that I have thought of as disembodied. A friend of mine who died who came back and was stroking my arm in such a way as I felt like there's no way in the world I made that up.

TGU: No, that's not necessary as a hypothesis.

R: In another instance, actually, a sexual contact, by a person from the other side.

TGU: What we would like you to do now: Take a moment, relive the easier of the two experiences and feel it carefully to see, was it actually physical or was there a second-body feel to it. Now don't answer that one too fast, because at first he might have said his ear was tweaked, and when he thought about it a little and we prodded him a little, it was a second-body experience. Now we're not saying what the answer will be, but we're just saying we'll see.

R: You know, the only thing I'm absolutely sure of is that my eyes were closed and I was in a very relaxed meditative state, and I felt the stroking of the arm.

TGU: And it felt like your physical arm?

R: It felt like my physical arm to the point where I had a startled response, opened my eyes to see who was there. And I was sure who this was because it was a reflection of the way I'd been working with somebody in the hospital before they died. I can't believe it's something I made up.

TGU: Why would you bother to believe it? [laughs]

R: But my understanding of things suggests that it would be extremely difficult for an energy that has now moved out of the body –

TGU: Yes, yes, yes. You are making a basic mistake here, though. You know, in another part of yourself, that in fact all the sensations that you could ever feel are actually put together inside your mind. It's much easier to manipulate the feelings that you feel inside your mind than it is to move the hairs on your arms. In other words, there's no reason to assume that it's physically impossible for a disembodied person to make you feel like they've touched your arm, but there's two ways to do that. One way is to touch your arm, and the other way is to, how shall we say, manipulate the neurons, so that you feel the same thing because it's indistinguishable for you. You see?

R: And manipulating the neurons would be somehow different than actual touch on your skin?

TGU: Well, we won't flatly say that it would be easier. But, there's no real need to go into the speculation. If you will remember Bob Monroe in second-body state pinching someone and then her having the actual bruise from the pinch, that would give you a sense of it. Certainly you know about poltergeists and an extensive literature of what can only be described as disembodied physical contact with the body. In those cases, there's no need to postulate that it's just a change in neurons. The bruises are there.

On the other hand, though, a bruise doesn't prove anything. You know that a hypnotist can touch you with a pencil, telling you it's a hot iron, and raise a blister. So, neither one is conclusive and in a way it doesn't matter. We would say flatly there's no reason at all for you to think that it's either, on the one hand, your imagination, or on the other hand, an impossibility. Why not just go more into the question of the meaning of the contact? That would be our advice.

R: Well, I understand the importance of that. But, it's very mysterious when you say you're not responsible for the tweak of Frank's ear.

TGU: Well, yeah. *We* weren't but someone else was. That's what we realized after we had to think about that a little bit. In other words, we're not the only game in town. There's millions of spirits, millions of extensions from our side to your side, that interact with you all the time.

R: Yeah, but I was so sure about the energy of the person that was stroking my arm.

TGU: That doesn't mean you're wrong. Why should it mean you're wrong?

R: Well, I suppose you're saying, okay this is possible, this is no big deal. And I'm saying, gosh I thought it was a big deal.

TGU: [laughs] Well let's make a distinction. Psychologically it's a *tremendous* big deal.

R: Yes!

TGU: But supposing you got a telegram and the telegram told you that someone you thought was dead was alive. The *content* of the telegram is a *tremendous* big deal. The fact that you got a telegram is no big deal. That's what we're saying. Although of course, in your case, it *would* be a big deal because no one sends telegrams anymore. [they laugh] The mechanism is not a big deal. The psychological importance is a *fabulous* big deal.

R: Well, so let's go back to Frank for a minute. What was going on with this?

TGU: It was just a little bit of help. He was drifting. That's all that was going on.

R: So there's somebody looking out for him besides you.

TGU: Oh, heck yes. You all have many angels. It's just we –

It was funny, really. We're having the most amazing experiences with you. [laughs] It's like the time you had us feel emotions. We were just trying to fit ourselves into the role of having tweaked his ear and realized, no, we didn't do that. It was funny.

R: Is there anything comparable that you've done with Frank?

TGU: Well, see, we tend to do the mental influencing, and to a degree the spiritual influencing. But, no we don't do windows.

R: So, those are such different categories of things that...Is there a – I don't know how to ask this.

TGU: Well, we know where you're going with this, we think. I don't know that that's too productive. Well, it may *become* productive. Go ahead if you want to. You're saying, do we have division of labor.

R: Well, I wouldn't put it that way. But, it seems like operating on quite a different level to be in a spirit world where you've used examples like poltergeists or something like that, playing around with material objects –

TGU: It's not harder than what we're doing. After all –

R: Oh, it's not any harder.

TGU: It's not any harder, no, of course not.

R: But it seems very different. One seems much more spiritual than the other. [chuckles]

TGU: Mm-hmm, and there's your word "seems" again.

R: Right, well at our end, one of those is very much more spiritual than the other.

TGU: Well, the way *you've* categorized it. But *we* say to you that your bodies are holy. They are as holy as anything else because they are manifestations of spirit. That's all there is. There isn't anything else. [pause] We know that seems contrary to fact but –

R: I guess maybe the distinction I'm making here is that some of this seems so sort of random, and really I used the word playing around, but it does sound like that. And the other is a much more – well, incredibly powerful experience of feeling a contact. I don't mean feeling in the physical sense but I mean all that it implies, a contact with the non-embodied state. This is not a common experience in the world.

TGU: Do you think what you're doing *right now* is a common experience in the world? [laughs]

R: Well, no.

TGU: But it's more common than is admitted, for one thing. We would argue that *most* people have that experience and either wall it off from themselves or certainly wall it off from most others. Just as you're not going to go around broadcasting it either. Although, you're doing something like that by putting it out on this transcript.

R: I think maybe Frank won't type this part up.

TGU: Well, not if you ask him not to. But you see the point. You don't really have the data on that because you have such a skewed sample. Most people either will not remember or will not want to talk about it. Or not dare, let's say, talk about it. But, if you're calling *us* random and playing around, we're going to be highly insulted. [they laugh] We won't say you're wrong, but we're highly insulted. But, to be serious and go back there, remember now that tweaking of his ear –

[change sides of tape]

TGU's Puzzlement

[As Frank]: I just said it was funny to feel them not know the answer to the thing about tweaking the ear. And I just realized they probably just went to each other and said, "did you do it?" "No, I didn't do it." "Did you do it?" "No I didn't do it." But *that* part's conjecture, I didn't hear that. But there was this real puzzlement. And then they said, "well somebody else did it."

R: Yes. For you, as you had the experience, it wasn't personalized to them, is that right?

Frank: That's right. I felt the tweaking of the ear and I did sort of feel that it was a quasi-dream experience, that's what it feels like. And they're right: The only thing that it did – because I didn't pay any attention to who it was or what – I knew that it was a bringing me back and I did go back because that's what I was concentrating on. It did, in fact, re-center me on that expanded state. Sounds funny to talk about being centered in an expanded state. Oh, that was the difficulty, is what they're saying. To be centered and to be in an altered state is an acquired accomplishment. Which is why it's difficult for us because we're learning more of it.

R: It's easy to just drift, when you're in an altered state.

[As TGU]: Yes, that's why you need to be operating with a surrogate left brain, as Monroe used to say. That's why it's been so productive these past few years, because it's the first technique to be invented in your time to allow you to both stay in an altered state and function as though you were not. A nice little trick. We would suggest that he did not come to that trick by accident. And not because he was a bright boy either. [laughs] He had help.

R: He had some help. Okay, are we ready to move on to another question?

TGU: Whatever you want.

Consciousness and the Body

R: I had some questions around the issue of how our consciousness connects to the human body. When an infant is born, is consciousness already surrounding the body? And also, before the baby is born, when it's in utero, is the consciousness already surrounding the body, but not in a way that the body tunes into it?

TGU: Tell us what you mean by consciousness.

R: I mean the part of us, what seems like us, that is not attached to the physical body but seems to rise and fall with it.

TGU: But you don't mean surely a sense of yourself as an individual, because, of course, a baby doesn't have that. So, what do you mean? Do you mean like a central receiving system for the various nerves of the body?

R: That might be the way to think about it. Is it there? Is it always there? Is it gradually as in a physical body you learn to come in touch with it?

TGU: We would say the consciousness goes over *first*, the physical body forms *around* the consciousness, and the consciousness learns to operate the mechanism. Now, there's a lot more to operating the mechanism than just learning all the nerves and muscles and the conscious and subconscious processes of keeping your diving suit working. There's – this may seem strange to you – interpreting the world *only* through the senses. That's very difficult. Because as you know, your senses are reducing valves, and they let in only a small amount of what's potentially there. And the whole point of your being in a body is to reduce the input to a very –

All right, we need to say this a little carefully. The whole point of being in a body – until now – has been to reduce the flow of input to something that could *only* be experienced by whoever was in that diving suit at that time, at that place. Because, to the degree that a person could have a focused experience, it would emphasize that individuality. It would shape the flower more elaborately, shall we say. Everything we're saying is also not true, it's so over-simplified, but we're trying to make a point here. Let's do this and then we'll come back with the caveats maybe.

You form a consciousness – that is to say *we* form a consciousness – it comes over to your side. The body forms around it. The mind forms – and see, a mind *forms, using* the brain, but not *dependent* on the brain. As the consciousness learns to live within the body, it limits itself more and more to sensory inputs, by design. That's what's *supposed* to happen. What's *also* supposed to happen is that the sensory inputs and the non-sensory inputs – what you today might call left brain or right brain differences –

Some societies have been structured in such a way as to shut down one side or the other side; some have been structured so as to help both function together. You know, societies, like individuals, are flowers. They have their own characteristics. And in order to manifest those characteristics, they suppress all contradictory characteristics. It's not one that's right and one that's wrong, it's just each one is out to show one thing, to be one thing. So, in your society, you will have in some social strata, people who *only* recognize sensory input, *only* recognize logic, and live according to what they sense. Whereas, of course, other do not.

Now, you have also individuals with very restricted minds. In other words, they might be autistic, might be retarded, might be physically handicapped so that they get very little sensory data. You know, they might be blind and deaf. In each of those cases, there is a consciousness functioning with severely restricted input, and we will tell you, as we have told you before, this is not a tragedy, this is just an experiment. Or perhaps we shouldn't say an experiment: a flowering. It's there for a reason. Does that change your view of it, at all? You're aiming for something. Show us what you need –

R: I am asking a very abstract question here, which has to do with how this process works – which is my main theme in life, I guess. You said the consciousness is formed to join this new physical life.

TGU: This is primary. Consciousness comes first.

R: Yes, okay. But, it's new at that point? It's a part of your consciousness?

TGU: That's right. Let's leave aside the question of reincarnation. Whenever a part of us is determined and formed on your side with certain characteristics, we take certain bundles, and this bundle is going to develop on your side. The external circumstances are chosen for just that reason, and therefore, the body is developed *around* that potential, just as the *family*, you might say, is developed around that potential. Now, sometimes we can't get exactly what we want, and so, we have to make do. We've talked about that. "We have this characteristic and this one and this one." "Well, we'll have to put up with that one because we can't..." you know. But, within those limits, the physical body has been shaped as closely as can be to provide exactly the experience that that incoming spirit wants and needs, and intends.

It isn't the other way around, which is the way it looks to you. You all tend to think, first comes the body and the brain, and then comes the spirit to live in it. But, that's backwards.

Souls

R: *Okay. I'm not asking that right now. I'm asking, this piece of consciousness, that comes to a new body here, is this sort of pulled from the body of consciousness from your side?*

TGU: Remember we told you we can do it a couple of ways? We can form a new bundle and send it across, or we can run it through a formerly existent life. And we've never been able to clarify that exactly, but we can use that to polarize this other life coming in. And we do that more often than not, we would say, actually.

That kind of polarization gives the new life more resources to draw from, because it gives it closer connections on our side. It gives it relatives, in a way. On your side, if you have relatives, you may or may not get along with them, you may not even like them, but you have certain things in common and you can count on each other for certain things. That's a loose analogy of what we're talking about here. If the new consciousness is formed through an older consciousness that's already been here (or been elsewhere; perhaps it was on Arcturus, you know) it seems to it that it knows more. It has more to draw on. It's the equivalent of the difference between what you call new souls and old souls. An old soul has been drawn through something else. A new soul may come in totally on its own, so to speak.

R: *First time in this physical.*

TGU: Here's the funny thing. They're *both* the first time in this physical. But the one doesn't *seem* like it's the first time because it has been sort of drawn through another. To it, it appears like it is the long end of a sequence. You know, it had all these so-called past lives. But, in reality, they're *both* new, it's just that the one has been drawn *through* the other ones. We're getting closer to an analogy you might like. It's been energetically connected. Oh, we thought we were close to an electronic analogy that you could have heard. But we can't find it at the moment. Anyway, you get the idea. You don't think that's central to what you're asking, anyway.

R: No, it's just my very limited visualization powers around something like that. It's as though a body of energy is coming across in some way to get attached to a physical energy, and that body of energy may or may not have been through other similar experiences of being attached to something physical.

TGU: You know, there's no reason you shouldn't think of that body of energy coming across as a baby, in the same way that its physical body will be a baby. That might help you a little bit. Because you in general tend to think of it as a fully mature, alive, alert, all-knowing, all-seeing, all-being [they chuckle] coming in and sort of getting stuck in this little baby that can't do anything.

R: Yeah, I think there is that kind of tendency, right.

TGU: Well, if you'll think of it as a babe in the woods coming into a baby, it might be a little more accurate. Think how lost *you'll* be when you come over here, until you learn the ropes. Same thing the other way around. It not only has to function by hooking up to all the wires that run the machine; it also is a bundle of energies that is for the first time operating together. And it has to deal with the other aspects of itself and learn to act together. Just as a baby doesn't know that its left foot has any connection with its right hand until it gets used to dealing with them *as one*, so your internal self, that came over from here, had to learn to deal with itself as if it were one. If it doesn't do that profitably, then you don't crystallize and we use those materials at another time. But, if it does crystallize, they'll stay together as one. [pause] We haven't made much progress on that, we know.

R: No, I think I'm following that. Let me move on to thinking about shared –

TGU: May we say, your going from one thing to another actually works very well for us. And then bringing it up again later at another session. That works very well for us, so you needn't worry about it.

Sharing Consciousness

R: I was thinking about consciousness shared in some way. Is that what we're dealing with in telepathy or the sharing of consciousness?

TGU: Well, the same old questions. What do you mean by "shared"? What do you mean by "between whom"? You know. Make a specific example. If you and Frank shared something telepathically – ?

R: Yes. Is this a shared consciousness? Is that a way to think about the consciousness issue? We share consciousnesses?

TGU: Well, we think the easiest way – not absolutely true, but the easiest to think of – is that you share a consciousness with something on the other side; he shares a consciousness with something on the other side; they can talk and bring it to each of you. You know, you can each send a telegram to the central exchange, which sends the telegram to the other.

However, having said that, remember we're always reminding you that individuals are a convenient fiction, not an absolute. So, for you to say, "do we share a consciousness" almost begs the question, because you can't help it, in a very limited sense. Really what it amounts to is, "is there a resonance sufficiently close that another person and I respond to the same stimulus at the same time." That's one way of looking at it. Anyone knows that not only lovers, but people who live together over a period of time come to intuitively understand each other well beyond predicted range, so that one can start a sentence and the other can finish it without any clues. It's just a matter of the resonance having been established so deeply that it just sort of happens without having to be worried about. We don't think telepathy is any big deal, because it can be the resonance on your end just strictly between individuals, so-called, at your level and/or it can be both of you being in good connection with your Upstairs, which passes the message.

Books

R: Oh, there was this question about a short book that Frank had in mind, I don't know why he emphasized the "short," but, he did.

TGU: We would say it's the book that he *doesn't* have in mind. That's the problem. He awoke with it and lost it. If he *had* it in mind, he wouldn't have a problem.

R: Is there anything you want to remind him about that?

TGU: Well, you see, he's becoming aware – almost for the first time – that in writing a book one needs to think about the audience's needs, rather than his need to express what he wants to say.

For just a moment, he had a glimpse of a possibility of speaking to people in a way that they might hear, and now has temporarily lost that glimpse, and we would assume that it stays lost for the moment because it'll come back in a more formed fashion after a while. And it's not a coincidence that he forgot; more like this was a metaphorical tapping on the shoulder and saying, "pay attention, but the time is not just yet," you see.

The simplest way to look at it is, he could take the ideas that we have given you over these times, put it into a very short book, by just removing all the examples and removing everything that isn't required in order to get the point across. And it would indeed be a valuable book. But, you're not quite ready to do that because you don't yet have the thing that will twist the kaleidoscope and make it all come out just right. Okay?

R: My inclination is to stop there, unless you have something else.

TGU: This is fine with us, we're glad to talk to you anytime.

R: Okay. Thank you for this interesting discussion.

TGU: Thank you for this interesting discussion.

Session Twenty-Two
March 26, 2002

Soul Mates and Twin Souls

R: All right. Let me let me start with something Frank and I were talking about the other day: Soul mates and twin souls. I was wondering if there was anything at all to this sort of idea.

TGU: Well, there's always a nub to any idea that many people have held, but the twin soul concept and the soul mate concept are firmly rooted in this individuality that we keep repeating is overemphasized. It's like one end of a magnet, and only looking at the North Pole and not the South Pole, which is equally valid. So if you take the concept of twin soul or soul mate and you look at it from our point of view, what is there? You could say that we group the energies and send them across. So maybe we group similar energies or even identical energies and send them across; you could look at that as soul mates. But does it mean more than that?

"Twin soul" implies that it's a soul that actually split in two in the beginning and it's usually seen in a romantic context, although not invariably. But a shorter answer than usual for us would be, no, we don't think much of either concept because it's a concept that can [only] appear if you look at something as if individuals were real. And we've said more than once that individuals aren't *very* real, they're more like a convenient fiction. If you *don't* stay within that fiction, what's left of the concept of soul mate or twin soul?

R: Well, I guess with soul mate it would suggest that there are individuals who, operating in 3D Theater are somehow meant to get together in some way.

TGU: If that didn't carry the connotation that it's only a pair (again, the romantic thing slips in there usually), we wouldn't have a problem with it. Obviously, as you can see in your everyday lives, whole groups of people come in to function together and often do something very elaborate. That, in a way fulfills your definition of soul mate. But soul mates means two people, and the two people probably have a romantic relationship. Again, we think it's a totally, inappropriately concrete idea of individuals.

R: Well, the definitions of twin souls that I've heard suggest that these two energies somehow entered into the universe together, as though there is a beginning entry into the universe. And so I wanted to ask you about that. Does that happen, or is this a phenomenon without beginning, without end?

TGU: We're aware of that speculation because Frank's read about that stuff, of course, but, it's not in our experience. That isn't to say "no, it's not so," it's to say it's not in our experience. We don't know. We'll welcome you pursuing it if you wish, but we don't have any more to say about it.

R: Well, it does bring up this other question that I was asking. Is it so that something happens like an energy soul enters into this at some point? Or is it as the Buddhists seem to say, that there is no beginning and no end to this process?

TGU: We need to know what you mean. What is it that it's entering? If you're saying a soul entering 3D Theater, which we know you're not, of course, we would know the answer. But you mean a soul entering – what, reality?

R: Yes, the moving in and out of various kinds of experiences. Is there some point at which that energy is not inside a system and then comes inside a system?

TGU: Isn't it another example of the misplaced concreteness of the individual? People are saying, "there is this individual unit that is somehow created, or at least somehow enters into our whole existence here," and we don't see any example of that. Where is the unit trying to come from? Where is a unit? We see ourselves as monads, and we see you at all levels as monads, and we don't see any reason to think that there's a level, either above or below, where you run out of monads. It doesn't mean it's not true, but *we* don't see any sense of it.

R: Yes. Although, I had gone beyond where people were talking about this and asking their own questions, so I'm responsible here for the questions.

TGU: As we understand the question, it is, are new energies created from somewhere else, or do they enter our reality from somewhere else? And all we can say is that we don't have any experience of that that we know of.

R: So within your experience it's all a recycling process of this energy?

TGU: Well, if you mean recycling between physical matter and nonphysical matter –

R: Or into other dimensions, and then back into the realm in which you exist, or –

TGU: Well, we wouldn't see it that way. We would say, we all exist in all places, and what recycles, if anything, is our awareness. You know, we put more awareness here or we move more awareness over there, but there isn't really movement. It isn't like we are going from one place to another place. That's why the movement of consciousness, as was reported by Bob Monroe, going here and there, that's why it's instant. Because there's not really movement. It's a movement of consciousness. But we *all* permeate the whole place, so it's just a matter of where we want to put our attention, or the whole non-place.

Boundaries

R: Certainly it raises the question of whether there are boundaries anywhere, and you're speaking as though there are no boundaries.

TGU: Well, what would be on the other side of a boundary?

R: I don't know.

TGU: That's our response. How could you have a boundary, how could someone recognize it as a boundary if there is one? Maybe there *is* one, but how would we know that it's a boundary? It isn't like there'd be a brick wall there.

R: Anyhow, you don't know from your own experience that there is such a boundary. You haven't become aware of that, anyway.

TGU: We would put it a little more strongly and say that we feel pretty confidently that there is none. Let's put it that way. That's more or less the same as you said, but changing the emphasis to say, we're pretty sure there isn't, rather than just only that we haven't had any experience of it.

R: Because boundaries, after all, are a characteristic of physical matter, so we tend to think in that way. We don't have to think about it.

TGU: Yes. But even the boundaries that you have in physical matter are actually illusory, or perhaps we should say *relative* boundaries. The boundary between physical matter and nonphysical matter is porous, although you may not realize it.

R: I'm trying to think of what that means.

TGU: Well, there's no absolute boundary between physical and nonphysical, as you see it. We are on both sides, which means you are on both sides, and that means that –

Well, okay. We've got ourselves in a little fix here. Let's see if we can get out of it. Remember we said you could look at physical matter reality as a wok, where Focus 35 as you call it, is at the edge, and it gets denser and denser in toward the middle, and we reminded you that mental states are still part of physical matter? But mental states are also part of our side – from a certain point of view. And so the closer you look at where the actual boundary is, the more it dissolves into ambiguity. There's not a hard and fast boundary, really. It's more like you go from where it's 60/40 in one place to 40/60 right next to what you're seeing.

R: Yes. The problem with that analogy is it suggests that there is an edge there somewhere.

TGU: Rather than quite an edge we'd say, a difference in emphasis. So that when you dream, you access the other side. And – remember the time we experienced the emotion with you? We were accessing *your* side. There's no hard and fast boundary between either, it's just we each have our center of gravity.

Now, it's convenient for speech and thought to *see* things as boundaries, just as we often said to you, you don't have a shoulder, you just have an area of your body that you *refer to* as a shoulder, but it's not quite as concrete as your language leads you to think it is. Same thing here. In fact, this sheds light on what you asked a while ago about the differences between us on our side. It's really a difference of emphasis. At any point between two different pieces of emphasis, you could draw a boundary. But you could draw it at other places, too, and it would be just as valid and no more. And no less.

R: I don't want to get caught up with physical analogies, but if we thought about something like the wok and at some point with the boundary not being manifest, there's something beyond the wok. Is that more like moving into another wok-shaped phenomenon or is it more like just extending the sides of the wok indefinitely?
TGU: More like the second, but even more like attenuating them so that they cease to be solid metal and become porous metal, or a metal that's half air, so to speak. Again, a physical analogy, but –

R: And yet you were saying within that realm, there are distinctions to be made.

TGU: Yes, but they're all *relative* distinctions. They're as distinct as individuals are, but no more. In other words, they are descriptions of convenience. So, what you say is Focus 12. There are no boundaries on either side of that, it's just that the center of gravity of a certain kind of attention can be called Focus 12, but you'll never find a sharp edge to it.

R: So in extending those boundaries we'd be thinking about a concept of moving to 43 and 58, if that kind of extension made any sense?

TGU: If it made any sense, and we'd find that 48 and 53 and all were so little physical matter and so much whatever we are that you couldn't really recognize them. That's why it sort of stops where it does. Now, maybe at another point in your gyrations, you'll extend it, you know, and you'll have Focus 100. And that won't mean that reality has changed, but that what is convenient for you to group under certain terms has changed. Another way of looking at that is, your ability to perceive differences and similarities will have extended itself to that point. We know that's wordy, but we're trying to be a little bit more precise.

R: I guess this goes back to thinking about a time when the universe maybe didn't exist, where the origins of the universe or something like that. That was part of my last question. Do those kind of boundaries make any sense?

TGU: We're glad to hear you see that immediately. Exactly. It's still a boundary, isn't it?

Time As a Dimension

R: So, okay. So then my question is meaningless, but I was trying to think about why in creation of this sort, time would be put into the picture at all. Was there a point of creation in which time didn't exist as a dimension?

TGU: Are you referring to time as you experience it in 3D Theater?

R: Well, in any sense, the way you experience it or the way we experience it.

TGU: Well, we are very pleased that you picked that dimension immediately, that in fact a beginning and an end is a barrier, a boundary, just as the brick wall at the end of the universe would be. You do understand abstractly, although we don't think you can really internalize it, that time is really a means of perception as space is.

It's as hard for us to answer that question as it would be for you if we were to say, "was there ever a time when the earth had height and depth but no breadth?" You know, without time, you don't have it all there, so how could that be? Now, that's not to say that time is what it appears to you, and you already know that it is not. But if you look at it as a dimension that organizes reality – and here we *can* use your time-space analogy, it'll work well enough – you have three dimensions of space and one dimension of time that you're aware of all the time. That is, every-body's aware of those unless they're –

R: Well, some parts of the globe still don't think in terms of time in the sense we do.

TGU: No. But they must *live* in time. They have no choice. We were thinking the only one who wouldn't, perhaps, be aware of the perception of time might be someone brain damaged. But a normally functioning person must, no matter how they *conceive of* space and time, live in those dimensions. There's no way around it. Just as you live in other dimensions without being aware of them. Anything that lives in *any* dimension must live in *all* dimensions. You just couldn't not do it. That doesn't mean you're *aware of* living in all dimensions. How could you live in a flat world that didn't have height? You see? Even if the height were 1/1000th of one millimeter, it would be height. Do you see what we're saying? So –

R: Once you've bought into the 3D thing, of course, that's true.

TGU: Well, we're using the 3D analogy because it's what you can really *feel*, but see, where we are it isn't like 3D – hmm. All right. Wait a minute.

This is going to be very difficult to explain. We'll take a shot at it. You mustn't think that we, on our side, don't have dimensions just the same as you do. The distinction is, we experience it all differently because we don't do it in time-slices or space-slices – but it's the *same* reality. It's the same place, or non-place, because there's no other place that there is. [pause]

We're trying to think of an analogy that would work in 3D Theater and we're not coming up with one. We're looking for something that would look one way to one person and another way to a person of more perceptive ability or at a higher level. Let's see. [pause]

It's absolutely true that we don't have four dimensions that you experience *in the way that you experience them*, but just as every one of you has to live in all the dimensions there are, so do we, and that's going to be really hard to explain. [laughs]

R: Yes. It's hard for us not to visualize you, in some sense, like a big computer in the sky, or in the library, or the Akashic records of some form that is a document –

TGU: Well, but see, all of those things have enfolded in them an intuition of dimensions. That intuition isn't wrong. It's just – it might take us a while to find a way to make it a little more vivid, but it's a *good* intuition. We *do* have dimensions. We *do* have duration, as we've said more than once. And the major difference is we're not dragged along by this concept of the moment, and we don't have too many consequences. [pause]

And the third difference, of course, is that we're all interrelated consciously more than you are. Well, let's go on to something else and come back to that whenever you wish.

Creation

R: Okay. Behind this question was the question, is this all an experiment of some sort? Has this all been put together to see what would happen?

TGU: "This all" means – our side as well as your side?

R: Well, you could look at it either way. Just take our side for the moment, it seems somewhat less abstract. I've had trouble with the abstractness once I get in to try to write about this.

TGU: It depends on how much you mean by "experiment." It should be clear to you that the physical matter universe is *created*. It didn't happen by accident, because there *aren't* any accidents. And anything that's created presumably was created for a purpose. But when you say "as an experiment" it implies a lot of insight into the motives of the creator. We don't know where that insight would come from.

R: Okay. But if there is a creator, one has to attribute some sort of motivation.

TGU: Well, yes. But there's a difference between attributing it and getting the *right* attribution, and, we're not confident that we would know what was in God's mind, if that's what you mean, using God as the creator. And we recognize – and in fact we approve of – the distinction between the two, that not every creator is God, given that you are creators yourself, and we're creators ourselves, and given that God as an idea has so many impossible characteristics imposed on it that for your time it doesn't work – although there was a time when it worked, and there may be a time again when it works. To say "experiment" sounds to us as to say, "we did this to find out either whether our hypothesis would be verified or maybe just to find out what would happen." That's the implication of the word experiment to us.

R: Well, I've gotten a sense from you that there are so many different ways in which this could be put together. I called it an experiment not in the sense of keeping track scientifically of exactly what's happening, but more that since there were an infinite number of voices that could be put together, calling it an experiment has to do with the notion that one is in some way keeping track of the various components of what all is happening, knowing that those components could all be different.

TGU: Well, that'll confuse [things] at the moment. What do you mean when you say, "it could all be done so many ways?"

R: Well, you've said there are an infinite number of realities. And –

TGU: But they're not alternative, they all exist.

R: They all exist. Yes. All right.

TGU: In other words, it isn't like there *could be* any of an infinite number of realities. We're saying that there is.

R: There is in fact. And as far as you know, there's no one keeping track of these in some comparative way.

TGU: Hmm. That's a new thought to us. *Maybe* there is. *We're* not it. [laughs] Why would one do that, we wonder. It seems to us that the one who's keeping track of it is all of us – "all" including you – but, really we don't know. We will say, by the way, just as an aside, we really dislike the word infinite, which is infinitely overused in your infinitely scientific world.

R: I meant it in a sense that one couldn't count them.

TGU: Yes. Well, that's the point that we're about to make. There's a difference between infinite as it is used and the word uncountable or innumerable. There is a serious difference between innumerable and infinite, and we're not accusing *you* of misusing it, but we're saying that we have a real problem with the way "infinite" is used. It really clouds scientific thought in your time. There will be a time when that word is not used anymore because it'll be seen how much damage it does. There's a huge difference between innumerable and infinite. And we would argue to you that infinite is a slight of hand. It's not that it has anything to do with what you are doing. [laughs] It's just that this is a convenient time for our editorial.

As to whether or not someone's keeping track – other than all of us together – probably that's true. We've been thinking about that while we've been talking. Probably that's true, because we often use the analogy of the kaleidoscope, and it changes all the time and we can't swear to it, but probably it's true because someone's looking through a kaleidoscope. And we think that's a very good insight on your part. Something was created, and something created what was created, presumably at least to watch it if not doing anything else for it. It's not something that occurred to us, though. [pause] You may notice that we're a less self-reflective bunch than you might have expected, and if this demonstrates that we're not all-knowing and not all-anything, then it's all for the good.

R: I haven't had the difficulty with that concept that Frank has had, apparently, but I don't want to hold you responsible for knowing everything.

TGU: Well, that remark is made as much for the readers as it is for you as an individual – but we *will* say that we're highly insulted that you don't think we know everything. [they laugh]

The Big Bang Idea As a Boundary

R: We're talking such big subjects tonight. I'm sort of ambivalent about that, but I wanted to go back to just pin down something that happened before. You've rejected the Big Bang Theory, because of the possibility that someone thought that the universe had been created out of nothing. So you weren't rejecting the idea of the Big Bang, but simply that there had to be something there before that? Have I –

TGU: No. We wouldn't quite put it that way. We would just say that really it's just – again, the whole idea of the Big Bang is a boundary, is it not? There is this boundary in time before which there was either nothing – and they seemed to look at it as nothing –

R: Well, it was a tiny, tiny, tiny little speck.

TGU: [laughs] It's so ridiculous. [they laugh] We're sorry, but it's so ridiculous. It's –

Really, we think that Bob Monroe's explanation is closer than science's, and that is to say, the emitter –

Now, this is an analogy, you understand, but the mechanism from a larger dimension projects a smaller dimension. If you look at it one way, you could say that it projects it and there's a time edge. If you look at it a different way, you could say it projects it as a time and a space edge. It's really not a meaningful distinction, but – be that as it may.

The Big Bang *seems* to be scientific because it spins elaborate mathematical rules and elaborate mathematical descriptions. But at the end of it, you come to a totally theoretical and totally stupid conclusion that there is a singular event made up of a singular and unobservable process. Regardless what it results in, the singularities are what should demonstrate the incredibility of the theory, and will. We're not really exercised about it, but we're just saying we don't believe in the Big Bang. The universe – every universe, any given universe, especially 3D Theater – was, indeed, spun from a higher set of dimensions. Let's put it that way. That's not at all true, but there's nothing that we could say that would be true. It was spun from something else that includes it. That spinning means that at one point it wasn't there and then it *was* there. So at least it was there nascently and then grew. That's *not* the same thing as saying it grew out of nothing, it's saying it grew out of another dimension.

R: I don't know that you would find Big Band theorists arguing with that.

TGU: Well, we suspect that they would argue strongly whether there were other dimensions beyond the ones they are trying to account for. However, if they wouldn't, that's good.

R: There's nothing about that perspective that excludes other big things going on.

THE SPHERE AND THE HOLOGRAM

TGU: That's right. In fact, we would argue if there's *any*, there has to be more than one. Now, from your point of view, there will only be one because you're only living in one universe at a time. But from a non-physical point of view, there will be others because every time we spin out a different place, there it is. But – they're not spun out of nothing. And they're not exactly spun out of no time. Well, it's difficult. Ask the question, we'll try and answer it.

R: I'm trying to think what the alternative is to thinking about it in that way. The universe seems, from whatever scientific evidence that's obtainable, to be changing all the time. That is, there's movement involved. You can argue for the unreality of physical matter but whatever is being measured there has that level of reality in it, that is measurable. And one explanation for all of this movement is the Big Bang.

TGU: Well, that's right. Well, that's one explanation.

R: What's another explanation?

TGU: Well – [pause] wow!

Movement – apparent movement – is, of course, a function of time. You know, that's tautological. If there's no time, there's no movement. Or if there's no *perception* of time, there's no *perception* of movement. Science doesn't have a mechanism, it has no ability to measure anything beyond the physical using scientifically approved methods. Agreed?

R: Yes. Although there are those who argue now that it's possible to make some measurements of the realms we're interested in, but I wouldn't argue with that for the moment.

TGU: Well, we need an approach here. Let's see. [pause]

It seems to you that all of you – each other, and yourself, your animals and plants and everything around you – move. It seems indisputable. And if we were to say to you that you *weren't* moving, you'd be perplexed. And yet we say to you that *nothing* moves. What happens is that your consciousness moves from one created moment world to the next. And you sort of fill the lines in between the two and conclude that you have moved and you have observed movement.

And we would say to you that's certainly *relatively* true enough, because you can function and you can measure all the movement and all that, but that *absolutely* it's not true at all. *Absolutely* it's not true. *Relatively* it's true. You can't tell that the sun revolves around the earth or the earth revolves around the sun. They're both equally partly accurate and partly inaccurate. After all, who's going to determine what's the center, you see. But that's a bias, that's a diversion. [pause]

For you to see these galaxies receding from each other, which is inferred by Red Shift and other very indirect, but ingenious methods, for you to infer that they are moving away from each other, you need to make certain assumptions, among them that time is what it appears to be; that space is what it appears to be. That is, some assume the entire universe is expanding, and the universe is the skin and the suns or the stars are various marks on the skin. As the skin expands, the distance between the marks gets greater regardless whether the marks are moving or whether they're just on a skin that's moving. But what if they're not moving and the skin isn't moving either? What if the *appearance* of motion comes because you're moving to – [pause]

That's not going to work. Go back. Point your question somewhat differently, if you can.

R: Well, I don't know that I can go ahead with that. Because I can give you all a lot of the indicators that we use that motion is occurring. And if you're saying that's not so, then I don't know what to do with that.

TGU: No. No. Give us – point us to what your concern is. You want to know – ?

R: Well, because the Big Bang Theory has been opposed as a theory primarily by the creationists.

TGU: Well, we wouldn't say that's true at all. In fact, Frank's reading a book about it right now, it talks about plasma theory. And plasma theory – to the limited extent that that *he* understands it – says that the universe is somewhere between steady-state and fluctuating, but it isn't created and it isn't destroyed, it just always is, and it's always in a state of change. Creationists should actually be in *favor* of the Big Bang Theory, if they knew it, because, of course, there's creation out of nothing.

R: Well, the creation was out of God.

TGU: Well, same thing. God created the world out of nothing according to them. Well, that's quite compatible with their beliefs.

R: Well, I mean, I don't think there's an argument about how –

TGU: *Ex nihilo.*

R: He doesn't need to explain himself to us to say how he did it. But my feeling about it is that this is a topic – I started out earlier saying I didn't really want to get into abstractions because they're too hard to write about.

TGU: That's right. But, you know, what you *could* do that would be productive for you and interesting for us, is find from time to time, anything more or less concrete that bears on it, and say "how does that relate to the question of . . ." You see, because it's very pointed that way. And it'll bring us the possibility, anyway, of grounding some of it. At the moment, we're floundering, as you hear.

R: Well, the only thing that we've got here, as far as I know, is that we've put new equipment on the Hubble Telescope and the telescope sees farther back into time, closer and closer to that time of the Big Bang Theory. Implied in that is the suggestion that ultimately it's going to be possible to move very close to that moment, those first three seconds that they have hypothesized.

TGU: If we had physical money, we'd lay a bet on that one, [laughs] because all that still implies *one* mode of time, *one* reality, *one* –

R: It doesn't in any way imply there isn't another reality.

TGU: Well, not directly, but woven into it is the assumption that there *was* a time, and there *is* a present, and there *will be* the future. And in some ways that doesn't matter, and in a couple of ways it *does* matter. If you're using an advanced telescope to find light as far away as you can, and you're inferring that this is the universe as it was way back then when that was sent, that's true within those assumptions. But if you destroy those assumptions, or step outside of them, what have you shown? You see? If you assume that, in fact, all moments of time still exist, that all moments of time, in all probabilities, in all dimensions, still exist, your telescope is still only going to show you the one. The data won't change. But the *meaning* of the data will change.

R: We can only measure this *one.*

TGU: That's where we began. We said your scientists are limited to –

R: I'm still wanting to change the subject.

TGU: Well, we haven't been very good on this one, so we'll gladly change the subject. But we do encourage you sometime, whenever some seemingly unrelated subject comes up and you get the inclination to connect it, there might be a reason you get that inclination. And go ahead and do it, and we'll see what happens.

[change sides of tape]

Time Travel

R: Well, the first thing that comes up is the issue of time travel. Is this something that you foresee as a possibility?

TGU: Well, you have to tell us what you mean by time travel. If you mean traveling in your mind to another reality, you're already doing it. We don't mean fantasy, we mean actually doing it. But if you mean taking your body and moving your body to another time, and having it function as an ordinary body, how would you do that?

R: Well, you'd have to deconstruct and reconstruct.

TGU: Well, there are a lot of serious problems with that. You're taking your mass out of one place, one time, and adding it to another time. And you say, "well, that doesn't make any difference. Next to what the world weighs, I don't weigh much!" But –

The only words that come to mind are inappropriate movement. We continue to say there is no movement, and that would be movement, but how are we going to explain the difference between your walking around or flying or doing whatever it seems like you do on the one hand, and *really* moving, which would be to take yourself physically –

It would be like – it would be like – it would be like – [pause] Well, we can't think of an example, but –

R: Well, maybe it wouldn't have to require that. If you think about the fantasies that have been written about traveling to places within the universe that we now can't imagine traveling to because of the time dimension. It would take too long to get there.

TGU: Well, now that's kind of a different thing.

R: Then that depends on the creation of something that will move, equipment or bodies or something, through space in a quite different way than we ever thought about.

TGU: [pause] Your assumption perhaps is that space is this extension of a uniform surface. And that's not true. Your assumption is that you move subject to the laws of gravity and electrodynamics alone, and *that's* not true. And your assumption is that your mental state has very little to do with how you're transported, and that's *very much* not true. And we don't know whether we'll be able to explain any of that, but we'll look at it.

When you travel, you're traveling through space dimensions and a time dimension, unless you're traveling instantaneously, which you cannot do. Agreed?

R: Mm-hmm.

TGU: Now, you *can* travel instantaneously with your mind – that's the only way – because you're not *moving*. But if you're trying to move – [laughs] (Just for the record, we'll say again, there is no motion, but we recognize you *have to* see it as motion.) If you're trying to move, you have to move through space *and* time. The more you move in some directions, the less you have to move in another direction to get the same result. Agreed?

R: Could we get specific about it? Suppose we wanted to go to Alpha Centauri.

TGU: Okay. Let's do it.

R: And starting from where we are now and what we know now, we don't know how to do that.

TGU: If you travel at the speed of light, let's say it'll take you four years. And so your question becomes how to get there in less than four years, or how to get there at all, or what?

R: Does your question imply that the trick here is just to think in terms of speed? I mean is this –

TGU: No. No. It doesn't really. Supposing you wanted to go to Alpha Centauri and arrive tomorrow, the easy way to do it would be to travel in the right direction for minus four years at the speed of light. Minus four years would correlate with the four years it took you to get there and you'd be there tomorrow.

R: But we have no idea how to move at the speed of light.

TGU: Well, supposing you wanted to travel at $1/10^{th}$ of the speed of light, it would then require going minus-forty years. And then that would balance out the forty years, and you'd be there tomorrow. And how are you going to go minus forty years? We're not about to tell you. We can't tell you, but just if you look at forty miles east as being minus forty miles west, could you?

R: It seems like it would be eighty miles.

TGU: Well, all right. But starting from ground zero, if you go forty miles to the east, that's minus forty miles if you're counting it to the west.

R: If you were counting it from here it's minus forty. If you count it from forty miles west it's eighty miles.

TGU: Well, yes. That's right, but that's forty miles away. You see, starting from your base point, if you're going somewhere, wherever you go in one direction, it's that many minuses in the opposite direction. That's all we're saying. Right now, you don't have any way of doing that. When you do have a way of doing that, then you will find yourself with the functional equivalent of time travel, and it will sort of *be* time travel. But what it'll really be is travel in eight dimensions instead of in three, you see. There are three dimensions of space and one dimension of time, and they each have a correlate. So you could look at it like three plus dimensions and three minus dimensions, and one time dimension and one minus time dimension. If you can travel in all eight – that is to say if you have eight vectors from the central spot and you can go in any direction you need to go to – you can either get somewhere in no time, more or less, or you can go a vast amount of time in no space or anything in between the two.

Only conceptual, we can't do any better than that. We're not technicians either, but this is the way you're going to do it. When you live on Mars, you won't be taking two years to get from earth to Mars, nor did you. Do you remember?

R: Well, yes. I mean I remember the experience.

TGU: And the experience was how long, or were you busy censoring it to make it probable?

R: Well, I'm working out the details and all. It's about a weekend.

TGU: Well, you can't get from earth to Mars in a weekend, can you? But they *can*. They did. Will. However you want to look at it. So that should tell you something. You *know* they didn't accelerate – well, you don't know, but anyway, but take our word for it. That's what you're going to wind up doing. It'll be child's play. Complicated child's play, but how hard is it to use the telephone? But it was not simple to *invent* the telephone. We're still a little off the beam here, this isn't quite what you asked. You asked about how you get to Alpha Centauri.

R: I asked you about the whole notion of time travel and whether that is something that's worth thinking about, and I guess you've said, yes, it is, and that actually we will be able to think up the kinds of inventions that could get us to some place that seems impossibly distant at this point.

TGU: That's right. And "impossibly distant" can be in time as well as in space. In other words, if you go in the negative direction long enough, you would be in the age of the dinosaurs. [pause] You see, here's the trick. All times and all spaces exist. They didn't cease to exist. That being so, there's a way to get from one to the other. Now, right now you can do it easily with your mind, because it's just a matter of moving your consciousness, because you exist in them all. But if you want to complicate matters and drag your body along – and there are reasons to do that – then you've got to find a way to navigate between them. We can't give you blueprints.

R: Okay. It seems like in previous discussions we've incorporated the idea of parallel universes, although I'm not sure that we have. We've talked about other universes as a possibility, innumerable –

TGU: Yes. Yes. And we would say the difference between innumerable universes and parallel universes is, again, a special example of that same fallacy that keeps coming in about misplaced concreteness of individuality. Someone who believes that this universe is real can stretch to believe in *another* universe, or maybe five universes, or maybe a hundred universes. And those are parallel. But once you've realized that they're innumerable, parallel becomes almost like small thinking, you know.

R: It's like twin souls.

TGU: It's like training wheels. The idea is a training wheel to stretch your mind to the point of realizing that there are, not infinite, but innumerable universes. Or, another way of looking at it, one universe with innumerable permutations. Exactly the same statement.

Suicide

R: [pause] We've talked to some extent about what happens when we drop the body. I was wondering what suicides might impact, if anything at all.

TGU: Might impact where?

R: In the process of dropping the body and moving to your realm?

TGU: Well, there are several overlapping but really different things that are encompassed in that word, and we just want to sort them out a little bit.

A suicide who kills himself or herself to save others or because it's an impossible situation and then they're trying to help, or because they misjudge their strength and they accidentally kill themselves – all of those things are different.

We assume you're talking about the suicide of the person who, for one reason or another, decides they don't want to live anymore, and they're not going to. We would argue that that is invariably destructive to the person's mission. Well, not invariably, but mostly, because when you want to pull the plug, *we* can pull the plug, and we will. And we will have a better view of "when" than you will on your end. Now, having said all that, we're going to take it back, because you have as much right to make that choice as any other choice, and in some lives, that is the appropriate end, and *we're* doing it, so to speak. So you also can't judge. That is to say, *you* [can't]. *We'll* judge all the time [laughs], but we have better data.

If a person, out of despair or anger or desire to punish others or whatever, chooses self-destruction, in defiance, shall we say, of guidance, of the higher self, of the rest of him or her, that has consequences. If that is the natural flower of the life, that has other consequences that are not nearly as drastic. Remember we said every death is a birth? Well, so when you kill yourself on this side, you're born in a certain amount of trauma on the other side – well, that's not the right way to put it. [pause]

It isn't so much the manner of arrival that's the problem, to the degree that there is a problem, as that the person went across to experience something and then aborted it. And yet, you could argue they made a choice, and that's what they went over there to choose.

R: Okay. Well, then, let me ask you about some distinctions like what we've experienced now, particularly of the Palestinian suicide bombers.

TGU: Well, they're not killing themselves to get out of life, primarily. They're killing themselves in order to kill others. They shouldn't be regarded so much as suicides as, shall we say, soldiers on a suicide *mission*. That sounds like playing with words, but motivation is the important thing there. Not that their motivation is *better*, but that it's different. Their motivation is to inflict damage, and the only way they can do that is by killing themselves. Their motivation is not, primarily, to escape life. That's the distinction.

R: To accomplish what they consider to be a more worthwhile goal.

TGU: With the *caveat* that, of course, there could be a tremendous amount of self-hatred as well as other kinds of hatred in there, too. And so that might be okay with them. But, yes.

R: I can see that there are a lot of distinctions one could make here. I'm asking over-all about the implications, and maybe there aren't any general implications, for the soul that's moving over.

TGU: Well, we don't see it much different from the soldier who's killing someone else.

R: So a person who is in tremendous pain asks the doctor to overdo the morphine, that's –

TGU: That's another case. That's a case of someone attempting to escape, as you say, intolerable pain, making a choice to do it. Again, the distinction is motive. It's one thing to escape *emotional* pain, a second to escape *physical* pain, a third to attempt to make others suffer, a fourth to escape the burden of choice. You could continue and every case really is different. In fact, we're going to back off our initial statement because the more we look at it the more we're saying, "well, it's a choice. It's your choice."

R: Well, you said that people who do that have, by definition, not accomplished their purposes in this life and somehow must face up to that by doing it over again, or whatever the implications are –

TGU: Well, that's rooted in a way of seeing things that think there's only one reality. That same person had *other* realities in which they *didn't* kill themselves, you know. In other words, there's that whole gamut. They died in childbirth all the way through they died at age 612, and everything in between. So to say that one particular iteration had to be relived, is based in an idea that says it's got to be done sequentially and there's only one running of it, and that's not correct. [pause]

Besides, it also implies there's only one correct mission, so to speak; one correct termination of the mission. Who's to say that Abraham Lincoln who *didn't* become president and instead, was a prairie lawyer and died in 1882 was less of a successful life for Abraham Lincoln than the one who was killed in 1865?

R: Okay. So that leads on to my next question. Is there a relationship between your idea about a person that's crystallized and a suicide mission? Is there some implication in suicide there?

TGU: No. No. Because there's too many possible motives. You'll find that almost all of humanity's religious and philosophical ideas are dependent upon their conception of the realities about time and space and other dimensions, other alternative realities.

Seth and TGU As Phenomena

R: Frank has asked what's the relationship between the process going on here and the process that was going on with Jane Roberts and Seth. Is there anything overall that you can say about that?

TGU: Well, sure. Jane Roberts had the ability to move herself out of the picture – that is to say, she had the ability to change her receptivity so that the energy that came in was not conducive to the continuation of her consciousness at that moment. Do you see? It was too discontinuous from an ordinary consciousness. She had the ability without fear to move aside, so to speak, and allow that energy to speak.

Seth, being purposeful, conscious, and intent on making certain ideas known, had an agenda to write books. He came in with all of that and, of course, set it up so that he had his willing assistants, Jane and her husband Robert. He then dictated those books and in the interstices of doing that, talked to them in an encouraging manner to assist them in their own lives, not only as a friendly gesture, but as almost a sort of payment for the work they were accomplishing.

But it would not be accurate to say that Seth was always there with Jane, because the difference in brain waves – that's a metaphor, but take it as a metaphor – was too great for both to be present at the same time, you see.

Now, what happens in a case like that, as happened with Edgar Cayce, is that over time, there's a sort of an accommodation, and it becomes relatively easier for the two to coexist consciously. And that becomes a matter of just how far apart they were when they started and how long it goes on and how willing they are, and other things. In Frank's case none of that applies, to his own initial confusion, because the difference between us and him is *nonexistent*. Well, that's not quite true; it's *more or less* true. There's so much overlap that the non-overlap is relatively small. So that when we say we're always here, we're always here. And when *he* says during these sessions, that *he's* always here, *he's* always here.

It's true, as you have observed, that he's not here in the sense that he thinks he is: that is to say, he hears, he listens, he participates, he throws in his own phrasing and things, he's actively participating, but his emotional makeup is slightly altered during the course of this. First of all, reactions are suppressed. And we don't mean that we're suppressing them, but the nature of the material, the nature of our interaction suppresses several aspects of his own personality. They aren't gone, but they're just not active.

So we don't come forth with a book to dictate, but in a way the only reason that Seth needed to do that was because Jane couldn't just sit down and write it, whereas Frank *can*, because we're right there, and the more receptive he can be, the easier it is for us to come through, the less need for these concrete distinctions.

So we would say those are the major differences between the two cases. Oddly enough, there's not much difference between his attitude and Jane Roberts's attitude. Her initial assumptions were quite different from his, but their attitudes and willingness and curiosity are quite similar, and necessary.

R: So Frank, if he wanted, could move completely aside and let some other energy come through?

TGU: Well, [pause] we doubt it, because you're asking him to be unaware of too much. The connection with us is strong enough that he won't lose the consciousness in the way that someone who is not consciously connected with the other side will lose consciousness if the energy pattern shifts. Can you see that?

R: But it's not just a matter of willingness to participate, but –

TGU: No. It's really a matter of, among other things, brain chemistry which is not an accident of course. [pause] If you're going to play the piano, you'd better have ten fingers. If you're going to play the piano *brilliantly*, it helps to have large hands than can encompass a greater amount. And if you're really going to play it brilliantly, it helps to have fast reflexes, accurate nerves, you know about that. So we're just saying willingness is absolutely essential, but not enough.

R: Is there anything special or different about energies like Edgar Cayce or Jane Roberts? When they move across, do they move into any special roles in your realm?

TGU: [pause] Well, if you have a very talented piano tuner, he doesn't have to continue to be a piano tuner all his life, but it's a waste of time to have him change oil in a car, so to speak. When you have a crystallized personality that has learned to hold that balance so clearly, it's a wonderful thing to shine other energies through, to help them get the abstract pattern that they will then have to animate. This is why when one person has become something it's easier for later people to become it. We can shine it from the personal. That can only be done by experience. The experience needn't be *external* experience, but it needs to be experience.

R: Does this have them participating in a particular role on your side, as the energy that moved across, or some variation of them?

TGU: They would participate in that they've acted those experiences and we can taste that. And they would be used, although not exactly participating, if we used them as a lens through which to shine other energies so as to give them the knack of putting it together in a way that'll function, you see.

R: I'm still not clear whether you're saying that that ability then exists in your realm, or that it's only resting in that bundle of energy as its functioning there?

TGU: Well, it's kind of a non-distinction really, because anything that exists on our side exists both in one place where it came from – you know, on your side – and also shared all through us. So again, be careful of the space analogy, like it's in one place so it can't be somewhere else. [pause]

Well, we can't think of a good spatial analogy, but if you go onto the other side it's true that you're an individual with that experience. It's also true that we as a whole have access to that experience. It's not the distinction that it might seem. It's both.

R: Well, is there some form of Edgar Cayce and Jane Roberts existing in your realm, or when their personality changed, have they moved on?

TGU: Remember, we said there's no movement over here, so they never left when they were on earth.

They no longer exist on your side, but they're still where they were on our side. But remember we said that on the one side, there is all of the personality that was formed and lived on your side. And that's *here*, but the underlying energy that went into that form and helped create that form is not the same thing, and it is not fixed. So it's back here. It's back here but it's not here bound to that form. It's bound to that form in 3D Theater, not afterwards.

So it depends on who you mean. If you mean the underlying spirit that for a while was Edgar Cayce – that spirit is wherever it is, it's not at all bound to Edgar Cayce. But if you mean the pattern, the crystal that was *formed* as Edgar Cayce, yes, that's still here, and yes, that's accessible, just as your friend Dave.

Difference in Questions

R: [pause] I think that's all the questions I have this evening. Do you have anything else you'd like to tell me about?

TGU: Well, this was a difficult session for you, and a difficult session for us, actually. And we think that the difficulty itself is useful in demonstrating the difference in what can be brought across depending on the nature of questions.

Some questions are inherently easier to be explained, even if they're quite different from what you expect, and even if they're quite removed from your ordinary perceptions. And other categories of questions get vague or *non*-answers, and it's hard for you to see why there should be the difference between those two kinds of questions. And we will say that as we explore that a little, the difference between the kinds of questions should become a little clearer, although that doesn't mean we'll get you clearer answers to certain kinds of questions.

We're looking at a boundary between the kinds of questions that can be *somewhat* answered and the kinds of questions that really can't be very well answered at this time. Now, when your consciousnesses are different, when the veil is thinner, that's another story. But at this moment, certain kinds of things aren't going to come across very well, if at all, just as eighty years ago, the whole ratio was different and there were many more things that couldn't come across. [pause]

We *do* appreciate your continued efforts here and we wish we could do better than we can at answering some of the questions that you have, because we recognize that the questions come out of a sincere desire to know. And all we can say is, we'll do our best, and you do your best, and we'll see what we come up with. Until one of us gets tired. [laughs]

R: Yes. Well, I sometimes feel that I get the answers and the difficulty is because I'm not understanding enough about what I'm asking. But there are other times when the material's at such a degree of abstraction that it's very hard to place it in the terms that we've been using.

TGU: Well, you're giving us too much credit there. It's also that sometimes you catch us thinking. In fact, you *set* us thinking, And we start saying one thing, and we realize that's not right. Why isn't that right? And then we correct it some. And sometimes at the end of an answer, we're at 90 degrees or 180 degrees away from where we were when we started. You wouldn't think that would be possible, but sometimes you catch us thinking. The one with suicide actually was a good example. [pause]

It's like we were *feeling* our way to the answer. No, it was like we had the answer, and then we were attentive to the successive feeling that said, "no, you're not taking this into account, or this or this or this." And as we paid attention to those hues, our stance shifted. That's all we can tell you at the moment. That's the process. So sometimes you catch us thinking.

[Although we didn't fully realize it at the time, this session brought our initial series of explorations to an end. Perhaps we required some time to absorb the concepts we had been given. For whatever reason, in the next few years we did many more sessions (including a set of 10 in the Monroe Institute's black box in 2004), but we never again did them on a regular schedule.]

Conclusion

by Frank DeMarco

Process

When I was young I didn't understand why Edgar Cayce had so many perplexities, hesitations, and fears about what he did. It seemed clear to me that he had been given a special gift: Why not just use it and rejoice in it? Why second-guess it all the time? Why wonder about its accuracy? Cayce used to say, apparently in a sort of teeth-clenched way, that if one child was ever hurt by the things that came through when he was in trance, that was the end of the whole business for him. I used to wonder, why? So it has been interesting to participate in this process from the inside; to exchange ideas and analysis with Rita, a trained psychologist who also knows *from her own experience* what I'm talking about. And it has been interesting to see how little of the reasons for my own perplexities, hesitations, and fears I have been able to communicate clearly, even to her. It gives me a whole different perspective on Edgar Cayce as a man.

I see more clearly now why Cayce did *not* see himself as a gifted seer, a favored communicant with the other side. Cayce was saved by his own humility. He knew the reasons for his own perplexities, hesitations, and fears. He was well aware how little he knew about what he was doing. He knew that every time he went into a trance, the information that came would come from somewhere beyond his control, which meant he had no way to filter it. The information came from someone (but he didn't know who) and it would be stated with great confidence (but he didn't know if the confidence was warranted) and it would supposedly be given with benevolent intent (but, as he didn't know who was providing it, he was forced to hope that was true). What's more, the information came to him while he was in trance, so he didn't even get to hear it as it came through. Talk about taking things on faith! No wonder he was worried! Plus, of course, his journey was so long. By the end of his life in 1945 he had come to integrate a lot of what his voice had said from trance, but in the early days it must have seemed to him a mixture of blasphemy and nonsense.

When I was young, reading about Edgar Cayce, I thought of him as one of a group of special men and women, set apart from ordinary men and women, who somehow had abilities most of us didn't have and didn't expect to have. Therefore I couldn't see him as a man, not really. Oh, I read that he had a wife and children and an external career as a photographer, and I read that he had his struggles on many levels. But the reality didn't really sink in. His struggles seemed almost irrelevant to his *real* story, which was "of course" that he could go into a trance and bring in medical and other information. And because I could not see Cayce as an ordinary man (with an unusual gift) I misunderstood everything I read. Certainly I misunderstood its importance for my own life. I would make a small bet that nearly everyone who reads about him or others like him misunderstands in a similar way.

Anyone who comes away from this book thinking, "wow, Frank is really special" is wrong except in the sense that we are each special. I will say it as clearly as I can. As far as I can tell, the information is available and can be retrieved by anyone who wants to try. We don't have to live as disconnected individuals on the long, hard, solitary Downstairs path. There's no reason you can't do what I learned to do, and there's no reason to think you won't be as good at it as anybody else. Only, don't think that acquiring access is going to solve your problems. It's more likely to give you a new set of problems to work on. Nothing wrong with that, just be prepared.

The one danger I see in this kind of work is that of psychic inflation. If you think that this work makes you something special, you risk turning it into a curse. It should be obvious that the whole point of the process is to bring information not from the part of us that is *in* time and space, but from the part that is *beyond* time and space. How can we do that if our ego needs are driving us to try to assure success?

I consider myself fortunate that the gift of being able to talk to the other side did not manifest when I was younger, particularly when I was still trapped in a succession of menial jobs. Had the gift come before I had made a place to stand in the world, the temptation to identify myself with the gift (that is, to take credit for it) would have been great. If I had allowed myself to measure my worth as a person with the ability to produce acceptable results, would I not have been tempted to cheat? In any case, the need for results would have put the cart disastrously before the horse. I might have done quite a bit of damage to others and to myself. This work has to come from the heart, not from the ego, and for most of us that will be a struggle. To the degree that the work comes from ego, the quality of the material is compromised.

As has been said more than once, our essential oneness is more evident outside of time and space than it is here. Therefore, it is true, though it has been expressed as a joke, that "you're special, just like everybody else." It's important to remember *both* halves of the statement. You, yourself, were specifically created to conduct the experiment of being you. No one else is you. Your choices *do* matter to the larger being on the other side, call it what we may. But by the same token, this is true of everyone else. This seems to me very close to the old Christian way of seeing each of us as God's children, as precious to him and as interesting, regardless of external circumstances. (It is also a damn sight more attractive to me than the idea that people are economic or political digits, to be *used* rather than valued.)

So, remember that you are unique and therefore special; remember that so is everyone else you will ever know. You are not insignificant. Neither is any of them, regardless the color of their skin, the sound of their accent, the content of their bank account or the clarity of their thought. This is not empty, high-sounding, meaningless sloganeering. If the guys may be trusted, it's a straight description of fact.

The Meaning of the Material

Not so easy to sum up the results of this exploration. Not so easy, particularly, to make it clear in advance to each of you who reads this book the importance of this information *for you.* After all, each comes to it with different assumptions, abilities, prejudices, emotional makeup, and educational background – to say nothing of life-plan and affiliations. Still, the attempt must be made.

The central problem with all this material is simply that the picture it presents is at such variance with the picture painted by "common sense."

Common sense says that the past is dead, the future not yet created, and the present moment is all there is. This material says the past is still alive, the future is already alive, and the present is as alive as either – no more, no less.

Common sense says that the present is the one and only present. What you see is what you get. This material says that this time, and all times, exist in multiple versions, with a version corresponding to the results of every possible choice made by every agent.

Common sense says that reincarnation must be true or untrue. This material says it's more a matter of definition than of an either-or choice. In any case, it suggests that our ideas on the subject are confused.

Common sense says that in this life we must be either individuals (as to all appearances we are) or in some mystical way all part of one thing. This material says, again, it's a matter of definition, and could be seen either way.

Common sense says that they on their side (assuming that common sense would concede that "they" exist) must be either individuals or in some mystical way all part of one thing. This material says that here, too, it's a matter of definition.

Common sense says "we" in time-space and "they" outside of time-space are different beings. This material says the difference between us could be considered more a difference in emphasis than a difference in kind, with the major difference between us being the difference between their turf (non-material reality) and ours (time-space, or what I call 3D Theater).

Common sense says that life consists of good things and bad, or problems and opportunities, stemming from the conflict of forces. This material says that we – and they, working with us – plan our lifetimes both beforehand and during the lifetimes. All our problems are opportunities, because they are all chosen by us in the planning of our life.

Common sense says that conscience (if it exists) is something like a scorekeeper or a nag. This material says conscience is a homing mechanism.

Common sense says that our health, like other aspects of our lives, depends on many things over which we have little or no control. This material says we have far more control over our health than we commonly suspect, and that how much control we have depends on our state of being.

Common sense, for many people (not all) argues that improving the world is done primarily by interaction with others. This material says internal work is as effective as external work, and often more effective.

Common sense for many says that to overcome disaster or even to lead a successful life, we must do many external things (although few agree on what specific things). This material says the most effective thing we can do, in the face of disaster or in ordinary life, is to hold our center.

Common sense says that the meaning of the manner of our death is confined to this side. This material says that how we die here is the equivalent to how we are reborn into the other side.

And so it goes. Everything common sense says that is based on our assumptions about time and space falls down if those assumptions are incorrect. That includes questions about good and evil and about our emotions (gradients between what is and what we prefer, they say) and the meaning and nature of our lives. They see our lives as lived in different versions, equally real, with us choosing versions as if wandering in a maze of freedom. It even affects their view of extraterrestrials, for they are as close to them – as much a part of them – as to us. In short, our lives appear quite different to them than they do to us.

Now the question is, what are we going to do with this information? How can we check it, expand upon it, use it? That, dear reader, is at least partly up to you. Fortunately you are not alone, however much you may sometimes think so.

About the Author

Frank DeMarco was co-founder (in 1989) of Hampton Roads Publishing Company, Inc. and was Chief Editor there for 16 years. Among the scores of authors whose books he edited are F. Holmes (Skip) Atwater, Richard Bach, Robert Bruce, Robert Clarke, Michael Langevin, Joseph McMoneagle, Bruce Moen, Peter Novak, George Ritchie, and Colin Wilson.

The Sphere and the Hologram is his fifth book. Previous books include:

Messenger: A Sequel to Lost Horizon (1994), a novel carrying James Hilton's classic 1932 tale of Shangri-la into the 1960s and 1970s. How do you weigh the outer world against the inner world? What would be important to you if you could live forever?

Muddy Tracks: Exploring an Unsuspected Reality (2001), a non-fiction account of various psychic explorations and experiences including Shirley MacLaine's first Higher Self Seminar, several Monroe Institute courses, and various individual explorations. If I can do it, you can do it. What does that mean to the world around us?

Babe in the Woods (2008), a novel about a group of two dozen people who attend a week-long residential course designed to bring them to states of higher consciousness. Sometimes when you go exploring, you get more than you bargain for.

Chasing Smallwood: Talking with the Other Side (2009), another non-fiction book, which started out as conversations with a past-life individual about 19th-century America and progressed to a discussion of the huge task ahead of us in our time.

A sixth book, *The Cosmic Internet*, also scheduled for publication in 2009, continues themes introduced in *Chasing Smallwood*, as other historical individuals add their perspective and opinions.

In addition, three books of poetry, "The Marsh," "Death and Resurrection," and "An Unsuspected Life," are available as downloads free from Hologram Books, www.hologrambooks.com.

About Hologram Books

For a complete list of titles available from Hologram Books,
and for Frank DeMarco's weblog called "I of my own Knowledge…"
go to www.hologrambooks.com.